JOHN AND ERICA PLATTER
AFRICA UNCORKED

SPAIN
ITALY
MEDITERRANEAN SEA
MOROCCO
TUNISIA
ALGERIA
EGYPT
RED SEA
SAHARA DESERT
ETHIOPIA
EQUATOR
KENYA
ATLANTIC OCEAN
TANZANIA
ZIMBABWE
NAMIBIA
MADAGASCAR
MAURITIUS
REUNION
SOUTH AFRICA
INDIAN OCEAN
N
W
E
S

JOHN AND ERICA PLATTER

AFRICA

TRAVELS IN EXTREME WINE TERRITORY

UNCORKED

KYLE CATHIE LIMITED, LONDON

DOUBLE STOREY BOOKS, A JUTA COMPANY, CAPE TOWN

First published in 2002 in Great Britain by
Kyle Cathie Limited,122 Arlington Road, London NW1 7HP
e-mail: general.enquiries@kyle-cathie.com; website: www.kylecathie.com
And in southern Africa by
Double Storey Books, a Juta company, Mercury Crescent, Wetton 7780, Cape Town, South Africa.
e-mail: doublestorey@juta.co.za; website: www.doublestorey.com

ISBN 1 85626 440 8 (Kyle Cathie Ltd)
ISBN 1 91993 007 8 (Double Storey Books)

All rights reserved. No reproduction, copy or transmission of this publication may be made without written permission. No paragraph of this publication may be reproduced, copied or transmitted save with the written permission or in accordance with the provision of the Copyright Act 1956 (as amended). Any person who does any unauthorised act in relation to this publication may be liable to criminal prosecution and civil claims for damages.

9 8 7 6 5 4 3 2 1

Text © 2002 John & Erica Platter
Photography © 2002 John & Erica Platter
Cover photograph © 2002 Dennis Gordon

Project editor Sheila Davies
Copy editor Stephanie Horner
Editorial assistant Sarah Epton
Designer Vanessa Courtier
Production Lorraine Baird and Sha Huxtable

John and Erica Platter are hereby identified as the authors of this work in accordance with Section 77 of the Copyright, Designs and Patents Act 1988

A CIP catalogue record for this title is available from the British Library

Colour separations by Scanhouse, Malaysia
Printed and bound by Star Standard, Singapore

CONTENTS

*All roads lead to
Mukuyu winery near
Marondera, Zimbabwe.*

This is the story of a quixotic quest, the search for the wines of the African continent by a battle-hardened journalist and his writer wife.

John and Erica Platter have been South Africa's most consistent, most comprehensive wine-commentators for 20 years, stern critics of dodgy wines, bold heralds of talent well-deployed. They have witnessed, wet-nursed even, the emergence in the past few years of Africa's first great wines: Cape whites (initially) and now reds of stellar quality.

Why have they then turned their energies to what looks a far less congenial job? Tracking wine in bush, desert and jungle is very rough shooting in a trade where the birds are usually driven tidily over the guns, corks already drawn.

And why do I feel this, above all books about wine I have read in a decade, gets closest to the heart of the strange passion which all wine-lovers share?

The thread that ties together the characters and places you meet in this book is not really the continent. Africa is the difficult, extreme, violent and deeply human location. It provides endless colour, adventure, beauty, hardship and absurdity. The true defining thread, though, is the challenge of producing one of earth's most precious and refined, yes, even sacramental, products when everything is stacked against you. Yes, it's booze. But so is whisky, arrack, beer…

And beer is so much easier. Why persist when Cerberus in the form of a doubtful pong and worse headache stands between you and desired oblivion? The same loony logic will make a gardener try for the perfect peachy petals of a rose in tundra or steaming swamp, or a musician write a concerto for a full orchestra and comb and paper.

What did Samuel Johnson say of a woman preaching? That it was like a dog walking on its hind legs. It is not done well, but we are surprised to see it done at all. Tanzania's wine in a nutshell.

No. Hilarious as it is to read the Platters' careful-stepping notes on fiercely 'rustic' wines (in normal wine-talk the most imaginative language is kept for the best: here it evokes the most obnoxious brews) the real point of *Africa Uncorked* is the dogged persistence, passionate aspiration, desperate longing or crazy courage it takes to be a winemaker when nature says don't bother. And in Islamic countries where it puts a price on your head.

Take Islam. Take Algeria, where the Platters' journeys begin. What was once the world's fourth biggest vineyard has been decimated, pulled up, shot up and on top of that foully slandered by the French who created it and were once its best customers. To the militant Islamic Front wine was the symbol of everything they loathed and feared. On one of their first visits John and Erica needed an armed escort. They might prudently have tasted in flak jackets. But the oenologists included young women in designer jeans. Shades; no *burkhas*. There's progress for you. And you read it first here.

Morocco is ambivalent, legalistic. The French are moving back in. Tunisia is settled and worldly. Egypt is a mad collision between Islam at its puritanical toughest and the latest stylistic wrinkles from Bordeaux. A fervent Islamist wants his share of wine alright, but has the faith and patience to wait for the promised supply (served by dark-eyed and available maidens) in the gardens of Paradise. Meanwhile he quotes the Pharaohs in evidence and keeps an eye on the refrigeration unit.

The tropics set other tests – for grapevines as well as their long-suffering proprietors. The vine needs the winter to rest. Where there is no winter, or only a hiccup in the rainfall, it sickens, tries to flower and fruit non-stop, and soon dies. For all the heat, whether dry, damp or saturated, the grapes don't ripen. Hence the paradox of having to shovel in sugar to make up for grapes that can still be green and already be rotten. Not that good tries are missing. Intelligent not-quites are surprisingly frequent, and there are just enough Eurekas to keep the show on the road. It is startling what ampelographers you'll find in a clearing in the bananas, dreaming their dreams, with their Jancis Robinsons propped open at M for Merlot.

So in Kenya, Ethiopia, Tanzania, Zimbabwe (where armed thugs are a special problem), but above all in the East African islands, Madagascar, Réunion and Mauritius, the would-be wine-grower heads for the higher, drier and maybe even cooler ground. In Réunion, whose Pinot Noir and Chenin Blanc have the distinction of being *produits de France*, the Platters follow demented mountain roads to 1200 metres to find vineyards on the lips of volcanoes. In Madagascar a thriving foie gras industry gives the wine an improbable partner. (In Zimbabwe one recommended accompaniment was five aspirins.) Mauritius still has an aristocracy in its plantation houses, but not too proud to import grape concentrate to ring the changes with paw paw juice.

Everywhere John and Erica went they found hope triumphing over experience. Fag ends of brief colonial histories (Ethiopians still eat *spiggttii*; Namibia enjoys German food) colour the often knockabout efforts of fanatics of the vine.

There is almost enough detail in the Platters' faithful records for a travel agent to base the ultimate wine tour on their pioneering. Air travel (terrifying), road conditions (what road?), accommodation from luxurious to 'sleep standing up', menus ('barbed wire and grilled goat') and of course wines are chronicled with frankly astonishing good humour. The bonne-bouche comes at the end: a privileged peek at some exceptional South African winemakers, their vineyards and wines. Followed by a round-up of what not to miss on Africa's entire Carte des Vins.

It was the elder Pliny, I think, who advised travellers in the ancient Roman empire to carry with them a flask of *conditum*, usually a mixture of honey and pepper, to mask the taste of too-local wines. The Platters learned the same lesson: their recipe, a bottle of *liqueur de cassis*. Only for emergencies, though. John and Erica are the world's gamest guinea-pigs. How about this for positive thinking? 'The finish hangs about awkwardly, but give it a spritz and away you go.'

Hugh Johnson

This is not a wine guide. Even we, champions of most about this continent, must concede that there'll probably be few followers in our footsteps right through the A to Z – Algeria to Zimbabwe – of African vineyards. Not for the wine alone, that is.

We relish the idea that our continent once led the viticultural world; that strap-hanging is not a product of modern transport but was invented by the Pharaohs' foot-pressing cellar rats; that the one book the Romans didn't burn when they sacked Carthage was written by Magon, an African agronomist; that France et al. were snoringly asleep when North African wine societies had been into vertical tastings of Muscat d'Alexandrie for centuries. But wine is no longer Africa's strength, and three millennia is far too long to leave a World Series comeback.

While there were brief flickers of fame in the Cape in the eighteenth century, and in North Africa in the early twentieth when winemakers from Algeria frequently won France's premier *maître de chai* titles, old reputations don't cut it for new consumers with the world on the tip of their tongues. North Africa has been off the main table for decades, and even South Africa, back in favour after Nelson Mandela's release, soon found the fashionable flavours of freedom finished rather short.

But there's something about winegrowing that seems to burrow deep into people's systems. You may think you have got rid of it, but it lurks, a bit like bilharzia. A decade after he'd ripped out the vines he'd planted overlooking the flamingos on Lake Naivasha, a Kenya farmer was e-mailing us: he wanted to start all over again. And he wasn't the only one. As the new millennium began, all over Africa a wine revival was under way.

It's true that you have to be prepared to drink – and journey – more adventurously in search of good wines in Africa. Everywhere but the far northern and southern extremities of the continent – and sometimes there, too – winegrowing and making is a battle of the eccentrics against all odds: climate, soil, antiquated technology, politics, market forces, and even religion. It's as far from Burgundy or California as bungee-jumping is from croquet. That's its charm for us, and that's what this book is all about: Travels in Extreme Wine Territory.

Wine tasting in Africa is not a gentle ramble through the usual vineyards or maybe, if you can stand the excitement, marking wines up or down on a sensory scale. There's nearly always an edge. Squashing up with jerrycans of petrol (in Zimbabwe), being deafened by outrider sirens (trickier parts of Algeria), toasting passing elephants. Surviving border crossings, cyclones, mosquitoes, leeches and in some cases, the wine itself…

We are into such masochistic pleasures. We are the sort whom friends ring to share their horror travel stories. Trapped by the notion that a purely aimless holiday is somehow wrong, we always trump up a reason for our alternative choice of destinations, Gabon, for instance. Lately it's been birds, and wherever we go, a truth prevails: rare birds dote on swamps, blasted heaths, impenetrable forests, thorn thickets and septic tanks, all in areas where the 'best available' accommodation, is often a case of endurance rather

Top: *Our first home in the Cape, La Provence; John, Erica and Cameron in wine-farming days at Delaire, Stellenbosch.* Middle: *Camping at Tamanrasset; tea mid-Sahara-style – water straight from boiling-hot jerrycans.* Bottom: *Our first patch of vines, in Franschhoek; John makes his first wine at Delaire.*

than enjoyment. Like the Russian-built hotel in the highlands of Ethiopia, squat as a Steppe, pungent with sewerage and fish oil. But the more challenging such trips, the more perversely worthwhile they feel, and the more elated we are by such small miracles as a decent espresso. Here's where Ethiopia strikes back: its wild coffee beans are the best.

It all dates years back, to our 'honeymoon' – a 17,000-kilometre drive through 19 countries from London to Nairobi, via the Sahara, with a detour to Abidjan and the West African coast. We took our temperamental Land Rover through sandstorms, past dead camels and burnt-out cars (did this mean we were on the right or wrong route?), stopped at 41 border checkpoints and a million road-blocks manned by police in mirror glasses.

We'd started off with the highest hopes and standards. John, brought up in Kenya on old-fashioned safaris – starched napkins, clean cotton sheets, comfortable canvas arm-chairs, impeccable cuisine – insisted on proper beds, seating and gourmet food to see us through the Sahara and beyond. I had never been on a camping trip in my life, and knew no London shops except those so famous I happened to read about them.

Folding beds and director's chairs from Harrods, printed curtains and sheets from Liberty, tinned camembert from Fortnum & Mason…. It melted the second we hit the Sahara. The furniture bit the dust shortly thereafter: sleeping bags on the sand were easier to manage. Weeks later, in some oasis or other, two overlanders emerged from a large truck, and sat down in a pair of chairs that looked uncannily like the ones we'd ditched en route. We sauntered over to enquire. 'You won't believe,' they said. 'There we were driving along, middle of nowhere, and suddenly we saw these chairs. Just sitting there.'

Not long afterwards, almost by default, and to pay the bills on the little Cape grape farm we'd escaped to from Johannesburg, we began to write about wine. John, a foreign correspondent who'd covered wars and coups in nearly all the countries we'd 'honey-mooned' through – and more – wrote a column for the *Rand Daily Mail*. Jointly we concocted the first South African wine pocket guide, which became an annual undertaking.

It grew and grew – more and more wineries, thousands of tasting notes. Eventually, the urge to stop assessing wine by stars and numbers and get back to writing about it as reporters, and as an adventure, became irresistible. So off we went and here they are: the people and places working to reclaim Africa's ancient place on the world wine map, and stake out some unlikely new territory. Yes, if the continent were a festival, wine would be playing the fringe in most regions. But there are so many other shows in town in African wine countries. And the backdrops! Where else in the wine world do you get your vineyards patrolled by lions or fringed by lemurs? Vineyards in Phoenician mosaics and Egyptian pyramids? Vineyards in volcanoes overlooking tropical island beaches? Africa's wine regions are not monocultures but a moveable multicultural feast.

This is the diary of our travels, from one end to the other, through the continent that grips and infuriates and exhilarates us like no other – using our own peculiar route map, with wine as the beacon. This was our Year (or two) of Drinking Dangerously.

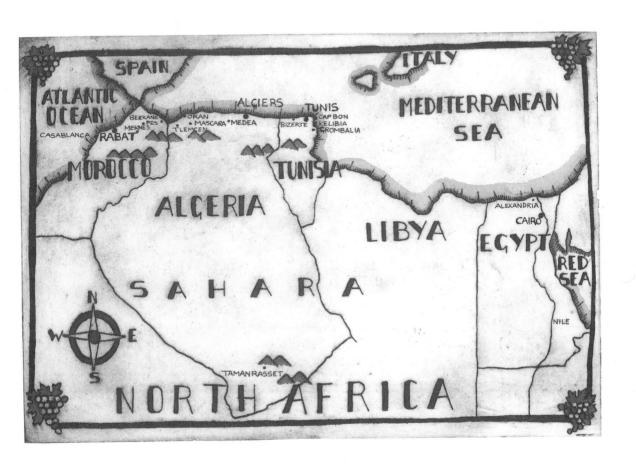

MOROCCO

Les Celliers de Meknes
vineyard in Morocco's
palm-fringed riposte to
the Côte d'Or: Les
Coteaux de L'Atlas.

It sounded promisingly exotic, but Casablanca to Meknes is not one of the world's great train rides. Industrial slouch, monotonous eucalyptus plantations, bare brown hillsides, heat and dust…. On the map, it had looked as if the railway line wound through wine country for at least some of the three and a half hours of the journey. But perhaps it once had; perhaps it once again would.

The landscape began to change after independence in 1956, when Morocco became an official Islamic state. French colonists who had farmed wine here since 1912, expanding the national vineyard to 50,000 hectares, packed up and left. They, like the Phoenician and Carthaginian invaders in 1200 BC, had originally taken one look at this corner of the African continent and licked their lips. Real estate, wine estate — location is key. And with a double-dose of sea and ocean, classic Mediterranean climate, high-altitude mountains, lime-rich soils, Morocco might be God's own vine country.

Taking that one step further now, to grow and market wine in a Muslim community, was a delicate matter. Other crops are simpler. And those who put their trust in France, which at independence took in 95 per cent of the 3 million hectolitre crop, had not foreseen the European Union. Forget old bilateral arrangements; Morocco's wine exports to Europe were turned down to a trickle — an annual allowance of 80,000 hectolitres. Local growers took stock and action. Vineyards were burned and replaced with cereals, apples, timber — or the wastelands we'd seen from the train. By the 1980s the industry faced collapse. State takeovers of vineyards, cellars and the négociant business put the patient on life-support. But only 8000 hectares of vineyards remained by the 1990s. Hardly any new planting had been done; most vines were pensioners. National production had shrunk to 300,000 hectolitres. Shock treatment was needed.

It took the intervention of the late King Hassan II — the maker of modern Morocco, and no stranger to a sybaritic life — to put a stop to a gathering fundamentalist momentum that wanted to outlaw the comforts of alcohol altogether. Low vineyard rentals were dangled in front of foreign and private investors prepared to plant at least 100 hectares of classic varieties per year to revive and modernise the industry. The scramble for international customers was on, the re-greening of the countryside had begun.

Meknes was where most of this renaissance was happening, the wine centre of this country which sometimes still pretends it's not a wine country, which continues to conduct a schizoid affair with the grape. It's an ancient sprawling hilltop city, with high stucco walls – and the old fort's ramparts – in shades of sedate brown and corn matching much of the countryside which is strung with olive groves and the occasional line of palms breaking up gold wheat fields and vineyards. Donkeys are still beasts of burden, moving slowly, if at all.

It was the last city we'd trundled through in our Land Rover 25 years earlier, before climbing the chilly Atlas mountains, and heading south into the dunes of the Sahara. We drank thick red wine at our last lunch in Meknes, and took away a couple of bottles, too – fortification for the trials ahead. In the desert this rapidly turned to *glühwein*; and our jerry-cans of water on the roof-rack got so hot that we simply poured straight from them to make tea.

Hidden agendas

Now navigational skills were again needed as we battled to find the headquarters of Les Celliers de Meknes. This firm, we knew, has the largest share of the domestic market, huge stretches of vineyards, and wineries with all mod. cons. But it appeared invisible. Our taxi driver stopped and started, back-tracked and circled, consulted umpteen long-robed, fez-wearing citizens. Eventually, with an irritable wave, he deposited us in a dusty backstreet. We thought he'd simply given up and abandoned us. There wasn't a sign of any sort in sight. We chose one anonymous door to knock on and ask for directions. 'Come in,' said a smart secretary. We'd stumbled into Les Celliers itself.

Behind the bland, unmarked exterior were gleaming labs and maturation halls, spotless tasting rooms, bustling women in white coats with French doctorates, Montpellier-trained winemakers fluent in esoteric tasting patter, sharply-suited executives on the phone to New York organising launches… all the dynamism of a modern, internationally focused wine company. But outside, there wasn't a hint of what was happening within, so as not to offend the devout. This wine capital is still a very traditional Arabian city of minarets, mosques and droning muezzins.

Young marketing manager Reda Zniber's studies at the University of Florida in Miami hadn't covered the peculiarities of popularising wine in a religiously sensitive state. He can't use conventional media advertising. Sports sponsorship is permissible, but must be approached crab-like, if not in reverse. Linking wine to high-visibility football,

Incognito – Mehdi Bouchaara outside the anonymous headquarters of Moroccan wine giant Les Celliers de Meknes.

athletics and tennis, is out of the question. He deliberately has to choose fringe sports, with fewer fans to risk offending. So Les Celliers had sponsored the Moroccan rugby team in the World Cup. 'We were eliminated, but not before we beat Uruguay 21–3,' Reda reported with satisfaction.

The adopted son of the founder and president of Les Celliers de Meknes, Brahim Zniber, Reda introduced us to Omar Aouad, the CEO, and his assistant, Mehdi Bouchaara, a formidably slick duo. They'd just won a bruising war against Les Celliers' rival, Sincomar, formerly a state-owned virtual monopoly. The diminutive Bouchaara, in a fashionably crumpled ivory linen suit, explained: 'They said they were going to kill us with cut-throat prices. So we said, okay, one of us is going to get killed.' He added, deadpan: 'So now Les Celliers has 85 per cent of the market and Sincomar has 5 per cent – a total reversal in a couple of years.'

Reda was also seething: the national airline, Royal Air Maroc, which had previously served Sincomar wines, was still keeping Les Celliers off its list. We'd been astonished, flying in, to be offered only (mediocre) French wine. His goatee quivered with indignation. 'It is so ugly.'

We asked Mehdi Bouchaara to clear up another mystery: the country's per capita wine consumption. We knew there were religious sensitivities, and had been warned not to pry too deeply, but the discrepancy between official and international statistics was too wild to ignore. Could he enlighten us?

'Of course. Naturally. Everyone in the business knows. Officially, Moroccans drink zero. But our per capita annual wine consumption is 1.4 litres. The government doesn't want to admit we are a leading Islamic wine producer – and expanding! – and that it's not only tourists who drink wine.' We churned around the figures: about 3 million tourists a year… 400,000 hectolitres of wine…. 'If our tourists accounted for this figure, we'd be facing an invasion of drunks!'

While insisting that Morocco was the most most advanced in wine quality among Arab nations, Omar Aouad also conceded that Tunisia is the most tolerant of alcohol. (Neither country seemed prepared to acknowledge that the big brother between them, Algeria, crippled by its decade-long civil war, was stirring now and could dwarf them both.)

Aouad had driven a recent overhaul of Morocco's wine legislation; it was now, he proudly told us, 'the strictest in the world, even more strict than France. Some French experts came recently and said we were "stupid" – too hard on ourselves. But we are determined to make modern quality wine to the highest international standards.'

Their new AOC (Appellation d'Origine Contrôlée) wines would have to clear a bar pegged much higher than the old colonial wines. No chaptalisation, for example: 'It is absolutely forbidden. If even one bag of sugar is found, the company is dead.'

No additives whatsoever, including acid. We couldn't help looking sceptical and asking: 'Even in a bad year? No tweaking?' Reda was adamant: 'No, you don't get a true flavour. It's cheating.'

Aouad continued with the recitation of new rules: no pumping up production with excessive irrigation; yields restricted to 5.5 tonnes/hectare (the norm is double that and more). 'Not difficult because it's dry here; we depend on wells but only to avoid stress.' Produce over the limit, and your entire crop could be de-classified. And the premium-quality flag would not fly above any old fruit salad. Wines would have to contain at least 60 per cent of the 'noble' varieties to qualify for AOC status.

He paused dramatically, about to bring in the trumpets… 'and we have introduced a "first growth" which we predict will become famous in the world, like the Côte d'Or in Burgundy. Our very own Les Coteaux de l'Atlas!'

The Mondavi of Morocco

This new appellation singled out – would give ultimate cachet to – parts of two adjoining areas east of Meknes: Beni M'Tir with red, lime-rich soils and sandier Guerrouane, both between altitudes of 600–700 metres in the cool Middle Atlas foothills. Les Celliers already owned 1000 hectares of these prime patches, and another 1500 nearby. They were turning out a million cases of wine a year. Company president Brahim Zniber, a Muslim who may drink a toast, at a wedding, or the beginning of the harvest, but that's about all, according to Reda, was well on the way to becoming one of the largest private growers and producers in the world.

So we were very keen to meet Zniber Snr. As head of both producers' and négociants' organisations in Morocco, he was reputed to be the Robert Mondavi of the region, with a similar mission to the Californian eminence, to make his region's wines 'valued around the world'. But an interview with him was impossible: we had applied too late, a month before our visit. 'Even I have difficulty getting an appointment,' his son said.

Though Brahim Zniber started his working life in a vineyard in 1946, his tentacles stretch way beyond wine; he'd become Morocco's top business tycoon. Les Celliers was only one of his 25 companies which produce and sell everything from Coca-Cola to export fruit and vegetables, cereals, furniture, toys, insurance and day-old chicks. But vines remain his first love, his 'veritable passion', and Reda whipped us out of the city, to have a look at the new Coteaux de l'Atlas vineyards.

Within minutes we were striding over pudding-rich soils amid hectares of neat young vines, the mountains on the horizon. Down the road at Boufekrane was a Les Celliers satellite winery: regiments of shiny stainless-steel tanks, the maturation cellar lined with new oak barrels. The vineyard rows ended in lofty date palms ringed by pink and red geraniums. Still on Zniber property, we passed a milling crowd of workers. Some held placards in Arabic script. Reda snorted: 'Strikers! They just want more, more, more. I don't want to stop the car in case I lose my temper!'

Mehdi Bouchaara later gave an indication of Zniber Snr's attitude towards his workers. 'When I first came here, fresh from Paris business school, I thought: Wow! We can really score on efficiency, we can make money. If we use mechanical harvesters… and I did a proposal. But Mr Zniber would not accept it. 'What do I do with the 1000 pickers?' he asked. "Drop it!" So we did.'

Old cuisine, new generation wine

Back in Meknes, at the Palais Tsarrab restaurant, we tasted Les Celliers *vins de cépage* – the company's first unblended, classic-variety wine range. First a Cabernet Sauvignon rosé, from the vineyards we'd just visited. Rosé is the regional *vin ordinaire* – appropriate for the climate, cuisine, coastline and 90 per cent red/black grapes. But we were to find

that all over North Africa, rosés and their paler gris siblings – designed to disappear down the throat rather than linger on the palate – rarely impressed. This one had the personality to partner anything on the table.

'Morocco is one of the world's mother-cuisines!' pronounced Reda. There were little dishes of grilled brains and liver; chicken, and egg and herb *briouats* (deep-fried pastry triangles or rolls); minced lamb or kefta kebabs; mini-pastilla pies filled with quail meat, eggs, almonds and sugar. 'Moroccans love sugar. And smoking,' said Reda, puffing away. Soft, sweet prune fruit jumped out of the next wine, a 97 Merlot. Serial salads and vegetables – chick-peas, whole green peppers, aubergines, stuffed tomatoes and more – came and went. Low divans lined one alcove in the restaurant, and no wonder some sated, suited lunchers had stretched out on them, taking a siesta before returning to work.

Lunch with Reda Zniber of Les Celliers de Meknes and other Moroccan dishes.

Later, the serious tasting in Les Celliers' lab began with a frankness unusual for a wine company. 'Probably the worst white we make,' said Reda, pouring a non-vintage Guerrouane Blanc. 'The whites could improve 100 per cent, the reds about 20–30 per cent.' Mehdi Bouchaara added: 'There are honourable whites in Morocco. But no great whites.' Reda was right; the subsequent wines got better. Even a *vin de coupage* (a blended Chardonnay, 90 per cent Moroccan-, 10 per cent French-grown) showed some pleasant nutty depth. We raced through two more Guerrouanes – rosé and gris, the first from Cabernet, the other from Cinsault: no-frills quaffing. But the star remained the Merlot we'd previewed over lunch. The Cabernet was promising; the Syrah, though pleasant, lacked oomph. Finally we peeked at two 'experimental, future flagships': Cabernet Sauvignon and Syrah barrel-matured for 9 months. Fruit and oak were in harmony, the colours better and deeper. But were they high-profile enough?

Winemaker Oussama Aissaoui, very proper and earnest, and lab chief Dr Haida Hanine – dashing driver of a black 4x4, the top Moroccan woman in the wine industry – were optimistic that their continuous experiments in vineyard and cellar would pay off. 'A winemaker never gives all his secrets,' said Oussama. What about the wines they bought in from vineyards not under their control? He was tactful: 'An old winemaker may not be very scientific, but he often has The Feeling….'

Later, in London, we did an update with Les Celliers' UK rep, David Gill of BottleGreen. The Safeways chain was selling the 2000 vintage of these wines, fronted by evocative desert labels – nothing like the Meknes region they came from! A Cabernet-Syrah was the most characterful, a Cabernet-Merlot more straightforward. A Grenache-Cinsault and a Carignan were more cheaply priced to reflect their lowlier status. The Grenache perhaps should have been left at home.

Return of the French

Nature generally smiles on Meknes, but also dishes out the odd frown. Its lime-rich soils – the calcium contributing to crumbly friability and aeration – also have high pH values, which promise healthy low-pH wines, with keepability. But climate and variety are more crucial to wine quality than soil, and Meknes is not only dry, there's the Chergui summer wind too, to bash and – as eminent Bordeaux scientist Professor Denis Boubals noted – to grill the vines. He prescribed drip irrigation and strong trellising, but otherwise gave it an outstanding bill of health as a fine wine region.

The sites specifically enthusing him were on the Domaines Delorme property, a private, 1053-hectare French investment in partnership with the state. Moroccan production might never climb back to the booming 1960s, when North Africa's exports led the wine world, but as soon as the government re-thought its post-independence, hands-off-our-land policy, foreign investors began to sniff. We whizzed past Domaines Delorme the next day, along the Fes–Meknes–Rabat road. It's a merger of four separate colonial-era estates: Delorme, Meunier, Vincent and Emmanuelli. Cabernets Sauvignon and Franc, Syrah, Merlot (which Prof. Boubals considers the ideal variety for Meknes) and Chardonnay had been added to the existing mix of minor red varieties; new-oak maturation was introduced in 1997.

Later we met vini-viticulturist Christophe Gelly, who'd been furiously replanting and cellar-building here since 1994. The fruits of these labours weren't ready to roll, but he promised that one day he'd bring them to South Africa for us to taste, because he'd heard we have such good golf-courses. (Perhaps not good enough, we haven't yet played a round with him.)

The incoming traffic also included French heavyweights William Peters and the world's second-largest wine company, Castel Frères. By 2001, when we sampled the latest

الدارالبيضاء
CASABLANCA

شركة إستغلال
م ميناء الصيد البحري ش

PLOITATION DU **R**ESTAURANT DU **P**OF
S.A.R.L. au Capital de 520.000 DH
 : Port de Pêche de Casablanca - Tél.
31101304 - N° : d'Identifiant Fiscal : 01
2 - R.C. / Casablanca : 45 131 - C.N.S.

Spécialités de Poissons

515527   Le   23.05
                   Table N°

		2
DE CALMARS		1
E CREVETTES		1

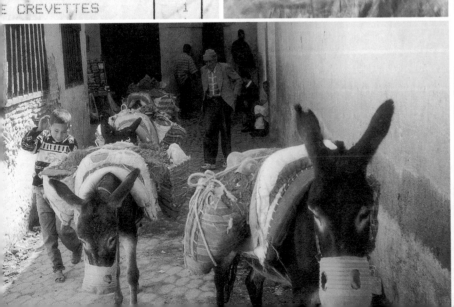

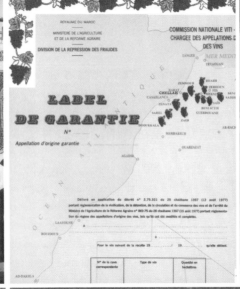

ROYAUME DU MAROC

MINISTERE DE L'AGRICULTURE
ET DE LA REFORME AGRAIRE

DIVISION DE LA REPRESSION DES FRAUDES

COMMISSION NATIONALE VITI -
CHARGEE DES APPELATIONS D
DES VINS

LABEL
DE GARANTIE

N°

Appellation d'origine garantie

Délivré en application du décret n° 2.75.321 du 25 chaâbane 1357 (12 août 1977)
portant réglementation de la vinification, de la détention, de la circulation et du commerce des vins et de l'arrêté du
Ministère de l'Agriculture de la Réforme Agraire n° 860-75 du 28 chaâbane 1397 (15 août 1977) portant réglementation des régime des appellations d'origine des vins, tels qu'ils ont été modifiés et complétés.

Pour le vin suivant de la récolte 19............ 19............ qu'elle détient

N° de la cave correspondante	Type de vin	Quantité en hectolitres

Quand mon verre est plein je le vide...

Quand mon verre est vide je le plains...

Top: *John trainspotting;*
Casa's market;
gateway to Fes;
Morocco's eastern
and central wine
regions; winemaker
Said Ibnaiche and
John at one of the
world's largest cellars.
Middle: *Our favourite*
Casa restaurant; en
route to Volubilis;
Berkane town of
clementine; pun-fun
mural at Aït Souala
Co-op.
Bottom: *Carrying the*
shopping, Fes-style;
remains of Roman
days at Volubilis;
Berkane's co-op
and lab.

vintage, Castel had poured £10 million (US$15 million) into their Atlas Vineyards venture at Beni M'tir, and British supermarkets were gobbling up the results. Nick Tatham, of Lane and Tatham Wine Brokers, arranged a tasting at Sainsburys' headquarters in London for us. Rachel Griffiths, the chain's North and South African wine buyer, was enthusiastic; even the picky UK wine press seemed reasonably enamoured.

The Atlas Vineyards Merlot 2000 was delicious: approachable, juicy as any easy Chilean seducer, but with more grip and structure. Atlas Vineyards and Sainsburys Cabernets 2000 showed even more potential. Two Syrahs perhaps needed to shout a little more Syrah (spices, tar, ripe black fruit) but were more than good quaffing. These were oak-chipped. A barrel-matured Private Reserve 99 El Baraka – Arabic for worthy, prestigious, abundance, blessing – was a more serious Cabernet-Merlot blend.

When these vineyards mature, when Castel bottles in situ rather than in France (there's always a quality loss when wine has to travel long-distance in bulk), what quality levels will they reach? The challenge will be to carve out their own profile. But they should certainly be in the ring with the New World competition.

Big, bigger, biggest

Back in Morocco, and the ancient world, our next visit was to the scene of a much earlier colonial invasion – the Roman city of Volubilis, 30 kilometres outside Meknes. But first we called on the giant of Moroccan wineries: the Société Coopérative Vinicole d'Aït Souala, which taps into 4000 hectares of vineyards. In the 1940s, this was the largest cellar in the world. It is now only third or fourth, according to winemaking director Said Ibnaiche, but by any count anywhere, this is mass production. 'Awesome' might have been the word before it was stripped of its gravitas. This is beyond big.

The buildings sprawl over 5 hectares; each tank holds 60,000 litres; 40 kilometres of internal piping converge in a spaghetti junction of monstrous complexity. At harvest-time, 1000 extra workers are drafted in to pick 24 hours a day. ('Machines are not illegal,' said Said, 'but for us they are forbidden. We like to make work opportunities for the people.') The *daily* crush in 1999 was 2000 tonnes from 15 varieties. The leading players – Carignan, Cinsault, Grenache, Alicante Bouschet, Syrah – each have their own premises.

A handsome, burly man, highly regarded by his peers, Said had been in the business for more than 20 years, his viticulturist for 35. Vineyards surround the winery and roll over the horizon. Most vines are around 20 years old, but 25 per cent of the Carignan is well over 50, still producing deep colours and 12–14% alcohols. These Moroccan traits (he was emphatic) had in colonial days given many French wines 'chaleur' or warmth.

Guerrouane is their biggest appellation (2400 hectares); its grapes have 'the most striking flavour profile, very fruity, banana, raspberry'. Its Carignan – the star Moroccan variety in his opinion, offers 'vanilla without the wood'. Of the tank samples we tasted, it did stand out – plum-coloured, sweet, quite soft. But Said was making no labels of his own; he blended according to customer demand, mostly (80 per cent) for Les Celliers de Meknes.

On a scale of wineries, starting small with boutique cellars, this behemoth was a mall. But a rustic one, with a grapey mural painted near the entrance above a bit of word-play:

Quand mon verre est plein

Je le vide

Quand mon verre est vide

Je le plains

(When my glass is full, I empty it. When my glass is empty, I complain about it.)

Old invaders

The landscape around Meknes captivated the Romans in the first century BC and you can see why. Lively rivers wriggle through immense blond and green plains. Vineyards, olive groves and wheatfields undulate into the distant Middle Atlas mountains. A little boy wearing a fez cajoled a floppy-eared donkey carrying panniers of straw up a rocky path. There were wild red poppies in the grass. Biblical, we thought, but of course now we were in the land of the Koran.

Here was where the Romans built one of their finest colonial cities: temples, villas and basilicas with a view. This was a neighbourhood which supplied the Colosseum with lions. Volubilis is still an extraordinary sight, perhaps even more exquisite now it's in ruins, a fallen beauty. Arches still arch triumphally, cobbled streets are lined with graceful colonnades. Mosaics, the interior décor rave of those times, have survived the centuries: they celebrated the gods and the bounty of the countryside – those unfortunate lions, various gazelles, birds, snakes, grapes. The urban living here had been splendid; now the remains of those days stand alone and abandoned.

Today there are tour buses. The rather bizarre (extremely luxe) Hotel Volubilis Inn commands the hillside above. Guests like to ride down in togas and chariots… but we had a longer distance to travel, and a train to catch from nearby Fes.

Once there, we sipped avocado milkshakes in the Medina (the old town), nibbled on fresh dates and pastel pink and green nougat, and thought: is this not a *most* exotic wine route? Sheep trotted down the mazes of alleys like pet dogs. Small donkeys operated as rubbish-removers and taxis. Blue-eyed carpet salesmen beckoned us into blue-tiled doorways. 'We are Berbers. We do not do business like this,' one said, making snaky hand movements. A perfume merchant with an American accent and portraits of Bill Clinton and Robert Redford on his walls boasted: 'I do not have ordinary people here, I have stars. President Clinton is my best customer. Everybody needs aphrodisiacs.'

We did all the usual Fes things, including trying on a fez or two; watching leather workers leap across cauldrons of boiling dyes in every colour of earth and sunset; peeping into mosques and madressas; buying local fast-food – warm roasted pistachios, fresh cherries. In the evening we sat on the street at the Brasserie-Café de la Renaissance and drank thick dark coffee in tiny glasses. Shoe-shine boys darted about. We ate chick-peas, and the tiny savoury pastries called *briouats*.

Between the desert and the deep blue sea

There were a few tense moments when we stumbled onto the midnight train and found one of the four bunks in our *couchette* occupied by a strange man in his underwear. John: 'Why are we doing this?' Erica, lying down firmly: 'It's too late to mind who's sleeping with us. Good night.'

It wasn't an auspicious start to a journey that many locals seemed to regard as distinctly eccentric. Berkane is the last outpost of Moroccan wine, 550 kilometres from Rabat, in the corner of the country between the tail-end of the Rif range, Algeria and the sea. It had been clear from the dubious looks of the men in Meknes that they thought this was going far too far. Now, had we been sportswriters, it would have been a different story – Hicham El Gerrouj, the country's world champion middle-distance runner, was born and bred here in the back of beyond. But wine writers? They'd shaken their heads. *Normalement* people of our sort gave the way-out wine fringe a miss. And even the train wouldn't get us there: Berkane was 60 kilometres beyond the end of the line! Such negatives, of course, only strengthened our resolve. We'd be tramping fresh ground. Squashing into a steamy, shuddering little space with a snoring stranger merely added greater texture to the rich fabric…

At Domaines de Chaudsoleil outside Berkane, vineyards amid mulberry, olive and citrus groves in Morocco's remotest wine region on the Algerian border.

The train stopped amid the dusty sprawl of Oujda just after dawn. Overnight, wheat-fields and vineyards had become sand dunes and desert scrub; the air was bone dry and already shimmering with heat. The next station would have been Tlemcen, an Algerian wine-town on our agenda. But right now the borders were closed; the neighbours were not on speaking terms.

We and our sleeping partner decanted wearily onto the platform, along with a group of black Africans. Leg-ironed, manacled, and chained together, they were marched off by armed guards. No one seemed to know why. The local co-op winery had sent a car to meet us, and had devised a 'programme' of daunting density and length. Our driver barely slowed down to point out the roadside tree with which he'd recently connected ('I was unconscious for three days').

We were nearing the Mediterranean now: the beach resort of Saidia ('The Blue Pearl') and the Spanish duty-free enclave of Melilla. Smuggling is big business here; bottles of black market petrol and other contraband were being flogged along the road. We dropped down into the Moulouya river valley where, sheltered from the scorching hinterland by the Beni Snassen mountains, Berkane dozed in a giant bowl of fruit.

Mulberry trees and groves of *picholine marocaine* olives lined the roadsides; neon orange globes lit up glossy dark green citrus orchards. Berkane calls itself the Ville des Clémentines; a giant tangerine presides over the traffic circle in the centre of town. Rolling out in all directions, row after row of emerald and lime green, were hundreds of hectares of – mostly State-owned – vineyards between the desert and the sea (deep blue, of course).

We drove out to one of the largest properties, Domaines de Chaudsoleil (an under-statement) with Mostafa Laridi, the 30-something chief of Berkane's Coopérative Vinicole des Beni Snassen. Some of the vines – at a venerable 60-plus – emphat-ically outdated him. He pointed out one block of very elderly Carignan which still produced an astonishing 16 tonnes/hectare (40,000 hectolitres). Teenagers – 12–15-year-old Cabernet Sauvignon, Syrah, Cinsault, Tempranillo, Mourvedre, Grenache and Alicante Bouschet completed the red wine varieties. The slew of unremarkable whites included Clairette Blanche, Pedro Ximinez, Folle Blanche, Farane and Grenache Blanc. They are irrigated – the annual rainfall here is a mere sprinkle – by a complicated arrangement of canals and furrows.

Locally-trained, French-finished vine-wineman Mostafa Laridi: fashioning floods of the stuff which is taboo in his family's household.

Compact and sturdy, with a flashing smile bracketed by deep dimples, Mostafa was modern, dynamic, and chafing to make similar wines. He was another symbol of the cultural conundrum of wine's place in an Islamic society. His family grows table grapes, but wine is taboo in their household. So why did his father encourage him to do a horticultural engineering degree (at Morocco's King Hassan II Agricultural College) followed by a diploma in viticulture and oenology at France's Montpellier University? For economic reasons, Mostafa explained. His father knew there were not many winemakers in Morocco, so his son would certainly find a job.

Drina Fadoua, Mostafa's wife (an arranged marriage), thoroughly current in her repartee and sleek striped trouser suit, allows no alcohol in the house. Her husband might be turning out 40,000 hectolitres of wine a year in the enormous plant a few steps from their front door, but he drinks only at the winery or in his laboratory, for tasting purposes. A gift of our own Chardonnay had to be hastily palmed to the nightwatch-man before we were welcomed into the Laridis' home for freshly squeezed clementine juice and *beghrir* (pancakes).

There are two schools of thought about the soil. One winemaker said it was too rich in potassium. 'So the grapes encounter a blockage in ripening. The tannins are green.'

Another insisted the soil was very good for traditional varieties. 'And we specify what we want to buy.' The co-op made wines *en vrac* (in bulk) for such buyers, and tankered them off cross-country, over desert and mountain, to be tweaked into négociants' ranges. A varietal (single-grape variety) brand existed only in Mostafa Laridi's dreams. Some all-sorts blends – one named Ali Baba – had been bottled here in the past, but now the only Beni Snassen Domaines de Chaudsoleil wines available directly to the public were a rosé and a gris.

We tasted some Syrah – old fashioned sweaty-saddle stuff. The Cabernet Sauvignons were bright and light (though firm), with restrained sweet-spicy scents, and cried out for a relaxing dose of oak. There was a very dry, light, highly perfumed Muscat d'Alexandrie. But we were specially taken by a pale apricot-pink gris. A match for the catch from both Mediterranean and Atlantic waters, a partner for a picnic. Or, as Mostafa put it, a child of the beach.

Action man

Jacques Poulain might have matched that description too, in a thoroughly grown-up way. A muscular, mischievous Frenchman, in earlier days he'd probably have been an explorer (though not a missionary), or even (was there much of a difference?) an adventurer-pirate. Now he's a pioneering winemaker – and surfer, snow-boarder, rally-driver, rugby front-row prop – in the vanguard of a wine renaissance in a deeply Muslim society. And he was making the most interesting wines we encountered during our North African travels.

The odds in Morocco are precariously stacked, but that was why – with the help of some marital imperatives – Jacques had left France and come here. After working for 10 years at various quite grand châteaux (including Giscours in Margaux and Beau Séjour in St-Emilion), he had eloped with the wife of a Bordeaux vineyard owner. Her parents live in Morocco.

'I pinch her. I am a *dangereux* man,' he said (superfluously). He was in his early 30s, she in her mid-40s, between them there were five children, and now he surfed the breaks off the beaches of Mohammedia, between Rabat and Casablanca, 'three times a week at least, every morning if possible. It's cool here, a good trip. I could not make wines in Meknes, it is too far from the sea'.

He was enthusiastic about the wine potential, too: 'Nature does very good things in the vineyards here. We have a very, very big possibility to make good wines.' It was his job to make this happen, and increase the (then only 10 per cent) market-share of Thalvin, a 50:50 French–Moroccan partnership founded in 1930 and now owned by Serge Baconnet and Laraki Abdelouhb (distributors of Pernod-Ricard, Ballantines, Grants, Campari etc). The winery – Jacques had been made a director – was at Domaine des Ouled Thaleb, just inland from his favourite surfing beach, and near the town of Ben Slimane.

We drove down wide boulevards fringed with podgy palms, purple bougainvillea, tamarind, fig and orange trees. Horse-cart taxis clopped sedately past. The shops' arched entrances and arabesque windows were outlined in green and black mosaic tiles. We might have slipped back a century. Some parts of the cellar looked fairly antique too. But lurking within was – we had a feeling – our best chance of finding that rarity in North Africa: a good white wine.

Great white hope, ripe reds

Though Morocco is lapped by an ocean and a sea, and awash in superb fish, we'd looked in vain for a decent white tablemate. The only one we fancied was labelled Semillant. It had nothing to do with the Sémillon grape but was, we later discovered, Poulain's mix of three varieties – Clairette Blanche (more opulent here than usual) Mayorquin (found in southern France) and Maccabeo (often partly guilty for poor white Rioja).

It was so much more agreeable than the rest that we became determined to track down its maker. We besieged the Agriculture Ministry in Rabat. Who, what, where was Thalvin? Why had it not been mentioned in any of the official literature? The man from the ministry eventually volunteered to drive us there himself.

In Jacques' cellar we sampled pruney, minerally inky, spicy Cabernet-Merlot of international potential; a super dry rosé which had French and UK importers panting; a saucy Sauvignon-Ugni Blanc blend. 'Here you get a very, very good result with Ugni, richer, more concentrated,' said Jacques. But by far the best of any North African white wine we tasted was his first Thalvin CB Chardonnay, from 5-year-old vines. It had all the sass and finesse of a top California example, could have outclassed most from South Africa, and when we tried to re-taste it later in London, was unsurprisingly sold out.

Its sleek bottle and modern, minimalist label dominated by the initials CB (Chardonnay Barrique) infuriated our minder from the ministry. He himself was visiting this winery for the first time, and he wasn't happy with everything he saw. The CB label was not patriotic or historic enough, and he took great umbrage at an old French sign in the winery extolling Cabernet as a 'Bordelais cépage des grands crus'.

'What is this?' he spluttered furiously at Jacques and the sign. 'We do not have to . borrow a variety of Bordeaux… we have our own… we are proud of our history.' Jacques remained imperturbable, already a veteran of such clashes with the old guard. 'I can swim with him, it's okay,' he whispered later. Later (3pm) at lunch at the very good Restaurant au Port in Mohammedia – which the Thalvin gang use almost like a canteen – the fonctionnaire seemed happier and had a dozen oysters. But we'd noticed with some alarm during the wine tasting earlier that he'd not been spitting.

Top: Trellising-talk:
Jacques 'Dangereux'
Poulain of Thalvin and
grower Abdelsalam
Moulbled; wheat, vines
and soil like chocolate
at Rommani in the
hinterland of Casa.
Middle: Flying back to
visit 'the best vineyard
in Africa'; salads and
spice in the Casa
market.
Bottom: New vine-
yards at Rommani –
'like the best of
Pomerol?'; Abdelsalam
Moulbled grows table
grapes too.

CB
Initiales

VIN VIEILLI EN
FÛTS DE CHÊNE

MIS EN BOUTEILLE
AU DOMAINE
PAR THALVIN
1993   DOMAINE DES OULED THALEB
BEN SLIMANE - MAROC

12% vol. 75 cl

SYRAH

1999

Morocco's wine
labels – except for
the CB Chardonnay –
don't cut many edges.

On the way back to Rabat, he sent a cyclist flying off into a roadside stall selling mint tea, and brought oncoming traffic to a tyre-burning halt by jumping the red lights. 'No problem,' he said, pronouncing his words carefully. 'We have practice of this every day!'

Most of the Thalvin wines originate from the 'traditional' Moroccan varieties – Carignan, Grenache, Alicante Bouschet, Cinsault and Tempranillo. Where Jacques Poulain was making the difference was in his vinification and vineyard techniques. He'd brought a very expert, Bordelais obsession about ripe tannins in red wine to the task. Just a bit either side of the cusp, he said, and a wine misses the point: it's coarse, green and puckers your mouth if unripe; it's flabby and spineless if over-ripe. These defects can be partially camouflaged by winemaking tricks, but real class is mainly about ripe fruit and ripe tannin before vinification. Jacques was the first winemaker we met in North Africa who worried openly about the problem.

'Everything else in the grapes is ripe, but the tannin is green,' he said, explaining that in hot climates you can get sweetness in grapes without physiological ripeness. So he'd applied various 'defensive measures'.

In the vineyards, he was manipulating irrigation, not to control the yield but to soften the tannin. 'We do it every three days, according to taste, just before we harvest. I think before long I will be able to prove a breakthrough.' In the cellar, he shunned the traditionally employed practices of long fermentation and strenuous pumping over to maximise colour and extract. He fermented at especially low temperatures, 12–14°C, to minimise tannin uptake. He showed off a cooling gadget he and a colleague had invented – and were thinking about patenting. Simple, mobile, inexpensive and very efficacious, he grinned.

Underground, where he kept his Chardonnay in barrel – next to a small wine library and tasting room – we asked whether we might visit what we'd tasted – the Chardonnay and Merlot vines. They had to be exceptional to produce such maiden wines. 'Too far today. Can you come back?' We were off to Tunisia the next morning, returning to Casablanca only to pick up our flight home. But that meant a day-long stop-over. And Casa hadn't been our favourite Moroccan city – industrialised, fishy-smelling, so disappointingly un-Bogart and Bergman. Jacques rescued us.

'I will be at the airport,' he said. 'I will take you to the most beautiful vineyard in Africa.'

An African Romanée?

And there he and his white Toyota Landcruiser were, and this was Jacques in rally-driver mode – safe but speedy. We drove for hours, the Atlas mountains hazy on the horizon, over crags and down gorges into the hinterland of Casa. Finally, we came over

D'ACCÈS À BORD
NG PASS

SAGER/name of passenger   اسم المسافر

TTER   *

من

UNIS

الى

ASABLANCA

CLASSE   درجة   DATE   تاريخ   DEP/flight   وقت

73   Y   03JUN   06H30

MENT/boarding   ركوب   SIEGE/seat   مقعد

06H00   10E

باب   HEURE/time   ساعة
OIDS/weight   الوزن

a crest and did a double-take. A vast, thick-pile carpet of vines – Syrah, Merlot, Cabernet, Tempranillo and Chardonnay – staggeringly precocious, brilliantly healthy – undulated into the distance, surrounded by oceans of golden, waving wheat.

'I told you! The best vineyard in Africa!'

'We will meet a nice old man of the soil,' Jacques said. Abdelsalam Moulbled is an aristocratic wheat baron whose huge farm borders the Moroccan Royal Family estate on this cool 800-metre-high plateau. Here, with Thalvin, he had established 150 hectares of vines; this was the home ground of the stunning Chardonnay and infant Merlot we had tasted at the Thalvin cellar. Jacques compared the *terroir* to the best of Pomerol but added: '*Attention!* There's something extra here!' Oenologist Christophe Gelly, visiting from Castel's Domaines Delorme near Meknes, was equally impressed.

We were intrigued to hear that the area and the nearest village were named Rommani, pronounced exactly as in Burgundy's Romanée. Might these wines one day become as famous as those on the Côte de Nuits?

The vineyards were laid out meticulously, trellised, with ample irrigation on tap: a huge investment. And virtually problem-free, Moulbled told us, except the birds eat the grapes. That's why he keeps the wheat. Jacques had coached workers in modern pruning and canopy-management techniques to maximise ripeness, minimise yield, concentrate fruit. This looked like an enduring source of very serious quality wine.

Moulbled, nearly 70 but a lot fitter and more agile than his friend, the late King Hassan, is an old-school farmer, up before dawn – today, he said, to organise the spit-roasted baby lamb (milk-fed only) for Jacques' friends. The lamb was the centrepiece of a late lunch; we lounged on divans around a low table in the salon, under a ceiling so intricately moulded and carved it had taken a team of craftsmen six months to complete. Eating was hands-on and in. Everyone dug into crannies and crevices, using their fingers as scoops, and triumphantly deposited the choicest morsels on our plates, whereafter we were watched beadily until we'd consumed every bit.

Jacques had brought some of his older, all-Carignan, Siroua Rouge – a fine violet-ruby colour, rich and concentrated, certainly one of the better traditional labels we tasted in Morocco. But the main accompaniment for most of the party was Ballantines whisky, practically neat.

One of the other lunchers, whom everybody called 'Sheik' was fascinated to hear we were from South Africa. 'Do you know you make this amazing chemical that can cover money notes and make them invisible to airport machines?' No, we didn't. 'Shall we go into partnership? You find it, I'll organise the money!' He laughed jovially.

Jacques dashed us back to the airport through the gathering night. What remained the most remarkable wine find of our North African travels had came at the eleventh hour in Morocco.

Eager to return, to see how the vines and wines were doing, we made plan after plan to revisit Jacques, but logistics and timing scuppered each one. We kept exchanging disappointed faxes and e-mails, we in our feeble French, Jacques in his idiosyncratic English. However, he wrote reassuringly about the Rommani vineyard:

Grapevines of Moulbled gave grapes of incredible wealth…futures wines are magnificent…you are always welcome here, we wait for you of firm foot….

ALGERIA

From tin back-packs in-
to trailers – harvesting
Algerian-style.

We have visited Algeria three times, which might seem a little excessive given that we've not once been to, say, Guinea Bissau. But the first time might have been the last. If ever a straw could have broken a camel's back, it happened here.

We got a parking ticket in the Sahara.

The temperature had been over 45 degrees, hot as harissa. We'd been slogging our way south, day after day. Over dunes fluted like pastry crusts; over seductively cinnamon-coloured, treacherously soft sand fields; over, most tortuous of all, the desert at its stone-hardest, beaten by the wind into infinite sheets of corrugated iron. We were hurled around the Land Rover like socks in the tumble drier.

Beware! Camels! We'd been amused by that sign at the start of our trek. There were plenty, saddled with rich red and orange rugs, bearing blue-robed, white-turbaned travellers smoothly past like a flotilla of yachts. But ominously, there were also heaps of scoured camel bones on the side of the road. What road, in any case? There was only one on the Michelin map, but on the ground a maze of tracks veered about wildly horizon to horizon, and we didn't know whether the skeletons were marking the right route, or the wrong one. The sand-storm season was about to begin.

So we were on our personal rims, drained and exhausted, when we crawled into the oasis of Tamanrasset. We'd covered 2127 kilometres of desert from the Morocco–Algeria border.

Panting for shade and icy drinks, we parked under a dusty tamarind, collapsed into a café with a humming fridge, and chilled out. Emerging four Oranginas later, we found a beaky little man in royal blue fastening a document in Arabic onto our sand-caked windscreen. Lurking behind the branches of the tamarind tree had been a No Parking sign. Ludicrous to us, a triumph to the only traffic officer in this one-camel town.

We protested, we laughed. He remained unmoved. Well! we fumed. Don't think you're going to find us visiting this part of the planet again!

Right and wrong. We didn't return to Tamanrasset – so remote that most Algerians never get there, fly if they do, and are deeply impressed by those who travel overland. But we were, a couple of decades later, with quite different challenges in place, about to drive through this troubled part of North Africa for the second time. 'Isn't it too dangerous?' asked Cheryl Carolus, a fearless, fiercely gritty leader of the anti-apartheid struggle, and at the turn of the new millennium, South African High Commissioner in London, Ambassador to the Court of St James. 'Wow,' she said. 'Be careful.'

Another year on we made a third sortie into Algeria. And though this time we were able to visit some vineyard regions that had been no-go areas before, different dangers lurked. We flew into Algiers on September 11 2001. The World Trade Centers and the Pentagon had been blown up while our Air Algérie flight was in mid-air.

War and peace

Those who prefer their travel diaries light and their wine stories frothy should be warned: the Algerian wine story is unavoidably serious. Sentenced to death, terrorised and traumatised, their vineyards ravaged, their cellars in ruins, wine people here were in the frontline of a war zone – the decade-long 'troubles', as Algerians refer to their civil strife.

It was a religious war, essentially, and decadent wine was at the core of militant Islam's quarrel with a louche, secular society ordered, in Algeria's case, by an equally militant military. Most commentators had been unanimous: in heading off what they considered a Taliban-like attempt to seize power and return Algeria to the Middle Ages, the military had themselves not been blameless. It was estimated that 100,000 people had been killed in the years of domestic strife – and we were frequently told that a shadowy figure named Osama bin Laden had fuelled its flames.

But by the end of 1999, the pitched battles and massacres were over, and 'we are starting to breathe again,' said the Algerian Ambassador to South Africa, an old friend (and former weapons instructor) of Nelson Mandela. Of course we should go to taste his country's wines on the spot. No one else had done so recently, it was true, but we should not concern ourselves. We would be 'looked after'.

We boarded an ageing, battered Boeing in Nice on a grey, drizzly morning. (Air Algérie's new fleet is a vast improvement.) There were no tourists making the hour and twenty-minute hop across the Mediterranean. Only us, and returning Algerians. There'd been reassuringly intrusive pre-flight security searches – El Al couldn't have done better – in a cordoned-off cargo area of the airport. Two hours late (on time for Algeria, actually, said a fellow-passenger) we taxied away, the loose carpets underfoot sliding this way and that. John alerted his neighbour – who'd just lit up – to the no-smoking sign. He took a lung-filling last puff as we lifted off and then obligingly, with leathery thumb and forefinger, squeezed the life out of the cigarette.

September 11, 2001, and still safe to fly. But by the time we landed in Algiers, suicide-bombers had struck the US.

'It's so hot here and there are sandstorms everywhere. They're even predicting an earthquake.' Our friend Abdelrazzak Osmani had telephoned from Algiers the evening before. He broke free from the cordon at Algiers airport – the non-travelling public were held well back from the Houari Boumediene arrival buildings – and rushed to welcome us. Our security detail, instantly suspicious, froze into a shield. We were already in the polite but firm grip of the police and the Algerian wine authorities – the Office National de Commercialisation des Produits Viti-vinicoles (ONCV). Razi – and we – learned that our programme was very chargé, and we didn't see him again in Algeria.

From now it was armed escorts and, in the wilder areas, military outriders in siren-wailing convoys. We were certainly 'looked after'. But there was no other way to get around.

Between me and my God

ONCV's human resources manager, Mohamed Rashid Salem, a national bridge player and equestrian dressage competitor, hosted our first meal in Algiers. Dining out was possible, he said, but safer in our hotel – the majestic El-Djazair, established in 1889, which everyone still called by its colonial-era name, the St George.

All intricately carved arches and grilles, lacy balconies, trellised verandas, and richly painted tiles, the hotel is a reinterpretation of the Moorish palace which once rambled over this site, high on a hill overlooking the port. Before becoming a grand (now State-owned) hotel, it was a superior boarding house, accommodating the overflow of visitors to wealthy expatriates. André Gide, Rudyard Kipling, Simone de Beauvoir all stayed here and walked in its palm avenues and lush botanical gardens. It was briefly General Dwight Eisenhower's Allied North African campaign headquarters during the Second World War (you can still stay in his bedroom) but we needed Mohamed's view on more recent history.

He ordered a Gris d'Algerie. That will be perfect, he said, but it had a depressingly stale bouquet. (Two years later, it smelled exactly the same. Old and neglected.) Why was an otherwise excellent hotel – a chic Chinese restaurant among its assets – serving such over-the-hill stuff? Why were the wine authorities allowing such a poor show? Let alone locals, the few visitors who braved Algeria deserved its fresher, fruitier wines.

Our conversation was inevitable. It was as if everyone had prepared for the same exam question: *Wine in a Muslim society: discuss.* They answered not to us but to the fundamentalists in their midst and in the tense aftermath of civil war, their views carried extra resonance. One diplomat had earlier roared at us: 'I raise a glass of red wine every night and drink to my personal crusade against the tyranny of religious extremists!' But Mohamed's delivery was more sombre.

'I believe,' he said, 'that wine is a personal matter between me and my God. And in my view that is the opinion of the vast majority of Algerians living in the cities. A lot of women drink wine and smoke too, though not much in public. The Koran, as interpreted by the Prophet, does not specifically refer to wine but says, "Do not pray when you are drunk." It also states there are benefits and disadvantages with regard to alcohol and that the disadvantages outweigh the benefits. But remember, the Prophet was himself only interpreting the scriptures. He was not God. And at least he recognised there were some advantages. Others interpret the Koran even more progressively.'

He continued: 'In modern Algeria, we have had a very hypocritical situation. The civil war was an attempt to impose one religious creed on our cosmopolitan society. Algeria has been at the crossroads of history – Berber, Phoenician, Roman, Arab, Ottoman… we are a very mixed people. Thank God this war did not succeed.'

During the war, he claimed that the fundamentalists were drinking wine themselves. 'All know it. We know from our distribution networks, even from the refuse collected, of empty bottles.'

His parting warning was not to wander anywhere near the Algiers casbah. We didn't. And our personal armed policeman, Anwar, escorted us into our hotel bedroom, this and every other night.

Before

We'd researched the available facts on Algerian wine before our trip, but they were skimpy and dated: visiting writers had been neither welcome nor safe in the country for a decade. Samples of Cuvée du Président, the most widely available red – at diplomatic functions at least – had not provided much enlightenment. This mix of also-ran southern French grape varieties wasn't about to receive any gongs. Was it the country's standard bearer? If so, Algerian wines were stuck in a time-warp, we pre-determined. How have the mighty fallen. Or would we find some of the vinous glories of Algeria's past alive and well?

Glory there certainly had been – before. 'Before' was Algerian shorthand for a multitude of meanings. 'Before' meant pre-1962 independence from France. 'Before' was when Algeria had been carpeted with vineyards, wall-to-wall, 360,000 hectares of them. 'Before' was when Algeria was the fourth biggest wine producer in the world, behind France, Spain and Italy. Prior to the Second World War, the flow of wine from Algeria to France made the colony the world's biggest 'exporter', too. And it led the North African trio of Algeria, Morocco and Tunisia which together represented two-thirds of the international wine trade. 'Before' was when Algerian wine's chief raison d'être was to beef up and colour not only lesser French domestic wines but, specially in poorer vintages, some rather grander Rhône and Burgundy labels too.

The old phrase *vin médicin* was still used by Algerians (and Moroccans) with pride, signifying not nasty medicine but the health-boosting tonic, the sunny ripeness their wine could inject into pallid, underpowered French specimens. Today all this would have been decried as a gigantic con, or (even trickier) a huge admission of inadequacy in 'French' wine.

After losing this jewel in its wine empire, a fifth of its entire crop, France character-assassinated Algerian wine as rough and tough! Yet the wines of Mascara, in the hills around the 600-metre-high mountains behind Algeria's western coastal city of Oran, had been winning prizes in Paris since 1858, just three years after the famous Bordeaux Grand Cru classifications were finalised. Mascara had official status, as French Vin Délimité de Qualité Supérieure, on a par with the metropolitan wine regions.

Halcyon days for wine, but not for Algerians, and the new firebrand leaders of free Algeria (promptly allying themselves to Moscow and Beijing) weren't interested in conserving the 'traditions and culture of the oppressors'. But this was a short-term back-view. Algeria's ancient association with the vine, like everywhere else in North Africa, made France look quite *arriviste*.

Even earlier

The first wine made in Algeria flowed from a blend of two cultures: those of the indigenous fair-skinned Berbers – hunters, pastoralists and by 3500 BC agriculturalists – and the Phoenicians. These mariner-traders were a *mélange* themselves: Canaanite stock infused with the exotic flavours of immigrants from Egypt, Crete, Mesopotamia. Sailing the Mediterranean from their city states along the Syrian shore, en route to the rich mineral fields of southern Spain, they sheltered from storms and foraged for supplies on the North African coast. These travelling salesmen soon began to trade with the locals; when their city state of Tyre was taken by King Nebuchadnezzar in 573 BC, Phoenicians emigrated to North Africa en masse. Within a century, the indigenous Berbers were working for these new masters, establishing vines among other crops.

Rewind – today's Algerian oenologists on the spot – and round the 'tank' – where their counterparts made wine 2000 years ago.

Mosaics and pottery show that Algeria was making wine long before it became the Roman outpost of Nova Africa. Under imperial rule, however, both markets and vineyards expanded – even Roman slaves were allocated a monthly amphora of wine.

All this was brought to life for us by driving out to the fabulous coastal Roman ruins of Tipaza, an hour west from Algiers. We had coffee at a café on a vine-draped terrace built into the ramparts of this once glamorous town. It's a 70-hectare UNESCO World

Heritage site now, swarming with archaeologists. (The Romans followed the Phoenicians, millennia after the first prehistoric inhabitants.) We wandered through an ancient arena with raked seating, and tunnels: we could almost see the gladiators and lions, hear the roars of the crowd. There were altars for sacrifices to the gods… graceful ochre columns round theatres and temples, basilicas and baths… a necropolis.

Bloodsports spectators, in the time of the Emperor Claudius, would have walked the same cobbled street as we did, down to the winery overlooking a bay of brilliant blue. Our modern Algerian wine friends posed for a photograph around a massive amphora. This fermentation tank was more or less 2000 years old.

The state we are in

If Algerians are famously frank, then few were more so than Abdelmadjid Merabet. He came to personify for us the modern Algerian survivor: cosmopolitan, charming, often secular, sophisticated and cynical but, despite two long wars in half a century, military coups, long dictatorships, nationalisations, authoritarian economics, he was still optimistic, full of laughter – much of it at himself.

Old pro of Algerian wine Madjid Merabet: 'I will explain you everything', he said. And did.

Chunky, compact, in his fifties, with wiry, salt-and-pepper hair brushed back hard, Madjid smoked 60 Malboro a day, though you rarely saw a pack. He kept the cigarettes loose in his jacket pocket, extracting one to light with the end of the last, a feat of seamless motion he sometimes managed with one hand. His breakfast quota was five fags, mitigated only by strong black coffees.

'I will explain you everything,' he'd said in mock confidential tones. 'It is a very interesting story. Many *bouleversements*.' And he had seen it all. A consultant to ONCV now, he had been its director-general in the early 1990s and earlier its production chief. He is a Dijon University-trained agronomist, skilled oenologist and all-round viticulturalist with (like many heavy smokers) a decisive palate.

'Ah, in Europe, Algerian wine has cornered the couscous market,' he said with a sad laugh. Brand loyalty for cheap wines among the many North African emigrants to Europe had been a double-edged thing, soaking up some quantity but stigmatising the labels, jamming Algeria into a low-rung rut. 'Not good business.'

But it was a lot better than some years before. Madjid and colleague Farouk Mechik – another charmer, the longtime ONCV marketing chief – had flown on many missions to Moscow to salvage what they could of the shattered Algerian wine industry, by selling to the Russians in bulk. At half the international price, but not in money, in exchanges, related Farouk. He still speaks some Russian: colleagues refer to them as Mechikski and Madjidski.

France – as every Algerian in the wine business corroborates with energy – had reneged on a pre-independence deal to continue to buy much of the Algerian crop. In some years, to make way for an incoming harvest, the Algerians were hurriedly forced to dump as much as 20 million litres of wine banked in overflowing tanks.

'They embarked on a deliberate campaign to discredit Algerian wine – the French press called it "*le pétrole rouge*", said Madjid. 'Can you believe that?' barked Farouk.

The French version of these events, naturally, goes rather differently. Huge deposits of oil and natural gas in the Sahara had given independent Algeria a strong hand against its former colonial power. In 1971 President Boumediene summarily nationalised the petroleum industry, sending international companies, including the French, packing. Algeria joined its Arab neighbours in the oil squeeze that shook the world and sent oil prices – and inflation – soaring, unsettling markets everywhere. Paris decided all bets were off. The wine treaty was redundant.

By then anyway, the mass, almost overnight 1962 flight of a million French colonial *pieds noirs* (wearers of black boots) had denuded the Algerian wine industry not only of its key players, but its thirstiest consumers too. And according to the French, Algerian wine quality slumped without their expertise. So the wine deal was off on two counts.

The caravan moves on

From Algiers, with Madjid, Farouk and other ONCV honchos, we flew to Oran. Very cosmopolitan, lots of cafés, any excuse for a party, we were told, but we apparently had no time for such frivolities. All we saw of this famously sophisticated seaside city was the airport before we were whisked into the hinterland.

We were met by the regional wine director, Mustapha Oukil – pronounced, appropriately, O'Keele. An elegantly tailored gentleman of Old World charm and sleek, middle-parted hairstyle, he had a fondness for lengthy debate which we'd always thought Irish until we met the Algerians. Also on the plane was ONCV Director-General, suave, chain-smoking Said Mebarki and his boss, burly Yahia Hamlayoui, an economist. He had a bone to pick with us – the standard of South African vine cuttings. 'We found them unacceptable. Diseased, even though they were sold to us as virus-free. We had to discard them,' he grumbled.

This entourage and the security-detail – bulging, bulletproof jackets, sub-machine guns clicking from safety to cocked and back – did not add up to your usual placid vineyard excursion. This was wine reconnaissance in armed force.

Waahwah! Waahwah! Waahwah…

Escort vehicles, front and back, switched on their sirens, motorbike outriders sped into position alongside our rapidly moving cars. We swept down the main boulevards of small towns that might have been in the rural south of France, lined with rotund date-palms and buildings roofed with terracotta tiles. Bleached shutters shielded arched windows from the North African sun, the wrought-iron balconies remained defiantly elegant. Old women in long robes scattered, small donkeys loaded with panniers of straw lurched out of our way, men in suits at pavement café tables stopped suspiciously in mid-sip of their mint teas. We sped on.

Remains of the heyday

Vast empty fields rolled to the skyline. Some fallow, sprinkled with grazing sheep; some ploughed. The soil looked deep and dark; it was earmarked for cereals. Or potatoes and onions. Or anything but the vines which once marched in bright green formation all over this western part of the country.

Facing a new millennium, all we could see was Algeria's tragic past and fragile present. How trivial the problems of most winemakers elsewhere seemed. Life and death, struggle and survival – they weren't clichés here. There was blood in these fallen vineyards; they were casualties of international politics and internal power-struggles. All that remained on this section of the road to Aïn Témouchent, about 75 kilometres from Oran, were the ruins of this once vibrant wine region.

There was Domaine St Jean, and Clos St Jules and St André and St Louis – wineries all reduced to faded lettering on abandoned shells. Some dated back to the 1870s, when many French growers abandoned their phylloxera-ravaged properties and re-grouped in the healthy climate of their colony across the Mediterranean. Three lofty cement tanks, silhouettes on the skyline, were the last lonely entrails of a cellar picked clean by forces beyond any winemaker's control.

Madjid, and we, became more depressed by the kilometre. We'd known there had been decline and fall, but the vast, tragic waste of what happened to agriculture here, and most devastatingly to wine, is almost incomprehensible, even when you see it. Madjid wiped away tears as he pointed out the skeletons of cellar after cellar. It was the first time in years he'd driven this route.

'Look at my wineries,' he mourned. 'All closed. I made wine in all of them. I knew all the cavistes.' In the 40 years since independence, the number of operational wineries nose-dived from 3000 to fewer than 50. The pathetically shrunken vineyards were down to 37,000 hectares, one-tenth of former times. Production had plummeted to 450,000 hectolitres. Back in Algeria's wine heyday, they'd churned out 21 million hectolitres annually, some three times more than South Africa currently produces!

Killing agriculture

The story our new friends told, in the eye of the storm, radically revised our definition of wine industry politics. Stand accused, they charged, Houari Boumediene: socialist,

CABERNET - S
CLONE 15
PG:140Rg CL:101

Top: *Traffic goes by at a clop near Mascara; room service at Hotel El Djazair; here we lunched on mechoui and tasted a young super-red; Gaiti Tayb, taste-arbiter at the Mohammedia winery.* Middle: *Tasting again; remains of colonial times; Moorish grace at the El Djazair; modern varieties, modern field researchers at Ain Temouchent.* Bottom: *Tipaza's Roman ruins; grape security; Mustapha Oukil; riding to work.*

soldier, dictator, second President of the new republic (and military backer of the first, Ben Bella, from whom he seized power in a 1965 coup).

Under Boumediene vineyards quickly became post-colonial victims, and the wine industry an economic and cultural nightmare. He ignored the facts: that viticulture in Algeria supported two-thirds of all workers in agriculture; provided half the country's export revenue; was still second only to oil as an export. He targeted industrial development as the overriding imperative of his régime. Agriculture became the dirt-poor relation. While industry was encouraged with incentives, including a special living allowance for those who moved into the cities, farmers were actively discouraged from expansion and directed to forget about their export markets.

Religious and anti-alcohol strictures, the easiest scapegoats for Algeria's wine decline, in fact were minor culprits. Boumediene, in the analysis of a leading Algerian economist, killed agriculture; he was one of Africa's visionary frauds and he failed to deliver Algeria's fabulous oil wealth to the people.

Algerian dates, once *premiers crus* in their field – 'the best in the world', every local told us, exported in massive quantity, suddenly disappeared from the international market. Not far from Oran, we raced through the village of Misserghin, where clementines were first developed by Père Clément, a green-fingered monk. Orangina, the hugely popular soft drink that international beverage mammoths have fought over tusk and claw, was Algerian-born. 'We were citrus pioneers. Then *pfouff*! Farmers were not allowed to export that either.' Olive production was the next to collapse – Algeria had formerly been the world's largest exporter of olives.

The previously French-owned vineyards and cellars had been nationalised and organised into collectives after independence; the land was redistributed, mostly in 3-hectare portions. But farmers were not given the title deeds – only the usufruct – and few had the urge or, on this micro-scale, the means, to make investments and improvements. The agricultural rout was almost complete.

Families abandoned the countryside and flocked to the factories. Those who stayed, struggled terribly, Madjid told us. 'This vine is old. I am in deficit. So – wheee! I rip it out!' was the refrain he heard over and over, from demotivated growers. The government, belatedly realising some of its mistakes, about-turned in 1986 and allowed wineries and farms to be privatised (Algeria is very paradoxical, said Madjid), but by then farmers were almost terminally demoralised.

Cut cut cut

Post-colonialism and politics shrank Algeria's wine-growing areas. Civil war almost wiped them out.

In 1990 the Islamic Salvation Front (FIS) swept to power – on the back of 'bread riots' – in local elections. Then came what seemed like the final blow: The vine is forbidden by God, FIS announced. Paradise was lost to both winemakers and growers, it preached.

'Everywhere, it was cut, cut, cut,' said Madjid, recalling the inexorable uprooting of vines, even in arid, rocky regions, where only they and the most tenacious olives and resilient aloes are reasonably at home. By the end of that year, only 102,000 hectares of vineyards remained in production, and about 60 per cent of these were politically and religiously correct table grapes. More wineries were dragged into the casualty department: with so few grapes to process, hundreds of *caves* were decommissioned.

While Algerian wine was stemmed to a trickle, blood flowed relentlessly. Civil war had effectively been declared by the military-backed government, against the militant guerrilla supporters of FIS, which was banned. Then the more extreme Armed Islamic Group (GIA) entered the fray. Appalling crimes and massacres were committed on all sides.

It is scarcely possible to imagine wine being made in such circumstances. Serge Hochar's gritty stand at Château Musar, keeping Lebanon on the world wine map while his country was engulfed in war, is perhaps comparable. The winegrowers of Zimbabwe have run the gauntlet of armed land-invaders, assaults and death threats. But in Algeria, the scale of intimidation and terror was enormous. ONCV extension officers visited outlying areas under armed guard, but were never safe. Madjid's closest friend was shot dead en route to Mascara. And still, committed winemakers and growers hung on and prayed.

By the early 1990s the mainstream guerrilla movement's cause had been muddied and indiscriminately bloodied by ravaging bandits, many high on drugs, locals allege, and available to act as mercenaries for the highest bidder. These rogue forces pushed the wine industry almost to the point of no return. In 1994 growers in Mascara were issued a chilling warning if they attempted to bring in their harvest: 'Cut one grape and we cut your throat. And your wife's and children's.'

Terrified, most complied. In just 15 days, farmers ripped out 3000 hectares of vines. The huge local co-op closed down. And then the cavistes in more isolated cellars also took fright. In one month, 300 wineries closed their doors. The battered wine community seemed finally beaten.

Stand or die

Crisis meetings were called at ONCV headquarters on the quayside of the harbour of Algiers in January 1995. Should it, too, abandon business? Wine had become a dead loss at home, and practically extinct in export markets, for while it had been fighting for its life locally, new wine countries, new technology and new consumer tastes had revolutionised the wine world. Algerian production and morale were at break point. Outside the boardroom, atrocities multiplied. The ONCV itself had been targeted. The civil war seemed likely to drag on and on.

It was then that D-G Said Mebarki took a decision which he acknowledged to us was crazy in many ways. He summoned up the defiant slogan of the martyrs of Algeria's own revolution as they faced French firing squads.

Mourir pour mourir, autant mourir debout.

If they died, they would die standing up. With honour.

He explained: 'I forgot politics and took a decision as head of a company employing 1200 workers, as well as all our growers, and their families.' Over the next few weeks, into February 1995, ONCV hammered out the blueprint for an extraordinary, high-risk rescue operation.

'With hindsight,' said Mebarki, 'we can find plenty of reasons for the decision to throw everything behind our last stand. But at the time, nobody but we were saying or believing such things.' He was threatened in Parliament by a fundamentalist MP who accused the ONCV of 'creating a new politics of wine just when we thought it was finished'.

To challenge the climate of fear and despondency, and the anti-wine propaganda of the time, the ONCV diverted massive investments into establishing its own new vineyards. 'We decided that even if the private growers did not come with us, over the next six years we were going to plant our own 10,000 hectares.'

The first pre-emptive move – to halt the feverish ripping out of vineyards – was to double the price of grapes. Then ONCV announced an ambitious planting programme, guaranteeing to back all farmers brave enough to join it. Generous (50 per cent) subsidies for fertilisers and pesticides; interest-free loans, repayable after the harvest; the hands-on assistance of *ingénieurs* (technical officers) were all offered to winegrowers.

Not more Gris! But salvation is at hand: ONCV's experimental vineyard of classic varieties, inland from Tipaza, heralds new varieties, new styles.

Then nature dealt a helping hand. A 10-year drought had crippled those who'd replaced grapes with cereals and other crops. And meantime, privatisation was claiming its own victims. Strings of factories closed, thousands lost their jobs. So many who had flocked from the farms to seek their fortunes streamed back to the land, susceptible to ONCV's blandishments.

'Their alternatives were closed,' Madjid told us. 'So they took courage and came back to the vine. Their experience and traditions remained.'

Back from the brink

ONCV's pioneering grower-partners became the wine industry's most fervent public relations officers. The national harvest, though still piteously reduced in comparison to the peak years of the past, rose by more than 100,000 hectolitres. Over *radio trottoir* (the pavement, or bush telegraph) the good news was broadcast.

Finally, in 1998, the Algerian cabinet gave ONCV its moral and public support, stressing viticulture's importance to Algeria's economy. 'They backed the challenge we had issued,' says Mebarki. More good news for wine arrived with President Abdelaziz Bouteflika, a former Algerian Foreign Minister and United Nations General Assembly chairman. Though his accession was fraught with controversy – the not-so-subtle pressure of the military persuaded all six of his election opponents to withdraw before polling – his Ministry of Agriculture publicly recognised the revival of the wine industry as a national priority.

'We began to breathe again,' said Madjid. 'And once we were sure we had official support we were obliged to move very quickly.'

By mid-1999 the ONCV had already bought 48 farms, mostly in the west of the country, not far from the Moroccan border, a total of 26,000 hectares. In Mascara, they planted 1000 hectares of new vineyards. At Bentata, within view of the Mediterranean, ampelographer (vine expert) Miloud Saadani, director of the new planting projects in western Algeria, showed us another fledgling vineyard of 300 hectares and insisted on discussing its merits in English.

All over the wine world, including here in Algeria, students turn grape-pickers at harvest-time.

Our fractured French improved in North Africa; it had to. Supplemented with hand signals and theatrical facial expressions, it got us by, but initially we struggled with technospeak. (It was some time before we realised that *goutte à goutte* had nothing to do with taste and everything to do with drip-irrigation.) But soon we were fluent enough to notice that Madjid, doing duty as translator, didn't always relay what we said. We asked blunt journalists' questions; he swathed and softened them in elaborately polite language. 'What Monsieur and Madame mean is…' It was reinterpretation rather than direct translation, and it worked beautifully, though it was sometimes difficult to keep a straight face when the gap between our straight-talk and Madjid's flowery delicacy yawned specially large.

However, when it came to the winery side of ONCV's mission to recover lost ground, he was frank: modernisation is crucial. Algeria's cellars had become a disaster area: underequipped fossils. Cement ruled, in industrial-sized tanks; cooling and cellar hygiene verged on rudimentary, oak barrels or even chips were a rarity. To morph old wineries into models for the new millennium, functioning to a total 2 million-hectolitre capacity, would be a gargantuan task. And even this might not be sufficient to handle the volume of wine destined to flow again!

The pace was slower on this front, and when we revisited in 2001, only four old cellars had been recommissioned. The focus still remained making bulk, all-sorts red blends, and rosé, in an era when single variety wines make the most profitable fashion statements.

Staffing was another challenge. Algerian winemakers had once been leaders in their field. Madjid Merabet's mentor, Papa Dahmoune, creator of the famous Cuvée du Président, was judged the best *maître de chai* 'in France' in 1926. Some of his students, now the old hands of Algerian wine, remain to lend their experience to the modern renaissance. But many abandoned their careers when their cellars were closed. Training a new generation is urgent: young Algerian *ingénieurs*, 20–30 annually, are being sent to the University of Bordeaux for one-year oenology diplomas. 'We cannot lose any time,' said Madjid, explaining why they were not targeting the four-year degree course.

We were seeing the start of a renaissance, and our first visuals of a battered wine industry began to take on a rosier tint.

Into the hills of Mascara

Next day, we travelled to Mascara through valleys of olives, climbed steeply, then stopped high above a lunar landscape. Stony hard, bone dry. Even a goat would starve. Madjid observed a few minutes' silence. It was right here, on a field-trip for ONCV, that his closest friend, a fellow oenology graduate, had been shot dead. 'By terrorists. For nothing.'

Mascara is one of the five Algerian wine regions, all west of Algiers, to have survived 'the troubles'. They roughly correspond to former French appellations (when names like Rabelais, Picard, Renault featured on labels) but now Algeria has its own Appellation d'Origine Garantie status. There is Medea, the Coteaux du Zaccar; coastal Dahra, Coteaux de Mascara, and, hugging the Moroccan border and the sea, the Coteaux de Tlemcen. There are two tiers of wines: a generic coteaux label, and, supposedly a notch up in quality, château or domaine labels – which don't signify that the wines come from a single property; only that they are the pick of a region's crop.

It was in Mascara and Tlemcen that ONCV had decided to concentrate their biggest vineyard expansion programmes. The target was 15,000 hectares by around 2008 (to complement the 10,000 hectares private growers would be urged to plant). In Mascara, the heavy-bearing 'traditionals', Grenache and Carignan, accounted for 70 per cent of the new plantings. Near the small town of Hadjout – just inland from the Roman ruins of Tipaza – we visited another young vineyard, 116 hectares, surrounded by the abandoned remains of formerly thriving wineries. The richest colonials lived here, said Omar Fodil, ONCV director of 'new projects'.

Trellised, irrigated Cabernet Sauvignon, Merlot and Syrah (it's all dryland bush-vines in Mascara and Tlemcen), were bearing formidably – up to 12 tonnes/hectare as against a low 4 tonnes in Mascara. But the classic varieties make up only a third of this new venture; the rest consists of the usual minor suspects.

Tramping through newly planted Carignan, Grenache, and Cinsault we admired the surrounding drystone wall, built from the rocks removed during soil preparation. Most attractive, but that's beside the point. Algerian soils are good, the climate generally favourable, and vine diseases common in many other parts of the world present only minor problems. Here, the biggest pest was *sanglier*, wild boar, which is inordinately fond of a diet of grapevine.

In a much older vineyard in the same locality we tried to break down Algerian resistance to the idea of marketing fashionable Syrah as a single variety or, more sensationally, a single vineyard wine. These *super-vieilles vignes*, up to 80 years old, had to be among the most precious antiques in the wine world. The cachet, marketing prospects and proximity to European markets seemed irresistible. Maybe, by claiming seniority, they could even reclaim this grape from Australia, we ventured. As Argentina had appropriated Malbec, New Zealand Sauvignon, and so on?

This not entirely whimsical idea unleashed an explosion. 'Don't you know that two Algerians equal three political parties?' Farouk shouted above the uproar. Exchanges of views here routinely come from poles apart. In this instance we were the other pole.

No, no, no! was the local consensus. They'd tried it and it hadn't worked. Picking and fermenting the mixed salad of grapes together undoubtedly produced 'better' wines than picking varieties separately and blending, if at all, later. Never mind that this bucked contemporary international trends. In any case, they were adamant, separate picking would be a nightmare in these jumbles of vines, unified only by age. But the prize is there: the fundamentalists haven't wiped out all Algeria's wine treasures.

Meantime, the good old recipe would be followed, and Hassen Daoud, a deputy D-G of the ONCV, was particularly averse to any new-fangled ingredients. 'No, never,' he said, 'will we use cultivated yeast. It would destroy our reputation for natural wines, it would change the unique Algerian taste.'

'Tradition and our culture – the vine, the olive, and our cuisine – must be our guiding marketing themes,' Farouk reminded us. 'But the loyalty of the Algerian consumer is a blessing and a curse. He doesn't like change. If I offer him a Mouton-Rothschild claret or a Mascara red, he'll always take Mascara – because it's Algerian.'

We would have taken one too, at the traditional lunch of *méchoui* – a spit-roast lamb borne whole to the table, and eaten standing, with a knife to hack off suitable bits, your hand to dig into the most succulent corners, and raw onion to cut the crispy fat. Never has a dish so screamed for a good slug of red. Especially in the circumstances – we were eating at the co-op in Mascara, on top of a stretch of cement tanks! There were bright pink and blue plastic anemones on the table, crusty baguettes, many glasses, but no wine.

It had all been sent off to ONCV headquarters. Maybe there was still a little in one tank…. Madjid scurried off with a jug, but the dregs had long since oxidised.

Applying Mascara

This party never skirted around issues, and tangents were surely invented by an Algerian. So we were prepared, later over dinner, when Mustapha (by now O'Keele to us), asked: Mandela, what is he really like? We threw out a string of superlatives: a man like no other… led us away from the precipice of racial war…inspiring, magnificent in every way… etc.

'Well,' said O'Keele. 'I have three daughters. Beautiful daughters. Before Mandela, I would never have allowed them to marry a black man. Now? No problem. Mandela changed my world. The world.'

There was impeccably fresh fish, succulent local prawns, and a scattering of the fabled Coteaux de Mascara bottles on the table. Happily, the ubiquitous, stale Gris d'Algerie had not made it to this gathering of ONCV top brass, though we did learn it had no excuse to be so unfascinating. Its grape mix is part Spanish grape Meseguera; part Clairette; part Chardonnay; part Aligoté and even (together about one-third) Grenache and Cinsault.

But it was the serious stuff we were drinking tonight. A Domaine El Bordj 94 from Mascara, selected from the very vineyard sites, since replanted of course, which produced prize-winning wines in France in 1858. It's an interesting merger too: mostly the two Algerian staples, Carignan and Grenache, with a mixed-spice sprinkle of Mourvèdre, Cinsault, Alicante Bouschet, Syrah and even Cabernet Sauvignon. Also a splash – about 5 per cent – of 'indigenous' whites – Farranah, El Moui, Tizourine. A local Chianti?

Our favourite was classified only as *vin de table* – Domaine Ouzera 96, from Medea, the hilly region behind Algiers which had become a renegade hide-out and was still too dangerous for us to visit, even with an armed escort. Some Cabernet Sauvignon stood out from the usual crowd. The grapes had – unusually – been pressed in separate batches. It snows in Medea, and the summers are relatively cool at an altitude of 1200 metres. In the past some growers accessed their ravine-hugging vines by cable car.

ONCV hoped to relaunch Algeria internationally with such wines – red only, to preserve their image (and because 90 per cent of the grapes are red/black). These might or might not, like the domestic labels, be vintaged. Farouk explained this curiosity: 'There would be too much demand for the good years and we are not organised enough.' As a virtual state monopoly, ONCV could afford such vagaries. But for how long?

The boss, Yahia Hamlayoui, a brooding presence at the table (since promoted to a post of Cabinet standing), was emphatic. The Algerian wine landscape must change and become more competitive to suit the country's transition from a command to a mixed-

Top: Farouk Mechik, Hassen Daoud and a boar-proof vineyard wall in Mascara. Middle: Inspecting a very vielle vigne; antiques of Algerian wine-making; awaiting the mechoui: the lunch-table above the tanks at the co-op in Mascara. Bottom:Olive groves outside the winery; main men: including Said Mebarki, D-G of Algerian wine (third from left), and Yahia Hamlayoui (extreme left).

demand economy. Foreign investors would be welcome to set up in Algeria now, lease land, and even qualify for state-incentives. They could establish their own vineyards and wineries, or embark on joint ventures with the government.

Old comfort zones, new horizons

Wine activist Jabulani Ntshangase was the first South African to take this bait. In 2000 he began structuring a historic collaboration between Africa North and South with wineries in Mascara and KwaZulu-Natal, and plans to bring some of South Africa's hottest young winemakers to work harvests in Algeria.

We had tasted right through the range and the regions in 1999, and repeated the exercise in 2001 with the latest vintages at ONCV's flagship Mohammedia Winery and bottling plant just outside Algiers. It was pushing 8 million bottles a year, just under half the total exported, and had grown (enormously) from the original *cave* founded by Catholic monks in 1908.

By this time, we were, men and women alike, on four kisses terms – for friends you haven't seen in a long while, we were instructed; two only if you bump into them regularly. So the greetings took (pleasant) ages. First there was the plant's director, Ihaddadene Boussad, who overwhelmed us with a deeply local gift – a Desert Rose, a fabulous multipetalled bloom of gypsum, naturally created and crystallised by Saharan sand and heat. Then there were *les girls*: there are more women in the upper echelons of the Algerian wine industry than anywhere else in Africa, perhaps the world. The laboratory at Mohammedia is headed and run by women. White coats over their blue jeans, Hakima Oulamara, Sabrina Mekaoui, Kahina Fridi and a bevy of other young beauties assessed the wines super-professionally with John and dapper Gaiti Tayb, the French-trained oenologist in residence, an enthusiastic taster and debater. He was under no illusions. The hammering the wines get from transfer by tanker over long distances in high temperatures before blending, filtration and bottling means a safety-first approach, and therefore highish doses of sulphur. And foreign supermarket buyers, who've done so much to shape and cater for modern wine tastes, had been too jittery (and far too well-supplied elsewhere) to risk visiting Algeria.

So we were tasting, and they were churning out, wines which conformed to a dogeared pattern, all from the same basic mix of minor grape varieties. Bulk blending blurred the regional and climatic variations which could have pumped some individuality into the bottle. Even alcohol levels were uniform, at around 12.5%. All understandable, in the circumstances. But the designer labels-in-waiting Farouk Mechik displayed were clearly intended for new, more daring vintages. They featured by far the most chic, modern variations on the desert/Mediterranean themes we saw anywhere in North Africa.

At both official tastings, Medea wines showed the benefits of a slightly cooler, gentler ripening season at altitude in a hot country. But we also liked the flavours from Coteaux de Tlemcen, which, Gaiti said, was only to be expected. In technical terms (and laboratory tests) this area produces the highest dry extracts of all Algerian wines, which generally means a deeper, more substantial flavour profile.

Later, in the garden of the El-Djazair, the girls took off their coats – and gloves – at a tasting organised for the local Press. They felt John was far too harsh on their wines, and surrounded him like a flock of (politely) annoyed birds. He didn't look as though he minded.

'Les girls' – a bevy of formidable feminine palates at work in the laboratary at ONCV's flagship winery near Algiers.

The comeback

Breaking back onto the world market is the mammoth task ahead. Wine faces the same dilemma as Algerian dates and olives: rebranding. Should they dust off old laurels or grow new ones? Emphasise region or variety? Play the *vieilles vignes* trump card or hide it until a new deck of plantings comes on stream? Push the Mediterranean connection? 'We are in a phase of maturation of our international strategy,' said Farouk.

The country's bulk wine image will be difficult to budge; its labels, apart from old campaigners like Cuvée du Président, are obscure; its winemakers unknown. And the perception still exists that Algerians are all anti-alcohol, and that those who don't drink can't make wine. The wry local response to this points to a time and place for everything; pray during the day, drink at night.

But perhaps a smarter response would be to organise an international roadshow – with women drivers! Like winemaker Ramilla Ramguendez. In her twenties, she heads Algeria's latest organic wine – *vin biologique* – project. The personification of cool in her flares, camisole top and designer sunglasses, she travelled with us on our 2001 visit.

We no longer needed police escorts, though ONCV's security chief, Rafik, was again an alert presence. (To our mutual delight, in the lobby of the El-Djazair we bumped into Anwar, our constant armed companion on our previous trip. He was guarding the visiting Belgian Foreign Minister.) Ten people had been killed the day before we arrived, in an area where fundamentalist extremists were still terrorising the locals. We were assured this was an isolated incident. But to us Algiers did seem more relaxed, livelier, sprucer. The heat was, if not off, at least turned down.

Maker of the most promising new-generation Algerian wine we tasted, Ramilla Ramguendez.

Ramilla has no escort when she visits Mascara to tend 'my vineyard', or the Cave de Bourkika to tinker with 'my wine'. We made that 70-kilometre trip with her, visiting the 170-hectare Bellalia vineyards in full harvest swing en route. Young students on holiday had been drafted in as casual pickers and two fearsomely villainous-looking guards were posted in a high lookout shack ready to pounce on grape-robbers.

She drew a sample from the (old cement) tank. It was a revelation: a thoroughly new-generation 2001. Powerful, gutsy, high-alcohol, strongly fruity, with some rare limpidity, showing what individual attention could achieve. Though it featured the usual Algerian mix, each variety had been vinified separately before blending. She checked on it regularly, and in between, it was looked after by the winery's headscarfed chemist, who had never drunk wine in her life, but had an excellent nose. 'A very good babysitter,' Ramilla said. With more selective picking, modern cooling, barrels, who knows what she might pull off?

Last taste

The winery here also makes a pastis called Narval after some obscure Polar fish 'which is, like this, always needing ice', we were told. This was the apéritif before our *méchoui* 2001. It is impossible to escape from the Algerian wine route without this roast lamb extravaganza; this one was exceptional and accompanied by a flood of wine. We'd recounted the story of our 1999 dry lunch in Mascara to cries of horror: It is a crime, *méchoui* without wine!

We returned to Algiers on a slow scenic road hugging the sea. There were kilometres of ice-creameries, and no wonder. It was so hot that everyone left car engines running and air conditioning on however long the stop. Small farms were planted with vegetables right down to the beach. Trucks loaded with green peppers trundled by. Flocks of sheep added to the weekend traffic jam.

We passed Madrague, a fishing village where we'd lunched on 'prawns and sauce' at Le Sauveur restaurant. This time, our seafood fix came at the more sophisticated Fantasia in Algiers. And the night before, the fish grill had been smoking under the stars beside the pool at the South African Ambassador's grand residence. His Excellency, the super-suave Moe Shaik, had picked up a lot more French since our first visit. Formerly the ANC's chief 'spook' – his term – running underground intelligence operations, he was now flourishing in the diplomatic air, and there were many speeches after dinner extolling North–South contributions to 'a new African millennium'.

Stirring stuff, but the *dîner de résistance* was on our last night, home-cooking by Fatima and Nawal Merabet, and this time too, our old friend and interpreter of Algeria's wine dramas, Madjid. Taking a break from the ONCV to recover from heart surgery, he'd played a supporting role in the kitchen to produce a culinary array that again underlined the pity of Algeria's virtual disappearance from the map during its 'troubles'. While Moroccan food is fashionable, Algerian food, equally exciting, is just about unknown.

At the Merabets' house opposite a mosque we had *chorba* (green wheat soup) with Algerian spring rolls or *bourek*; a delicate white-sauced, handmade pasta speciality of Algiers called *richta*; a dish of chicken and green olives from the west; lamb with prunes and almonds from the east. The Domaine El Bordj flowed, just about everyone smoked. Then to finish, melon and fabulous marzipan fruits. And dates from a desert oasis. We hadn't quite made it back to Tamanrasset, but near enough.

TUNISIA

Vineyards tumble down to Raf Raf beach near Bizerte.

Director-General Fethi Askri leant over his desk at wine industry headquarters in Tunis – L'Office National de la Vigne de Tunisie – and spoke confidentially. He had a theory that the vine had even deeper roots in Africa than any of us yet knew. That the mother of all vines might be found on this continent!

This was no crackpot speaking: this was the national wine chief, an eminent, widely published ampelographer. He had travelled all over the continent on research missions, living in huts, conversing with *petits Congolais* (Pygmy had long become an unacceptable name), tracking the grape into the depths of the jungle and bush. But though his search had proved fruitless – most of the local rumours of venerable vines had ended up in the grounds of mission stations, where Catholic fathers had planted the ingredients for celebrating Mass – he still had history on his side.

Tunisia had once led the wine world, and we were here to investigate what had happened to the vineyards and cellars of this beautiful little Mediterranean-rim country in the interim.

On the Carthage line

If there's one name which sticks out in BC wine literature, it's Magon. This super-agronomist, the viticultural guru of ancient times, was a Tunisian or, more precisely, a resident of Carthage. His theories were practised in the flourishing vineyards of the region; many are still in use today (close-planting, for example). When the Romans sacked Carthage in 146, they burnt its many splendid libraries too. But they took care to make a translation of Magon's *Treatise of Agronomy*, and thereafter plundered his viti-vinicultural ideas to propel their imperial wine diaspora.

No wonder the D-G saw red when *arrivistes* like Europe – let alone the New World! – questioned Tunisia's wine background. A small, round, bouncy man, Askri was our first official call in Tunis, and he immediately, emphatically – there should be no misunderstanding about this! – launched into a wine-history lesson. The Romans? *Pfouff!* They learned from us. The Ice Age pushed vineyards south from the Caucasus, and the Phoenicians brought vines right here, to Carthage, 3500 years ago. Long, long before the Romans came!

We'd already inhaled the perfume, tasted the fruits of descendants of the vines he was convinced were imported from the Phoenicians' Middle Eastern home region (round modern-day Lebanon). Muscat Sec de Kelibia, a light, dry, aromatic Muscat, today comes from vineyards planted practically on the beach, toes in the Mediterranean, in the neighbourhood of Kerkouane, a fifth-century BC Carthaginian site northeast of Tunis. It's no longer what it was – a palmy seaside resort – but one pink-tiled bath stirred our imaginations. Here some antique beauty might have lolled, lazily sipping her wine, contemplating the electric-blue view. Preserved in the Bardo Museum outside Tunis are mosaics of the same period, superb depictions of its rich wine culture.

We'd caught our first astonished sight of Carthage the evening before, from the window of a little train which trundles across the manmade Lake of Tunis on a long causeway. We had fled from the grand hotel the Tunisian diplomats in South Africa had recommended – clearly overestimating writers' finances – soon after we asked the price of their rooms and were corrected by the concierge: 'We do not have rooms, monsieur, madame. We have suites.' We scuttled out of town to find a less opulent base.

The remains of ancient Carthage, a pillar here and a ruined wall there, flashed past amid plush villas, embassy residences, the Presidential Palace, smart hotels. Modern Carthage is a chic seaside suburb, its fabulous name preserved in five stations on the line, including Carthage Hannibal. (We found a hotel more appropriate to our means a couple of stops further on.) However, as Askri was the first to concede, while history looks good in brochures and on labels, Tunisian wine can't rest on desiccated laurels.

He proudly announced that his office had launched, in 1999 – he paused for maximum effect – a Ten Year Plan! This campaign to boost Tunisia's 17,000 hectares of vineyards was operating on two fronts – improving the quality of traditional varieties (Grenache, Syrah, Carignan, Alicante Bouschet, Cinsault, Mourvèdre, Clairette, Muscat); and accelerating the planting of classic, or what he called 'universal' varieties.

The UCCV, the Tunisian winemakers' union, had already put the beginnings of this grand scheme into bottles: various co-ops had contributed to the making of the country's first classic *vins de cépage* – single-variety Syrah, Chardonnay, Cabernet Sauvignon

Five centuries BC pink was THE bathroom colour and Muscat grapes already grew on the beach near the Carthaginian resort of Kerkouane.

and Merlot – to celebrate the union's 50th anniversary. Before their neighbours, it seemed, Tunisia had got the modern wine message: all-sorts, mystery blends of lesser grape varieties weren't going to cut it in the twenty-first-century wine market. Even if they were the 20 per cent cream of the crop allowed to flaunt a Tunisian Premier Cru tag; even if they did come from the Coteaux de Carthage or d'Utique. (Utica started off rather like Cape Town, only a great deal earlier, 1100 BC, as a halfway-house on a rich trade route – between the Phoenician home ground and Spain.)

So, Fethi Askri beamed, he would give us Mohamed for a day or two. Mohamed would take us to some of the vineyards and wineries. *Non, non*, it would be too difficult for us to drive ourselves. *Par exemple*, without Mohamed how would we find, in the deepest countryside, the two farmers he'd already lined up to epitomise the best of the old and the new? In any case, Mohamed was *un caractère* – 'that is why I have chosen him'. He would add more flavour to our schedule. We would see.

We had already seen. From the moment he came to pick us up – so immaculate in an Armaniesque linen suit we initially thought he must be the D-G himself – and took us to the national wine office in Tunis, it was clear that Mohamed Chekir had more than his driving skills to offer, though these were considerable. We had to beg him frequently to have mercy on the accelerator, but he was a fine judge of slipstreaming and taking the narrowest of gaps; he also avoided tollgates with great cunning. Muttering about the *péage* (highway toll) in a manner so similar to the French pronunciation of pH that we thought he'd launched into vine-speak, he would veer suddenly off the highway into the *garrigue*, tear over obscure sand roads, and make a triumphal, free, re-entry into the traffic beyond the toll-booths.

But most importantly, he was a man of his stomach. Via Mohamed, every few hours, we could be guaranteed of sampling yet another Tunisian delicacy. The suit became progressively more rumpled after we left the city and proceeded west into the back-woods of the Tebourba region.

Ancient and modern

Lean and long Faisal Mzlini, wearing a wintry hat with ear flaps more suited to the Russian steppes than scorching *Tunisie profonde*, was waiting for us in his 7-hectare vineyard. Precision-planted rows – not a leaf out of place, not a single stray weed – of Cinsault, Carignan, Alicante Bouschet and the Sardinian grape Monica (which he called Monique) marched up and down gently rolling slopes. Faisal was 'the best young *viticulteur*' in these parts, according to our briefing, and certainly his young vines looked splendid and his technospeak – rootstocks, soil composition, pruning and canopy management – was all new-world, even if his varieties were not.

The embodiment of quite another era was nearby farmer Al Haj Mohammed Souissi, wizened as a walnut, turbaned, tending his nearly 9 hectares of Monique and Cinsault. These were notably healthy too, but they were real oldtimers, planted, so he claimed, in 1946. They had the thick, gnarled trunks of ancient trees, and their roots looked as if they went down for ever, but they still produced a respectable 6–7 tonnes/hectare, for a product which this devout Muslim – who'd made the pilgrimage to Mecca – had never drunk in his 80-year-old life.

Next we sped off to the village of Thibar, a Roman outpost in the second century BC, 140 kilometres west of Tunis in the Beja-Jendouba wine region. It was far enough from Mohamed's breakfast to necessitate stopping for a considerable snack en route. In the bustling provincial town of Beja we had a *café direct* (nearest local relation to a cappuccino) and traditional pastries, *m'kharek* (plaited, honeyed) and *zlabia* (a lemony whorl), both deep-fried to order in gigantic cauldrons. Mohamed had a quick smoke-break – a puff or two on the traditional water-hookah – and, fortified all round, we ventured deep into rosé and red wine territory. Merlot, Cabernets Sauvignon and Franc, and modern Mourvèdre had recently joined the region's 1000-hectare mix of traditional varieties.

Thibar's most recent colonists had been religious. The winery of Domaine de Thibar was formerly a cloistered Catholic monastery. A mosque, with muezzin, peered over its walls. Viticulturalist Moez Ayadi and *cavistes* Noureddine and Habib Khemeri were as cheerful as the wines' packaging. This depicted a jolly Bacchus holding an amphora on his shoulder, in a sort of javelin-hurling pose. Its contents appeared to be cascading all over the place. He sported a bracelet of vine leaves and grapes, should there be any doubt of his identity. The heavenly background was a very lurid blue.

The young team here was obviously doing its best, but the winery equipment was outdated, the tanks cement, the bottling hall sauna-hot. The oak barrels were mostly rickety veterans of decades of Thibarine, a wine and herb liqueur as demanding as Fernet Branca, though some had played an undiscernible role in the making of a very rustic, low-alcohol (11%) red blend named Château Khanguet. (Naked in its unpolished glory, read John's note.) It tasted a bit like a gravel farmyard, and whether the slightly sweet overtones came from Grenache, Alicante Bouschet or our first meeting with Monica (Munica/Monique) we weren't certain. 'And don't forget the 2 per cent Pinot Noir!' urged Noureddine hopefully. Whatever, it called for a hearty dish of couscous. Monica was again a bit-player in the earthy Clos Thibar rosé, with Cinsault and Carignan, which Noureddine pronounced 'the best in Tunisia', but which we found a little too feral for our (doubtless effete) palates.

Our return loop to Tunis provided yet more evidence that if it's great Roman ruins you want to see, uninfested by tourists, don't go to Rome, come to North Africa. The town of Dougga took us just off the main road and way back in time. There were evocative arches and baths, temples, theatres and ancient brothels; a very fine capitol (dated

OINE
N

كالة إحياء التراث
التنمية الثقافية

№ 585953

1.000 DT

Ste de Dougga

26 ... 1999

يوم التصوير

الرجاء الاستظهار بهذه التذكرة عند الطلب صالحة ل
sition. Il n'est valable que pour une seule visite le jour de son émission

6 V/A/M/000 TVA comprise au taux de 6%

Top: *small vineyard on Cap Bon; palms and vines along the Med.; individual bottling for Sidi Saad Rouge; 'best young viticulturalist' Faisal Mzlini.*
Middle: *Jean Boujnah, Tunisian wine independent; permission to snap the sights; off to the shops; Domaine de Thibar viticulturalist Moez Ayadi; his monastery-turned winery.*
Bottom: *New barrels at Bir Dressen Co-op; BC and AD ruins at Dougga; grapey traffic circle at Grombalia; 'best old viticulturalist' Al Haj Mohammed Souissi and matching vine.*

AD 166) with soaring fluted columns; and nearby, a third-century BC pre-Roman mausoleum. Young Tunisians were clambering about, lapping up their history.

We noticed how unusually neat the roads through towns and villages were, and wondered why they were all called Boulevard de l'Environnement. The indispensable Mohamed enlightened us: President Ben Ali had enforced this uniform nomenclature, decreeing that towns which did not keep their main drags clean would be fined. Visitors should not take away a filthy impression of Tunisia.

It was now stinkingly hot and eating couldn't have been further from our minds, but Mohamed declared himself faint with hunger so we stopped for a late lunch. Tunisia is very strong on roadside food. No flabby hamburgers, wrinkly sandwiches or micro-waved monstrosities here. Every village and byway is lined with small butcheries and al fresco barbecues; you choose your hunk of lamb in the former, it's grilled in the latter, and served with a fresh salad of tomato, onion, green peppers, chillies and caraway seeds called *méchouia* (confusingly similar to the name for a whole spit-roasted lamb in Algeria), olives, pitta bread or baguettes.

An independent

Strength restored, Mohamed drove us on to Montfleury, on the outskirts of Tunis. Here we met cynical, amusing Jean Boujnah, the businessman of the world who heads the country's biggest independent producer-négociant business. Established by French immigrant René Lavau in 1895, SICOB (La Société pour l'Industrie et le Commerce de Boissons) was producing 4 million bottles annually at the large, modernised cellars of Tebourba, Fouchana, and here at Montfleury. The technology in the bottling plant was impressive, and the labels as slick as the boss.

One of those authority-challenging, go-getting entrepreneurs, Boujnah is the sort of rebel character every establishment-dominated industry probably needs. For example, he felt that the name 'Carthage' should belong to Tunisian wine in general, and not remain the sole property of the national co-op, UCCV. So he'd cheekily named one of his reds Cuvée de Carthage, reproduced an ancient mosaic on the label, and sent a batch to the US. The wine was sold and drunk without fuss, but when he tried the same in Europe, UCCV claimed its trademark. 'We have a big fight.'

He was the first to offer an explanation for the absence of oak in local cellars, beyond the 'it is our tradition not to use wood' line. For the prices that local and export Tunisian wine fetches, it doesn't pay to import expensive barrels, let alone mature wine in them. His La Vieille Cave Grand Vin Rouge (Carignan, Syrah, Merlot blend) made by oenologist Noureddine Megla was good as it was. And who needed wood for vin gris, like his supple, agreeable El Kahena, a blend of Cinsault, Carignan and Mourvèdre? Or for the amiable, ubiquitous Cristal Blanc white blend (Ugni Blanc with a splash of Pedro Ximinez,

Chardonnay and local grape Beldi)? Or for the biggest seller, the Koudiat rosé? Private cellars such as his are in the minority in Tunisia (the UCCV produces 65 per cent of all wines), and specialised vinification of small parcels virtually unknown. But a handful of other mavericks are bucking bureaucracy, among them the Tardi family. In their vineyards in the north of the country, near Lake Ichkeul, the watery, marshy setting of Tunisia's only national park, they were giving classic varieties, including Pinot Noir, a go.

North Africa's Cape peninsula

Next day, Mohamed introduced us to another institution of Tunisian cuisine – *le restaurant populaire*, the equivalent of a working-man's café or *routier* pit-stop. *Salade méchouia* was the constant on the menu, but Au Bons Amis, packed from its pavement tables to its enclosed veranda and into the depths of the kitchen, specialised in a hearty casserole of chick-peas, beans, braised lamb and potatoes.

We were now in Grombalia, in the heart of the vineyards on Cap Bon, the 25-kilometre wide peninsula southeast of Tunis. Though it features many more olive groves and gentler mountains, the combination of cliffs, sea and vineyards reminded us of South Africa. (There's more symmetry: Tunisia and South Africa own the extremities of the African continent, both in wine territory: Cap Blanc and Cape Agulhas.) A gigantic bunch of cement grapes adorns the traffic circle in Grombalia centre; the biggest event of the year in this Muslim country town is the annual wine-harvest festival.

We spent the morning visiting a series of wineries old and new, starting in the Mornag area 20 kilometres out of Tunis. Just about every growing thing here, vines and olives apart, was pollarded, and we drove between thick hedges of aloes and prickly pears, all given the flat-top treatment. There were sheets of wild red poppies, white lace-flowers and yellow fennel.

At the purple (they all appeared to be purple in Tunisia) bougainvillea-draped Cave Coopérative Bir Dressen we saw our first and only new *barriques*. These were labelled Vicard, France; when we asked for details – forest, toasting, grain – no one knew. The winery gleamed with stainless steel and the bottling plant was ultra-modern, except for one small corner. There sat a couple of men on a low bench surrounded by double-handled, small glass flagons of wine. The sort of shape that has lampshade-base written all over it. This was the Sidi Saad Rouge, which obviously had to be labelled by hand.

In an attractive subterranean tasting cellar, we clearly disappointed our hosts by trilling over the sort of Dry Muscat they'd been making for centuries (*Great bounce!* read our notes) and remaining rather tepid about the newer-generation, oaked reds. A 98 Merlot with a walnut nose tasted curiously volatile and sweet-shoppy at the same time, but when we hazarded this opinion we were firmly rebuffed. This was the effect of new wood, we were told. We retailored our remarks to the safer realms of 'most interesting' and 'very different'. To those compelled to score every wine let's say that we might have rated the best of these reds, a 97 Cabernet with 6 months oaking, 14 out of 20.

At the nearby Cave Coopérative Semmech, we found rampantly moustachioed cellar chief Noureddine Benzurane, a veteran of 30 years in wine, beaming and cooing over his latest acquisitions, two 40-ton Italian roto-presses so new they were still wrapped in plastic. 'What improvements we will now be able to make!' He was practically dancing with excitement. Hayrel Ben Naceur, his young University of Barcelona-trained oenologist, was enthusiastic too. It was he who'd fine-tuned the *vins de cépage* that Fethi Askri had so delightedly shown us as examples of Tunisia's wine renaissance.

'Mes Bebes!'
Noureddine Benzurane
welcomes his new
machines.

This co-op had been in business since 1948, and now had 160 members tending 1600 hectares of vineyards. A conversion to new 'universal' varieties had begun; 180 hectares had already been planted (and trellised: machine-harvesting — socially unacceptable in other North African countries — was going to be introduced). All these innovations because the Germans demand it, they're our top consumers, Noureddine explained.

Equally intent, if not more so, on raising the national bar to international heights was our next stop, Domaine Magon. It was newly planted as immaculately as we imagined the famous old Carthaginian wine-fundi would have demanded. The rusting, flapping sign was a relic of its past: now it represented the sort of joint venture Tunisia has been encouraging since it opened up its previously socialist economy to private investment. (A policy that saw the country's growth rate become the highest in Africa, after Mauritius.) At Domaine Magon, the local:foreign ownership ratio is 66:34, but it is German money and markets that drive the engine. Other partnerships, including a Tunisian–Sicilian one, were in the pipeline — looking ahead to 2007, when the country's 'association' agreement with the EU was due to become a full free trade agreement, with all customs tariffs scrapped.

With the aid of a formidable German machine that could plant 3 hectares or 10,000 vines a day, 240 hectares of red varieties were being established to transform Domaine Magon: Syrah, Merlot, Cabernet Sauvignon and Pinot Noir. They looked superb: extremely vigorous and healthy; the best vines we saw in Tunisia.

Top: Plodding through
the Muscat at Raf Raf
Middle: The German
machine that plants
10 000 vines a day;
Taking a break from
weeding the vines at
Domaine Magon,
colonnades of cement
tanks.
Bottom: Old sign, new
Tunisian-German initia-
tive; the Tardi vineyards
near Lake Ichkeul in
the north.

All the modern techniques of canopy management and stress alleviation were in place here, and needed to be. Though most of the country's vineyards are moderated by maritime breezes — 'strong winds', clarified this project's savvy viti-viniculturalist, Hedi Grayaa — even late spring, as we found, can be searing. Old laws forbidding irrigation have now been relaxed, but there was a small difficulty with the computer-controlled irrigation system, tapping a number of wells and boreholes. The builders inexplicably forgot a door; they'd entombed all the machinery, and when we visited, they hadn't yet tidied up the hole they'd had to break into a wall.

شركة الإحياء والتنمية ال
ضيعة ماڤو
القبّة ـ بني خلاد
S.M.V.D.A
DOMAINE MAGON
KOBBA = BENI-KHALLED

Machines didn't rule altogether, however. These vineyards were being weeded by hand by families of peasant workers – men, women and children. They were lunching on baguette sandwiches, sitting in the blazing midday sun under little tepees fashioned out of branches and black plastic, topped by layers of the grass and weeds they'd been clearing.

The Med washes both ways

We drove back to the decidedly other-worldly sophistication of the seaside resorts on the Gulf of Tunis – La Marsa, Sidi Bou Said, Carthage – where café society throbbed, and included women. Tunisia's first post-independence leader, President Bourguiba, who assumed power in 1956, had liberal ideas not only on wine but on women, too. Or perhaps more correctly, as it was related to us: Mme Bourguiba insisted.

Older women in Tunisia, especially outside the big cities, still wore the *hijab* (veil) but Bourguiba, describing it as an 'odious rag', banned it from schools, and we saw few younger women in such traditional dress. Over and over we were told by Tunisians that it was 'the emancipation of women' which distinguished their country from the neighbours, and made it 'more progressive'. Mini-skirts on the streets, bikinis on the beaches, these were common, but not the point: it was Tunisian women's professional, economic and political clout that made the difference.

It all seemed very French. Or Italian. And Tunisia was the only North African country we visited which didn't take this observation as an insult. 'My country,' its suave Ambassador had remarked, briefing us before we left home, 'is not like the others. The night-life… at 10 in the evening it has only just begun! Here in Pretoria…' he'd sighed and diplomatically left the sentence unfinished. Whichever end of the continent, he led us to understand, Tunisia was livelier, more cosmopolitan, more urbane.

We wouldn't have to tiptoe delicately around the subject of wine, to avoid either colonial or religious sensitivies, certainly not. We would see – and did, at wine industry headquarters in Tunis – a famous photograph of President Bourguiba, pointedly planting a vine. We would see that Tunisia was the most secular state in North Africa, and that wine had been completely outed. It was a proud national tradition, widely and openly drunk 'as in any other Mediterranean country' (and starting long before Italy, or France).

Out of Africa?

At our small hotel, the Plaza Corniche at La Marsa, much wine was consumed, and the underground disco vibrated all night. 'Yes, this place is not for the old, not for the quiet!' confirmed the manager, Abdessar Ayed. But it was a small price to pay for the fantastic enclosed garden, and the open air restaurant, lit at night by millions of white fairy lights wound round towering date palms from the oasis of Gabes. And the neon turquoise of the view from our balcony.

We were initially mystified by the colour of the Tunisian stretch of the Med. Why did it somehow appear a more iridescently kingfisher hue than the neighbours'? Eventually we decided it must have something to do with the power of contrast: of blue sea and brilliantly white coastal architecture, exemplified in the next historic suburb along the Carthage line, Sidi Bou Said. Aquamarine shutters, casements, balconies and arched doors decorated with brass and iron studs are set in shimmering white walls; a rampage of purple bougainvillea deepens the effect. It all looks too picturesque to be true, but it's real enough. People are living here – and amiably putting up with the busloads of tourists who converge to drink mint tea and smoke hubble-bubble pipes at 'the oldest café in Tunisia'.

One of the grandest blue and white edifices of all, high on a hill looking all the way to Italy, is the American Embassy, where we were invited to dinner. (Courtesy of our friendship with the Ambassador's husband, an old journalistic colleague from Cape Town.) We drank California wine, and our table-neighbours included the editor of the leading daily newspaper in Tunis, visiting honchos from the US State Department and the Pakistani Ambassador, an admiral with whom Erica talked cricket all night (she is obsessive about the game). Excellent company and wine, but the food was nowhere near as good as that on the vine-covered terrace of the Plaza Corniche.

En l'honneur de l'Ambassadeur Robert Oakley et Mme Phyllis Oakley, Secrétaire d'Etat Adjoint

L'Ambassadeur des Etats-Unis d'Amérique Madame Robin Lynn Raphel

prie M. et Mme Platter de lui faire l'honneur de venir dîner le jeudi 27 Mai à 20 heures

R.S.V.P.
782.566 poste 4450
789.037

Résidence
Sidi Bou Said

Our invitation to a diplomatic dinner with a view in Sidi Bou Said.

There, the debonair, bow-tied *maître d'* would bring along a little folding sort of luggage rack, snap it open, and deposit a great plate of just-caught raw fish for us to inspect and select: swordfish, tuna, merlou, rouget, sea bass. The minute it had been grilled he would glide back, dissect it with a fork and *spoon*, and present it to the table, majestically deboned. It was he who'd first recommend the Kelibia Dry Muscat to us: a charmer of a partner for fish.

The hotel was owned by André Backar, a Tunisian who'd become a highly successful Wall Street broker, and was once rated the 12th richest man in the world by *Fortune* magazine. Mme Backar was apparently the decorator, and she'd modelled her ideas on New York's Tavern on the Green. The accessories included American signs in the bar – Fifth Avenue, Broadway – and the flags of US states flying round the pool, where most superior little *amuse-gueules* accompanied every drink: warm broad beans, chunks of cucumber, minute minced lamb *boulettes*, small squares of local cheese and *tajine* (not a stew or its cooking-pot in Tunisia, but a sort of pastry-free quiche). We'd initially been drawn to the place by the naïve painted statues in the garden. They reminded us of works by South and West African artists.

Where are they from? we asked. From Africa, came the reply. But, we said, this is Africa. The helpful hotel employee looked perplexed, then pointed vaguely south. No, no! I mean they are from *Africa*-Africa!

This hyphenated manner of describing sub-Saharan Africa – a them-not-us figure of speech – was new to us, but only underlined what we could see, literally: Sicily, 80 kilometres from our room. And what we'd observed – the links did seem much closer with Mediterranean Europe than the African continent. The Medina in Tunis was the most haggle-free we encountered in the Maghreb, and the salesman from whom we bought a superb carpet looked at us with bewilderment when we asked if he drank any wine. *Bien sûr!* A little – three or four glasses – a day. To take away the stress.

Meantime, there were more Tunisian vineyards to explore. We drove up to the seaside hamlet of Raf Raf in the Bizerte region northwest of Tunis. Here plodding horses ploughed Muscat d'Alexandrie vineyards which swept steeply down and around Raf Raf's crescent-shaped bay and silver beach. The Hotel Dalia served the freshest skewers of grilled prawns, brought in by the fishing boats rocking on the shore. But no wine, no beer. We asked the waiter why not. With a slightly disapproving look – clearly the louder, looser effects of alcohol were not lost on him – he replied firmly: Because here we are *très calme*.

Passionately green

Communist Green, free-spirit eco-wine-maker Amor Jaziri.

Closer to Tunis, a half-hour east of the capital, we tracked down Amor Jaziri. A respected research scientist and top UCVV official for 30 years, his training included stints in Paris, Dijon and Montpellier. Now in his mid-fifties, he'd 'retired' to a 14-hectare farm near Jedeida – which calls itself the Town of the Artichoke, sporting a colossal sculpture of this spiky vegetable on the main street.

'Wine is still my life,' he said, but at last, he made it clear, he was living *that* life, making *that* wine, his way. A sturdy, blue-eyed Berber with a dreamer's approach – *L'amour et la passion du vin* was the heading on his wine brochure – he was also (still) a Communist, and his strong, pleasantly rowdy opinions had a distinctive spin.

As did his Almory wines (a compression of the first names of himself, his magistrate wife Alya and daughter Rym). He poured a surprisingly gentle, light-coloured 2-year-old Carignan-Syrah blend into large glass tumblers without ceremony. There was a mound of black olives on the rickety table to nibble with crusts torn off a baguette drenched – not drizzled – with his own olive oil. The oil was green, fresh and scratched the throat properly. (Rather too much North African olive oil tastes stale, looks yellow.) The wine was very light, juicy, simple but good. 'Like the pinot of the Rhine,' he said.

He also made a rosé from Grenache, a white from a Muscat he called Raf Raf (Muscat d'Alexandrie habituated to the beachside *terroir* we'd visited earlier) and a Vin de Pays Almory Village ('convivial par excellence!') from Carignan and Cinsault. The wines on his list didn't seem to coincide directly with the rows of vines outside, hazy in the Mediterranean heat, which included one of the few patches of Chardonnay in the country, and some Alicante Bouschet too. Beyond, rolled hills covered in ripe wheat fields and waving, silvery olive groves.

'People and the earth must be in harmony, otherwise the wine will be no good,' he said. 'Same for olives,' and he nodded vigorously. Here was the Tunisian pioneer of *vin biologique*. He made his own compost, and shunned all chemicals – in the soil, on his vines, in the making process – except traditional copper and sulphur, which he used sparingly. He had an abrupt view of oak: 'An additive, hides faults and cheats the consumer. *Pfouff.*'

For his annual pilgrimage he headed to the Semaine Verte – Green Week – in Berlin, where environmentally sensitive oenophiles gobbled up his production. Charter plane-loads of European sun-worshippers decant on Tunisia's coast continuously, and German parties regularly visit him at his tiny, challengingly rustic winery and olive-mill. His open-air recycling and bottling plant consisted of two cheerful women sitting under a tree, scouring away with bottle brushes. Having dextrously uncorked the used bottles with a loop of wire.

Just as we were about to leave, Amor answered the inevitable question. How to reconcile the drinking of wine with Islam? Leaning through the car window, he pronounced solemnly: 'Man and wine – neither must be a slave to the other.'

EGYPT

*Three different ways
to get to the Pyramids
of Giza...*

Logically, we should perhaps have begun our African wine quest in Egypt. Here, at least five millennia ago, the culture of the vine had first taken root on the continent. Ancient tomb paintings show, step-by-step, the whole winemaking process from vineyard to table. How the grapes were trellised, how they were crushed – by foot, with workers holding onto the sort of overhead strap contraption still used in some traditional cellars in Portugal – and wrung out in sacks, like laundry. How the wine was stored, vintaged and signed. (The personal cult of the winemaker is very old indeed.) And how lavishly it was consumed – with bejewelled socialites depicted in dainty mid-vomit; not a social gaffe in those days – at the banquet table.

But where, in modern times, were these once-illustrious wines of the Nile delta, savoured by the Pharaohs and Cleopatra?

It took Europe many centuries to catch up to Africa, and the New World many more, but in the meantime, the ground beneath Egypt's vineyards became shakier and the climate supporting its wine traditions far more inhospitable under the influence of Islam and the invading Ottomans. Tom Stevenson, in *Sotheby's World Wine Encyclopedia*, wrote: 'Foul-tasting Egyptian wine should be avoided at all costs.' This was the consensus on the fruits of the State-owned and -run vineyards near Alexandria. We pushed them to the bottom of our itinerary.

But as a new millennium began, we heard tantalising murmurs of a revival. The industry had been privatised. The French were being consulted. A week after the September 11 2001 aerial attacks on New York and Washington, we flew into a Cairo jittery with rumours of Egyptians among the suicide bombers. What we found was probably the most dramatic symbol of an African wine renaissance on the continent – in a country whose national airline serves no alcohol (while heavy smoking appears almost obligatory).

We left the many-storeyed pleasure palaces on the banks of the Nile glittering brilliantly behind us as we took the new Ring Road round this most insomniac of African cities to the suburb of El-Giza. It was no less noisy than downtown – the hooter is a crucial component of every Egyptian vehicle – and at just before midnight no less busy. 'We have a 24-hour rush-hour here,' said our driver proudly.

Policemen were unclogging traffic jams; pavements were thick with men drinking coffee and mint tea, women carrying babies and baskets; shops teemed. Fine gold jewellery winked next to shelves of turkeys and piles of fresh pomegranates. It was all tinselly lights and commercial action; nothing wasn't being bought, sold or bargained over. But where were the stars of the show? The Pyramids? The Sphinx? In the hot-soupy, electric smog, they were invisible.

Erica, on her first visit to Egypt, was dismayed. She hadn't picked the hotel because it was just off the Cairo–Alexandria highway en route to the vineyards; and near the headquarters of the company resuscitating Egyptian wine. She'd been seduced by the name, Sofitel Le Sphinx, and the swimming pool – in the brochure overlooked by the Pyramid of Cheops. Had the camera lied?

Fortunately, in the morning, some visibility returned. Proceeding to the buffet for the national breakfast of *ful medames* – slow-cooked, garlicky, lemony beans with pitta bread – past the indoor pool (featuring an island topped with a white grand piano and – later – slinky *chanteuse*) we saw a faint triangular outline and cheered.

From El-Giza to the vineyards at Abu El-Matamir is about 160 kilometres on what's known as the 'Desert Road'. Once a camel track, this is now a double-lane highway, joined via toll-booths festooned with pillars, statues and relief carvings – transport system meets temple. Deserts, as we'd discovered 25 years before when we drove across the Sahara, are sometimes soft and sandy but very often hard and stony, or along this route, a gravelly mix of both, like a monumental building site. Some strips have been reclaimed by canals and irrigation piping: here were citrus orchards, peaches, prickly pears, mangoes, bananas, and huge maroon dates hung from the bright orange chandeliers of many palms. But mostly, the road is lined with *allées* of advertising billboards (many hand-painted) touting just about anything.

Date palms off the Desert Road between Cairo and Alexandria.

Lacoste, Diesel, Gucci; the latest Nokia cellphone; Michelin tyres, Krups coffee machines; jetskis, ice-cream, American Express. We flashed past a giant message from a local company: *Our executives would like to thank our mothers for washing our clothes in Persil.* Beyond this border, the landscape stretched out flat and lifeless, horizon to horizon. Our driver stopped every now and then to ask for directions. He seemed rather like the saleswoman in the duty-free shop at Cairo airport, who'd told us firmly that no wine is made in Egypt.

We turned off the highway onto a narrow road which dawdled between dusty villages, maize fields and conical towers pierced with small holes. John thought they were graves. They turned out to be pigeon lofts. Pigeon-droppings have been the traditional manure of Egyptian vineyards for centuries. Birds are bred by the flock for the pot: *hama mahshi* – pigeon stuffed with cinnamon-spiked rice or minted cracked wheat – is the local celebration dish.

Caught behind ponderous lorries we exclaimed at the view: nondescript from the front, such vehicles changed personalities at the back. Mudguards and tailboards were brightly painted – op-art patterns, lotus flowers, hieroglyphics, camels – and hung with shiny tin ornaments which tinkled and swayed over potholes, around donkey carts. Handsome white-turbanned men spread maize cobs out to dry in vast yellow sheets on the roadside.

Up came small faded signs showing bunches of grapes, and, at last, the one we'd travelled from the Cape to Cairo to find: Gianaclis, Vineyards for Beverages. It looked far from promising as we wove between mud cowsheds and chicken runs wondering, not for the first time on the African wine route, what horror of a cellar lay ahead. And why we weren't cruising lazily down the Nile. But a sprucer sign, indicating another turn onto a marginally less trying road, kept our hopes up.

The instant-fix winery

Quite suddenly, there was a substantial canal. Men were fishing, women washing, kids playing in the slow-flowing brown water; a live illustration of the adage that Egypt is a gift of the Nile. Pied kingfishers hovered and dived as they do throughout Africa. We came to a bridge and a small settlement – mud walls, flat roofs, a few tall date palms, very quiet. Word of mouth at street corners steered our driver to a vacant lot scattered with rubbish bordering a high blank wall topped with barbed wire. We suspected we'd arrived because of the piles of broken green bottles, but still… could this really be Egypt's flagship winery?

The driver shouted our identities over the wall. An iron gate creaked open. We drove up a ramp – the same way the grapes had been arriving until three days before. The 2001 harvest had just ended. Strong whiffs of fermentation wafted about and over the wall came the Muslim call to prayer.

A beautiful young Egyptian woman greeted us in exotically accented English, then amiable, self-effacing, equally youthful winemaker Sébastien Boudry appeared. He's French, from the Perpignan area, and became sheepishly vague when we enquired how long he expected to be working at this parched outpost. He'd been seconded here to the Gianaclis Winery by Al Ahram Beverages' technical partners, Groupe Ginestet of Bordeaux, in 1999.

'*Ça dépend*,' he said. 'It's okay here. I live in Alexandria on the sea, less than 100 kilometres away. We go to the beach, we swim, there are good restaurants and cafes….'

But, he smiled, there was also Gehan, our meeter and greeter, an administrator at the winery. She and Sébastien had recently married – 'the first multi-racial marriage in Alexandria in three years.' He was learning Arabic, she French and 'English is now our home language!' Was Gehan a wine-drinker? 'Oh no,' he said. 'Except champagne, sauternes… expensive stuff.'

Apart from a few *stages* in Bordeaux, where he qualified at the city's famous oenology faculty, this was Sébastien's first job after military service – 'a big opportunity for me'. He had formidable support from Groupe Ginestet (its properties include Chx Chasse-Spleen, Gruaud-Larose, Haut-Bages-Liberal), with regular visits made by its technical director, Bernard Laurent, but he'd been the point-man in the dramatic revival of Egyptian wine. When he arrived, he found a wreck of a winery, woefully unequipped to handle grapes in searing temperatures. 'That first vintage was chaos….'

Al Ahram Beverages Company (ABC) bought State-run Gianaclis in March 1999; the Ginestet tie-up was finalised two months later (there's no French investment, only a technical and management contract); Sébastien had three months to revamp the winery before the harvest. He spent US$3 million (over £2 million) in key upgrades: enormous, automatic closed presses that limit oxidation – and, like washing machines, practically clean themselves; a centrifuge to clean the grape juice before fermentation; cooling jackets for every tank, controlled from his laboratory; insulation for the roof over the tanks.

A cooling system that takes a whopping 20°C off the grape temperatures – they arrive at 37° plus – was the most crucial innovation but there were vital small adjustments, too, like picking into crates rather than a trailer, so berries wouldn't be crushed and oxidise between vineyard and winery.

Nothing was spent on fancifying the buildings; no confusion about priorities here. 'It looks like a gasoline station, but it works,' he said. With a drastically pruned staff of six, he now produced 30,000 hectolitres, the equivalent of about 4 million bottles (half table wine, half spirits). And in just two years the wines had become unrecognisable.

The 2000s eclipsed the vintage before; even better 2001 samples confirmed this was no fluke. Given the previous rampant bacterial levels and the near-vinegar state of the old wines, just a strong dose of cellar hygiene would have made a startling difference. But in fact the new wines stood out among many suspect whites and rosés churned out all over North Africa. The instant-fix here could be a regional case study.

Deeper into the desert

Sébastien was still dissatisfied. 'The problem is the grapes.' His team could advise and cajole but, ultimately, improved fruit quality would only come from better vineyard management and classic grape varieties.

Zamalek

Fax _____
Other _____

Date	Follow-up	Notes
		Soup
		Lentille Soupe ورق عنب
		Apetizers
		Vine leaves ورق عنب
		Tahina طحينة
		Ta mix salad green أو خضراء
		Main Course
		Pigeons فريك / رز
		Rice or Ferik
		Molokheya ملوخية
		To drink
		Kasab قصب

طحينة

الرشيدى الميزان

Sesame Paste
TAHINA
الجـــودة تراثنـا

CONFISERIE EL MIZAN
since 1889

Ingredients: P
Free from blea

750 Grms Gro

Keep away fro

Valid One Yea

MAKERS O

EL RASHIDI
6th Of Octob
Telephone: 011

Made in Egypt

Top: *Winemaker Sébastien Boudry and John inspect the vines; Sébastien in his 'gasoline station'; preserved on papyrus — . picking, treading and pressing the Pharaohs' wines.*
Middle: *On the right road; 'Here's what you must eat tonight… we'll write it down for you' – local advice on local specialities; inside the cellar; and looking out; we bought this tahina opposite the Sphinx, to make hummus back home.*
Bottom: *Gianaclis winery from over the Nile; safety-first for cellar-hands; newly-married Gehan and Sebastien; the mournful Sphinx.*

'Here, at this time, in the vineyards, you have one vine that is black grapes, the next that is rosé coloured, another that is white, *pfouff…* all planted together, it's crazy.' They're still trying to identify the varieties. 'We call our red wine Cabernet Sauvignon but in the vineyard there is a maximum 20–25 per cent of Cabernet vines, and maybe a bit of Merlot. We are just lucky there are no regulations about this yet.' He was having to blend in other unknown varieties, even some Muscat de Hambourg – a red Muscat – and it was a tribute to his skills that the powerful flavours were held in check (though he makes some specific Muscat wines that aren't so shy).

The dry white was labelled 'Pinot Blanc' but Sébastien was convinced that the majority variety was Chasselas – Switzerland's staple white grape, here in the desert! Its Egyptian name is Gazazi. But is this so strange? Perhaps not, according to Jancis Robinson in *Vines, Grapes and Wines*: 'Chasselas may be the oldest known grape variety cultivated by man. The leaves, red-veined and emphatically five-lobed, bear a strong resemblance to those painted on the walls of the burial grounds at Luxor and similar vines are said to thrive in Egypt today.'

The latter, at least, Sébastien confirms.

Another grape variety in the 'Pinot Blanc' is known locally as Samos, perhaps imported by this wine venture's founding father, Nestor Gianaclis, from his birthplace of Greece – where it is related to – perhaps even synonymous with – Muscat à Petits Grains, a more subtle member of an unsubtle grape family. And as if this wine were not already unique enough, it also contained Thompson Seedless table grapes!

'We will make our next big step soon,' said Sébastien. 'We will plant our own vineyards. We've been making our research.'

That research had revealed that Nestor Gianaclis – and perhaps the Pharaohs whose wines he set out to revive – could have sited their vineyards more advantageously. Most vines were planted on land with a very shallow water table – less than a metre deep. 'The roots cannot penetrate and they also sometimes rot,' said Sébastien, which partly explained the curious fact that even in the Egyptian heat the grapes don't ripen properly. They must be chaptalised by at least 1 degree to reach 12 or 12.5% alcohol. Then, because the sun tends to strip them of natural acidity, they need freshening with tartaric acid, a double manipulation!

So the search for ideal (in the circumstances) *terroir* had broadened: 400 hectares in an even more desolate area, Wadi Natrum, had been staked out. This is roughly halfway between Cairo and Alexandria, west of the 'Desert Road', on slightly raised ground with a water table 2 metres deep – or more. But before plunging into planting, they would establish a nursery, to find the most suitable varieties.

Sébastien was keen to try Cabernet, Merlot, Tempranillo, Syrah, Grenache, Sangiovese and Chardonnay. That eventually would make the current 800 hectares of straggly old vineyards – 20 per cent red, 80 per cent white – redundant except for distilling. It was all still on a minuscule scale, but he was optimistic: 'If we can make our present wines from such poor grapes, we can make much better wines from new vineyards in the future.'

And so to those 'present wines' – which he compared to vins de pays. 'We couldn't be making world-class wine'. He'd laid out the range in his laboratory. Unusually for this part of the world, there were standard tasting glasses. 'When I first came, they used a tea cup for tasting.'

The Château Grand Marquis Pinot Blanc 2000 and 2001 (Chasselas and Thompson's Seedless, 6g/l sugar) were plumper and friendlier than the same vintages of Cru des Ptolomées Pinot Blanc, a Chasselas-Muscat blend. Sébastien was achieving marginally more palate weight and feel by leaving these wines on their lees for nearly a year in tank – a risky enriching process in these climates without perfect temperature control. The Rubis d'Egypte Vin Rosé (a blend of white and red wines) was deep-coloured, dry and palatable, if a touch bitter in the aftertaste. An Omar Khayyam Cabernet Sauvignon 2000, with a worried turbanned sage peering from its label, was quite soft, but unremarkable.

The flagship was undoubtedly the Château Grand Marquis 'Cabernet Sauvignon'; De Ginestet is a strapline on the label, presumably to offer reassurance of French involvement. Sébastien's use of oak chips here made an instant difference. In the future, he plans to barrel-age the wine. There wasn't much Cabernet Sauvignon character of course, since that grape features only marginally in the wine's make-up. But a tank sample of the 2001 showed how much quality had improved since privatisation.

Such a respectable red would have rescued our dinner on EgyptAir, and back in Cairo that night, we hankered after it. We ate sizzling kebabs and stuffed pigeon in a neighbourhood restaurant where we were the only non-locals, and Sprite, Pepsi and Al Ahram's Birell non-alcoholic beer the liquid choices. It's still rare to find wine off the beaten tourist track.

King Tut's cellar

Next morning we rewound through the millennia to the tombs of Africa's most ancient wine growers, makers, collectors and consumers. The crush of buses at the Egyptian Museum in Cairo appeared to contradict what we'd been told – that tourism had plummeted 30 per cent in the week since the suicide bombings in the US. It was King Tutankhamun's gold they were all after.

We took a look and reeled – no books or movies prepare you for the immense quantity of this treasure, the gorgeousness and glamour of every piece. We tore ourselves away to get back to the wine trail, to rooms full of phallic-looking, long-BC clay amphorae, with rush and mud stoppers. We also examined King Tut's own wine collection – some of the 36 special vintages which accompanied him into the grave in 1352 BC. (Surely the most venerable form of BYO – bring your own?)

In another gallery, we were staggered by the oldest wine grapes we'd ever seen – ever would see. Vintage 1200 BC from *Vitis vinifera* of the 18th Dynasty, found in a tomb at Thebes, near the Nile riverside town of Luxor, about 700 kilometres from Cairo. Of course, these were by now very desiccated indeed, all pip and no flesh; but we only had to join the dots between them and the papyrus paintings next door to be able – almost – to taste the juice, smell the perfume. Pergolas pendant with ripe bunches, feasts overflowing with wine: the artists who conjured suitable after-lifestyles for the Pharoahs (and the less lofty) were master illustrators of sensory pleasure.

Egyptologist Nahed Al Amer seemed perplexed by the subject of our travels. Waiting for us to take photographs, she studiously dipped into her pocket Koran. We had the fleeting notion that we were such unholy company that she was doing a spot of on-the-job decontamination, but we nevertheless pressed her for more ancient wine history.

When Tut's tomb was discovered in 1922, some of the amphorae still contained 'traces' of wine, she said. This had to be the longest finish of all time – 3274 years – we said. Wine was the brainchild of the Pharoahs, she said. Hang on, we said. Of course we would relish flying such a banner – Wine is an African Invention! – but Hugh Johnson, in *The Story of Wine*, confirms that Egyptians were not the first to grow wine (though they were 'the first we know of to record and celebrate the details of their winemaking in unambiguous paintings').

We debated back and forth, but Nahed's nationalism was as unshakeable as her anti-alcohol resolve. 'No, no,' she wagged a finger at us. 'It is not always easy, but I am waiting until I get to Paradise where the Koran tells there are rivers and rivers, jars and jars of wine. It's difficult….'

She was equally firm when we visited the Pyramids of Giza and (surprisingly small by comparison, a dinky toy lion) the Sphinx, which gazed mournfully over the tourist buses directly at a Kentucky Fried Chicken outlet. No slaves had set foot on these building sites, Nahed maintained. The work was all done by volunteers; there had been no slavery in Egypt. 'The idea was that if you helped to build a house for a god – which is what the Pharaohs were – you would be saved from your own sins. So 30,000 citizens, including of course mathematicians, engineers and astronomers, built King Cheops his home for the next life. We don't have that sort of motivation today!'

New motivations

Disbelief must have been written all over our faces the moment Fatenn Mostafa said: 'We're Pharaohed out, we Egyptians are completely Pharaohed out. Trust me. We've had enough.'

A long pause. A wide, patient smile from a young woman more or less the same age as Egyptologist Nahed, but switched on to quite another channel. Fatenn wore her hair loose and shoulder-length; the knit top under her fashionably skinny cardigan was cropped to reveal a sliver of taut stomach. She shopped at Zara, the Spanish instant-chic chain busy storming the world, smoked many Marlboros, and was as relaxed as she was in charge.

We were still awed by the Tutankhamun marvels that had transported us to the impressive orderliness of the Egyptian wine scene 3350 years ago. Its labelling system foreshadowed current international wine laws. The wine's regional provenance and vintage were embossed on each amphora. The star oenologist of the time appeared to be one Kh'ay, who signed nearly every 'bottle' we saw. (Young Sébastien was stepping into very ancient desert boots.) But there seemed to be a rather French disdain about grape varieties. The ancient Egyptians didn't specify which grapes had gone into their wines — just as makers of red burgundy feel no need to identify it as Pinot Noir.

This was one tradition Fatenn seemed happy to continue, but for the rest, she was frankly fed up. Modern Egyptian consumers, she was convinced, wanted to move on. As the CEO of Egypt's only wine company (Gianaclis had swallowed up Obélisque, a firm making wine from imported grape concentrate) she'd decided to change the labels — radically.

Pyramids had been brushed almost out of the picture. Just the faintest outlines remained on one or two labels, appropriately lost in what the tour guides call 'humidity haze'. Altogether abandoned were the labels featuring grapey, winey scenes copied from Pharaonic tomb paintings.

'But they're unique!' we protested. 'They're beautiful! And they're yours!' Fatenn regarded us understandingly. 'Yes, I know. Maybe, in time, we'll reconsider. But for export wines only. To be frank, for people here it's become a bit, well, kitsch. We've even got the Pharoahs on Kleenex now.'

The label change was an outward symbol of the profound restructuring of Egypt's wine image which Fatenn was directing for Al Ahram Beverages Company. Al Ahram may mean 'pyramid', but it was clear that seizing the moment and owning the future epitomised this firm's activities. Since 1996, when chairman Ahmed Zayat returned home with his Harvard PhD, MBA, and extensive experience on Wall Street, to wheel and deal in a business arena newly re-opened for privatisation, ABC had acquired a monopoly in the beer, spirits and wine markets, and a leading edge in the non-alcoholic beverage

Switched-on Egyptian wine CEO Fatenn Mostafa in the boardroom amid the tools of her trade.

sector. In 2001 *Forbes Global* magazine rated it one of the top 20 small companies in the world.

Zayat bought Gianaclis Wines from the government in March 1999 and poached Fatenn from the top international echelons of Coke to re-invent Egyptian wine and re-launch 'the legend in a bottle'. Daughter of a diplomat, she speaks German, French, English and Arabic, grew up and worked in Vienna, and spent long, mind-stretching stints in Japan. Of all the wine executives we encountered in Africa, though she'd been in the game just a couple of years, she was probably the wittiest, smartest and gutsiest too.

She was facing the toughest of challenges as a young woman in an old Islamic world, planning and executing a grand-scale rehabilitation of vineyards and cellars, actively pushing their generally forbidden fruit. Gianaclis might be the only wine show in town, but it's ranged against fierce opposition nonetheless. Could – should? – the wine message be heard above the muezzins calling on every corner, five times a day? Egypt, while among the most cosmopolitan of the MENA (Middle East and North Africa) countries, is still a traditional (and polygamous) society in many respects and home to the militant Egyptian Muslim Brotherhood, for which wine is more than a taboo.

The wine-drinking pavement café-society of cities like Alexandria had been dwindling for years. As writer Adel Darwish put it: 'Those marble table-tops running with beer and wine were pushed behind wooden shutters'. Fatenn and her Gianaclis team (strongly featuring other switched-on young women) were battling to open such shutters. They'd targeted the 6–7 million tourists drawn to the Pharaonic splendours in a good (calm) year. The range was selling at around 62 dinars (US$14.60 or £10) a bottle at Sofitel Le Sphinx, and on the Nile river boat *Scarabee*. A floating dinner, with band and belly dancer, was just the way to pass the night in Cairo before catching the 1am Johannesburg flight.

And they were wooing local consumers too: launching a wine magazine, setting up a network of private home deliveries throughout Egypt (a potential market of 67 million people), whisking food and beverage managers off to Bordeaux, founding a Wine Academy to train sommeliers. Working to make wine more fashionable than the current craze – *shisha* – hookah water-pipes. These had gone upwardly mobile, from scruffy corner cafés to designer restaurant-bars like the Abou El Sid, where the smokes came in flavours from 'wrigglis' (chewing gum, we assumed) to peach, cappuccino, canteloupe, and 'our own cocktail'. (Our meal of warm vine leaves was equally good.)

Gianaclis was looking over the border, too: ABC aims to 'refresh' the entire MENA region's 350 million Muslims. These are challenges not attempted since the Prophet's times in the sixth and seventh centuries, after which clouds of prohibition had hovered intermittently around the Middle East and Mediterranean coastline. More recently, there'd been the 33 'dark years' (as ABC's annual report put it) of nationalised underproduction, when the wines nose-dived into vicious volatility. But right now, the old euphemisms

– 'an acquired taste' or 'best avoided' – emphatically no longer applied. Quality had made an about-turn.

We drank the top of the range, 2001 Château Grand Marquis Pinot Blanc, over a working lunch in the Gianaclis conference room. The unmarked offices are difficult to find (or target, perhaps?), on the third floor of a building in the plusher part of Cairo. Double-glazing and air-conditioning muffled the cacophony of hooting, the honks of the Nile river boats, the nasal muezzins.

The wine was perhaps even nicer than when we'd tasted it with Sébastien the day before, and Fatenn took a satisfied, proud-mother sip when we complimented her. She asked: Which North African country has a better white wine than this? Answer: Morocco. What alcohol level do you think our 'champagne' should be? A Gianaclis sparkler was in the pipeline. She was wondering whether it should be light – about 8–9% – or more conventional – about 11.5%. Answer: aim higher, towards champagne.

Nestor the Greek

Nestor Gianaclis had started his wine company 120 years ago, aiming for what others believed impossible, but he regarded as inspirational. And far from trying to disown or downplay a foreigner's ideals and role – the more usual refrain in modern Africa – Fatenn Mostafa wanted to restore and revive them.

She even referred to him by his first name: 'I wish I'd known Nestor – he was a great man. His idea, when he began planning vineyards in 1882 – he didn't plant until 1903 – was to replicate what the Pharaohs did… a great, great idea. I found that one day browsing in an antique shop in Alexandria. I paid a lot for it.'

She pointed to a 1931 red and gold calendar, featuring a formal portrait of the fez-topped *héritier du trône*, Egyptian Crown-Prince Farouk. Nestor Gianaclis, a tycoon of many parts, was the purveyor of quality tobacco to the Egyptian royals at the time; this was part of his celebrity sponsorship campaign. It would have been another matter to find a frontman for the passion he'd laboriously, tenaciously, turned into a wine business. But 1931 was a significant vintage nonetheless: the year Gianaclis wines won their first international awards at an exposition in Paris.

Fatenn told the story as fondly as if Nestor had been her grandfather. If he had done it so could she….

A maverick, in the manner of all pioneers, he dreamed of re-creating the legendary 'light white wine' Cleopatra is said to have served Caesar, and the rich reds that were the tipple of the god-kings, the Pharaohs. Nestor's readings showed that the best Egyptian wines had come from Lower Egypt, on the western edge of the Nile delta, inland of Alexandria (hence, Muscat d'Alexandrie).

He bought land there, on the sites of ancient noble estates. Hungarian, Italian and

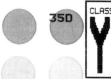

EGYPTAIR مصر للطيران EGYPTAIR مصر للطيران

DESTINATION	FLIGHT	DATE	CARRIER
JOHANNESBU	MS0877	20SEP	EGYPTAIR

	35D	CLASS Y	NAME PLATTER E	SEAT 35D

GATE 7	TIME 0100	SQNR 093	CODE US

نفرتيتى

نبيذ أبيض فاخر

NEFERTITI

Grand Vin Blanc

EGYPTIAN VINEYARDS COMPANY شركة الكروم المصرية

French viticulturalists were enlisted. Soil tests showed good pHs, enough lime. Vines were imported. The network of canals was tapped. Summer and harvest temperatures – well over 40°C, fermentation could be completed in a single day! – were challenging, but it cools down to 10°C in winter, so vines can rest in dormancy. Within two decades Nestor planted 73 grape varieties and built the huge winery we'd visited the day before.

His labels plundered the past with some of the names and ranges we'd just met: Cru des Ptolémées, Reine Cléopatre, Nefertiti Grand Vin Blanc and even Omar Khayyam Cabernet Sauvignon. After raising an eyebrow at the Persian poet's convenient relocation to the Nile, we were told: 'Omar belongs to wine everywhere.' Absolutely. Especially while, in all respects vinous in his homeland, he remains for now a prophet only beyond.

Nestor's holdings eventually extended to over 8000 hectares, wine tycoonery off the Pharaonic scale. But his empire crumbled overnight in 1966 when President Gamel Abdul Nasser, undaunted by the Suez Canal débâcle, embarked on a spree of summary nationalisations. In State hands, wine quality crashed, becoming a virtual advertisement for abstinence. 'One of the world's weaker wines,' wrote a Cairo magazine kindly. Sales plummeted. Yields dropped to 2 or 3 tonnes/hectare; the area under vines shrank to about one-tenth of the spread the Gianaclis family had once controlled.

'They moved to Syria and founded new businesses and you won't believe this,' said Fatenn, 'they were nationalised again! Now they're back in Greece – and still claiming compensation from the Egyptian government.'

We who enjoy wine with our oases and pyramids, our ta'amia and tajines, owed them a great deal, we decided. We raised our glasses: 'To Nestor!'

Top: Anti-alcohol warning from Egyptologist Nahed Al Amer. Middle: Millennias-old wine bottles; Egyptian vehicles are best viewed from the back. Bottom: The sort of label Fatenn is changing; the Pyramids of Giza in typical Cairo 'humidity haze'.

ETHIOPIA

John had been to Ethiopia on many journalistic assignments – coup attempts against the little Lion of Judah, Emperor Haile Selassie, grand OAU summits with Idi Amin having the entire continent's leadership rolling in the aisles when he told his sworn enemy, Julius Nyerere: 'You're so beautiful, I'd marry you except for your grey hair.'

But the vaunted thirst of newspaper correspondents doesn't always extend to the wines of countries that – how shall we put it? – don't quite make the oenological A-team. (Wine made from honey – *mar tej* – has been the national drink for centuries; wine made from grapes is much more nouveau. It's been around only since the Middle Ages, popping up in the form of Communion wine for the Ethiopian Orthodox Church. Catholic missionaries later planted their own vineyards for the same purpose.)

So the first Ethiopian wine he ventured to taste was at the Kakamega Golf Hotel on the Kenyan tendril of the great rainforests that stretch through central and west Africa. (Which we were about to slosh through in pursuit of the Great Blue Turaco and other significant birds.) The wine list had it down as Gouda Red, and at first we thought a cheese had blundered into the wrong company. But no, it was just a spelling idiosyncrasy – it ought to have been Gouder (or Guder), after a vineyard which was once the heart of the Ethiopian wine industry. The list also punted, under the heading of Champagne, something which instantly took our fancy: Mole and Chando (Germany), it said. We ordered it, agog to see whether it could possibly be a geographically challenged Moët, but the mystery was never solved; stocks had run out.

The Ethiopian red it was, then, to accompany a menu which started with Baked Bean on Toast (yes, singular) in a deepest-Africa dining room wallpapered with scenes from Nordic fjords and autumnal forests. From the lines of malevolent vultures on the roof, seemingly waiting for us to drown as we swam in the pool below, to the pungently fragrant bedding, it would be putting it mildly to say the Kakamega Golf Hotel had character. So, too, did the wine. Six years later, we followed it to its source.

The Gouder vineyards are in the Ethiopian highlands 135 kilometres west of Addis

Ababa, near the beautiful volcanic crater lake of Wonchi. Add a spritz of Ambo mineral water to the wine from these rolling slopes and you'll not lose the local flavour – it comes from hot springs nearby. At 2005 metres towering 400 metres above Europe's highest wine skyscrapers. This altitude – grapes give way to coffee further down the road – and temperate climate (annual rainfall 900mm, temperatures between 27.5 and 10.5°C) produce a fairly conventional viticultural result: one crop a year. But 170 kilometres east of Addis, at the Upper Awash Agro Industry Enterprise and the Zwai Horticulture Development Enterprise fringing a lake in the Rift Valley (altitudes 1100–1650 metres), the norm is two harvests a year: November/December, and May/June.

Crates of grapes from these outlying areas were being unpacked from trucks when we visited Awash Winery – the only one in the country – in Lideta, a suburb of Addis. It was a fruit salad – familiar varieties like Chenin, Grenache, Ugni Blanc, Petit Syrah and Barbera, as well as some new to us – Dodoma Altico (Aleatico), Tikur Weyn, Key Dubbi and a couple which might easily have slotted into Ethiopia's list of about 830 birds (30 species are endemic) – Debulbul Attere and Nech Debulbul. Seventy-five hectares of these super low-yield 'local' varieties – reputedly of Mediterranean origin – make up most of the national vineyard.

The 'European' grapes in production at Awash covered about 30 hectares, but the future lay in a nursery block of 100 different varieties. Undaunted by the ravages of famine, border wars and former dictator Mengistu's disastrous 20-year rule (he fled to and still lives in Zimbabwe as a guest of Robert Mugabe), Ethiopia's wine industry is actively seeking partners to push through major plans for expansion.

The Awash river is the life-support of these vineyards, and we could have done with a dive into their irrigation ditches ourselves before bumping and grinding onwards – the road was topped with molten lava from the nearby and still-smouldering Fentale volcano – to the Awash National Park. It was approaching 40 degrees, and we were extremely thankful not to be staying in the tin-can caravans in the Park (great position, overlooking a plunging gorge, but temperature within just about boiling point). The market town of Nazret is the better bet for wine and wildlife, particularly if you have an interest in Ethiopian music and the provocative, wildly shoulder-shaking local dancing. Our room at the Plaza Hotel opened onto a courtyard which was the venue of non-stop day and night gigs for tireless trumpeters, singers, drummers and maestros of sundry wailing instruments.

But what are sleepless nights when your wine route also offers encounters with Afar tribesmen, hairstyles à la Sphinx, razor-sharp scimitars sheathed in goatskin tucked into their belts, AK-47s over their shoulders? As well as entry to Emperor Haile Selassie's old palace (now the University of Addis), with a tour of his private quarters – turquoise bidet, bullet-riddled mirror – thrown in? Superb traditional arts and crafts – jewellery, marvellous comic-strip historical paintings, superb basketwork and textiles? Sight of that

blonde temptress the Gelada baboon, black-maned Abyssinian lions, blue-winged geese (nearest relatives in the Andes)? And fabulous rock-hewn churches and castles…

… and the best coffee in Africa

Coffee was Ethiopian-born, in the province of Kaffa – apparently discovered by a goatherd, who noticed how frisky his charges became after chewing certain local berries. It wasn't until the thirteenth century that this stimulant made the cross-over from food to hot drink, and it was only in the fourteenth century that coffee hit Yemen, which now, much to Ethiopian chagrin, claims it as its own! Every little hut in the highlands is fronted by a couple of coffee trees. An Ethiopian coffee ceremony is as elaborate as any Japanese tea ritual, and espresso-cappuccino machines crank away in the tiniest bars in the deepest outback. At every hotel, even the dodgiest, tables were exquisitely dressed with flowers minutes before mealtimes. Coffee cups, wine glasses, place settings on snowy cloths (locally grown and made, every bit as fine as Egyptian cotton) were surrounded with swirls of freshly picked lilies and hibiscus, and scattered with canna and rose petals.

Italy occupied the country only from 1936 to 1941, but it bequeathed a thing or two: when we visited the Illy coffee operation in Italy, we were told that wild Ethiopian Arabica beans were a highly prized ingredient of their top blends. And you still find classic Italian ristorantes in Addis, and *spiggttii* and *makkarronnii* on the menu of every rural eating house. (Ethiopian spelling is superbly alternative, and flourishes in hand-painted signs for products like Massey Ferguson tractors – *Maassi Fargisan* – and even hair-salons – *barberry* here.) 'Russian' salad is ubiquitous too – another reminder of the socialist past? – and uniformly ghastly. We found the best home-grown accompaniments to local food were the Gouder Red (gold medal from Bulgaria in 1979, Leipzig in 1980 – Mengistu and the Soviet Union were close comrades) and the Awash Soave. However, it's the national dish, an incendiary stew called *wot* (or *wat*), based on a killer mix of chillies, herbs and spices called berbere, which most sorely cries for the intervention of wine, Ambo water or Bedele beer – or anything liquid at all. It's served with *injera* – tripe-textured pancakes made of tef, a grain often used for cattle-feed, rolled up and piled onto trays like in-flight hot towels. We consumed a lot of *wot*, but it was a challenge.

Awash in wine

As was the Awash Winery, founded in 1943 by Greeks and Italians, but more recently reminiscent of an old Soviet-era factory. Even some years after Mengistu was booted out of the country, the most minor decisions (might we take photographs?) had to be referred to higher authority than the – most friendly, courteous – winemakers and chemists we met. Concrete and glass-fibre ruled, and the wood vats we saw were antiques, but since our visit there's been an injection of stainless steel, newer oak and Italian machinery.

The key staff had trained either in Russia or Italy – white-coated beverage technologist Yegezu Mershabayu, for one, had studied at universities near Moscow and on the Black Sea. 'I'd like to come to South Africa to see your vineyards and wineries,' he said. And he was very keen for an outside opinion, obligingly pulled a few corks for us to taste – plain drinking glasses suffice in his laboratory. We were a little sparing with our praise; perhaps we'd have been more forthcoming and generous had we visited Ethiopia *after* some of the decidedly rustic wines we tasted elsewhere in Africa.

Besides, there was uncertainty in the air. The staff knew Awash was to be put up for sale after decades as a state-owned and -run facility. That period may have provided cushy jobs – but it did nothing for morale. Clearly, Awash was in a technology time-warp, 1950s–60s equipment and plumbing – and consequently hygiene – wouldn't have passed in a top New World winery. There were many dank and grimy corners; the pipes and pumps needed an overhaul.

What changes would new owners make? Who would keep their jobs? The Italian consultant oenologist who'd been helping for several years had already packed his bags. His wines, sadly, lacked passion: there was a very commercial, factory quality to the range.

But the entire industry was on the verge of even bigger upheavals. Even the Government 'Ethiopian Fruit and Agricultural Division' which had been responsible for grape supplies, dealing with the agricultural co-operatives in the provinces, was due for a major overhaul. Land privatisation in Ethiopia will begin as well now, Mershabayu told us. No one seemed to know the full implications of that. For the time being, however, the show went on, producing 2.5 million litres of wine annually, mainly for local consumption, plus a risky-sounding (we didn't taste it) apéritif named Kilikil, vermouth, grappa and vinegar. Doing our sums, we realised that such volume couldn't possibly be produced from local vineyards, and it wasn't: raisins were being imported from Turkey (also Pakistan and Greece) to be rehydrated and fermented into wine.

Packaging featured both recycled and new bottles, and in neighbouring Kenya we were to hear (doubtless scurrilous) complaints that Ethiopia has been stealing used bottles. It's a three-day overland journey through the desert from Nairobi to Addis, surely a deterrent to any smuggler, but it's true that glassware is scarce and valuable in East Africa.

The whole range had won a Golden Europe Award for Quality, in Paris in 1996, which perhaps goes to show, yet again, how unavoidably subjective wine judging is. The conclusion of our own foray was that while wine is not yet Ethiopia's strongest point, it certainly adds to the fascinating flavour of this enchanting, naturally splendid country.

KENYA

Yatta's strikingly healthy Cabernet Sauvignon vineyards – a promising future for Kenyan wine?

Kenyan wine used to be something of an oxymoron, with even the most patriotic locals turning up their noses at such home-produce. Those were the days when the only vines in the country were the odd few patches of table grapes, and winemaking came closer to home-brewing. John's father, in memory of his Austrian-Italian roots, planted a few vines on their cattle farm in the Rift Valley at Gilgil, almost on the Equator, turning out a liquid which both son and long-suffering neighbours took pains to avoid. The only 'wine' produced in any quantity didn't come from grapes at all.

We remembered the Editor of the *Nation* newspaper, Joe Rodrigues, a Goan transplant to Kenya (his brother remained in India to become army chief of that country) whipping out a mystery vintage during one of his wife Cyrilla's famous prawn curries and challenging us to guess its origins. With our tastebuds by this time in abject surrender we roamed the world: a lesser Monbazillac perhaps, or some obscure sticky pudding product of Australia, Sicily or even South Africa (its tropical fruit scents rose above the cardamom and coriander)? We knew that Joe, then a leading light in international journalists' organisations, jetted all over the place in the interests of press freedom; this had to be a souvenir of his travels, and to us, the wine equivalent of one of those stateless unfortunates unable to find asylum anywhere. We were stumped; he was gleeful.

'Platter,' he crowed, 'have you learned nothing since you left the newsroom?' He had been a mentor since John's first foray into journalism as a rural agricultural correspondent, reporting on cattle sales, and thereafter through the ranks to the *Nation's* hard-hitting political column, 'On the Carpet'. Kenyan novelist Ngugi wa Thiongo was a fellow-reporter.

Wine mischief

'It's Kenyan. It's paw-paws!' Well, of course. Papaya 'wine' was then, still is (though much drier than Joe's sample) the pop-hit of the country's leading alcohol importer-distributor, Kenya Wine Agencies Limited (KWAL): 50,000 cases churned out in a good year;

tourists the biggest fans. But such an imposter had never been allowed onto the list of Kenya's largest single consumer of wines, the Muthaiga Club, the guava pink-stuccoed scene of much languid debauchery, the old colonial headquarters of the spouse-swapping White Mischief set (hoary old motto: are you married or do you live in Kenya?). Still isn't. But Yatta Vineyards Ruby Cabernet and Colombard are now full members of the club. (Not permitted through its portals had been the *Out of Africa* crew, who'd wanted to film their Muthaiga scenes on the actual spot; a replica of the club had to be built elsewhere for Meryl Streep, Robert Redford et al.)

In Kenya, wine is now wine: made from classical *Vitis vinifera* vines, KWAL's mostly imported from South Africa, and planted between 1992 and 1995. There's a way to go, as readily acknowledged by the country's 'Mr Wine', fun-loving, savvy Paul Chemng'orem, head of KWAL. But Faith Rutto, the company's softly spoken, charming chief food technologist-turned winemaker, is ratcheting up the standards.

'Bring up some Cape wines so we can sample them here; we'll make a day of it out at Yatta,' Paul bawled down the phone to South Africa as we finalised our itinerary. He was going to invite Nairobi members of the International Wine and Food Society. 'The oldies we'll put on (tractor-drawn) trailers for a trip around the vineyards; give them some champagne beside the river half way to keep them cheerful.'

Paul, like John an old boy of Nairobi's Duke of York School, is an accountant – he worked at the Central Bank before becoming a liquor merchant – and looks much younger than his 45 years. He's headed KWAL since 1990, and steered it through privatisation and public listing. After nearly three decades in the comfort zone as government-monopoly importer and distributor of much besides wine, this was a radical change, and Paul found that KWAL had to square up to tough competition.

'Big-time smugglers,' he said indignantly. 'Of spirits and wine, and you won't believe how brazen they are… whole big containers, marked wrongly, phoney invoices. We have bribery-prone customs officials. We might as well have no import controls at all. But we, KWAL, have to go through the proper channels, keep our books straight. We've reported it to the authorities umpteen times. Nothing gets done.'

Until recently, Kenya's best 'wine' was made from paw-paws, and tourists loved it.

Fighting off these 'mafias and the rest of them' hasn't kept him from driving – perhaps it's spurred him on – his pet project: establishing Yatta Vineyards and making wine at KWAL's downtown Nairobi headquarters, a vast winery, distillery and multi-purpose bottling (fruit juices etc.) operation, plus bonded warehouse and duty-free outlet for the capital's diplomats. His travels round the wine world have fired him up: next step is a dedicated winery amid the vineyards. And he turned our reconnaissance trip into a party-cum-marketing exercise, taking the opportunity to persuade Nairobi's gourmet élite – heavily cross-pollinated with the Muthaiga club membership – that home-grown Kenya wines are worth supporting. Nothing, he asserted, builds consumer loyalty like a walk through the vines and a tasting in situ, with the winemaker wisecracking away as the wine takes effect.

Obey your thirst

So out we drove to Yatta, a relatively dry, high (1500-metre) plateau at the base of Ol Donyo Sabuk mountain, just over an hour east of Nairobi. Past the shanty towns sprawling round the capital, via Thika – where Elspeth Huxley's famous flame trees and bucolic settler-farming way of life has been overtaken by urbanisation and overpopulation – and Kikuyu coffee plantations to the more romantically 'African' setting of the Kamba district. Here 50 hectares of cattle country had been picked as a vineyard site after five other locations around Kenya were researched.

The instant reaction was that it had been an excellent choice. The health, vigour and good husbandry of this gently sloping spread of vineyard was impressive. And strikingly framed by a wilderness of long grass, scrub and thorn trees, with a river where – as Paul had promised – we paused for champagne.

They were about to harvest – end-February to March; getting the grapes off before the 'long rains' began. (Kenya has 'short rains' too, around November.) Merlot and Pinot Noir had been disappointments, but neatly trellised Cabernet Sauvignon, Ruby Cabernet, Muscat Alexandria, Sauvignon Blanc and Colombard presented probably the finest vineyard spectacle we'd seen in the African tropics. Drip irrigation had been installed and used expertly. The pruning was equally systematic, though perhaps not ruthless enough. But large, deep green leaves canopied inviting, small-berried, unblemished blue-purple bunches, with a light yeasty bloom. The picky might have pointed out that few vines featured a minimum of 15 leaves ripening each bunch – today's vogueish rule of thumb for quality fruit. And the Cabernet, ripening splendidly and already tasting succulent, was a bit too laden – though no more so than in many of the world's much longer-established wine regions.

Frederik Kibet, the vineyard manager, started with the help of a South African consultant but had been flying solo with his staff of 12 for several years. He gazed fondly at and stroked his vines as if they were his children. And later, enjoyed what they produced with at least as much devotion – a true wineman.

Faith, in green battle-fatigue slacks, presented her wines: Yatta Vineyards Colombard, Muscat and the first two of her Ruby Cabernets, 99 and 2000 – both briefly aged in American oak barrels. They were as refreshing as her own absence of hype and unpretentious tasting remarks – 'This is a very young wine, its sharpness should fade in another six months' she commented on her Colombard 2000, before echoing what she'd written for the back label: 'A promising white wine, quite enjoyable after a hard day's work.'

Paul had given a carnival air to the proceedings – white marquees flapped gently under the wattle trees, a live band from Nairobi serenaded us; lamb and chicken sizzled on the barbecues; white-toqued chefs fussed over the coals; pink cloths on the lunch tables for 80 or so guests. The Yatta wines did duty and only the gathering evening clouds dispersed us. Otherwise we might have stayed on, mindful of Paul's old Chemng'orem family rule: If you get drunk, you don't go home. Depending on your interpretation of this maxim, it might have been related to the large red signs blaring above several of the hundreds of roadside beer halls between Nairobi and Yatta: Obey Your Thirst.

Both Faith's and Paul's forebears come from the Rift Valley near Lake Baringo, traditional Kalenjin pastoralists every bit as warrior-like as the more mythologised neighbouring Maasai, whose preoccupation with ochre-smeared sartorial niceties amuses the Kalenjin. The agricultural hoe, *jembe* in Swahili, was always regarded by the Kalenjin as an object utterly beneath their aristocratic concerns with cows and goats. The tractor and plough are, however, a tolerable improvement; and of course without these advances on the *jembe* there'd be no modern *pombe* – booze, or *divai* – wine.

When Paul, the epitome of modernity, announced: 'I'm a traditionalist,' he'd switched contexts to extol 'the great Kalenjin contribution to Kenyan cuisine', a specially slow-grilled kid goat – *Koriama* – reared in the Tugen valley beside Lake Baringo. Like many a wine appellation, *Koriama*'s name has been much abused and passed off at many of the roadside braziers all over Kenya offering *Nyama Moto* – roasted meat. Scandalous, said Paul. We hoped the Yatta wine appellation would remain safer.

Pioneers, Mondavi and bubbles in the bath

Naivasha, our destination the morning after, is one of a string of beautiful lakes along the Rift Valley. You drive out of lush, green, cool Nairobi at 1800 metres, through junky shantytowns and onto the edge of a majestic escarpment. After a couple of hours via a winding, cliff-hugging road that Italian POWs built in 1943–5, you descend to the warmer valley floor pocked by old volcanoes. Zebra and giraffe wander about freely. From their cool, high-ceilinged timber house built into and around big boulders under yellow, umbrella-shaped acacia thorn trees, John and Elli D'Olier look back at an extinct eruption called Longonot and thank it for their good volcanic soils. Out west they gaze over hills that head toward the Maasai Mara Game Park. Wildebeest (gnus) and water-buck, with their white lavatory-seat backsides patrol the sparse bush that slopes to the water's edge. An occasional giraffe glides by and gymnogenes work the huge trees for fledgling snacks.

Here, in hippo territory, the D'Oliers planted wine grapes in 1982. They made their public début – a Kenya wine first – with their Naivasha Dry White in 1985. Their lakeside vineyards of Colombard, Sauvignon Blanc, Cabernet Sauvignon and Carnelian

Top: *John D'Olier
pulled out all his vines,
now they're back;
alfresco lunch for the
foodies at Yatta
Vineyards; KWAL wine-
maker Faith Rutto.*
Middle: *A Kenyan wine
lake...; evidence of Yatta
manager Frederik
Kibet's care for his
vines.*
Bottom: *Lake Baringo,
home territory for
Faith, Paul and Kalenjin
pastoralists; their
neighbours, the
Maasai.*

(a curious Californian cross between Grenache and Ruby Cabernet) eventually stretched for 30 hectares. It all looked idyllic, but the realities were more problematical.

This is beer country. Along the Equator, it's always been said, the safest investment is in a brewery. And when the staff parties around Lake Naivasha, usually thumping all-night, all-Tusker lager events, converted to wine – to 'champagne' in fact, and in magnums no less – John and Elli D'Olier weren't convinced that they were witnessing a dramatic diversification in consumer tastes. Nor did they conclude that they'd been wrong to sales-target only tourist hotels and expatriates. No one in Kenya had made sparkling wine before – nor has since – so it seemed ominously likely that it was the D'Oliers' Naivasha Vineyards bubbly which was fuelling these local festivities.

'As soon as we came back from a holiday at the coast and heard the reports of "champagne parties" we realised we must have left the store open,' recalled John with a loud laugh. 'We had this promising assistant, an ex-policeman, only a lad, who became so keen on the whole business and started reading books on wine-making, that eventually we thought we would put his name on the label as the winemaker. Though he was still learning – just as I was – we thought this would be in the spirit of *Harambee*.' That's Swahili for 'let's pull together', the national motto launched by Kenya's founding president, Jomo Kenyatta.

*John and Elli D'Olier –
incurably bitten by the
wine bug.*

'We should have realised he would now think it was *his* wine. Especially when he inscribed a couple of magnums and presented them to me! For my birthday, with his "best wishes", said John, with more laughter. 'I left it for a while, couldn't spoil the fun of it too soon, but do you know what it costs just to import a magnum into this country, let alone fill it? So eventually I had to say, let's talk this thing over.' He 'was retired' a year or two later but not before claiming copyright fees. 'You'd better pay me for wine with my name on it,' he insisted.

Californian wine icon Robert Mondavi had arrived unannounced here, having heard about these Kenya pioneers, keen to taste. Now we did likewise, on the veranda, the moon out, hyenas baying. An 88 Blanc Fumé –'undrinkable at the time we released it, it was so acid' – had more or less survived; it had some stern flinty life left and surprised even the D'Oliers who'd not sampled it in years. 'Must have pulled out a lucky bottle,' said John. Then what he called a 'gumboot' Cabernet 96. Elli slapped him on the wrist. 'John, that's not smart marketing.'

Not always satisfied with the performance of his grape crusher and de-stalker prior

LAKE
NAIVASHA
VINEYARDS
MÉTHODE
CHAMPENOISE

D PRODUCED BY
ASHA VINEYARDS LTD.
620, NAIVASHA.
F KENYA
750 ML

to fermentation in tubs, John and his team would sometimes retread the grapes. 'Some of the juice would overflow into our squelching gumboots,' he explained, adding that yeasts perform such a powerful cleansing job during alcholic fermentation that any bacterial problems are swept away. It's *after* fermentation that wine spoils easily – specially in the presence of air or the absence of sulphur.

Besides, the home-grown lamb – Elli is the livestock manager, handling a herd of Jersey and Friesian cows – camouflaged any wine faults. It was basted in a rich mix of heavily garlicked lard, mild American mustard, liquid coffee and sugar; beneath this caramelised crust, the meat was tenderly pink. And it was served with a prune and port sauce. A dish to reduce most wines to insignificance.

Mondavi, in Kenya to contribute a case of his Reserve 89 Cabernet to a Richard Leakey wildlife fundraiser, had complimented the D'Oliers on their 'Fumé' – the Sauvignon Blanc – before he knew that the vines had been propagated from his own Sauvignon block back in Napa! Elli, a fellow-Californian, had brought the vines to Kenya. (She emigrated here in 1979, met John on a blind date at the Muthaiga Club, and doesn't hanker after her homeland. 'Kenya's a place where you have time to have friends,' she said.) Mondavi promptly invited the D'Oliers to lunch on their next American visit, and they've framed their photograph of the occasion. 'Such superb, super wines,' sighed John.

But the vineyards which Mondavi had inspected had now gone. 'We grubbed up the lot, most of it in 1992. Had to. They changed all the rules overnight.' 'They' being the Kenyan Government. John reeled off, in the best tradition of farmers anywhere, the crippling tax burdens: 30 per cent on everything imported (glass, corks etc), 45 per cent for excise, 18 per cent for VAT… 'it was hopeless, we couldn't compete against imported stuff. And the exchange rate of the Kenya Shilling was all over the place, we didn't know where we were.'

Still, the wine bug lurked in his bloodstream. And out at the back of the farm, beyond the hippo trails, behind fields of onions and the cattle paddocks, he'd just planted 2 hectares with 10,000 Tempranillo vines – the variety which makes some of Spain's most serious red wines. Never tried in Kenya before. In their first leaf, they'd taken very well. He'd imported them from Italy, on the recommendation of his German friend, Wolfgang Shaefer, an international tropical wine consultant who'd spent 10 years in neighbouring Tanzania in the 1980s.

'He should know… I just hope the vines bear,' John was still the laid-back risk-taker, incorrigible dabbler, smitten oenophile. 'I'm going to add some Shiraz – Wolfgang's favourite – and a little Cabernet. These will be Reserve wines, a hobby, without the pressure to sell at vast profit. I suppose I'm a sucker for punishment, and by now, an encyclopedia of errors!'

We'll know how well the new vineyards have worked in about 2006, when John will have to dust off his – mostly home-made – winery equipment. He's hoping not to attract too much attention from anti-alcohol neighbours: this young vineyard is very close to a new, white-domed mosque, in a village that's recently sprung up on his boundary.

'If I can just remember all the mistakes of the past, we should be on to a good thing,' he said. But he *was* on to a good thing. We'd tasted it before the lamb, some of the famous ex-cellar hand's wine – the Millésime 92 Jua Kali (Hot Sun) bottle-fermented bubbly. 'We degorged and bottled this in the bath, froth flying everywhere,' recalled Elli.

Aphids in my apples

In the Kinangkop hills above Lake Naivasha, via a maze of rutted farm tracks dissecting small garden plots, we found John Waweru. Vines, Paul Chemng'orem insisted, could and should be grown as a 'peasant crop' too, and Waweru's three rather straggly rows were evidence. They were trained haphazardly, alongside potatoes, apple trees, beans, peaches, mulberries, peas, more beans; a few chickens and two cows seemed contented enough. Each stockaded homestead in this crowded area – once the site of vast white-owned farms – was similarly closely planted. John had been a schoolteacher for 14 years before he 'retired' and since, he said, he'd never worked so hard. Life was difficult but he had only one complaint: 'Corruption. You can't get anything done. It's our No. 1 problem.'

But make that two. He'd thought of something else. 'The aphids – and right now mildew too – in my apples,' he said, puzzled by the arrival of strangers, off the beaten track. Beaten just about irreparably, in fact: it took us 40 minutes to negotiate the road from Naivasha – a 10-minute drive not so long ago. 'But I have a neighbour, Billie Nightingale, I was there yesterday and she lent me some spray against mildew.'

Why wasn't he growing more grapes? 'I can't get the right varieties, what's available here doesn't seem to grow very well.' Would he be interested in trying different vines, or had he given up on them? 'Of course, send me some from South Africa.' He assembled his family around one young healthy vine for a picture, and we promised to be in touch.

A few isolated farmers opted to stay out of the settler-to-peasant resettlement schemes of the 1960s; our old friends Ted and Billie Nightingale chose to stay on. Ted, who gave up polo-playing only after his 80th birthday, had died a few years ago aged 92, but Billie, a serene 89, was going strong. We bumped up the road to the typical, sprawling, tin-roofed Kenya settler home her family had built in 1909. For the past 20 years, the Nightingales have produced beautiful white table grapes – and Kenya's finest export turkeys.

We strolled down to the vines, trellised high, bearing massive bunches, all under fine chicken-wire mesh to keep out the birds – and flying, reddish Sykes monkeys. 'We picked two and half tonnes of grapes last year,' said Billie. 'They were magnificent.' John wanted to know the variety. 'Oh, John, don't ask me that… Ted knew all the details.' Ted had been in the élite British Political Service in the Sudan, eventually becoming Deputy Governor of Africa's largest country. He'd told us about a lethal Sudanese tipple – a cocktail of Cypriot sherry and methylated spirits. 'It took them weeks to recover. They called it the Father of an Axe.'

Billie Nightingale and the best table grapes in Kenya in the Kinangkop hills above Lake Naivasha.

From Billie's sweeping lawns we saw the swathes of powder blue lake below, edged by the greens of the famous Naivasha fever trees – and spotted a tell-tale clearing: more vineyards? (Trees can only be cut down by special presidential permission in Kenya.) We'd earlier heard about the Morendat Wines of the Rift Valley, made enquiries, and been told in uncharacteristically unfriendly terms: no entry. However, we later bought a bottle each of red and white – in Naivasha village's main pub, the Bell Inn, famous for its greasy chicken pies. The wines didn't seem to have travelled the 5 kilometres particularly well.

I'm one of these stubborn buggers

Next day, with Paul Chemng'orem, we headed east from Nairobi. We were on the track of one of the most interesting, contentious men in Kenya. Richard Leakey, palaeontologist, politician, conservationist; the mover and shaker with only one kidney – transplanted from his brother – and two artificial legs ('at least I don't get cold feet'); son of Drs Louis and Mary Leakey, whose diggings in the Olduvai gorge in Tanzania had dramatically advanced the case for man's origins in Africa; descendant of missionaries who were buried alive by the Mau Mau, facing Mount Kenya, home of the tribal deity Ngai. And much more. More stories had been told, and legends invented, about Richard Leakey than seemed reasonable.

For years we'd watched his career with awe, dismay and perhaps an even keener interest than most followers of African affairs – John and he had been contemporaries at the Duke of York School in Nairobi in the 1950s. He was a skinny fellow with a permanently faraway look, obviously at odds with the confining strictures of school, more interested in the bush and snakes than organised sport, or exams – which he never seemed to pass anyway. Richard, schoolmates predicted, would not take after his brilliant and often controversial parents. Nor was there an inkling that the rumpled, wildly white-maned Leakey Snr's genius for provocative publicity and a very political take on all things Kenyan would become Richard's trademark too, though he was hardly likely to be entirely apolitical either, and dramatic events had always been a fact of Leakey family history.

But he had outdone them all – for ballsy public commitment to Africa. And been badly beaten up twice for his pains, his car set alight once. He'd scratched around in the searing northern Kenyan deserts, closing the gaps in his formal education and collecting doctorates as well as fossils, and spearheaded the country's fight against the ivory trade, helping, ultimately, to secure a resurgence of the continent's dangerously dwindling elephant populations. Even the many adversaries he's collected in the ensuing scraps acknowledge his canny grit; and he enjoys the respect of millions of Africans in and well beyond Kenya.

It was the latest news in his gaudy career we were after, though. He is growing and making wine. And remarkably, here bang on Latitude 1 South, he's gone for Burgundy's 'heartbreak grape', the notoriously fussy, site-specific, cool-climate Pinot Noir upon which many a producer's hopes have foundered, even in near-ideal temperate climes. What's more, his winery has no electric power, no cooling system, barely any running water.

Wine stories don't often come as wild as this. But initially and uncharacteristically, though we spoke several times on the phone, he seemed determined to keep us away from his vineyard. His brothers call him the showman of the family; it was he who conceived, for the elephant-conservation cause, the extraordinary giant public bonfires of government-owned tusks. But now he was all excuses: I'm not ready… it's very modest… we're still on bucket technology… let's wait for your book's second edition, I shouldn't show the cake before it's baked….

We were just as determined to nail him down. To find out how and why he'd become not just a fancier but a grower, and a serious one. When we finally pen-etrated the protective perimeters of his private life, the answer was succinct: necessity. And his reticence was understandable. 'Without my name on it, nobody would be interested in this wine,' he said. (Not quite true; whoever was making equatorial Pinot would have had *our* antennae quivering.) But his wine would carry extra baggage: people ready to mock a premature or faulty release, to accuse Richard of trading on the Leakey name. Which was why he'd proceeded with such stealth: when we visit-ed in early 2002, almost no one in Kenya knew he'd already filled his first 1000 bottles.

Cheese, wine and Richard Leakey in full flight.

The genesis of his maiden 2001 vintage of Pinot goes back to the collapse of his kidneys in 1979. His younger brother (and sometime polit-ical foe) Philip donated one of his kidneys to keep Richard alive. Convalescing in France after the transplant 'I began to appreciate wine. I didn't have access to the grand labels but there was a variety of many good and inexpensive ones. And the prospect of drinking expensive poor wine for the rest of my life back in Kenya was appalling.'

Eventually he succumbed to our persistence, and we met at the main gate to the Nairobi National Park on the city's outskirts, one of his old haunts as a former Director of the Kenya Wildlife Service – from which he'd since graduated in public fits and starts to Head of the Civil Service and Cabinet Secretary. This is the most powerful 'non-political' job in the land, with constant, direct access to the President; an extraordinary position to achieve for a member of such a (numerically) small and politically insignificant community, and 40 years after independence!

However, he had just resigned, and as he drove us in his white Range Rover up the dirt road into the Ngong hills, he explained that this latest and, like the others, sudden departure had been 'by mutual agreement' with the President and had not dented their 'personal relationship at all'. But we paused the politics; we were at his vineyard now.

Château Leakey

It's on an eastern escarpment of Kenya's grand Rift Valley, within sight and sound of Maasai herdsmen whistling their cattle and bleating goats into the *manyattas* – traditional thorn and-dung stockades – on the dusty brown plains, and overlooking the dry river beds which unfold along the rift. Buffalo, eland and hyenas roam, and as he goes to sleep on the windy cliff, Richard hears elephants trumpet and lions roar. Not your average patch of vines.

He launched into its history. 'Fifteen years ago I managed to get 12 Chardonnay vines from California and planted them at my old home in Karen [a Nairobi suburb]. But it was damp and they suffered terribly from mildew. I gave some cuttings to my older brother Jonathan at Lake Baringo – hotter, lower in the Rift Valley – but in two years they'd curled up. I had one vine left when I was finally driven insane by advancing suburbia, discos and barking dogs. Try handling that lot – and rowdy week-long weddings among the neighbours – with my shingles! I took a cutting from that solitary vine with me when I sold there and bought this farm – 105 acres – on the Ngong.'

He acquired more vines from France and Italy and planted them on steep, west-facing slopes, each row on a separate terrace buttressed by walls of stones. 'And here at last the vines seemed content,' he said in a phrase redolent of Karen Blixen. And, it seemed, he was content too. With a nod to *Out of Africa*, he could easily adapt Blixen's immortal line: 'I had a farm in Africa.'

But why Pinot Noir? 'Well, I'm one of these stubborn buggers who don't like to be told it's impossible. They all said you must do tests for this and that and everything else. I didn't want to go through all that… I said "leave me alone… the test will only show it can't be done". And by the way, the Pinot vines love it out here.'

He'd christened the vineyard Ol Choro Onyore, the Maasai name of his Ngong ridge, and each wine was to bear the Maasai name of a berry tree. But he'd been so cagey about this visit that we were still wondering whether we'd get to taste the fruits of his labours.

The vine repertoire has grown steadily but not largely. Now covering, or rather plunging precipitously 2 hectares down the slope, are Cabernet Sauvignon, Sauvignon Blanc, a Muscat or two, as well as Pinot and Chardonnay. There's basic but adequate trellising; electrified anti-baboon fences and gates. The soil, dark and friable, has an ideal neutral pH. However, the happy circumstance of a vineyard on a hillside out of the lee of the regular winds has a drawback: the regular early morning mists here aren't blown away quickly enough to prevent some mildew.

Minute crops of tiny, thick-skinned berries, with their high skin:pulp ratios, are guarantors of concentrated fruit flavour — but only if the vines aren't over-stressed. And they have been at times during Kenya's fierce droughts. 'So I'll install drip irrigation soon — not to dilute the flavour mind you, but to tide the vines over the worst dry periods. I do think so many growers in Africa use water wrongly. The grapes lose flavour and the definition of the variety is lost in the wine. You couldn't tell Cabernet from Shiraz or Sauvignon from Chardonnay,' he said. 'I'm a bit worried about my Chardonnay actually… not because of any dilution, it's the one wine where I think a bit of oak might suit it quite well. But we need to sort out our cooling system. And we shall.'

Here's the scientist, the farmer, the wineman rolled into one. 'Actually, what's kept up my enthusiasm is my daughter Louise's love of wine. She's absolutely passionate.' Louise was away in Britain, just having finished a PhD (in palaeontology, did we need to ask?) but he proudly showed her immaculate vineyard records, in a neat, small hand; almost every vine had a documented history. 'We know now, exactly 154 days from pruning, it's harvest time in our conditions,' he said.

Not to strain his legs — he'd been confined to a wheelchair the previous week with back trouble — we drove the few metres from the house down to the vineyard. After a crash in a light plane he'd been piloting, he'd had both legs amputated below the knee. President Moi had come to see him in hospital. 'I'm praying for you,' said Moi, the practising Christian. 'Don't bother,' replied the straight-talking atheist Leakey. Moi's biographer Andrew Morton says Moi was deeply wounded. 'I gave my legs to Africa,' Richard later wrote grandiloquently, in one of his resignation letters.

Self sufficiency

We walked, he slowly and with a stick, to the winery to see the 'bucket technology' he thought would amuse us. Scores of brightly coloured, spotless plastic buckets, stored in readiness for the vintage in a few weeks. A tiny press, tiny filter. The cleanliness was no accident. 'I believe hygiene is one of the keys to decent wine,' he said — advice most of the world's wineries could take to heart.

But he was expanding — unconventionally. Bales of straw were stacked, like giant bricks; each side was plastered with cement, making very thick but very light walls. It's a

GILGIL COUNTRY CLUB

John Platter _____ Date J

3 Tuskers Shs 150 –

Signature _____ Total _

have another

Top: *One Kenyan drinking hole; and another; Richard Leakey's straw cellar; doum palms, Samburu Reserve.*
Middle: *Richard Leakey and Kenya's Mr Wine, Paul Chemng'orem; beers in John's child-hood village; we might have stayed at home; first editions inLeakey's wine library.*
Bottom: *Roadside shopping; John Waweru's family and their best vine; Ch.Leakey; on the Kenyan bird-trail, John, marathon-man Bruce Fordyce and Cape wineman Gyles Webb discovering signs of wine.*

novel idea – for wineries at least – publicised only 6 months earlier in California by Paul Draper of Ridge Vineyards. A simple, quick and cost-effective cool-storage and sound-proofing system. Richard led us through to his wine library, the vintages neatly ordered and tagged – though not yet labelled.

Lighting is powered by batteries, charged by a windmill feeding an alternator, which lights the house too. 'Free,' he beamed. 'And we get no power cuts,' a reference to Kenya's chronic energy shortages. He returned frequently to the self-sufficiency theme.

'Provided the wine's reasonable, drinkable… and I hope we're getting there; provided the wine's okay, I have to be sure about that first' (he cut the air with an open hand for emphasis, making a speech) 'then I think we can release a little to the local market, to a few game lodges perhaps. I find the wine perfectly drinkable – no headaches afterwards, no tummy troubles the next day.

'Obviously the name should help. But I'd like to be able to recover our costs from sales and put the balance, our own wine on our table, for free. At least I don't want to worry each time I open a bottle of bought wine and don't finish it in one sitting that I'm wasting $15' (The Kenya Government's almost extortionist, multiple taxes on imported wines virtually quadruple their landed retail cost.)

'You see, I've been on a civil servant's salary most of my life,' he added, with a chuckle. He laid it on thicker. 'We go out to a restaurant perhaps twice a year.' Clearly meaning in Kenya. He's in such world demand as a speaker – with at least some attendant dining presumably? – and doubtless can name his price, except on those occasions when *he's* fund-raising for causes back home. 'In fact it's been a problem in the past… fitting the harvest between some of my overseas commitments. But now Louise has finished her PhD, at least one of us can be here.'

The comprehensive, 'subsistence' philosophy has shaped their farming for some years. Vegetables are planted between the vine rows. The sheep and cattle (local Borana crossed with Charolais) provide meat, milk and cheese. Chickens do their two-piece bit, the dam is stocked with tilapia. All waste is converted into gas and channelled back into the home to run the freezers and cookers. 'Smell this,' he instructed, lighting a hob; there was a brief whiff of bad eggs that blew off in a few seconds. And the by-product, cakes of con-centrated fertiliser, goes back to feeding all kinds of plants and (strictly indigenous) trees.

But for its silhouette on the ridge, you'd hardly notice the rambling house – huge windows surveying Maasailand, minimally furnished, gigantic fireplace, occasional rug, walls of well-used books. It's built of whole stones collected from the cliffs, a natural dusty buff colour. 'We want for nothing here,' he said, 'but we usually come out only for the week-ends.' His wife is curator of the Coryndon Museum in Nairobi, where they have an apartment, from which until recently, he'd been at the President's beck and call.

In the wine library he'd slipped us a bottle of the Pinot and a Sauvignon Blanc. The

Chardonnay wasn't 'quite ready' and the Cabernet Sauvignon 'too tight still'. A pity, but two was better than none, and perhaps he was right not to show us.

We gathered in the kitchen, he pulled up a chair for himself ('sorry about my legs'); we leaned around the big working space with its built-in hobs. Then he shuffled over to a fridge and said: 'I spend most of my life hearing people tell me what I shouldn't eat and drink'. He hauled out a large yellow round of Tilsiter cheese, mild, soft, chewy, cut a few generous chunks of cholesterol and invited us to help ourselves. For the first time in any African wine country outside the Cape, we tasted from large handsome Riedel glasses with a decent swirling bowl – the bane of dishwashing kitchens everywhere.

The Sauvignon was ample, clean, fresh and quite fleshy – untypical Sauvignon, but a satisfying, grapey mouthful. The Pinot was discernibly itself – on the palate – and unexpectedly full; clearly the product of well-ripened, clean berries. That showed in the surprisingly intense ruby tint.

Settings – leave aside fine cheese – do have a way of conditioning palates, so we sniffed and swallowed more deeply. Was the implausibility of it all tricking our senses? Were we being seduced by the powerful presence of Leakey – no longer a dreamy, skinny, unfocused schoolboy but a battle-scarred heavyweight politico? By the majesty of the Ngong vistas and the legends of Maasai in the gorges below? We'd like to think not. The crucial berry ripeness was confirmed in 13%-plus alcohols – without sugar assistance from chaptalisation! And without the aid of oak, the winemaker's trustiest crutch.

Here was a signal achievement, discovery wine, a coup. Certainly the most interesting, drinkable red we'd tasted in the tropics. But the bouquet might need some work; it lacked nose-power. He almost seemed grateful for the suggestion.

'Absolutely, absolutely,' he agreed. 'We'll have to go on experimenting. If we don't go on exploring, we're dead.' The cooling system he plans to install will go some way towards preserving essential fruity aromas. And with just a little tuning and more luck with the weather – and further dogged work in the vineyards to improve the canopy and see off the mildew – Kenya and Richard Leakey could very well be heading towards an international icon label, the ultimate *garagiste* wine out of Africa. On our next visit, will we be able to afford it?

TANZANIA

On the Morogoro road: cashew nuts with your wine, anyone?

The warning was an unambiguous African perspective on the dangers of *pombe*. Wine is included in this generic Swahili word for alcohol, which, claimed the poster, contributes directly to Tanzania's deadliest modern killer: Aids. Why? Because pombe gives you a 'craving for love-making' – *huongeza tamaa ya mapenzi*.

It was spelled out in bold comic-strip style by Mohamed Charinda, one of the founders of Tanzania's famous Tinga Tinga (tractor – let's skip the subtleties) school of art. Charinda had depicted the swift descent of plump-bosomed ladies of the night, swinging to the beat of central Africa's high-life music, to skin and bones under grim blue sheets in hospital wards. And issued a final dire reminder: There is no medicine for UKIMWI – the Swahili acronym for 'loss of protection in the body.'

Was this an unfortunate augury for Tanzania's latest attempt to revive its wine industry? We searched out the artist himself on the outskirts of the coconut palm-fringed port of Dar es Salaam. This means 'haven of peace' and it is indeed much less chaotic, noisy and congested than most big African cities. In a riotously primary-coloured side street, the artists congregate in makeshift shops and corrugated iron stalls, hung with canvases flapping in the breeze, connected by a maze of narrow, dark backrooms. Many seemed exhausted by their labours and were dozing on the floor in their bright *kikois* – the sarongs uniformly worn along the East African coast. But Mohamed, a Muslim teetotaller, was extremely chirpy.

Shirtless, and wet with sweat, he smilingly allowed a very pregnant woman at his side to explain his didactic message: 'If you drink *pombe*, you want sex too much. All the time.' She rubbed her tummy and rolled her eyes. There were hundreds of similar works; the artists' colony was taking Aids and booze very seriously indeed. But it's an original Charinda now in our possession.

This art interlude had come after our trip to the Tanzanian winelands, but Mohamed would have been pleased. There'd been no time for partying, nor for heeding one of the favourite Swahili aphorisms along this humid tropical coast: *Haraka, haraka hana baraka*

– to rush is unseemly. It was rush rush from the start. Moses Kagya had already become a long-distance friend and he was at Dar airport at midnight, after our five-hour Tanzania Air delay, still as jovial as his e-mail messages. The next morning, we had to make a dawn start for the long journey into the interior.

Looks good but doesn't even fly to its own capital city!

Try, try and try again

Moses is a maths boffin with an MBA from the US; with his German partners in Tanganyika Vineyards, he's spearheading Tanzania's wine revival. Another one: there've been several 'new beginnings' in the country's curious wine history.

German viticulturalists began growing grapes before the Second World War when Tanganyika, as it was then known, was a German colony. Those small-scale vineyards were dotted around the Usamabara hillsides just south of Kilimanjaro, Africa's highest mountain, then rather more 'snow capped all year round' than it is these days. A little wine is still produced there, but it's for home or, at a couple of mission stations, Mass consumption. Sister Happy, we were told, was the best known of these 'winemakers', but Tanzania is huge – larger than Nigeria, three times the size of Italy – and time and distance constraints didn't allow us to meet her. Our focus had to be on Dodoma, in the centre of the country and centre, too, of its contemporary wine culture. Here other missionaries had first planted vineyards in the 1930s. And here, Tanzania's bigger wine boom had begun in the 1970s.

This was when the parastatal Dodoma Wine Company was launched. It reached a peak production of 3500 tonnes (about 2 million bottles-worth; though much of this went to distilling and spirits production) before sputtering out in the mid-1980s, finally collapsing in the general inertia and corruption that overwhelmed Tanzania's government-run agricultural co-operatives. Rather bafflingly, it was then taken over by the Prisons Department, which had little interest in vines and no money to pay farmers. Most plots reverted to subsistence maize, millet, beans, cashew nuts and livestock; those who retained vines picked them as table grapes. (Tanzania has often been characterised as a 'barefoot economy' – the vast majority of its 35 million citizens scratch out a living on the land.)

Now Moses Kagya was on a wine rescue mission here, in partnership with a retired German banker, Rolf Gieseng. They'd launched Tanganyika Vineyards in 1996; their Dodoma winery was being supplied by a handful of growers in about a dozen surrounding villages of the Gogo tribe. Moses knew the area well from the days of his former job as the chief civil servant in Tanzania's Capital Development Authority. This was no money-raising outfit; it was charged, from 1974, with relocating the nation's capital from Dar es Salaam to hot, dusty, drab Dodoma, almost a semi-desert town, ringed by statuesque grey boulders. Now Moses makes the 6-hour, 500-kilometre journey from Dar to check the winery and jolly along his growers.

Parliament sits in Dodoma for several months of the year. But there's no buzz — except from the clouds of mosquitoes at dusk. Not even the national airline flies to the Tanzanian capital! The runway, almost in the middle of the sprawling town, is an unfenced field grazed by goats; we'd had no option but to drive.

The road shimmered in the heat. An occasional shower of rain cooled us and Moses' white 4x4 off a bit. An inordinate number of snakes slithered across the road; scores had been run over. Traffic and foliage thinned as we climbed up from the tropical-coast palm and banana belt toward the African savannah — vast rolling plains of scrub and thorn trees under billowing white cumulus clouds. We talked non-stop, munching cashews and stopping for Cokes, water and whole, peeled pineapples. Moses, the socialist technocrat-turned-capitalist businessman (his other ventures include road construction) frequently wandered off the subject of wine. Like most Tanzanians, he's an eager philosopher — and an unrepentant fan of the late President (Mwalimu — 'Teacher') Julius Nyerere, the literary scholar-statesman who translated two of Shakespeare's plays into Swahili and who, towards the end of his life, admitted his doctrinaire policies had failed his country.

Occasionally, a red-robed herdsman would burst from the bushes, waving a stick or spear. Parts of the long, often very straight, raised road formed a dam wall and herds of cattle were drinking the coffee-coloured water. We were at the southern extremes of the Maasai grazing lands that reach far north into Kenya. Years ago Nyerere had tried to get the Maasai to wear trousers and give up their traditional skimpy red shoulder cloths. Across the border, Kenya permitted — even encouraged — such outfits. Good for tourist photos. But Nyerere disapproved of tourists flaunting their wealth, 'corrupting' his countrymen; better, to his mind, poor but proud self-reliance. We foreign correspondents had closely followed this intriguing war of the wardrobe. At the time, many nomadic herdsmen simply slipped over the border to dodge the trouser police, and now it was clear this had been another of Nyerere's lost causes.

Moses said the Maasai hadn't changed in another respect: 'They still believe every cow placed on earth is their God-given present, and it's their inalienable right to retrieve them from all the other tribes.' They continue in their ancient rustling ways. We briefly wondered if Moses would be able to convert them to Chenin Blanc. 'No, they'll always prefer blood'.

Moving the capital had not signified any presidential ego-trip, he explained. It was just that Nyerere wanted the government to get closer to the people. He lapsed into a reverence unusual today; people are now much more cynical about their leaders. Nyerere, he insisted, had been Africa's most engaging and eloquent statesman — engaging in the sense that he connected with people. It was his verbal dexterity and honesty that allowed him to juggle, for two decades, a devout Catholicism with fervent Marxism and an admiration for China's Chairman Mao. Nyerere had called his system African Socialism – *Ujamaa*. 'A more humane form of coerced collectivisation than Mao's but disastrous nonetheless,' said Moses. 'A visionary prig' is how Xan Smiley, of the *Economist*, a veteran Africa hand, once described Nyerere.

'That's not quite fair,' said Moses. 'Unlike nearly all the other rulers in Africa, Nyerere at least admitted his mistakes and did a u-turn on Ujamaa. And he remained a man of very modest personal tastes, completely uncorrupt. We loved him.' Tanzania's current President, Nyerere protégé Ben Mkapa, has privatised much of the economy.

Barbed wire and grilled goat

In his retirement, Nyerere became a farmer and lived both at his remote birthplace at Butiaba on Lake Victoria and at Dodoma. He was specially fond of indigenous trees, and though he didn't drink, took a personal interest in winegrowing. But all was not well in the national vineyards. As was instantly evident to a young German viticulturalist and oenologist, fresh out of Geisenheim Viticultural Research Institute in the Rheingau winelands, Wolfgang Shaefer, who came to Dodoma in 1978 under a German aid programme to establish a vine research station. 'They were trellising their vines with barbed wire!' he told us.

He and his wife Mary, an economist who worked for GTZ , the German overseas technical aid programme, were taken 20 kilometres out of Dodoma to a 40-hectare piece of barren, dry land, very red and sandy, no water, no house. This is your plot, they were told. 'We just camped in the bush,' said Wolfgang. They dug a well and built a reservoir. And a house. And got a vine nursery going within a year. Later, a nursery for their two daughters too – both born in Tanzania. 'It was like 100 years ago, when we all had to be self sufficient.' Malaria was a constant threat.

But soon Wolfgang was monitoring more than 300 varieties of vines and rootstocks. 'The vine grows easily anywhere it's not too wet, nor too dry. But we had a hell of a time dealing with nematodes.' Shiraz, Tempranillo, Grenache and Carignan all looked promising, especially Shiraz. 'Certainly more promising than the red wine grapes the Fathers were using.'

And here begins one of those earnest – sometimes deadly – viticultural disputes from which laypeople can only stand back to enjoy. The Italian Catholic Passionisti Fathers – who came to the area with the vine in 1934 – insist their variety is Aleatico, an Italian grape (also known in Corsica) which, ordinarily, gives an unmistakably spicy Muscat flavour to its wines. It's sometimes even called Moscato.

'Try it for yourself,' Wolfgang suggested. 'See if you get any Muscat flavours. I don't think it's Aleatico at all.' The Bihawana and Veyula missions near Dodoma and elsewhere

Top: *Father Sergio
Teani. 'Listen to the
wine!'; evensong above,
Veyula mission's cellar
below. Peanuts and
cashews are more
popular cash-crops
than grapes.*
Middle: *A wine which
dances off the tongue?
Winemakers' meeting:
Tanganyika Vineyards
winemaker Kato
Archad and Father
Sergio Teani.*
Bottom: *The Passionisti
Fathers' vineyard near
Dodoma; a wine-
warning from the
Tinga Tinga artists.*

grow this grape – whatever it is – as do Tanzania's small-scale peasant wine farmers. It produces Tanganyika Vineyards' Makutupora Red; the Makutupora White is a dry Chenin Blanc. And Fr Sergio Teani of the Veyula mission, his mournful, saturnine features straight out of an El Greco painting, was adamant when we visited his winery and vineyards. 'What do these Germans who only came here the other day know?' he demanded. 'We know what the first Fathers brought – Aleatico!'

His winery under the Veyula seminary (they were chanting at evensong above as we tasted below) is cramped but a model of modesty. 'When I leave, they must be able to continue – not too many machines is better. Ha?' His main complaint seemed to be with his fellow Fathers, who refused to chop down the gorgeous, shady flamboyant trees bordering his tiny and ordered, 1-hectare vineyard. 'Their roots,' he said pointing at the trees, 'they are a 20 metres long and they a suck, steal all the water from under my vines. Wine is water. You understand?' Nor had his prayers for good weather been answered this latest vintage. 'We had hail, such big stones, I never seen anything like that in 30 years.'

He'd made only 2000 bottles: but of every hue. 'When the grapes are dusty, it is hard to clean them… so, it's simple, I make a rosé, then you don't see the colour! Ha ha.' He had mightily pungent grappa too ('not Mass wine!'), made in an alembic pot still. In neatly stacked rows, he'd labelled his production *Divai Nyeupi* white wine in Swahili (or *Nyekundu* – red; *Divai* is among the words Swahili and Malagasy have in common.) Each time Fr Sergio passed around a glass, he'd say: 'Listen to the wine, it's very good, very young.' The Passionisti brothers were not going to go short.

Back in Dodoma, we looked over the bare essentials Tanganyika Vineyards winery (no cooling but clean), then repaired to taste at our no-name hotel, an extension of the premises of the local Vocational Education and Training Authority. It had the air of a basic old government rest house and cheerful staff. We sampled the wines with a hearty pile of well-hung chunks of goat, spit-roasted in the beer garden. Blue, red and yellow light bulbs were strung among the trees. Miaowing black cats had to be fended off with goat morsels, and Moses pointed out heavyweight Tanzanian politicos whispering in corners.

Winemaker Kato Archad, a chemist trained at Dar University, had learned his wine-making in Thailand. He was trying to solve the problems of two vintages a year, one 'dry' in August/September, the second and slightly more abundant 'wet' one in March/February. His farmers produced not much more than 3–4 tonnes/hectare over both crops combined. He thought rather than blending the two 'vintages' he should perhaps consign the 'wet', poorer quality one to distilling wine (Moses Kagya was actively seeking out such markets).

An even bigger problem was to get the farmers to synchronise their pruning – and the harvest – whichever the season. 'I get odd crates of grapes at unpredictable moments without notice from the farmers,' said Kato. He shook his head. But he understood. Since

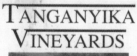

TANGANYIKA
VINEYARDS

P.O. BOX 1565 DODOMA/TANZANIA

CHENIN BLANC

ol   DRY WINE   0,751

MAPADRE WAPASIONISTI
(PASSIONIST FATHERS)
← VEYULA

POMBE HUONGEZA TAMAA YAMAPE

CHUMBA CHA KUPIMA DAM

TUJIHATHARI NA UKIMWI HAUNA DAW

their loss of confidence first in Dowico (Dodoma Wine Co) and then in the Prison Service, the remaining farmers had become cynical. They pruned to outdo *one another*, aiming to ripen their grapes irregularly so as to get the best prices on the table grape markets. 'We need more patriotism, more protectionism and more patronage – the Ps,' he said. 'Take that down in your notebook.'

Kato and Moses were trying to coax the farmers to take Tanganyika Vineyards more seriously. The trouble, as they confided, was that dry local wines weren't exactly taking the markets by storm. The posher lodges in Tanzania's great game reserves – the Serengeti, Ngorongoro Crater, Manyara, around Kilimanjaro, and the beach resorts on the spice island of Zanzibar – tended to keep their dollar-waving clients happy with imported wines. 'We're in 2002 and I still have 1996 wines in the tanks,' said Moses. 'We'll probably have to bottle sweeter wines to lure the locals.' Kato wasn't so sure. 'Maybe we should give them the faulty high volatile, vinegary wines Dowico used to give the locals. They drank that, they could taste it! They don't congratulate me for making cleaner, proper dry wines.'

Kato's Chenin was clean and enjoyable – well-chilled. A roughish finish became evident as it warmed. A touch of sweetness might have been useful to round off the edges. The Makutupora Red was drinkable too but the robust goat flavours – and textures, this was no kid – would have overwhelmed any wine. But – Wolfgang was absolutely right about the 'Aleatico' saga – there was no hint of Muscat. The waiters brought blue soap suds on saucers and a bowl of hot water in which to wash our hands. Then we downed a few soothing beers.

Renaissance and revolution

What, we wondered, had happened to all Wolfgang Shaefer's experiments 20 years ago to broaden the vine and wine choice? Where were the Syrah, the Carignan, the Tempranillo (which he'd persuaded his Kenyan friend John d'Olier at Lake Naivasha to plant)? Unfortunately the brave new wine world Wolfgang had hoped to pioneer had not materialised. He had not renewed his contract after five years: the Dowico officials actively kept him out of their winery, as they drove it into bankruptcy. Giving technical support to growers had become more and more difficult and he was even barred from advising farmers who left the co-operative system.

He and Mary did stay another five years in Tanzania; but this time Mary was the 'bread-winner' as the region's German Aid representative, and they were based at the coastal town of Tanga. 'We made the most beautiful wine from passion fruit,' Mary recalled. 'The purple variety – not the yellow, which is too acid. We even made champagne from it.'

Wolfgang translated his Tanzanian experience into a thriving international tropical viticulture consultancy (now based in Frankfurt) advising projects in India, Venezuela (wonderful Tempranillo vineyards practically in the sea), Thailand, Taiwan, Vietnam, Myanmar – anywhere, it seems, but the vine's natural home. The great and still elusive trick, he says, is how to manipulate conditions to compensate for the 16 hours of daylight a vine prefers – and gets in temperate summers and can't, in any season, in the tropics – to ripen grapes for top quality wine.

But just before our Dodoma trip, he e-mailed to say that the German government, with Tanganyika Vineyards, had decided to fund a revival of his more promising experiments 25 years ago. By 2003, new young vineyards of various vine types, imported from Europe, will be planted at Dodoma – on Tanganyika Vineyards' own 14-hectare parcel of land already earmarked for the purpose. The winery will be up-graded. In a few years, we should be able to taste Tanzanian Shiraz and other modern classics. 'I'm really very excited about this… I know they can produce good quality fruit there. Specially in the dry season,' wrote Wolfgang.

As we drove back to Dar we passed through the town of Morogoro, surrounded by the rugged, secluded hills that Nyerere had allocated for the secret training camps of the African National Congress. Here they'd also made wine. Bongi Njobe, a young ANC guerrilla who'd fled apartheid South Africa, and obtained a horticulture degree from Bulgaria, was put in charge of fruit growing.

'The best paw paws we sent to market, but there was always a pile of ripe and over-ripe ones. They'd ferment on their own. So we decided to filter the stuff – bottled it and forgot about it. Then, going on exercises into the mountains one day, someone thought we should take it along to quench our thirst. We drank so much of it – it tasted so good – we could hardly get down. We were tipsy! After that, we thought, hey, we should do this more often. So we organised some proper yeast, improved the filtration with more rackings – all very simple. After that, the weekends were more fun. But we had to be careful when the bosses, like Oliver Tambo, came to visit… the war effort could have foundered… we didn't want to betray the revolution.'

Years after those heady Tanzanian days, Bongi Njobe became South Africa's Director General of Agriculture.

MOZAMBIQUE
CHANNEL

N
W E
S

GRANDE
BAIE

PORT
LOUIS

LA
BOURDONNAIS

PIETER
BOTH

MAURITIUS

CUREPIPE

BLACK RIVER

SOUILLAC

ANTANANARIVO

ANTSIRABE

MADAGASCAR

FIANA

AMBALAVAO

ST DENIS

BRAS
PANON

SALAZIE

REUNION

ST LEU
CILAOS
ST LOUIS

LA PLAINE
DES
PALMISTES

PITON
DE LA
FOURNAISE

ISALO

TULEAR
TOLIARO

INDIAN
OCEAN

MADAGASCAR

A few visits to this 1600-kilometre long island adrift in the Indian Ocean build strong resistance to surprise. 'Mad', as those bewitched by its crazy individuality know it, is something else. So when a British wine magazine published an article claiming that Madagascar might be the motherland of all vines, pre-dating the usual suspects (Mesopotamia, the Caucasus, even the Himalayas) we couldn't instantly dismiss it. Not because we didn't know the place; because we did!

The South African botanist credited with this major discovery – a Dr Sam van Busuck – didn't ring true; his research – DNA tests and carbon dating on ancient Zinfandel and Chardonnay vines – sounded dodgy. Less implausibly named was his colleague, one Professor Zina Magee, quoted as saying the vines were found to be generationally anterior to European vines… making Madagascar the birthplace of *Vitis vinifera*.

But though the magazine's issue date was 1 April, Mad is a world so out of this world you don't lightly dismiss even the most outlandish tale. When you look into the bulging, confiding eyes of the unique lemurs (new species are still being discovered in the forests) there's an eerie sense of communing with very distant relatives, the presimians. And if Mad grows some of the most bizarre plants on the planet, why not vines of extraordinary antiquity?

The mainland is a mere 560 kilometres to the west. But as the locals say: Africa is another continent. The Malagasy people, their language, architecture, looks, and mores, are traceable to Borneo in Indonesia. The boffins now seem agreed that the world's fourth largest island, floated away from Africa – its western coastline fits into Africa's southeastern coastline as snugly as a jigsaw piece – in the Gondwanaland continental drift, about 160 million years ago, time enough to endow Madagascar with its fabulous level of endemism and speciation.

A vast unspoiled garden of plenty, of coastal plains and forested uplands, awaited the first migrants. Unsurprisingly, they stayed. It's believed they'd sailed from the Pacific via Indian Ocean 'stepping stones' – India, Sri Lanka, the Maldives, the Comores. They came

The Chan Foui family vineyards in the valley of Ambalavao.

in waves, starting about 2000 years ago, some settling along the way, others hitting Africa, before subsequent generations took to their outriggers again, and landed in Madagascar.

Walk down the noisy, chaotic streets of Tana, as the capital, Antananarivo, is called (many Malagasy names are so long they are routinely shortened); mingle with the beautiful, distinctive people and you instantly see that these theories are not far-fetched. So what about those vines?

There was indeed, we discovered, a bit of (rather sad) Chardonnay on the island, being clucked and worried over by Chinese viticulturalists. They kept asking us anxious questions, like parents consulting the doctors at an ailing child's bedside. 'What can we DO about them? Why do they look so SICK?'

But both they and the vines (imported from South Africa) were relatively recent arrivals. Reluctantly, we had to accept the facts: we weren't going to find a world viticulture first here. However, knowing Mad, there'd be no shortage of wine eccentricities. We rather hoped we'd be able to offer some advance on Dervla Murphy's discouraging comments on the wines some years before. 'Superlatively undrinkable,' she'd written.

And in 2001, on our second visit, we'd know the pitfalls. We hadn't, our first time in Mad. Soon after touchdown we'd been in trouble. From our bus, bowling from the airport over the potholes into central Tana, Erica enthusiastically photographed the moving feast: fat ducks waddling and swimming in the rice paddies; squacco herons stalking through drifts of lilac waterlilies; washing drying on the banks of pungently littered canals; green, red and orange Citroën Deux Chevaux; green, red and white painted carts (the colours of the national flag) drawn by hump-backed Zebu cattle.

Very home-made sausages hung out within arm's reach of the traffic; there were precarious pyramids of bright red tomatoes and live turkeys tied in heaps or dashing between the cars. Equally photogenic was a pink and white colonial building, cheek by jowl with the Reserve Bank, which looked – as confirmed later – closed and out of funds.

Erica aimed her camera. A whistle shrilled out. A thin, vexed face with a black beret nearly covering the eyes, rose to the window and hammered on the glass with his whistle. 'Me police,' he cried. 'You out.'

Apparently, this was the presidential townhouse – a no-photo zone. The President at the time, Albert Zafy, was not in – upcountry somewhere, probably wisely, because legislators were trying to impeach him. John leaped out of the bus in hot pursuit.

'Not you!'

'But I am her husband!'

We were marched through heavy iron gates into a charge office at the side of the presidency. Erica's fractured, injured-party French, which included protestations about 'notre Président Mandela' loving it when people took pictures of 'sa maison', was not helpful. Apologies and declarations of innocence worked better. She was 'released' to retrieve her passport from our bus, which had disappeared into the babel of Tana.

John was held as a sort of deposit and escorted over various grunting prostrate forms under blankets down a dark corridor and into a padded and windowless room. Out of the gloom loomed a brigadier wearing sunglasses, a red beret, and massive, drooping epaulettes. Then a translator, then a CID man – joining the rather pleased-with-himself original apprehender.

The offending Pentax lay on the table, lit by the single bulb. We'd already removed the spool and now they unrolled the film and held it up to the light. The brigadier shook his head and pronounced: 'We five cannot solve this problem.'

A fair start – at least John was included in the negotiation. But he hadn't understood the logic of the brigadier's thinking. He was free! Smiles all round, eternal fraternity sworn in franglais. And we'd know to expect the unexpected next time….

Mad soup

The night before we left for our second visit to Madagascar was one of those that guarantees a morning after.

We caught South African wine eminence Michael Fridjhon in a rare moment of repose. Then Chairman of the Trust taxed with the 'restructuring' of the South African wine industry, writer, judge, importer, consultant, show organiser – Fridjhon could juggle in a tornado. But he and wife Janice, head of her own PR company, were both at home – a mansion built by one of the gold-digging Randlords who put the mining camp of Johannesburg on the map. We ate in the kitchen, impeccably. Michael outcooks most chefs in the country. We drank equally splendidly. Buckets of champagne; exquisite burgundies, two bottles of Château Figeac. It was fabulously excessive and very unwise.

Mad is a test of nerve, health and shock absorbers if you, like we, are always travelling off-piste. We ought to have been keeping ourselves strong and fit for the inevitable rigours that lay ahead. Too late. We tottered onto the Air Madagascar flight the next day feeling as fragile as the filaments in a lightbulb.

The plan was to head straight into the field: the nearest vineyards are a mere 110 kilometres from the airport at Tana. We anticipated making first base, the spa town of Antsirabe, before dusk. There we'd have something restorative – a bowl of soup, perhaps – and an early night, so as to be fresh for our morning appointment with the maker of Mad's one and only 'champagne'.

We hadn't even got through passport control before we began to revise this best-case scenario. In triplicate here meant our forms were ever so slowly handled by three different officials, all sitting in the same glass and plywood cubicle. We added another hour or two onto our ETA at Antsirabe.

There was one consolation once we were finally on the south-bound highway: it was removing us from whatever dangers might lie in wait had we stopped over in Tana. (More whistling policemen? Other state-security-threatening photo opportunities?) But the basic principle of travel round this enormous island is fly where you can.

Mad roads are maestros of deception. They may be grandly marked on a map as Routes Nationales with encouraging single-digit numbers – the RN7 in this instance. But they can and do peter into sand tracks, descend into mudslides, disappear down lorry-eating potholes. Factor in the national driving style – it's practically a contact sport – plus thick tropical night and torrential tropical rain. A policy of better late than never urgently needed to be adopted.

Big city life in teeming Tana, the Mad capital.

We stopped in a dot on the map called Ambatolampy to have a Fresh (Madagascar's ready-mixed shandy), and suggest a slightly less dynamic approach to our driver. The whole village had gathered in Au Rendezvous des Pêcheurs, a roadside inn owned by an Albanian, known for its fish dishes and large TV set in the dining room. Chairs in neat rows, the locals were getting their nightly fix of Mad's most popular soap opera, an apparently addictive saga of forbidden love.

We continued our journey more sedately, avoiding hump-backed, long-horned Zebu cattle and the immensely long-legged, long-necked local chickens (do they put them on a rack and stretch them?) which – like most animals on this island – appear to be a breed apart. Surely the toughest birds in the world, not born to be grilled.

It was 10pm when we found La Calèche, our B&B, a colonial confection of verandas, pillars, wooden shutters and French doors. Our host, Eddy Marzel, was small, dark and handsome. He looked like one of those whip-slim characters that canter through Dick Francis books, and indeed he was: a 'gentleman rider' as his Britanny-born partner Véronique put it, a top amateur jockey. Hotels and restaurants were his *métier* – most lately he'd been 'development manager' of the Arhotel, Antsirabe's most modern. At La Calèche (meaning horse-drawn buggy), he and Véronique were going solo; it had been open only one day and the blue and yellow rooms smelled of fresh paint, crisp new cotton and just-sanded floors.

We had a THB – Three Horses Beer, known by its initials – and relaxed. We were in competent hands. Eddy's wine list was reassuring too. St-Emilion, Côte du Rhône, Vins de Pays d'Oc, a decent little range. The local complement was a work in progress, he said. 'But…' He loaded meaning into that one little word, and we would soon establish why.

He disappeared into the kitchen and came out bearing what we'd been panting for, bowls of steaming soup. We'd feasted on porcini at the Fridjhons' the night before; here was a bit of continuity. Cream of mushroom, it looked like, the broth thick with stems chopped into chunky rounds. We dug in ravenously. After a couple of greedy slurps, we revised our first impressions. If these were mushrooms, then they were a brand we didn't know, which was more than likely given that there's greater biodiversity in Madagascar than anywhere else in the world except the Amazon rainforests. You name it, Mad probably has more of it, and it's likely to be unique. With 20,000 species of beetles, nearly 12,000 varieties of plants (with a uniqueness factor of 80 per cent), 1000 different orchids, 30 species of lemurs… if there's one place on earth where you might find a mystery mushroom in your soup, it's here.

But no. The texture wasn't right. These were more rubbery than most fungi we knew. They didn't smell of clean compost heaps or leafy autumnal forest floors; they gave off a slightly sweaty, animal aroma. They tasted like that too. Sort of. On the other hand they might have been the tentacles of some sort of Mad squid…. To tell the truth, we were stumped: not quite sure what we were eating or whether – after the first few spoons – we'd be able to finish it. It tasted odder by the second. Questions would have to be asked.

'What an interesting soup! Such an unusual flavour and feel! What is it?'

Eddy and Véronique, and our Malagasy friend and interpreter Vy Raharinosy (a philosophy student who excused himself from the table later to go off and read a bit of Hegel and Heidegger), smiled. 'It is a local speciality. A great delicacy. You said you wanted to try traditional dishes. What do you think it is?'

We ranged far and wide: Octopus? Brains? Tripe? Gizzards? Sweetbreads? Vy's look, as we finally ran out of ideas, contained the merest hint of nudge-nudge-wink-wink but was enough to alert us. He pointed down at his lap. Definitely below the belt.

Our hosts in Antsirabe, Véronique and Eddy (married since our visit) Marzel, provided a stunning tasting of local delicacies.

Cow's testicles! Erica blurted over-excitedly. (Well, who's not had trouble with the French feminine and masculine?) But no, they weren't even bull's balls. With great delicacy, our new friends now fell silent. It was up to us to choose the most acceptable word for what was floating in our bowls. Which was unavoidable and obvious now we came to consider it. (There'd even been a bit of hair on one of John's morsels.)

There were Zebu penises in our soup. In Madagascar, this gourmet delight is called *soucril*. It translates better into French than English: *zizi de Zébu*.

We went on to Eddy's next courses – grilled Zebu steak, *parfait de gingembre* – both exemplary, and discussed the other culinary attractions of the area. Antsirabe is famous for its duck, and Eddy likes to serve the local *magret de canard* with a pumpkin preserve, fresh foie gras, and a red wine ('Bordeaux of course') sauce. It's also known as *la ville des légumes*: we'd seen, en route, lit by little flickering candles, thatched stalls stacked high with aubergines, carrots, cabbages, and elaborate arrangements of tomatoes. And piles of persimmons, loquats, apples, tangerines, strawberries, guavas.

We tried not to sound like squeamish foreigners (*vazaha* in Malagasy). After all, we are committed to our continent's cuisine. You will never catch us ordering pizza when we could have *wot* or *bredes chouchou* or *pepeta* or *harira* or somesuch authentic local flavour. We have eaten anything and everything all over Africa. But the fact remained that we were not strong enough for this, our very first dish on the Madagascan wine route. We beat a rather ignominious retreat to bed.

Magician, not winemaker

Next morning we met Antsirabe's Mr Wine. Stéphane Chan Foa Tong's light frame was weighed down by a multitude of woes and three jangling bunches of unmarked keys which he carried in a basket. Madagascar is famous – or should be – for its woven raffia baskets but Stéphane's was made from orange plastic. Each time we came to a door he dropped the basket, kneeled down and sifted through the 40 or 50 keys.

He was showing us around his country estate, at Soafierenana, 20 kilometres from Antsirabe off the same RN7 we'd negotiated in the rainy dark the night before. We followed his weathered pick-up onto a deeply rutted, dried mud cart-track, bumping between clusters of huts, plots of maize, cassava and apple trees, rampant banks of mauve cosmos and a lot of ducks. We passed a typical highlands house – triple-storeyed, narrow, medieval, with rose brick walls, terracotta tiled roof, wooden balconies. A small sign offered Wine for Sale. A wizened old man filled your own container from a plastic drum. It had the look and smell of the sort of stuff to be avoided this early in our travels.

The track dead-ended at Stéphane's winery, next to chicken runs and a tractor shed. During the harvest, he camps in a loft where he's rigged up a basic laboratory, bathroom, camp-bed (with mosquito net) and a table made from a black and yellow metal billboard advertising Pirelli tyres.

'Anywhere else, I'd be considered a magician, the way I can make wine under these conditions,' Stéphane said. 'All those people in Europe have classic grape varieties, they wouldn't have a clue here. And I would need satellite tracking to catch all the thieves around me.' There was a suggestion of the heroic last stand about him, and he was dressed for the part – denim jacket, checked shirt, cords, boots – the pioneer farmer character in any number of old Westerns.

Stéphane and his wife Denise are locally born and bred but their parents were from Canton; part of a small wave of immigrants who took flight from the Sino-Japanese wars in 1936–7. It was yet another Mad surprise to find that the island's wine industry is dominated by these transplanted Chinese, who've been the leading growers and winemakers since the departure of most French colonists in 1960. They speak Malagasy and French and though one told us *chez nous* was Hong Kong, this seemed more a reflection of ancient history than current circumstances.

'I've never been there,' said Stéphane. 'I go for holidays to France.' Which is where their children were studying. And from where another unexpected influx of settlers might have come had the Nazis triumphed in the Second World War. When the Germans overran France, thereby also becoming rulers of French overseas colonies, they seriously considered moving the entire Jewish population of Europe to Madagascar.

Stéphane didn't look his 52 years but he talked the tribulations of a lugubrious lifetime. A mutter about the '*dégradation de moralité*' of our age was his stock phrase. He was patient, sad, matter of fact, sharing a universal predicament. 'There are too many people in this world, not enough jobs.' But not much at all had been going his way, he led us to understand, ever since he bought 14 hectares of vines from a departing French colonial in 1972.

'The birds take a lot, disease takes its share and in some years, like 1985, there's a 100 per cent loss due to the weather. Generally about a third goes away with the thieves. Sometimes I even buy back my own grapes that are being sold on the side of the road. I have four guards day and night when the grapes ripen but it doesn't help much.'

The winery seemed less problematical to him, though it would have given New World oenologists migraines. Some of the tanks could be approached only from a space in the roof. We clambered up a rickety ladder, hauled ourselves through a trapdoor, and then stepped shakily from beam to beam, trying to grasp the intricacies of his winemaking system.

Outside was easier to understand. Eucalyptus trellising poles soared crookedly above the vines, giving the vineyards the look of a forest defoliated by Agent Orange. They rotted and had to be replaced every five years or so – but concrete poles were too expensive, Stéphane said. Signs nailed onto the poles gamely warned thieves they would be prosecuted. He shrugged his shoulders. *Dégradation de moralité*.

Here was a small patch of Alicante vines. But – there were no level playing fields in his life – 'Petit Alicante, you understand?' Not the Alicante Bouschet that features in some southern French wines, which is humble enough. There was also Seyval-Villard, a white grape mongrel best relegated to distilling, and Couderc, yet another hybrid. Many vineyardists would have cringed at the straggly, weed-choked unruliness of it all. But could they claim anything like Stéphane's problems?

'We can't get spares for our equipment, because there's no foreign exchange….We can't earn foreign exchange because our vines are hybrids and so the wines cannot be classified as wine – in the EU at least….We can't import classic vine varieties because there's no foreign exchange….We can't import tractors. The (former) President said:

"You have the terrain and you have the labour, what more do you want?"....We have to bribe officials for permission to do anything....We don't have any rat poison for our stores. We have to put everything under drums cut in half....'

No wonder he sounded so mournful. Even a magician would be hard-pressed to conjure anything, let alone a living, out of this. We felt faintly apprehensive about what we might taste once we got back to the business end of the operation in town.

Downtown

Antsirabe was once a glamorous spa resort (its name means 'the place of much salt'). Its Hôtel des Thermes, looking like a faded imperial palace, perches on a hill above hot sulphur baths reputed to alleviate rheumatism and liver problems. Vizy mineral water – the local equivalent of Vichy – is equally healthy. The French military academy here once trained officers from all over former francophone Africa. Trimly uniformed soldiers still dash about in drab army vehicles, but most of the traffic is more colourful.

That afternoon we clopped down the wide boulevards of the French quarter and the narrow cobbled streets of the Malagasy old town in Eddy's own *calèche*, visiting the markets and craft workshops. Jewellers cutting and polishing – Mad is naturally encrusted with every sort of stone. Women squashed around large tablecloths embroidering for chic French stores – their eyes last only seven years on this job. Young girls cramped into little black holes off crooked lanes, arms and legs pumping old Singer treadle machines, churning out 80 straw hats a day, sold for 50p each in local markets.

Hats are worn by everyone but each region has its own brand. In the deep south, the hats were almost brimless, like pudding basins, made from raffia leaves. Around Antsirabe, made from long ropes of wheat or rice-straw, they sported dashing trilby, Homburg and Stetson-style brims.

In muddy alleyways and the dirt of the central *taxi-brousse* (bush taxi) station, everyone was playing *pétanque*. Vy told us that Madagascar was the current world champion. (And that Mad's most famous athlete was world kickboxing champ Parfait Rakotonirina.) We felt rather squirmingly Royal-

Top: Platters in hats from the deep south. Bottom: Taxi! Poussepousse pullers wait for a fare.

party-at-Ascot as the local kids waved and shouted at us: 'Vazaha! Vazaha!' But if horsepower was uncomfortable, imagine manpower!

There are more rickshaws – *pousse-pousse* is the local name, very descriptive of the effort required – here than in any town on the island; 6000 we were told. They're the one man–two passenger (or the equivalent weight in shopping) taxis, used by everyone to go everywhere. The pullers – barefoot or in sandals made from car tyres – went slap slap slap up and down the streets. Passengers hail them by going Pssst! Each *pousse-pousse* had its name painted on the back of the seat: we spotted one in English – Not the Jealous One.

Manipulations

Stéphane is wine purveyor to the small, residual expatriate community here, plus some restaurants, a couple of tourist hotels. He blends, bottles and dispenses in a quiet street in Ambavahadimangatsiaka (the snappy name for the centre of town). Récoltant et Manipulateur his labels read. Grand Cru d'Antsirabe – Vins et Grand Mousseux – Rouge, Rose, Blanc, Gris is painted in bright primary colours outside his premises, alongside a caricature of the French drinking man: beret, baguette, Michelin-man stomach, swigging from a bottle with his pinkie up.

Through the loading bay, up and down vertical wooden stairs, ducking under low lintels, we proceeded deep into the labyrinth: through Stéphane's office (Dickensian), past his lab (Heath Robinson), motley tanks, barrels and wire cages full of bottles to a dank dungeon. Here was his wife Denise's desk, piled with invoice books. With an accusing look, she said: 'It gets cold and damp down here.'

Stéphane and Denise live above the shop, in a small apartment of tiled floors, family portraits, china ornaments, cut-out pinups in the bathroom and an embroidered cloth over the TV. Biscuits and oldfashioned, wide-rimmed champagne glasses were handed around. A cork was popped. We swirled and whiffed in a serious way.

'No, no, it's fine, you can drink it,' urged a French friend of the Chans, who was also tasting. We were too slow and unenthusiastic for him. He was talking to his dog a lot but soon held out a trembling glass for more. So did we: Stéphane makes unquestionably the best sparkling wine in all Madagascar. Probably the finest Couderc Blanc *méthode champenoise* in the world!

This is a grape that rates barely a mention in standard literature. It's related to the once popular hybrid, Couderc Noir, a nineteenth-century crossing of American *Vitis rupestris* and Eurasian *Vitis vinifera*. Though still rampant in many parts of France until the 1970s, it was regarded as an embarrassment. As Jancis Robinson says in *Vines, Grapes and Wines* it was best blended to mute its flavours even when intended for 'commercial consumption'. Here in Madagascar it still ruled.

Encouragingly, our first sniffs and sips of Grand Cru d'Antsirabe bubbly revealed only muffled hints of the 'foxiness' that mars so many American-based hybrids. The 2000 – made to celebrate the new millennium, one of the few Madagascan wines we came across that claimed a vintage – was a perfectly respectable combination of festivity and drinkability. But it cost about US$8/£4.45 a bottle, before tax, and the tax here was a whopping 185 per cent.

'It's mad, mad,' fumed Stéphane. But he'd increased production from 5000 bottles to

Top: Stéphane Chan Foa Tong's wine business billboard in Antsirabe; Bottom: Stéphane at lunch with his own liquid accompaniments.

50,000 anyway: if you want bubbles affordably here, this is the only answer. A work of art in the circumstances, we all agreed; motivation for this endearing, doleful winemaker to soldier on. We raised our glasses. He smiled and bowed his head. Merci beaucoup. On we went to his second-tier sparkler, an orangey 'rosé' made from the hybrid Seyve-Villard, another goodie by local standards.

Madagascar is probably the world's last determined redoubt of hybrid vines. Like its working museum piece, the Micheline, a railway coach and engine circa 1920s, with rubber wheels, that can still be hired for trips out of Tana, the island can be oblivious of time and fashion. The existing vines are hangovers from colonial and missionary days, when the hardiest, least complicated, most prolific vines were planted for basic purposes: sweet wine for Mass, cheap quaffing.

Today, hybrids don't make the cut for official EU quality wine status. But their partly North American makeup does lend a bit of credence to the April fool scientists: their *rupestris* or *labrusca* chromosomes could be more dominant and older than their Eurasian *Vitis vinifera* components.

Some allegedly better-born varieties can lay claim to antiquity too. The next wine we tasted was made from Viala, a white grape (related to Chasselas) confined mostly to Switzerland, but said to be among the very oldest recorded *vinifera* vines, spread around the Mediterranean by the Phoenicians. Strangely, this limp, light, low-acid variety was decidedly foxy. 'Gorgeous!' exclaimed the red-nosed Frenchman. 'A bouquet of framboise, do you get it?'

Stéphane put a few bottles of bubbly under his arm and we hurried back to La Calèche to tackle a buffet of regional specialities prepared by Eddy's elegant, silvery-haired mother, Elisoa Ravololomboahangy Marzel. It featured duck, pork, baby freshwater shrimps, *ravitoto* (stewed cassava leaves), vegetables too local to identify. We tasted a fine rendition of the national dish *romazava* (beef, ginger, leafy greens); just about every part of the Zebu other, thankfully, than the one we'd sampled the night before; little concoctions designed to cut high-fat dishes like *rougaille* salad, tomato, spring and red onion and chilli. We went back for more *varenga*, thread-thin, deep-fried beef, piled up like a delicate bird's nest.

Vary (rice) was not the supporting role here, or anywhere in Mad: it's always the main act. Rice is the national metaphor – half an hour is spoken of as 'the time it takes for rice to cook', seasons are described according to how high or what colour the rice is in the paddy fields. Two musicians played traditional kabosy guitars and sang softly. We took a few token sips of the locally recommended liquid partner for such feasting, *ranon'a-pango*. This is a doddle to prepare: scorch rice at the bottom of a pan, add boiling water, strain, serve warm.

Gratefully, we returned to Stéphane's wine; it continued to sparkle.

On road, off road

It's 240 kilometres from Antsirabe to Fianarantsoa, the centre of Mad's wine-growing region and the road is, typically, a challenge. We were nominally on the central 'plateau', but there was nothing flat about these highlands or the RN7. We wound up, down and around remnants of extinct volcanoes, granite outcrops surely related to Zimbabwe's Matobos, terraced rice paddies out of Chinese paintings, eucalyptus forests imported from Australia, Alpine waterfalls, Scottish moors (uncannily like Ethiopia, too). Little girls sold wooden chopping boards and Cape gooseberries along the roadside. Planted around terracotta churches with bell-towers were hedges of Mexican poinsettias.

The prevailing green of these highlands is dramatically gashed with the red, raw, bleeding-earth gullies called *lavka* – a result of the traditional practice of *tavy*, the annual slashing and burning of vast areas to re-grass pastures and open up more agricultural land. This is much frowned upon by the fleece-lined First World but understood by practical environmentalists: where there is extreme poverty, people will live off the land until viable, culturally acceptable alternatives emerge. However wounded, it's still beautiful.

The traffic was another matter. Zebu carts and wooden sledges slowed our pace to a century ago. Minibus *taxi-brousses* and station-wagon *taxi-bes* (literally big taxis) revved it up to the present. These were crammed too full for the doors to be closed. Their roof-racks were piled with giant baskets of rice, bundles of tethered ducks, crates of THB, rolls of plaited raffia. It looked as though anything, maybe even the passengers on the extremities, might shear off any moment. Swaying like full gospel choirs, these buses loomed round almost every corner of the narrow road.

Equally fearsome were the Toyotas or Hyundais flashing new 'garage' plates as they hurtled past. These signify that the vehicles belong to a 'deputy', an elected official. Deputies could drive their cars into the ground and us off the road at manic speeds, because such vehicles need to last only four years, until the next election. Then, we were told, instead of repairing the roads, the government gives the deputies new 4x4s.

Retiring shaken to the verge, we had lunch overlooking the rose-brick town of Ambositra ('ambush' it's roughly pronounced) where anything can be wood-carved. A balcony? A brilliant collapsible chair? A set of espresso cups? A mustard pot in the form of the lemur or the dead elephant bird – reputedly Sinbad's Roc, weighing in at 450 kilos, now a skeleton in the museum at Tana's Botanical Gardens? We considered our choices while – rather apprehensively – unpacking the picnic Eddy had rustled up for us.

Birdman Ian Sinclair, with whom we made our first foray to Mad, is Africa's most prolific author on anything with wings, and a veteran of thousands of take-away meals in jungles and swamps. He maintained (we could confirm) he'd never had a good packed lunch on an African expedition. But here was a masterpiece of the genre: rosy *magret de canard*, airy baguette, cerise radishes, ripe scarlet tree tomatoes, a fine bit of local Camembert.

DU RAISIN AU VIN
PAR L'AMOUR
DES PAYSANS DU BETSILEO

Our dinner that evening at the Tsara Guest House in the *haute ville* quarter of Fiana was a pleasure too. Once a basic hikers' lodge, this is now a stylish small hotel. Fat candles flickered in the twilight on the terrace; bundles of designer twigs and topiary trees in overscaled red clay pots were arranged in a V-formation like flying ducks, very Wallpaper. We overlooked terracotta church spires, red brick universities (Fianarantsoa means 'place of good learning'), cobbled streets, green paddy fields and red mountains. The manager was as sleek as a seal, and the chicken proved unrelated to the usual jaw-achingly chewy Mad specimen. There was espresso to finish.

We must do this more often, said a small boy who could barely see over the next table, and we agreed. But first, to pay for the day's gourmet experiences, we'd done some penance, at the (Chinese) Hotel Soafia and the (Trappist) Monastery of Maromby.

No free lunch

The historical role of missionaries in Africa generally gets scathing reviews, and the example they set in the vineyards makes a bad press worse. In Madagascar, Catholic priests were the fathers of the wine industry more than a century ago. They planted any old grapes, and glorified the result with the name of wine. At Monastera Masina Maria, 7 kilometres outside Fiana, they were also selling over the counter.

Father Badouin Mateva was manning the take-away bar: tapping wine out of a big blue plastic vacuum dispenser into the locals' bottles. Not all went home to drink their purchases. Turn-around and refill time for one happy customer while we were there was four minutes. The monks were clearly permitted to break their usual silence to provide the usual sales patter. Fr Badouin silenced us, in fact, when he broke into Flemish, fairly similar to Afrikaans, after asking where we were from. A Belgian, he'd been here for 43 years. He doled out tasting samples of Clos de Maromby.

The white was very dry, foxy-smelling, rather empty. The red, a half degree more alcohol at 12%, was similar. A pineapple liqueur, at less than US$1/£0.70, was the stand-out: spicy bouquet, limey finish.

Could we visit the *cave*, we asked? Maromby hardly hides its wine production; even its front gates make a branding statement. They are decorated with two large, wrought-iron bunches of grapes, artfully fashioned into the shape of Zebu heads. But when consulted, the chief monk, in a pink polo shirt, was firm. No, he ruled. The *cave* is in a restricted area.

The vines – the usual hybrids – were outside the 3-metre walls, topped with jagged broken glass, which enclosed (whence Clos) the monastery. High wooden lookout towers are occupied during the ripening season by monks with drums and whistles. God alone seems no deterrent to birds and thieves.

Back in town there was no water in the bathroom at the bizarre architectural folly that is the Hotel Soafia: China meets Gaudi on the *Titanic*. It teems with pagoda roofs, porthole windows with bamboo-etched panes, walls that veer arbitrarily into snakey curves or wild zig-zags. There's a swimming pool shaped like a soya bean, a garden bristling with more pagodas and Chinese lanterns, a disco, the whole catastrophe. The health club offers Gym Tonic – with a slice of lemon, we presumed.

It's so ghastly it's almost endearing.

Lemurs and le patron

So far we'd not found any wines which were going to give the great vineyards of the world much competition. But on the other hand, which offer lemurs more or less by the glass?

There are hundreds of small vinegrowers in the Mad highlands, and we happened on one of the most impressive by complete chance the next morning, en route from Fiana into Ranomafana National Park. To see – if we were lucky – the golden bamboo lemur, quite recently discovered here; also the broad-nosed gentle lemur – if very lucky – the rarest of all; and maybe some hot birds. (Ground rollers were the ones we were after, this reserve has them by the bucket.)

On the map it looked a small, quick, easy side-trip. Our guidebook described the road as 'good'. Perhaps it once was. It took us two hours to negotiate 30 kilometres of awesome potholes. We passed huge lorries in extremis – this outrageous relic of a route was the main commercial link to the east coast. They were rocking and rolling from one mud-bank into another. Some – we saw carcases – had slid over the brink.

The rainforested hills and ravines of the 41,600-hectare park were, however, fabulous. So was the most common chameleon – there are 55 species on Mad – a hectic mobile of turquoise, green and black, with orange spots. At the Domaine Nature lodge amid bananas, wild ginger and hibiscus on the edge of a cascade, a waitress called Tina served us chicken as tough as coir matting and extremely finicky freshwater crayfish. She reminded Vy, our translator, of something important.

Tina Turner comes from Madagascar, he said. Or her family did. Honestly.

So should we have been surprised that the guided forest walks ended with a stage show? Adorable rufous mouse lemurs, and a small cat called a *fosa*, the biggest carnivore on the island, were lured out of the forest. The guides squashed banana onto branches at camera height for the little lemurs; they sliced raw meat and threw it down for the *fosa*. The stars appeared and the cabaret began, in a clearing signposted Le Rendezvous de Nocturne.

Had we encountered more on our hike to this spot than a legful of leeches so blood-thirsty that they'd wriggled right through our shoes and socks, perhaps we'd have taken a less jaundiced view. But if we'd not ventured to Ranomafana, we'd never have seen the vineyard slope, swirled in morning mist, which led us to Jean-Louis Randrianahazo.

Previous pages
Top: *Mad bread is brilliant; Father Badouin gives John the Clos de Maromby wine-spiel; Mad grapes are the 'passion of peasants'; pharmacist Desi Mac, co-owner of Clos Malaza.*
Middle: *Stephane Chan and his hybrids; in Mad's enchanted spiny forest; a typical Highlands farm; village bar; Lazan'i Betsileo winery.*
Bottom: *Roadside wine stall outside Fiana; threshing the rice; national utility vehicle, the zebu-cart; octopus-trees in the spiny forest.*

Stop! we shouted. We piled out and headed for a high, narrow house, with children and grannies hanging out of every window. Madagascar very *profonde*. To the bewilderment of the men working in the vines we wanted to take photographs. Fine – the playback facility on our digital camera was a hit everywhere. But, they said, *le patron* lives over the hill. Would we like to meet him?

Bananas fall straight onto your plate at Domaine Nature lodge in Ranomafana National Park.

Off–road we drove, into the high grass and bush. The cattle track petered out between patches of cassava and we proceeded on foot to a bunch of ochre and rust houses (a bit like a Provençal *village perché*) set in pocket-gardens bright with marigolds and rambling roses. They clustered around a deep pit steaming with manure and hump-backed Zebus, securely barricaded against local gangs of rustlers.

A small crowd of children pushed us through a door, into a ground-floor room full of chickens and bags of rice. Brick outside, these houses are all-wood inside – even the (chimneyless) kitchens at the top, where the cooking fire is made on the floor. Beckoning us upstairs into the salon was village squire Jean-Louis. He motioned us graciously to the red Dralon three-piece suite. His wife – one of a bevy of Madagascan beauties who followed us up the stairs and craned through the door – bustled in and puffed up the cushions.

With his trim moustache, rice-straw hat and blue and white checked lamba, the local wraparound that serves as shawl, loin cloth, picnic blanket, whatever, Jean-Louis could have stepped off the Lazan'i Betsileo labels on an array of cobwebbed wines on his mantelpiece. (Except for his blue denim baggies and slops.) His wife swooped in again, and dusted the bottles off.

Lazan means pride in Malagasy and proud he was – of the co-op named after these highland people and their dialect. He grew grapes for the co-op, and had worked there for 20 years. He'd been a foreman in the winery, and still 'consulted' there part-time. Though a busy man, he said, he could spare just enough time to show us his domaine. Superstition or fady is a core influence on Madagascans and no one appeared to think that our arrival on Jean-Louis' doorstep was remarkable, or even a coincidence; it had been meant to happen.

We told him we were writing this book, someone had even talked of a TV programme. 'Oh, that's good,' he said, pointing to a TV set which we hadn't noticed in the corner (nor any signs of electricity). 'I'll be able to watch myself.' He grinned, revealing more gold filling than front teeth.

Did he make wine for his personal consumption, we asked, hoping for a sample? At 9 am, it was quite early to start tasting, but this was work not play. However, this was also an overly nosey question after such a brief acquaintance. In any case, there was the delicate matter of '*le bras long*', the long arm of officialdom. No one gives away secrets about the possible existence of taxable substances.

'No,' he said. 'I make no wine for myself. No wine at all.' But, he assured us, he had nothing against drink. So what was his tipple? 'Coca-Cola.'

Soon we and most of the village were marching out to his terraced vineyard, 20 minutes away, on a steep slope leading down to a stream. The vines were immaculate, weedless, trellised and interplanted with pineapples. He stopped to demonstrate how he'd be pruning for next year's bearers and shoots. Many of the poles were bent, and planted irregularly – the vineyard curved artistically around the hillside. But the scene reflected tender loving care and disciplined industry; Jean-Louis was understandably proud. Fruit trees fringed the vines, there was a luscious green vegetable and banana patch lower down, a rice paddy and small sugarcane field. Add the cattle and the chickens back home, and here was a working model of the sort of self-sufficiency we saw all over the highlands.

Going to and from his vineyard, Jean-Louis passed his family's mass tomb. A daily reminder of the importance of the ancestors in Madagascan life. Hundreds of forebears were buried there, wrapped in *lambas* and, yes, his family still disinterred ancestors on certain anniversaries, displayed the bones during long parties, rewrapped and returned them to the tomb. (They get cold, Vy explained, and need new *lambas*.) No one could be excluded from these *famadihana* parties, Jean-Louis said. 'But it's very expensive…so we can't do it often, maybe after seven or eight years.'

LAZAN'I BETSILEO

VIN ROSÉ

DU RAISIN AU VIN PAR L'AMOUR DES PAYSANS DU BETSILEO ÉLEVÉ ET MIS EN BOUTEILLE PAR L.B. S.A. à FIANARANTSOA

Was he the model for the Lazan'i Betsileo label? Our new-found friend Jean-Louis in his lamba and vineyard.

And did wine – *divay* is the local word – accompany these festivities? Not at all. But by now we weren't tax inspectors, so he allowed that it was sugarcane spirit – rum – that propelled the parties.

He took us through his vineyard calendar, which, as usual here in the tropical cyclone belt, meant picking in the rain. How did he determine sugar and ripeness? He eyed us beadily. Were we by any chance suggesting that he was a bit too rural to know what he was doing?

'I do not require a saccharometer,' he said. 'I know when to pick because I am an expert in wine. I judge the ripeness by the taste.'

Yes, he did adjust the acidity of his soils, with bought in 'dolomite' (calcium), and enriched it with Zebu manure. Yes, unfortunately, the grape varieties were not classic, but what could he do? Couderc and Petit Alicante were the available vines to people like himself.

He waved us off with a big grin and a last word: 'I am ready to star in your movie.'

The cold shoulder

It was a Swiss-run co-operative established in 1971, with backing from the Madagascan government, that began to cover the hillsides around Fiana in patches of vines. The idea was to diversify – to reduce the dependence on rice and launch an import substitution industry. With typical resourcefulness, local farmers took to the new project. Four grape collection depots within a 50-kilometre radius of Fiana fed into the central Lazan'i Betsileo co-op; its wine became the dominant label of the island.

Inexplicably to us the Swiss had stuck with the same dodgy old hybrid suspects that guaranteed local produce could never compare or compete with imports for quality. When the Swiss were seen off in 1984 by doctrinaire state control of almost everything, 625 small growers remained. Their vineyards average about a hectare each (after some head scratching, Jean-Louis owned up to 2 hectares).

Now privatised and wholly locally owned, the co-op is Madagascar's biggest single producer, making 2.5 million litres of wine a year, about half of it bottled (100,000 cases), the rest disposed of in bulk, much of it as distilled *marc* (brandy). The winery, stretched along a hilltop, rather Italian with its terracotta tiled roof, basked in morning sun. Turkeys gobbled in the yard, in front of a large, wobbly mural featuring happy peasants, bunches of grapes and a slogan testifying to the Betsileo people's love of the vine.

But the *maître de chai* was not available. Madame Joséphine, the co-op's PR, was *désolée* but no appointment had been made through the head office in Fiana town. A fine but obviously important point which seemed to override the visit made to the co-op by our London travel agent to pre-announce us! We said we too were desolated, but in the circumstances, seeing we had come from so far, would the *maître* not consent to see us for just a few minutes? We would wait until he was free. She darted off again, but returned almost immediately: He says he is too busy.

So Madame Joséphine took us on a short walkabout round the rambling winery. As a fashion statement, it would have been grunge. She answered our questions as best she could. When we got to technicalities, she darted off to the *maître's* office.

A sample of two wines was thrown into the $5 cost of this tour. We had already tried some of these labels and found them resistible, but perhaps they hadn't travelled well? She poured a 'Pride' of Betsileo Vin Blanc and Vin Rouge, in the tasting room overlooking vineyards and granite hills. The maître's office was now only three paces away, via an open veranda; Madame Joséphine could lean out and relay questions; a disembodied murmur delivered the answers.

The white was not fit for that tasting euphemism 'clean' (plain, inoffensive). It was more vegetable than fruit, more animal than herbaceous, beyond the cusp of decadence. Perhaps it had been open a while? The red had a watery orange edge, and its nose jerked ours out of our glasses. A rapid gulp confirmed both volatility and sickliness. We resorted to the saving grace of formal tastings and spat vigorously.

There's always tension between growers and the winery in co-ops, but here the husbandry of a grower like Jean-Louis clearly had been dishonoured. The tropical climate is difficult, the varieties antediluvian, other growers might take less care. But in an age of modern – basic – cellar technology and hygiene there seemed little excuse for quite such sad quality.

We hoped for better things down the road.

Big Mac

Which is the best wine in Madagascar? We kept asking, the locals kept answering, and we kept trying Clos Malaza. It didn't grab us by the throat, but yes, perhaps they were right: Stéphane Chan's agreeable sparkling wine excepted, this range did so far seem 'best'. Clos Malaza's vineyards were just 16 kilometres away, over the hill from Lazan'i Betsileo. We'd be there in no time.

Nearly an hour and a half later we were still in the back of beyond. In the absence of any signs, we'd consulted various drivers of Zebu carts, and after attempting one track which dead-ended on a riverbank, were (we hoped) on the right road. It was extremely photogenic: giant granite boulders, rolling green hills, wild flowers, rice paddies. It travelled abominably. Couldn't make up its mind: was it gravel, was it stone, was it sand? Should it sink into a sudden crater here or a muddy gully there? How narrow could it go? And so on.

We squeezed past a *taxi-brousse* that looked like some Guinness Book of Records attempt. It contained 26 people (that we could see) plus their baggage; no wonder it had given up while trying to climb a hill. Instead of the usual holding pattern in such emergencies – stones behind the wheels – the 'conductor' put neat wooden chocks in place. Clearly this had happened before.

Monday-best hats and lambas for market-day in Dambouimalaza.

The road became more corrugated and thick with pedestrians. The hills were alive with the sound of Zebus, chickens, ducks, turkeys. Everyone was in Monday best, streaming into the little village of Dambouimalaza for the big market day of the month. The older ones wore traditional straw hats and draped their *lambas* round their shoulders like capes. The young set wore their *lambas* like bandanas. There was much meeting, greeting, trading, socialising, flirting.

We threaded through this throbbing throng and the equally congested Zebu market on the outskirts of the village, spirits lifting when we saw the houses were fringed with vines. At last, in the lee of a small but rugged range of mountains, some serious vineyards appeared. We later learned they spread over 30 hectares of the 400-hectare property; there were also rice fields, essential oil-producing geraniums, 100 hectares of forest and two large lakes.

Excitedly, we drove past a couple of religious statues and into the courtyard of the Clos, formerly a Jesuit monastery. A lovely old building, festooned with creepers and carved balconies, round a central cloister. This, we could almost taste it, was going to be good. While we were busy the driver could change the wheel. Hardly surprisingly, we'd picked up a puncture.

We bounced beamingly into the reception area and introduced ourselves and our purpose to a man behind a desk and his colleague, a woman in a white coat, promisingly suggestive of proper laboratories and that sort of refinement. But no. They couldn't help. Only Mr Desi Mac was authorised to take people on a tour of the place, and he was at his pharmacy back in Fiana. (Desiré Mac Gui Chan and his brother – the label says Mac & Frère – started off at Clos Malaza in partnership with a Swiss investor, then bought him out.)

'Do you have a signed authority? Only yesterday, visitors from Africa came with the right form. Otherwise, it is forbidden.'

Fine, we said, might we phone him? No, we couldn't. Telephone lines had not yet made it to Clos Malaza. Cell-phones didn't work because of the intervening mountains. There was no electricity either, the whole outfit ran on its own generators.

'You must go back and get his permission. Then you may return here. I am just a salaried employee.'

There was no other road to go. We got back into the car. How silly to imagine that Madagascan wine producers would welcome visitors.... And we couldn't return; we had a firm (we hoped) appointment in the next wine region of Ambalavao later that afternoon.

The race was now on to get back to town before noon when the shops closed. (It's *déjeuner* between 12 and 2 all over the island.) At 11.59, after a hectic rerun of the Clos Malaza route, we rushed into Desi Mac's gleaming shop in the better part of Fiana and managed to gain an audience. Superb Chinese-dinner scents wafted through to his rather sleek office full of books, computers, a TV set (a soap opera flickered soundlessly), a substantial leather chair. His pharmacy degree from the University of Montpellier hung on the wall. We told him how devastated we had been not to see inside his winery.

Pity, he said. 'Because it is very *propre*. Not like Lazan'i Betsileo! I have put in stainless steel, tanks with adjustable fermenting caps, all the more modern, cleaner equipment, refrigeration. It is very inconvenient, this no phone, no electricity, almost no road. I have been speaking to the government about it for many years. But first, what can you do for me? We want to improve.'

He wanted us to recommend good varieties for the area. We discussed crow-scaring strategies – workers kept his birds at bay by running round cracking whips. He was anxious to find a new winemaker. He'd had bad experiences with two previous candidates: One was too young, the other drank. He'd had to take over!

He didn't drink wine himself, he said, just a sip or two, but his chemistry background had kicked in. There'd recently been a pharmacists' convention in Fiana, and at one of the parties, nothing but the Clos Malaza he'd made was served. His colleagues had pronounced it 'remarkable'.

The range featured Blanc Doux, Blanc Sec, Rosé, Gris and Rouge: Couderc for the whites, hybrids Petit Bouschet and Jacquez for the reds (Jacquez, with tiny, very dark red berries, is sometimes used simply as rootstock elsewhere, its wine banned in the EU). The gris, from Bouschet, we found marginally more attractive than the rosé, a blend of red and white: both were dry, clean and with less bottle variation than other labels. But nothing startling – yet. Though once we had met the very suave and smart Mr Mac, we decided to postpone judgement: bigger and better things must be on the horizon here.

Brothers breaking free

From Fiana to Ambalavao the route was blessedly easy, the only delay at a narrow bridge, where we waited 15 minutes for herd after herd of Zebu to cross. The passing show was a re-run of *Out of Africa* – wide grassland plains rolled up into green-blue mountains. Kenya's White Mischief set would have been at home. We rounded one of the escarpments and arranged below in an enormous bowl were millions of vines rimmed by more mountains, and the dozy town of Ambalavao. The name of the nearest range of peaks is Sleeping Lady.

Nothing happens here, said locals, but the winegrowers appeared more consumer-conscious than their colleagues further back. There were large signs advertising wines on the side of the road: Côte de Fianar, Château Verger, Domaine Manamisoa, Soavita. There were small stalls selling wine. For the first time we felt as if we really were on a wine route. Of course, it wasn't all plain sailing. We found the next winery on our schedule only because we had 4-wheel drive and binoculars.

Gazing down from a dauntingly eroded track on a steep hillside, we were convinced we were lost (again) until we spotted a lonely apparition, a three-storey pagoda-like mansion. It had to be the home of the ubiquitous Chan Foui family and we descended gingerly towards it. Chan Foui *père*, who'd started it all in the 1970s, was away on business that day, but two of his seven sons, Denis and Michel Chan Tzi Tong, crawled from under a vehicle they were fixing in the yard.

Their training in France was not in wine – Denis is an electrician, Michel a food technologist – but now they respectively handle these family vineyards and cellar and were thirsty for information:

– What is the price of a good second-hand tractor in South Africa – or a bulldozer?

– Where can we get more Merlot vines… or Chardonnay… or Shiraz?

– Is there a good epoxy lining you can recommend for our cement tanks?

– Do you have a good spray against cochineal?

The cochineal insect – it bores into grapes and vine leaves – was decimating yields. Next season, said the Chans, there was bound to be something else. Hail or something. Meantime, they were not only experimenting with noble varieties, they were trying different rootstocks too. Trailing clouds of dust we drove past dense, healthy hybrids to 2 hectares of experimental vines. An aspirational patch rooted in rich red-ochre Madagascan soil at the extremity of their 40-hectare spread of vineyards. The soil, they said, like the wine, needs acid adjustment. They shovel in half a tonne of lime per hectare.

The vines were babies, temperate-climate plants trying to find some seasonal rhythm in the tropics. They looked confused and rather sad: some budding, some trying to ripen, others losing their leaves, perhaps dying. But they certainly were Merlot, Chardonnay, Cabernet, even in their various deformities – and they would need the individual attention that thoroughbreds demand. This was the start of something serious. No quick buck to be had. Perhaps no buck at all.

Suddenly, it was easy to understand how earlier pioneers gave up and reverted to uncomplaining hardy hybrids. But the young Chans were themselves hardy transplants – they seemed up to the task: 'We will keep on trying. These noble varieties interest us.'

Above: The young Chan brothers, Denis and Michel, growing their experimental 'classic' vines by the book in Ambalavao.
Opposite Top: Sunset at Relais de la Reine in Isalo National Park; bottling-line at Ch. Verger; third-generation Madagascan Jean Verger
Middle: Chez Chan and the family winery at Ambalavao
Bottom: The smartest wine shop in Tana; welcome to the Fiana wine route; Frédéric Chaix: a new saviour of Mad wine?

Back at the farmhouse, we tasted in a large living-eating-playing-room. A couple of chairs and a sofa were scattered and battered about – any fancier furnishing was doubtless unwise, taking into account the small children with shiny black hair hurtling around on pushbikes. A TV blared loudly. Whiffs of soya sauce floated from the kitchen. On the walls here, as in the winery, was a selection of pin-up pictures. If the Chans were making money from their wine it wasn't on show.

A Côte de Fianar Vin Blanc was up first: mainly Couderc Blanc with a dash of Seyve-Villard and, in the circumstances, a good, drinkable result. The brothers maintain that the best quality grapes come from Ambalavao – lower yields than Fiana, though they're lumped together as a wine region. (Fiana or Fianar are colloquial names, Fianarantsoa officially.) Then came a Petit Bouschet – a respectable Madagascar red but spare and lean, as usual, on the palate. The Chans asked for our views – insisted. Perhaps, we suggested, they might

CÔTE de FIANAR

try a brief rev with oak chips in the tank? And a little residual sweetness, to plump out the wine? Neither idea was new to them, but would we send them more information?

Little wonder, with this kind of flexibility and enthusiasm, that the country's best red came from these young brothers – according to the pickiest French négociant in Tana. Stylishly wrapped in raffia, it was labelled Tsara Be (very good in Malagasy) Grand Vin de Madagascar, selected and reserved specially by La Cave à Vin de Tana. We were to meet Frédéric Chaix, of La Cave, later, and discover how remarkable this accolade was. Tsara Be was the only Madagascar wine he sold in his very upmarket shop.

We departed from the Chans as the sun set (pink, gold) behind Pic Boby, impressed by their brave and eager efforts to liberate themselves from their viticultural legacy.

When everything went upside down

'Maybe he was just trying to put off the opposition – he doesn't want anyone else to come here!' Jean Verger cackled with laughter. It was early the next morning, and we were in his living room on Domaine Manamisoa, also known as Soavita Estate and Château Verger, just outside Ambalavao. Battered but upbeat, this courtly old man was putting a cheerful spin on his son-in law Patrick Canone's comments on the trials of growing and making wine in Madagascar to *Océan Indien* magazine: that the whole enterprise was an endless struggle against the elements and the thousand practical problems of life in the bush….

French windows opened to the garden, birds sang, multi-coloured children splashed in the pool, vines marched around the house, there were mauve mountains on every horizon. And what the winery might have lacked in cutting-edge equipment it made up for in charm: roofed with bamboo and palm fronds, it was open-air conditioned; breezes ruffled through, and the morning sun filtered slatted shadows onto rows of large fibreglass tanks.

'Yes,' said M. Verger, 'even when everything went upside down' (he demonstrated expressively) 'we had this – no neighbours to disturb you, so quiet you can hear the birds, fresh air, nature….'

His grandparents had come to Madagascar from France and evidently prospered. Jean Verger himself became a successful *homme d'affaires* with interests in hotels, transport, rice, peanuts, and chose not to leave in 1960, when the island became independent.

'The French warned us we were on our own. But of course I was not going to move. I was not French! I was born here, I am the third generation of my family living here.'

The upside-down era arrived in 1972: 'Almost everything was nationalised!' and he decided not to battle the current. He sold all his businesses and went into partnership with a French expatriate who'd elected to take the Independence package offered to those who decided against repatriation – 100 hectares of land. On his particular parcel happened to be a small vineyard, established by Jesuit missionaries. It was obviously a venture crying out for expansion, development, Verger business savoir-faire.

There were now 25 hectares of vines, the business was wholly family-owned, and had been bottling for 15 years (previously, wine was made in bulk). They called their flagship wine Château Verger because the name was so 'bien connu from our business days you understand'.

Mindful of the necessity of confirming (and reconfirming) appointments here, we'd phoned the winery the evening before. But winemaker Patrick Canone flew in and out like a swift, too harassed to speak. Cellar technician Emile Rasolomandimby explained the basics, and the struggle to find empty bottles, which had to be recycled by cleaning laboriously by hand under the trees. He drew a few samples of Petit Bouschet, unpretentious, basic, light. The vineyards yield quite prolifically, in a good year – some 250,000 litres, or more than 10 tonnes/hectare.

But Emile couldn't give us the broader picture. About to retire defeated, we spotted Jean Verger in his car, en route to Fiana, and did the journalists' thing: feet through door, a stream of fast-talk, a determined effort to about-turn no comment into tell all. He agreed to stay his journey for a question or two.

We began on the whys and wherefores of the usual suspect varieties planted here. Well, said M. Verger, they grew. Unlike the Syrah they'd unsuccessfully tried. Did we have any noble varieties in South Africa? He was astonished when we reeled them off. 'No!' he exclaimed. 'Even Merlot?'

The gap between Madagascar and the African mainland is more than meets the eye.

Cool places, cool man

Having explored Ambalavao's valley of vines, we needed to get back to Tana: Africa's finest foie gras was waiting to be investigated, and whispers we'd heard about a new wine venture in a new wine area. We decided not to backtrack on the same road, but to head south to pick up a plane – and revisit our favourite part of the island.

We broke the journey at the Isalo National Park – more lemurs, more birds, and ravines, gorges and Jurassic-age sandstone ridges so wildly eroded they make a lunar landscape seem suburban. At the Relais de la Reine, sensitively sculpted into the landscape, expensively heeled hikers and riders came out onto the terraces and sat around their drinks expectantly just before sunset, like clubbers waiting for the cabaret. It was a hugely extravagant show, with the sun seeming to melt right into the rocks; they held their Campari and orange and purple colours for a good 15 minutes. Everyone clapped.

Very early the next morning we dropped into another world – huge empty grasslands, river beds steaming with mist, and then a mirage – surely? A conglomeration of brassy saloons and bars, restaurants and dubious hotels, hundreds of shacks and shops looming up in the middle of nowhere. It looked as unreal as a Wild West film-set – the archetypal mining boom-town. Sapphires were discovered here, barely hidden beneath the ground, in 1999; fortune-hunters, dealers and prospectors descended overnight from all over the world. When a car came rocketing dangerously towards us out of the mists, our driver muttered darkly: Nigerians. Police roadblocks suddenly appeared. Endless herds of Zebu, like the Serengeti migration, streamed along in the bush.

At last the sea slipped into view, but more road-trials were yet to come – the stretch between the steamy, gaudy port of Toliaro (with a hectic nightclub, the Zaza), and Le Paradisier. This was the perfect little scattering of huts on the dunes just above the highwater mark at Ifaty, where we were to overnight before catching the next Tana plane.

Sunset at Le Paradisier.

The road to Ifaty is not a road. Wasn't last time we passed this way either. It's 22 kilometres of corrugations, sand dunes, mangrove swamp, that sort of thing. It takes at the very least an hour and a half (if you are driven by a local who knows the detours of the day), and the barefoot patron of Le Paradisier, Daniel Burkhalter, used to send a light plane to fetch guests from the airport, all of a three-minute flight. But the (Russian) aircraft was no longer in operation, and a small dhow – a fishing armada of these clustered along the reef – wouldn't do. The tides and the Air Madagascar flights rarely coincide….

Daily essentials do, however, get to the hotel by sea – baskets of crabs and prawns, octopuses on a stick like a giant kebab, a fish so large it had to be carried by two little boys. Off the *pirogues* – here, canoes carved from mangrove trunks – up the beach between the palms and euphorbias – what a tradesmen's entrance! – came a constant stream of supplies which jumped almost instantly onto our plates on the high, wide-open veranda. The sea was exquisite – shades of turquoise and aqua washing into each other like a water colour, speckled with silver; the sunsets were by Delacroix.

Daniel, who is from Strasbourg, lamented his wine list and his struggles to build a cellar; even in a well on the property, the temperature went down only by a couple of degrees. He wistfully conjured up a little hotel in Alsace, Riquewihr it was, and a cool Gewürz and foie gras with my late wife….We understood. The swordfish carpaccio (dressed with tomato rather than lemon), the octopus salad with basil, deserved better wines than the locals on his list.

But quite matchless was Cool Man. That's more or less how you pronounce Kolomana, the name of the priceless old greybeard who took us birdwatching in the sur-real spiny forest inland of Le Paradisier. ('O' in Malagasy is always 'oo' unless it's the last syllable, which is regularly dropped: Isalo becomes 'Eeshall' and Ifaty 'Eefut'.)

He wore tractor-tyre sandals, immaculate black cargo shorts, and soon whipped off his many-pocketed khaki shirt, slinging an axe casually over his bare shoulder where, it seemed, the very sharp blade was in constant danger of drawing blood. We trudged through groves of baobabs hung with huge round pods like Christmas baubles covered in chestnut velvet; and through thickets of *didiera*, the octopus tree. This has giant wavy tentacles upholstered with vicious spikes. Another great big bristly bully of a plant, the *nato*, is a member of the rhododendron family. Though you couldn't be further away from a European shrubbery.

Cool Man studied the prints in the sand (*Ah! Le très grand serpent!*), then let out the most astonishing, raucous, cacophonic series of shrieks. Within seconds a dozen black and white birds descended on the trees around us in a furious clatter, cursing us coarsely for invading their territory. They were the endemic, rare and very strident Sickle-billed Vangas, a 'lifer' – first-time spotting – for us.

We were ecstatic, Cool Man was, well, cool. He foraged out a stinky fag-end, fitted it into an elegant black cigarette holder, and took a luxurious draw. It had taken four and a half hours of crawling and scrambling and fighting our way through the thorns; we were scratched, bleeding and pouring with sweat. But triumphant. Might we discover some equally fine wine rarities that night? We had the last of our booty to taste.

No. Our winning streak didn't hold. The bottle of Domaine Lovasoa 'Soaindrana' Vin Rouge we'd picked up just south of Fiana, was far from the exciting boutique wine we'd hoped it might be – on the evidence of the immaculate vineyards, the attractiveness of the roadside stall, and smiling staff. (Though they knew nothing about the wine except that it was red.) Clos Malaza Blanc Doux, with more than usual Madagascan substance at 12%, was better but: sulphur on the nose, some pleasant sweetness, abrupt finish.

And then onto a whopping, crushing 52% *marc* from Jean Verger at Ambalavao. Here was the kind of fieriness that banishes pain. A menacing dark brown, it smelled earthily grappa-like and took no prisoners. It induced instant philosophy. All kinds of intractable woes dissolved in the clarity of the Madagascar night sky.

Madame Josette, foie gras queen, some of her ducks, one of her delicious products.

Duck tale

Madame Josette Razafiarisoa is the foie gras queen of the island, the doll-sized dynamo behind Madagascar's most luxurious food label – Bongou – a play on the French for 'good taste'. We flew back to Tana from Toliaro for a tasting with this stylish, twinkling little entrepreneur, who didn't lose her composure in the slightest when her secretary locked us all in her office and couldn't find the key. She sailed on with her success story while we admired what had created it: ducks.

They were everywhere, wall-to-wall in the office, her house above the shop, her factory. They flew up and down the curtains, stood stiffly in rows in glass display cabinets (souvenirs of her world travels), were carved into lampstands and mantelpieces, fashioned into silver trophies, rested deliciously in any number of tins and vacuum packs. (A locksmith liberated us finally.)

At the height of the season in June, Madame's Société Bongou moves 700 ducks a week through its gleaming white-tiled premises. They arrive well-stuffed after 20 days on a special diet of maize, salt and (to ease it all down) oil, dispensed by the rural *gaveurs*. There are hundreds of small farmers in this duck-raising, force-feeding business, many trained by Madame Josette.

Widowed in 1982, when she was a secretary in a Mercedes dealership, she was galvanised by a client from the southwest of France. 'She asked why we did not make foie gras.' Madame Josette thought about it, and it made sense. 'Ducks, maize, these were things available *chez nous*.' She also discovered something new about herself.

J'avais le goût du risque. I had a taste for risk-taking.

Against the wishes of her family (all working with her now) she flew off to France to learn how. After stages around Toulouse, Brive, the Dordogne, Perigueux, she returned to apply everything she'd learned about French geese to Madagascan ducks, a Barbary cross. The business boomed, she won awards in Spain and Switzerland, and now 22,000 ducks produce 10 tonnes of foie gras here on the outskirts of Tana each year. (Approached extremely cautiously on the usual execrable road.)

She walked us through the – very slick – process. But spared no detail. We'd hoped to escape without a viewing of the corpses, but no, we were down for the complete tour – a sample came only at the end – in the company of five food technologists. It was all immaculate, and so were we, in white coats, shower-caps and shoes sterilised in a series of footbaths. If only the wineries we'd visited had been half as spotless. Madame should be made the Tzarina of Madagascar wine.

But, we asked afterwards, through mouthfuls of silky paté piled onto bits of toast, what about the suffering of the poor ducks? 'I do not like that,' she said. 'No. But there have been hard times in Madagascar. And I employ 50 people here, and at our boutiques in Tana and the airport. And we support all those hundreds of the small farmers. Animal Protection groups do not exist in Madagascar – for the moment.'

If anything cries out loudly for a fine wine partner, it's foie gras. Stéphane Chan's sparkling wine would have been the best Madagascan bet. But we were soon to discover, on Réunion island next door, a match made in the Indian Ocean. And at our next port of call in Tana, there was a glimmer of a local possibility on the horizon.

I'll show them

It was all very clear to Frédéric Chaix. Madagascar wine was an awful mistake, he told us in his chic boutique, *the* purveyor of fine French wines to Tana's high society and diplomatic corps. Outside is a dingy back street. Inside La Cave à Vins, wrought-iron racks display gleaming tiers of 500 (mainly Bordeaux) selections, many very grand indeed. Chaix, a qualified oenologist from Bordeaux, had been in Madagascar for eight years; it was now home. A fabulous place for his daughter to grow up; for the shooting, fishing, diving, great-outdoors things he liked to do. And here he was determined to make history. I shall explain, he said. But first a splash of lubrication. We sat around a barrel and he poured a Château Arnaud de Jacquemeau 95, a St-Emilion grand cru. The first deep whiffs after weeks of denial on the road jolted us back to the larger wine world. We were a captive audience. Prepared to believe that Mad wine's fiercest local critic might become its saviour.

Frédéric Chaix is establishing his own vineyards – nowhere near (much drier than) the island's traditional wine regions – at Itasy, about 200 kilometres west of the capital, on a high (1500-metre) plateau. They're mad, he said of the Fianarantsoa area. 'Wine is about two opposites: quality and quantity. You cannot do both at the same time. How can they grow those terrible vines? These hybrids… terrible, terrible. And they always chaptalise, they never get ripeness. In all this sunshine, can you believe? There's no passion, they're mad, *fou!*' The red wine we'd tasted at the young Chan brothers' winery outside Ambalavao was the only exception he'd made to his all-French wine rule, and we had the feeling that he might have preferred the attractive raffia sleeve to its contents. He took a deep, appreciative slug of the St-Emilion.

'I have spent years looking for a suitable place for vines… because I love Madagascar. I want to re-create my culture. French culture is unique. None of my customers here buys local wines. They are not noble; 10%–11% alcohols are miserable wines, not true wines. Perhaps I will not make a great wine, but I will make a sound, round, fuller wine, of irreproachable quality.'

Though his new vineyards are well into the tropics, with high summer rainfalls, even cyclones, he believed the cool highland air and drying winds would compensate. He certainly had the highest winemaking qualifications in the country. And self-belief. And French partners with 'connections to Château Cheval Blanc'. St-Emilion varieties plus Petit Verdot, would form the new joint venture vineyards on a 25-hectare lake-side property ('we will later build a tourist lodge'). The first 8 hectares of vines had already been planted. When we applauded his pioneering spirit, he roared with laughter. 'I am not a pioneer, just an egotist.'

REUNION

High-altitude wine-growing in Cilaos.

Réunion is not African. This rugged little blob anchored in the Indian Ocean between two member states of the African Union, the new name for the old OAU – Madagascar (700 kilometres away) and Mauritius (a mere 200 kilometres) – remains a province of France. With a phone system engineered to make Paris a local call, and a third generation now living off the French dole. 'The only European region south of the Equator! A secure and stable environment!' is how the island solicits investment.

Ask the Réunionnais – which we did, often – if they feel they are African, like the countries next door, and they look astounded. *Pfouff*! they retort, signifying both irritation (how can you ask such a silly question?), and disdain (us? Africans? please!). But were we going to let the idiosyncrasies of French national policy, not to mention the depths and shallows of its foreign affairs, determine our route? Were we to bypass the very sort of countryside (Réunion's vineyards are not for the vertigo-challenged) which had suggested our bumper sticker for this trip: A Year (or two) of Drinking Dangerously?

We were not. Réunion's footballers had shown us the way: they annually do battle in the all-Africa championships. Firmly inking Réunion onto our map, where we wanted it to belong – what could be more ludicrous, we asked ourselves, than its official designation as a wine appellation of France? – we flew onto the island and officially out of Africa. Instant impressions seemed to confirm that we had, indeed, landed in France.

The airport's name – Roland Garros International – transported us to Paris and the red clay battlegrounds of the French Open. (M. Garros, a famous aviator, was born in the capital of Réunion, St-Denis.) Phalanxes of Air France jumbos were connected via see-through passenger tubes to a prime example of terminal chic – tinted glass, brutal steel, soaring wood pillars suggestive of monumental palm trees. Passport control and customs were negotiated in minutes. At the airport bar, people were sipping wine – locally grown but sporting a sticker that said: Vin de Table de France. Some had clearly ordered the *Formule les Hauts*, which proposed a glass of sweet white with a *gâteau réunion du jour*. Even the *toilettes* smelled of coffee and croissants.

Outside, trim little white cars – Citroëns, Peugeots, Renaults – zipped along impeccably surfaced highways. No need for the expensive 4x4s imperative in much of Africa, where murderous roads keep the poor marginalised and only the elite mobile. Just before midday, just before Boucan Canot, reputedly Réunion's finest beach, we slowed to a chug. Streaming onto the highway, keeping the lunch hour sacred *à la France*, came car after car, all hurrying towards *déjeuner*.

The beach was overpacked, skimpy, the sand a collection of coarsely crushed shells rather than the drift of pale caster sugar we African beach connoisseurs know. It was adorned with some fantastic bodies, and others carrying the most fascinating swags and ruches of surplus flesh. Nearly all of them were topless.

But this isn't the Côte d'Azur. It has a different bouquet. Vanilla, wild ginger and curry. The beach picnics, unpacked from raffia baskets lined with palm fronds, are much spicier. Baguettes stuffed with *carris* – curries of anything from prawns to baby jackfruits; or *cabri masalé* – kid casseroled with Indian masala. Small *samousas* costing a couple of francs from push carts and smart pâtisseries. This isn't Métro either. Métro is the sign outside a restaurant which means its cuisine is French rather than Indian, Chinese or Réunion's distinctively Creole mix of the lot.

Reunion's beaches are less challenging than its vineyards.

The houses underline this island-style. From the overwhelmingly white-painted roofs – wooden shingles, corrugated iron, grand mansions, sub-economic apartments, all looking cool and freshly washed – to the colours of the walls. There are ketchup reds, egg-yolk yellows and every shade of pale and frothy milkshake. The wrought-iron balconies, the trimmings on gutters and verandas are as whimsical as the paper cutouts children make at nursery school.

Very pretty, very doll's house… in fact – we summed up, after just half a day – rather a toy-island sort of place. Early the next morning, we realised our mistake. This speck in the ocean is more impressively endowed than most full-scale countries. Its narrow frill of black and white beaches is the least of its attractions. It was the interior that grabbed us and shook us.

A formidably moustachioed helicopter pilot lifted us away from the coast over slopes of sugarcane and pink pelargoniums – Réunion is the world's leading supplier of geranium oil. We floated gently up to an innocuous green crest of hills, and then, without the slightest warning, tipped right over the edge. We had just climbed over the rim of one of the three great *cirques*, volcanic amphitheatres, on the island.

The ground plunged into a perpendicular abyss, 1000 metres or more. We dropped sickeningly down the side of the crater, skimming the tops of giant bamboos and colossal tree ferns. Almost at rock-bottom, we flattened out and headed along a river gorge. It was so dark and narrow we might have been flying through a tunnel. Long streamers of waterfalls rushed past the windows. The river dead-ended in a circle of towering dark cliffs over which poured more cascades.

Our pilot corkscrewed the helicopter slowly up through the spray, millimetres from the rockface and the water; we spiralled agonisingly out of the canyon and popped into the light. We were so terrified we were practically whimpering. Closing our eyes for a brief recovery period, we had to look down again when we caught a new note of enthusiasm in our pilot's commentary. He was extolling a local delicacy.

Réunionnais are as dedicated to their stomachs as any other Frenchmen. News of President Jacques Chirac's impending visit to the island was splashed over three pages of the local paper that morning. No mention of the chronic unemployment rate (higher than the Métro), crippling labour costs (French salary scales apply) and such matters. This report focused on more serious stuff. Where and what would the President eat? What and where had he eaten the last time he visited? There were menus, there were interviews with chefs, there were recipes. We learned that M. Chirac was keen on local *lentilles*. And so was our pilot.

We must be overflying Cilaos, known both for wine and the lentils which cognoscenti rate (almost) on a par with those from Puy in Métro France. A ring of mountains enclosed the remains of a volcano which collapsed into itself two and a half million years ago, leaving a shark-toothed mess of more peaks, sheer cliffs, forested chasms, a bit of a plateau on which the town huddled precariously, and some perilous little tongues of cultivated land – *îlets*. Réunion wine country was teetering on many precipices.

The grandmother of all wine routes

Piton de la Fournaise, the Peak of the Furnace, is the only active volcano on the island, and its pockmarked, porridgy swellings were all too visible from the air. They seemed to be heaving, though that might have been air turbulence. But the fumeroles – the wispy vapour trails which spiralled up toward us – were not. When this furnace is stoked – a couple of times each year – it lights up the night sky. Next door in the Cirque de Cilaos bits of vineyard have been known – and seen – to crumble away and vanish with rumbling echoes into the crevasses below. Just like that.

Winefarming here is clearly a risky business. Wine-drinking could be pretty hazardous, too, according to many locals. The new-generation wines were fine, but, they cautioned, we must strenuously avoid the 'traditional' home-brew sold at farm stalls: Don't touch it. It can make you go crazy. What they didn't mention was that we might be driven crazy just getting there: this is not a wine route for the fainthearted.

'A few bends' we were told, as we set off on the one and only road, which dead-ends in Cilaos. The N5 it was marked on the map, and though not as straight and smooth as the island's other national highways, we weren't unduly alarmed. The stories we'd heard about the little roadside shrines – adorned with desiccated flowers and forlorn candles – marking the spots of fatal accidents seemed rather far-fetched as we drove through homely little stands of bananas on a flat valley floor. But the minute we began to climb, the sky began to shrink.

Perpendicular cliffs reared around us. More shrunken wreaths and sad Madonnas. The road narrowed alarmingly, the gorges deepened and darkened, the hairpins became tighter, the gradients steeper. Just a knee-high wall and a few inches separated us from eternity. These were our reactions:

John (*testing brakes, checking steering, adjusting mirrors, twitchy*): 'The team-spirit thing was in trouble. Erica was white, a petrified profile staring over the edge. She suffers from vertigo at the best of times. She shuts her eyes in office lifts, you cannot drag her to a cable car. Otherwise an athlete of note, she gave up skiing before she started. The helicopter flip had almost finished her.'

Erica (*noticing John's hands were sweating*): 'Oh no, oh no. The last time this happened was in the Moremi Game Reserve in Botswana, when we were surrounded by a breeding herd of elephants. We took more than five hours to get ourselves out of that one; it was terrifying. But this is worse.'

Erica to John: 'Why aren't you hooting before the corners? You've got to hoot hoot HOOT!'

John (*let's not make a loud scene even if it kills us*): 'It's rude. And anyway we don't want to shock the other cars. They'll hoot if they need to.'

Erica: '*Rude? Shock?* I'll tell you who'll get a shock! We will when they crash straight into us!'

John: 'I don't think we'll have much of a crash at this speed.'

Erica: 'Any crash, at any speed, even if we were standing *still*, would send us plunging into that abyss! I'm on the outside edge. I'd go first! And we're in active volcano country. The road could collapse any moment!'

The end is nigh

And so we crawled on. And soon it was further down than up. No turning back. We stopped counting after about 200 parallel bends, and stopped awarding the title of 'mother of all hairpins' too; there were great-grannies here. Eventually, we saw the tips of a range of mauve mountains and above them, clear blue skies. Through pine forests, past waterfalls, the higher we got the more uncannily Alpine it became. Well into the two-hour haul we managed to find one 'viewsite' unoccupied and pulled in to pop our ears.

This was a holiday long weekend, and the roadsides had been colonised by cooking, eating, drinking, *pétanque*-playing parties. *Le pique-nique* is an art-form in Réunion, and this was splendour in the grass, or wherever: lacy cloths, proper plates and glasses, elaborate menus. Yes, confirmed our local friends: anything from rabbit curry to *rougail saucisses* (local saucisson in a spicy tomato and chilli reduction), and duck with vanilla. Accompanied by lentils, beans and *achards de légumes*, mixed-vegetable pickles.

Lubrication might be *dodo* – the Creole name for the local Bourbon beer – and *ti sec* – a little glass or two of rum, white or *arrangé*, flavoured with anything from coconut to vanilla. (Réunion's rhum agricole is the equivalent of boutique wine, handmade, in small quantities, from fresh sugarcane juice rather than the industrial-commercial way, from molasses; connoisseurs say it's the best in the Indian Ocean.) Wine-drinkers would be on cheap rosé from the Languedoc. Not the wine we were en route to taste: the vineyards of Cilaos would have to expand drastically if there was ever to be a hope of catering for the mass *pique-nique* market.

On we pressed, more boldly and fatalistically now, confronting oncoming cars – and even a big bus emblazoned with the owners' names, Moutosammy et Fils – head-on, hooting merrily. Whichever had the shorter distance to reverse to marginally wider ground, politely backed off though there was one rather long face-off between two logging lorries at each end of a tunnel. Yes, tunnels too. Vehicle loads here had to be minutely calculated: tree trunks a tad broader, piled any higher, would not have made it.

Vin de Cilaos: a handwritten sign on a trestle table, under a couple of striped umbrellas, at last told us we were getting warm. There were jars of jam and honey, bags of lentils, bottles of dubious shapes, sizes and colours. It was the first of many roadside stalls punting the (evidently) dodgy traditional wines; the first to issue that invitation to *dégustation* which is a feature of every self-respecting French wine village. Well-matured women in unsuitable mini-skirts, rouged to the eyeballs, stepped into the road waving bottles rather unenticingly.

We needed a slug of something to calm the nerves, but perhaps not this badly. And the vines couldn't be far away. But our spirits sank when we saw the first few spindly specimens climbing feebly up tottering trellises in bedraggled gardens. Had we forced ourselves up this terrifying road (and we had to go down it again!) to discover vineyards as ragged as these?

There were some particularly demented hairpins still to negotiate between hamlets, and we felt deeply for the young woman in the Auto Ecole car who was inching her way round a real terror just before the N5 merged with the main street of Cilaos. On the other hand, if you passed the test here, you were probably qualified to fly.

French wine

Jean-Pierre Dijoux met us beside the warm blue swimming pool of Le Vieux Cep, the best hotel in town: owned by his family, founded by his wife, run by his daughter. A heated pool on a steamy tropical island was the least of the anomalies here. The architecture was Alpine chalet-style, featuring wooden porches carved with bunches of grapes and vine leaves. Looming overhead was a massive curved wall of mountains, forested right to their peaks. We were (officially, disconcertingly) in France, but Cilaos might have been in Switzerland, too. Or the Alto Adige.

Le Vieux Cep – fittingly for the power behind the Cilaos wine industry – which this square-jawed, chunky little man is – means 'the old vine stock' (though we were soon to conclude that Le Nouveau Cep might now be more appropriate). At the hotel's front gate was this ode to the area, attributed to the Bishop of Réunion:

'The old vine stock sings of the native terroir, where our eyes are illuminated by a huge sky, heart and soul with the stones and wood, while a friendly sun takes flight over the vertiginous blue of our mountains.'

At 9500 kilometres and several worlds away from the French Ministry of Agriculture in Paris, Cilaos had, in 1998, become a wine appellation of France, entitled to emblazon this on its labels. And the quality upgrade that satisfied Paris enough to admit this far-flung wine region into the official French fold was the handiwork – the lifetime's work – of Jean-Pierre Dijoux. This retired maths master was a New World wine pioneer.

He'd persuaded – was still persuading – his neighbours to abandon the traditional but indifferent vine hybrids that were common in Réunion in the (very) old days and still survive in pockets and back gardens. Late-ripening varieties like Isabella and Couderc, modish in parts of southern France way back in the 1800s, had been planted here in the hope they'd outlast the annual cyclone season. Wines from such vines are disqualified from claiming any official French wine appellation.

With a note of satisfaction in his voice, M. Dijoux announced: Couderc is now banned. At the roadside stalls in and around Cilaos, locals were still punting the old sweetened, fortified, hangover-guaranteed, kitchen-garage-garden shed stuff, at 17% or more alcohol, but they could no longer call it 'wine' on their labels.

We told M. Dijoux we had almost succumbed and had a few nips on the way up; we commented on the extreme challenges of the road. He affected not to understand why we were so stunned by this bizarre bit of wine country. 'It is an everyday drive for me, why not for you? It is perfectly safe. The volcano is dead. Almost.' Of course he understood only too perfectly. Monsieur was far from rural. And he could sniff a PR opportunity in his wine route.

'This road registers in your head doesn't it? You can't doze on this drive, can you? Up

LE CHAI DE
CILAOS

MOELLEUX
Vin de Table de France

C

ÎLE DE LA RÉUNION

n bouteille à Cilaos, par les vignerons du Chai de Ci

1

NOM PASSAGER/PASSENGER NAME
PLATTER/JOHN

DE/FROM
ANTANANARIVO
A/TO
UU 0664 X 26APR X
ST DENIS REUNION
UU 0120 X 04MAY X
MAURITIUS

CIE   VOL   CLASSE   DATE   HEURE DEP.
CARRIER FLIGHT   CLASS   DATE   DEP. TIME

EMBARQUEMENT / BOARDING   SIEGE / SEAT

PORTE/GATE   HEURE/TIME

NB/PCS PDS/WT   N.ENR./UNCKD N° SEQ   NB/PCS PDS/WT N.ENR./UNCKD
****
IDENTIFICATION BAGAGE / BAGGAGE ID NO

or down. Do you have roads like this where you come from? No, I think you do not. So, you will remember the wine of Cilaos.' Yes, we agreed, whatever the taste. Continuing along the PR track, he stressed the altitude. We were now 1200 metres above sea level, nowhere near the tropical humidity zones at the coast, much better for vines. In fact, he pointed out triumphantly, the vineyards in Cilaos pipped Switzerland's loftiest (1100 metres). 'Perhaps the highest vineyards in the world!' he claimed enthusiastically. We didn't have the heart to tell him that there were even more elevated plantings in the Nyanga mountains of Zimbabwe; nor about the extreme-altitude vineyards in Argentina and Bhutan.

Whatever the relative claims, however, Cilaos was exactly our sort of wild and untrampled wine territory.

Le Chai de Cilaos

But where was the cellar, we asked? It was marked on our map and we'd driven round and round but we'd spotted nothing winery-like. M. Dijoux piled us into his very *sportif*, bright yellow Peugeot two-door coupé and drove all of one block. There indeed was Le Chai de Cilaos, but we hadn't been looking for a modest old Creole house, pale blue and cream wood, and we hadn't spied the discreet extension in the back garden. Like everything in this spa village of 7000 people, it was neat, orderly, small-scale, and slow.

The main attractions in Cilaos are the warm sulphur baths at the foot of one of the lesser gorges – more hairpins, very slippery, more driving angst; we'd sooner have been carried down in a sedan chair, as happened in the old days. Up in the town and close by the *chai* are the church and town hall, with a siren rigged up prominently on a tower, four loudspeakers facing all directions. 'For the cyclones,' explained M. Dijoux. 'We have to chase everyone indoors when the storms come.'

In the reception-cum-tasting room, we watched a video of the Cilaos wine story, starring M. Dijoux himself, resplendent in a huge straw hat, supervising the harvest. Then we went through to the winery, commissioned in 1994, a petite model of stainless-steel hygiene and order. The good winefarmers of Cilaos had not only begun ditching the traditional grape varieties, they had clubbed together to hire an oenologist, young Bruno Rangé, Montpellier University-trained and fired up by the challenge.

There were all of 11 growers of the 'new' varieties (rather more holdouts of the old). Together they'd planted a total of 9 hectares, barely enough to pasture a couple of Swiss Brown cows. The vineyards were all small – *morceaux* or morsels they called them – squeezed between orchards, next to chicken runs, under washing lines. They translated into an annual production of between 24,000 bottles (in 2000) and 33,000 bottles (in 2001).

But what was most significant was that the grapes were Pinot Noir, Malbec and Chenin Blanc. Incomparably more serious than the neighbours. Bruno had made three wines from these – off-dry rosé and white, and a sweet white.

M. Dijoux admitted to a preference for sweet wines: 'I was brought up on them. I know. I know. We Réunionnais have a very sweet tooth: even our Coca-Cola is sweeter than normal. But of course I understand real quality is revealed in dry wine.' He had a small, satisfied, proud-parent sort of smile on his face.

Bruno collected tasting glasses from his lab and popped a few bottles. Now, should we sniff and spit, or swallow? Wines so rare and remote that even many locals didn't know them? Réunion's independent TV channel, Antenne, was doing its very first story on what was going in and out of the new *chai*, and we collided with its cameraman at the winery door. He was astonished that journalists from South Africa had almost beaten the Réunionnais to their own story, and insisted on interviewing and filming us. This made it even less advisable to spit. Anyway, we were staying the night.

The very first sniff of these 2001s ended any qualms. These were real, unmitigated wines. Definitely to be swallowed.

The unique (in our experience) 70 per cent Malbec–30 per cent Pinot Noir blend of the rosé was light, and both earthy and fruity. (When the vines are older than their present adolescent six years, Bruno will consider a fuller red from the Pinot.) The *moëlleux*, a fresh, light, sweet and tingly Chenin was delicious on the spot, and months later, back home, with Bongou foie gras from Madagascar. The off-dry Chenin showed a similar lively, fruity complexity too. All three were elegantly matched by a label featuring an etching of the mountains surrounding the 100 square-kilometre Cirque de Cilaos, including the island's loftiest peak, Piton des Neiges (3000 metres).

Bruno, gold earring, manicured black moustache and matching goatee, represents the new breed of French winemaker: less insouciant guesswork, more reliance on the logic of maths and chemistry; a man after M. Dijoux's heart, perhaps. The spotless order in the winery, its 15 sparkling stainless-steel tanks with adjustable lids (all small, 2000 litres or less because the roads and tunnels are too narrow for bigger equipment) revealed an obsession with order and planning.

Winemaking in a cyclone

Like everywhere else in this sub-tropical Indian Ocean region, the cyclone season from January to April inconveniently coincides with the harvest. But it's not quite like the old days, when unprepared pickers dropped their baskets and secateurs and scrambled for home: they now stop harvesting before the storms hit.

'They're manageable, the cyclones – they needn't destroy the vintage entirely,' said Bruno. 'We get two or three days' warning, and know a week or so before that there's a possibility. Sometimes we're lucky and they miss us.'

The cyclone of 2001 arrived on 6 January. 'We were able to speed up the harvest

Previous pages
Top: *When the surf's up here at St Leu, it's a hot-wave spot; wine-maker Bruno Rangé; island style; John gets into the vanilla.*
Middle: *On the edge of the crater; etched on label and skyline, the mountains of the Cirque de Cilaos; Mr Wine of Reunion, Jean-Pierre Dijoux; Chai de Cilaos.*
Bottom: *More Creole style; Beware of the Volcano!; vineyards in the clouds; more vines on the edge.*

of everything that was nearly ripe – up to two days before the first winds hit us – which gave us just enough time to have pressed and stored and inoculated the must with yeast. When the sirens blasted their last warnings, we switched off everything, tightened and latched things down, boarded up the windows and doors, ran home and did the same – and waited it out. In the winery, fermentation progressed. We left grape juice and came back to wine!' Many winemakers describe their cellar technique as 'minimum interference', but this has to be the one to beat.

The vineyards are a tangled mess afterwards; punctured berries begin to rot immediately. But in a gentler year, some grapes do survive, and can continue to ripen if the vineyard and trellising are re-ordered. There's sunshine between the storms. If there are no more bad cyclones, they harvest again. In 2000, when serial storms tore into the crop, they darted in and out, picking in waves.

It's far from ideal. A fundamental of classic quality is to pick on *the* day of 'optimal physiological ripeness'. Not before or after. But this is a luxury in Cilaos. However, wines that emerge from such rigours have an extra dimension and M. Dijoux knew it. He wasn't short of marketing angles, only short of wine. Even at Le Vieux Cep they had long run out of their annual allocation, and his daughter, Jackie Chamand, wasn't happy.

'Everyone wants to know why we don't have it,' she almost wailed. Her father, being also, as he said, *un homme d'affaires*, is unafraid of charging top prices, and the 2001 vintage was pitched at around Ff50 from the cellar-door, treble that in restaurants. 'This is very authentic and artisanal – it has to be expensive,' he said.

Bruno had given the wines what he called *rondeur*, plumpness, by leaving just enough grapey, fruity sweetness (off-dry at 12 grams per litre of measurable sugar) to cover the brusquer acidities without flattening the palate. He'd chaptalised to raise the alcohols – to about 12% – though no more so than colleagues in a bad year in France. And then, he said, it was a matter of plain, standard, hygienic husbandry in the winery.

Not quite. That *rondeur* is elusive even in wines from ideal climates. In less skilful hands, these could have been very clumsy efforts. But he continued to deflect compliments. It was a tribute to the vine's remarkable adaptability, he insisted.

Vineyards on the edge

Now, where were these famous vines? We'd spotted only a few rogue specimens in backyards. M. Dijoux volunteered to solve the mystery, and we clambered into his 'work vehicle', a battered white 4x4 Land Rover. 'We're now going to see some really BIG vineyards,' he said. 'Le Coteaux de Dijoux.' Wine was not grown in any other area on the island, he said only half-jokingly, 'because there are no Dijoux there'. You do have to be a special breed of person to want to grow vines, and succeed, in the tropics.

Back down the N5 we drove, and just after an extreme hairpin bend he braked suddenly. The turnoff to his patch of vines was at such an acute angle that he had to overshoot, reverse, turn, and come at it from the other side of the road. We bumped down between large sisal plants and there, on a little spit of land between ravines, were his precious vineyards. With barely 2 hectares he was still the biggest *propriétaire* in Cilaos.

The modern Réunion wine industry is very much a work in progress, and M. Dijoux had clearly been the driving force. Much of his patch was given over to experiment. 'But I'm beginning to lose my energy,' he said slightly dolefully, wandering slowly up rows of different vine varieties, tapping the marked poles as he went.

'These are all the failures… *Chardonnay, NON!; Sauvignon Blanc, kaput!; Gamay, désastre!; Cinsault, pfouff!; Gewürztraminer, rien!*'

On he strode. In all he'd tried some 50 varieties over the years. He was possessed, obviously. But he'd narrowed them down to three. Chenin was always a likely, forgiving grape. But Pinot Noir and what he called Cot – Malbec. Not the first varieties that sprang to mind. When it comes to site, Pinot is probably the fussiest vine in the world, much preferring lime-rich to volcanic soils.

A man of his complexity naturally could not be expected to stop at grapes. Fringing, and sometimes invading, the vineyards were Brazilian cherries, macadamia nuts, all kinds of peaches, chestnuts, table grapes, sweet potatoes, pens of forest boars, strutting pheasants and ornamental Mallard and Macao ducks. Plastic loungers underneath the chestnut trees, overlooking a couple of ravines, were for 'long summer picnics'.

He took a few steps more to the edge of his vines, beckoned us to follow and parted some reeds: Whoah! A sheer fall into a jagged black volcanic chasm. 'Ha! *La précipice*. No room for error!' He waved across the valley to a scree of loose rocks also plunging away into space. 'Not so long ago, that bit just fell away. It could happen again any time, you never know.' His pale blue eyes gleamed; he was (wasn't he?) teasing us.

A settling drink seemed called for. We came to a *cave* in the hillside. Yes, his own personal winery of the rough stuff – the fortified red Isabella, precisely what he'd urged everyone to give up! He drew some from a leaky old barrel, filled a plastic cup. It was jammy, heavy, coarse, biting, heady.

'Very sugary, eh? And 18% alcohol, maybe more. Not good enough for the *curé* at Sunday mass any more, he'd throw it out, he's for the sophisticated new wine. But okay if you're working in the vineyards. Or it's raining.' And, he might have added, in a cyclone or if the ground wobbles under you.

Some of his trellising here is only about a half metre high. 'To keep the vines close to the ground, to minimise storm and rain damage.' So much for those contemporary boasts about 'hand-picked grapes'. Here you get down on your knees! M.Dijoux' craggy faced creased; he hadn't thought of that possibility for his back-label, and he rather liked it.

We stayed at Le Vieux Cep that night, and ate duck *carri* and gratin of *songe de bois*, a big edible leaf that looks like an elephant's ear. M. Dijoux found some 2001 wine for us. The downhill run next morning seemed surprisingly easy.

Active and passive

We wanted to walk on the crater of Piton de la Fournaise which we could practically see from our balcony at Le Vieux Cep. But by road there were no short-cuts. We had to re-wind down to sea-level, drive along the coast, and then head inland again, on the only road which bisects the island.

We took the turning to the volcano twice. The first time because we didn't listen to those who gave us a mist-warning. We said: mists? Just after lunch? With the sky empty and blue? So off we set, taking the usual bends up into yet another landscape – craggy moors complete with heathers, ericas, yellow gorse bushes and Swiss Brown cows with tinkling bells – another, chillier example of one of the island's 200 different microclimates.

The mist came barrelling after us. We crawled sheepishly back – on yet another of the dead-end roads so characteristic of Réunion. Fine, we'd go to the Maison du Volcan instead, a dramatic building, all angles, stone and glass, with a faint touch of the I M Pei pyramid outside the Louvre about it. It's reputedly a drama inside, too: simulations of great blow-outs of the past, including the 2-week-long spectacle in 1998. It was closed. We took off for the real thing again next morning, very early.

Close to, the mouth of the volcano looked much bigger than we expected. It's not the sort of dinky little opening made by one of those things you put into a pie to let the steam escape. It's the whole enormous filling of the pie, sprawling and spilling over its crust. A dark charcoal colour, it's wrinkled and pocked with great open pustules, and boils with red-orange rims. Little puffs of steam were rising out of some of these, it was too easy to imagine in lurid colour and heaving motion what was going on below – a boiling, roiling, cauldron of pressure building up to explode under our feet. The furies at their most elemental. But it all seemed so unlikely.

We and many other little white cars had parked amid the volcanic rocks in orderly rows. Young fathers hoisted babies into backpacks to stroll them across the dried lava. There were a lot of women with that impossible shade of orange-maroon hair you find only in France. It was all so safe. And anyway, this is the world's most god-fearing, compassionate volcano. During its last major blow-out in 1998, the boiling lava stopped millimetres from a shrine. In 1977 it forked considerably at the door of a church in which local villagers had taken refuge.

The last touch of cosiness was the Beware of the Volcano road sign – red flames spurting decoratively out of what looked like a ship's decanter....

Vanilla nose

With Natty Dread, Réunion's reggae king, making mellow in our tape-deck, we dropped down into sugarcane country on the east coast, and immediately noticed how sensational everything seemed to smell. Thickets of head-high wild ginger pumped out the most gorgeous perfume – tropical, floral, with topnotes of honey. And then there was the living trellising system of the *vacoa* (pandanus) trees, entwined with cream and white climbing orchids, with a bouquet of vanilla. This was because they were vanilla.

These Indian Ocean islands are international vanilla HQ: Madagascar is the leading world producer, Mauritius does its bit, but Réunion is highly disparaging about both, claiming its vanilla is the *grand cru*. Originally from Mexico, imported to Europe by conquistadors, this fragrant plant was rerouted to Réunion in 1820, and it was here that 'the world's vanilla industry was born'. So we were told, and this wasn't French chauvinism or Réunionnais sales-hype. A 12-year-old slave from this island liberated these scents and flavours for the world.

Edmond Albius worked in a sugar plantation owner's garden here. Observing that the vanilla orchids were sterile – the insect which pollinated them back in Mexico didn't emigrate with the plants – this curious and observant boy pollinated them by hand. His experiment in 1841 launched an industry.

Edmond was 19 when slavery was officially abolished on Réunion in 1848, young, free, reasonably famous, highly talented. But like many prodigies, he fizzled and eventually he put his dexterity to inadvisable use. He became a jewel thief, and not an especially good one either. He was caught, imprisoned, and died destitute. Vanilla, still grown and handled in an anachronistically artisanal way, has become one of the most expensive spices in the world.

Cinnamon sticks are still used to effect the delicate transaction of pollination. No way has yet been discovered of hurrying up the nine months it takes to coax the scent from a vanilla pod.

'There are more than 200 compounds in its fragrance. They need time and patience to develop, you know,' said a Réunionnais friend. He sounded remarkably like a winemaker doing the 'wine is SO complicated and mysterious' sort of sales spiel. It struck us that this last leg of the process was the equivalent of barrel maturation in wine. During which time, especially if they're new oak barrels, the wine picks up – yes – vanilla flavours.

MAURITIUS

Travelling the African wine routes was outlandish enough, but whenever we mentioned Mauritius eyebrows became over-exercised. Please! This palmy, balmy, fragrant fragment of lava floating in the Indian Ocean was surely on our itinerary because of the beaches. The diving. The palm hearts. The pink pigeons. That sort of thing? Because there are no Mauritian vineyards. Are there? No. But there are Mauritian wines, winemakers, and wineries.

The pigeons, recently snatched from the brink of extinction, are the blushing beauties of their family. The beaches look like coconut cream, feel like cashmere. Fresh palm hearts served with Mama Rouge – orange rock cod – are not to be missed. You don't even have to get your hair wet to explore under water, so consumer-friendly is the contraption devised by a Mauritian who clearly understood people like us – intimidated by diving, but frustrated by goggling: the foggy mask, the water up your nose, the inevitability of having to surface for repairs just when a shoal designed by Gaudi swishes past. All you do here is put a sort of square fish-tank over your head. And *walk* underwater! But – honestly! – we were there for the wine. To unravel the mystery.

It's a detail that's not given much play in the official histories, but it was a Mauritian-born man who was the father of South African wine in the seventeenth century. In the official books of the island capital of Port Louis, the son of a Dutch sea captain and his Indian wife (so the story goes) is the first recorded birth. Later, as the Dutch East India Company's Governor of the Cape of Good Hope – its halfway house on the spice route – Simon van der Stel led South Africa's earliest wine boom. The Muscat grapes which became a highly desirable, expensive wine in the eighteenth century flourished on his personal estates near Cape Town. The wine town of Stellenbosch was named after him. Enter a modern Mauritian connection.

One of South Africa's most charming beach-picnic whites is 'Vin d'Erstelle! You get it?' Asking the question, about the allusion in his own label, was Marc Wiehe, based in Stellenbosch since the early 1990s, but still as Mauritian as *mazavaroo* (a local chilli relish), and often as fiery. In 2001 his L'Avenir Estate won a gold medal for the second year running in the Chardonnay du Monde competition in Burgundy, and he decided the time had come to take his wines home. L'Avenir was on restaurant lists in London, New York and Hong Kong but at swish Mauritian resorts, Chevalier-Montrachet was easier to find. Only one, the very convivial and switched-on Sugar Beach, had previously sought out Marc's labels. So he was having 'a little tasting in the old family home, very informal old boy' (or ma chérie, depending on whom he addresses), 'and would you come?'

L'Avenir was already on our visiting list for the South African leg of this wine odyssey, Marc being one of the inkruipers (creepers-in) – outsiders who crashed the old boys' club in the Cape, and rewrote the wine list. Why not taste under rustling palms instead of Stellenbosch oaks? After we'd sniffed out Oxenhams, the island's leading producer, which turns out millions of litres of wine without a grape in sight.

Grandpère's last words

Oxenhams is an import-export-distribution enterprise established in 1932 by a man driven by a dream – or obsessed by a fantasy. It provided the backing for businessman Edward Clark Oxenham to pursue his life-long struggle to grow and make wine in the steamy Indian Ocean. He started off planting vines on the island of Rodrigues, east of Mauritius, but cyclones annihilated his grapes. Undeterred, he corresponded with oenologists from Burgundy, scientists from the Pasteur Institute in Paris, and consulted all the wine disaster literature. He concentrated on how the French had managed to make wine during their devastating phylloxera plague: they chaptalised on a grand scale. 'Eureka!' he is inevitably said to have cried when he cracked the conundrum.

Transferring his focus to Mauritius, he launched a new venture: wine-without-vineyards. But it was always a compromise, as his last words acknowledged. They've become local lore – an article of faith about the refusal to yield to the hopelessness of Indian Ocean wine-growing. (And a dig at the younger generation's substitution efforts – pineapple and guava concoctions.)

'Remember,' Grandpère said, after summoning his children to his deathbed in 1948. 'Wine can also be made from grapes.'

They took his exhortation to heart, and planted Chardonnay, Chenin Blanc, Syrah. No go again. But – 'all these new clones…' the grandsons still said wistfully, dreamily. When some magical anti-cyclone, climate-resistant vine mutant comes along, the Oxenhams will be waiting with open arms.

This is the ultimate family concern. Alan (marketing chief) and Steve (one of the winemakers), were our jaunty, jolly guides for the day. Their assorted brothers, the heads of various sections (they employ 208 staff), popped up as we proceeded through the premises, before peeling off busily. Brian in bottling, Frederick in production,

Christopher and Sylvain in accounts. Patrick, another oenologist, was away in Spanish wine country, and we didn't meet chairman Clifford or directors Vivian and Edward. But all were Oxenhams.

'We have our arguments' Alan said, and we could imagine – acute and grave accents flying all over the place, torrents of French spiked in the Mauritian manner with spicy Creole. Not, despite the Anglo names, English. They speak it fluently, but the pronunciation is definitely not pukkha or even (as John le Carré says) the 'bottled' version. Their colonial forebears – Britain ran this island for 158 years before independence in 1968 – mightn't even recognise their own name. It's 'Auxenum' now. 'Clee-four' if you're on tutoyer terms with the chairman. And this was Alan's description of the range named after *grandpère's* Eureka whoop: *Zeez eez for ze chip and chirrfool markette.* (Cheap and cheerful, Mauritian-style.)

Both tall and gangly, Steve and Alan epitomised cheeriness themselves. They were entirely comfortable making a product designed to send wine purists into deep shock. Equally comfortable had been Steve's oenology professor at Dijon University. During the final oral exams, the Prof. instructed: Never mind the syllabus. Tell me how you make your wine. Steve recalled: 'It was almost as if he wanted to learn from our experiences. And I passed!' Some starry French wine names were classmates of his; when he visits Burgundy, he stays with the Prieurs of Domaine Jacques Prieur.

Alternative wine

Now here we were in the winery, Steve shouting over the whine of a recently acquired centrifuge (hygiene is taken very seriously here, as is effluent grading and control) and the shrill clinking of bottles. A bin of purple juice frothed appetisingly. We stepped over thick pipes snaking between stainless-steel tanks. Men in white coats with clipboards marched about, or occupied heavy-duty desks. It was a normal, spanking-clean cellar anywhere, on a good day. Except there were no grapes.

These are wines grown in Spain and Argentina, made in Mauritius. The former, less climatically challenged wine countries supply grape-juice concentrate (the bulk variety is Malbec); at Oxenhams they do what Mauritians do so well in every field, from textiles to IT equipment – *manipulation* and *élévation*. Adding value to basic, imported raw material.

The concentrate arrives in 100-litre plastic drums, is reconstituted, hydrated, inoculated with yeast and fermented more or less as in any other winery. But the Oxenhams can skip the messy stages – de-stalking, crushing, pressing – and the fancy footwork normally required to extract colour from grapes. They avoid cyclones, droughts, frost, heatwaves, whatever. They can make their wine any time and get a better (cash and carry) price for the empties than others squeeze out of their grape skins – locals use them as water tanks.

But what do the wines taste like? Bland, it must be said of the Eurekas – pink and white – despite their excitable name. The instant we tasted them, we understood Grandpère's disquiet. There was an alarming blank on the nose. 'Our big difficulty,' said Steve. Without the distraction of fruity, flowery, earthy, just about any aromas, the slightest excess sulphur can and did stand out. This was why fellow winemaker Patrick was in Spain. He was giving a pep-talk to their concentrate suppliers. Motivating them not to strip the fruit and bouquet so bare. (His experiments with oak chips during and after fermentation hadn't filled the gap.)

But only 10 per cent of drinkers 'nose' their wines with any degree of expertise, and that number dwindles after the first glass. Few ultra-sensitive snifferati are likely to be caught dead wandering around in this area of the market. At around US$1 a bottle (the concentrate is not highly taxed) you forfeit the right to over-picky pedantry. In any case, the range had been a roaring success. So why worry about improvements? Because, we found, the Oxenhams subscribe to a philosophy Johnny Hugel once expounded to us in Alsace: 'The most important wine in your cellar is the cheapest.'

Le Jeroboam, their chic wine shop, carried many grand marques for hotels and embassies, but no less attention was being paid to the vins ordinaires. In Creole, which everyone here speaks – a mix of French, Malagasy and some African dialects – there are strings of phrases, songs and jokes about divin – pronounced dee-van. And though wine-drinking at 3.5 million litres a year is hardly riotous, it's a given with meals. Where it might accompany spicy Indian carri or gâteaux piment, Chinese noodles (mine), Creole vindaye or haute French ways with anything that swims. Or simply celebrate the pre-prandial sunset. (We were assured that the 'san-downair' was invented in Mauritius.)

For all these cultural reasons, Oxenhams' wines had flourished; the company was now pumping out 2.5 million litres a year under the Eureka, Chaptalin, Val Ory, Bordofin and Cordon labels. There were bubblies Decramon, Montrevel ('country sparkling liquors') and Kirvel (a local Kir Royale). And however unclassic the process, Grandpère's appetite for a challenge remained, as their power-point presentation reiterated.

'Wine runs deep in the Oxenham family culture. Much more than a tradition – a passion…we do not intend to sleep on our laurels….'

Or rest on them either, as Steve's latest vintage confirmed. We'd spotted a small, bright yellow French Vaslin wine press in a corner, and wondered. This is a fixture on wheels in garagiste cellars all over the world, but why here? Was this some sort of show-piece frippery? Certainly not, in a company with this ethos: We value modesty as a frame of mind. The Vaslin had recently made its début on the tropical fruit they call letchis here, litchis, lychees elsewhere. Each letchi had been prepped as carefully as if it was going in for major surgery: peeled, depipped, and 'second-skinned' to lose the highly tannic white layer immediately above the succulent flesh.

One of the Oxenham's popular wine-from-grape-concentrate labels.

Steve poured a sample. It was sensational! A ravishing, brilliant light gold, and the perfume came rocketing out of the glass like a glamorous Gewürztraminer or a fine Muscat à Petits Grains. No need to be coaxed by swirling. No need for us to affect delight and surprise. Here was a scent with such knockoutability it would need rationing. 'I thought you'd like it,' he said.

A splash of this into Oxenhams' Made in Mauritius, Grown Elsewhere wine would turn its colourless bouquet hot pink. Granted it wouldn't be all-grape. But on the other hand, it would be much more Mauritian. Eureka!

Round the island

Meantime, Marc Wiehe had arrived back on his home ground to organise the tasting of his wines, and he quickly whipped us around his old haunts.

Over the road from the reclaimed waterfront – chi-chi shops, gleaming hotels – throbbed the Port Louis market. A bouquet of dried octopus drifted past, moderated by diesel fumes from a bus that promised *Tomorrow will always come*. The octopus was being sold in the crafts section amid model galleons, and shirts with those loud tropical patterns that make your eyes whimper. Among the roots and shoots at Chez N Mootosamy, we found a hangover tisane featuring mangrove bark, mint and other mystery leaves. Even Marc's Creole was not up to them, but rose to the occasion when some youngsters tried to sell him bootleg Viagra. 'What a cheek old boy! Do I look as though I need it?'

We detoured round Parliament, an engaging little shuttered, pillared, veranda-wrapped building, and the fading beauties of old Creole mansions; circled the Champ de Mars, headquarters of the Mauritius Turf Club. Marc was put down for membership at birth. Under a giant banyan tree were wooden bookies' booths – Cyril Wan Kwan Wan, Laval Tack Shin…'Mauritians adore, absolutely *adore* gambling,' said Marc.

In the Robert Edward Hart Garden close to the bulk sugar terminal we were astonished to see – could it be? – Lenin. To be precise, his (colossal) head, growing up from the lawn. Out of sight and favour all over the world, here he was larger than life. Marc explained. Mauritius is a member of both the English-speaking Commonwealth and the Organisation Commune Africaine Malgache et Mauricienne (OCAMM), the francophone African community, and this was a typical example of island expediency.

'It's classic Mauritius. Anticipate every eventuality. Don't commit yourself. If the world returns to Communism, Mauritius wants to be prepared. That statue might come in handy.'

There were Hindu temples everywhere, bright as tropical fish, adorned with enigmatic deities in acrobatic positions. More than half of all Mauritians are Hindus of one sect or another. But more ubiquitous was Ralph Lauren. We'd not seen so much

Top: *Gentle ocean, manageable mountains: cyclones aside, Mauritius is remarkably easy-going; combing the beach, sifting the lagoon at Paradise Cove.* Middle: *Steve Oxenham draws some letchi wine; a family business - Alan (marketing) and Steve (winemaking) Oxenham; Port Louis pick-me-ups.* Bottom: *La Bourdonnais, the Wiehe family's quintessential sugar-plantation house; Marc and Hester Wiehe discover a Mauritian hamlet synonymous with their Cape wine estate.*

trumpeting of one man's name since we were in central Africa just before the self-coronation of Emperor Bokassa.

When the first Original Ralph Lauren Factory Shop popped up in a dilapidated blue building with a wooden balcony like a piece of grimy lace we stopped to take a picture. But umpteen little men on ponies subsequently galloped by – more polo teams than you could shake a stick at, symptoms of an island-wide style epidemic. Hundreds of famous designer labels are Made in Mauritius.

We called in at Marc's birthplace, the highest-altitude town on the island, Curepipe (at a modest 540m); saw its toy-sized Trou aux Cerfs volcanic crater; wondered why Mark Twain thought it the nastiest spot on earth. Especially after raving about the whole island: 'You gather the idea that Mauritius was made first and then heaven, and that heaven was copied after Mauritius.'

In winter every year, the Wiehes – an old and large sugar-farming clan – and the rest of local high society would move to the drier, warmer coast for a few months, to beach shacks known as *campements*. (If you speak of a 'villa', you are not Mauritian.) Marc recalled these great treks: 'It would take us three days to pack the lorry. Beds, chairs, linen, food, chickens, dogs, wine, the servants and their families, my parents and us eight children, everything. It was a major blurdy expedition, old chap.' (Marc's hot-Pom de terre accent – frightfully English phrases given an exotic French-Mauritian spin – was picked up in London, where he trained as an accountant and later worked, in the City, for an international sugar-broking firm.)

Fewer than 50 years ago the coastline began to change. Marc was by turns plunged into gloom -'Blurdy 'ell old boy! My father used to hunt here with his dogs!' – and then on a high. Waving his arms round the curve of Grande Baie, packed with Original Ralph Lauren Factory Shops and hotels, he cheered: 'Look at this! Mauritians are very, very industrious; they don't just have one job, they'll sometimes have three.'

And so, many of yesterday's *campements* had become today's starry resorts – and pretty staggering they are. Such a small island, such grand designs. Multiple man-made cascades, lakes, lagoons. Acres of marble floors. Only the thatch – sugarcane fronds – lends a touch of local realism. Nothing on the mainland comes close to so much collective opulence in such a compact space. If John hadn't been asked to give a wine tasting in the Oberoi Hotel (Thai architect, American landscaper, English lighting designer, *haute cuisine*), and if we hadn't been invited to dinner at Le Barachois, on a pontoon moored in the lagoon of the shiny new hotel Prince Maurice, we'd not have dared to venture in. The sommeliers were better dressed and far more suave than we were.

The pontoon bobbed and swayed, and some of the party felt quite queasy, especially when told of the lagoon's resident shark, cruising beneath. African big-game stories are big-fish stories here. Which was the most dangerous fish in Mauritian waters?

After much passionate debate it was eventually decided that a wahu edged out a barracuda. Said young Sébastien Leclezio, who'd recently returned from wine studies in the Rhône Valley to join the family import business: 'Oh, there is no question. A wahu can snap someone's leg off even after it's been caught and is lying at the bottom of your boat!'

Our encounters with local hazards were confined to the ferocious chilli sauce Marc had earlier insisted we dab onto the wild guavas which send locals into a hunter-gatherer frenzy after the cyclone season each year. We bought them on a remote beach, where they were piled up like old-fashioned sweets in a glass case fitted to an ancient black bicycle.

The fireplace which grew into a winery

As we'd criss-crossed the island that day, we'd not talked wine. But Marc insisted on asking one question: 'Would you, would YOU' – his gravelly voice rose – 'dare go into an artist's studio and tell him how to mix his palette?' The energetic blue eyes, the tanned face, the expensive shirt, the London commodities trader's bravura were all speaking. 'Winemakers are artists, they're prima donnas, especially when they're good. And François is good. Well, old chap, don't you agree?'

François Naude is the nice, steady pharmacist who one day, to his family's alarm, announced they were packing up in Pretoria and moving 1000 miles south to the Cape. There he'd work as a handyman, until he found someone who understood his compulsion to change his life, and was undeterred by his inexperience, or his age. He had no formal oenology training, but destiny called. He would advance his case via a Cabernet he'd cooked up in his kitchen. He was a winemaker waiting to happen.

At more or less the same time, 1992, Marc was also reshaping his life. Retiring early from the sugar business, he decided to holiday neither in Mauritius nor his ski-chalet in the Haute Savoie but at a health hydro in Stellenbosch. Here he succumbed to the charms of the 53-hectare farm which he renamed L'Avenir – the future. There was no winery: grapes were sold to commercial wine giant Nederburg. But there was a guest-house, rather too frigid in winter. Marc hired a handyman to build a fireplace. The handyman made kitchen Cabernet….

'Something happened in heaven,' said François. 'His Cabernet knocked me over,' said Marc. Within weeks it was decided: the estate must have a 25,000-case a year winery; Francois would design, build and run it. The big, beaming Afrikaner, built for a rugby line-out, and the raffish, debonair Mauritian are, temperamentally, surprisingly similar: prone to volcanic eruptions, cyclonic storms, dramatic passions. And addicted to hard work. François might very well, too, have been Made in Mauritius.

A major vineyard make-over began. Out went unfashionable varieties, in came the classics. But preservation orders were placed on Pinotage, the unique Cape-crossed red wine grape, and Chenin Blanc. François approached both like a besotted lover.

Give him a variety that others neglect… and he won't just send it flowers, he'll make a serious commitment, we wrote. The Pinotage, wrapped luxuriously in oak, abandoned its clumsy rural ways. The Chenin, the Cape's most common grape, was transformed into an uncommon beauty too. François deliberately nudges a percentage of the crop toward noble rot sweetness in the vineyard, to emphasise the grape's honey-tropical fruit richness.

New and foreign-speaking arrivals until quite recently were regarded with bristling suspicion by many born and bred into the Cape's vinocracy. (Bordelais incursions into Burgundy might have been received more warmly.) But François' talent was undeniable, and Marc's theatrical geniality soon made him a winelands 'character'. At dinner once – at Charles Back's Fairview Estate near Paarl – he suddenly announced to a table including Said Mebarki, the visiting head of the Algerian wine industry: 'Look here, Charles old chap, your Syrah is so blurdy good I shall just have to show you the hairs on my chest, old boy.' He ripped open his shirt and flashed.

What would he do in front of his – adoring – home crowd tonight, we wondered, as the 140 guests invited to the belated island launch of L'Avenir began to arrive. There'd be no shortage of lubrication. Marc had shipped a dozen cases of each of his eight wines! 'We're having a party old boy. Do you agree with me, one mustn't be mean on these occasions?'

A château in the cane fields

The Wiehe family seat, Château La Bourdonnais, is in the cane fields on the northern flats of the island. Mangoes that taste like rose petals, letchis that smell like the finest Gewürztraminer, vegetables and vanilla, orchids and anthuriums are now grown on this once sugar-only estate. The Château was named after Bertrand François Mahe de Labourdonnais, the eighteenth-century French ship's captain who kick-started the transformation of Mauritius from a settlement of pirates and slaves into a thriving agricultural and commercial community.

For the past 150 years or so, when Wiehes have had something significant to celebrate, they've come here: up the gravel drive, under a long archway of venerable fig trees to the Gone with the Wind plantation mansion built by Marc's great-grandfather, the Hon. Christian Wiehe. The formal salon, the lofty hallway and the dining room with its mural of a deer hunt (they still breed stags here) had been opened into one huge space for the party. Crystal cascaded from enormous chandeliers; the elaborate trophy the Hon. Christian won at the 1859 Inter-Colonial Exhibition for 'the best samples of sugar' glittered on a sideboard.

The deep, black and white tiled veranda was the place to cool off. It was dotted with tree ferns, pink and red anthuriums, old rattan chairs and the *gratin* of Franco-Mauritian society. There was a sprinkling of handsome young Indo-Mauritians – mostly sommeliers at the swanky hotels. There were waiters in the creamy toffee shades of Creole. The South African High Commissioner, burly, snappily dressed Louis Mnguni – a political science professor – stood out in this African country where black Africans are a rarity.

'We were here first,' said Jean-Marc Harel – lawyer, consultant to companies throughout Africa, owner of the not-implausibly named Paradise Cove Hotel (staff combed the sand twice a day), where we were staying . Unlike the mainland, and even the islands next door, and apart from creatures like the dodo (described in early histories as a 'feathered tortoise') Mauritius was uninhabited before the first European adventurers set up shop in the early seventeenth century. Now it's run by a canny, industrious Indian majority, with (largely) leftover British administrative institutions and jurisprudence, Creole soul and wit, Chinese grit and tenacity and French savoir-faire. An ethnic blend so mixed it makes a masala look one-dimensional.

High Commissioner Mnguni launched the tasting 'At the end of the day, we are all Africans' he opened, and after explaining that 'we've had a slight pause, but we're back in business now', he canvassed support for South African President Thabo Mbeki's grand vision of an African Renaissance. The Mauritians looked bemused. No wake-up calls needed here. Their scale-model island has been a lesson to the continent for years. Its forte is cajoling development aid from all-comers on the increasingly tenuous submission that Mauritius is an undeveloped Third World country.

'Look at all this,' Marc had said at the airport, waving his arms to take in spruce and spanking terminals. 'The Government here is *fantastic* at getting money. Brilliant beggars. This airport – a gift from China. The motorways – all from the EU. That hospital – donated by India. Our new satellite for tracking cyclones – from the US. And France! Pouring the money in!'

Marc Wiehe ready for wine-tasting at his family's old colonial home, La Bourdonnais.

Tasting à la Maurice

'Good wine does not have to be French! Africa must take centre-stage!'

The High Commissioner finished in rousing cheerleader mode, and the crowd responded: the serious business – the partying – could begin. Mauritians are prodigious party throwers and goers; the word 'festive' could be their copyright. When they invite you to a wine tasting, *attention*! These are not effete and short-lived affairs. Evenings stretch into elongated nights, stamina is needed. The first corks were pulled at La Bourdonnais at 6pm, things began to hot up around 10pm and were still cooking at 2am.

Sheer volume of numbers and national exuberance made the tasting unusually noisy. There was a bit of a hush for a short general introduction, and that was it. No one interrupted the free flow of wine or conversation with an agricultural or technical drone, or a string of adjectives limper than a garden slug. Out and about streamed snacks to match each wine-flight. Smoked swordfish; tuna carpaccio; spicy potato *samoosas*…. No pallid old water biscuits here, Mauritian tastebuds would be outraged.

When twilight washed into night and the lights went on, the whole house shimmered and sparkled, floating in the darkness like a liner on the ocean. It was extremely glamorous and sultry hot, and the Chenin Blanc tasted cool and good. Close to midnight, to cries of appreciation all round, the Pinotage came out blazing. At 1am people were still calling for — and being found! — more bottles, to partner trays of ripely stinky cheeses. Long after we retired, they were still partying on.

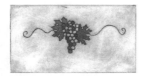

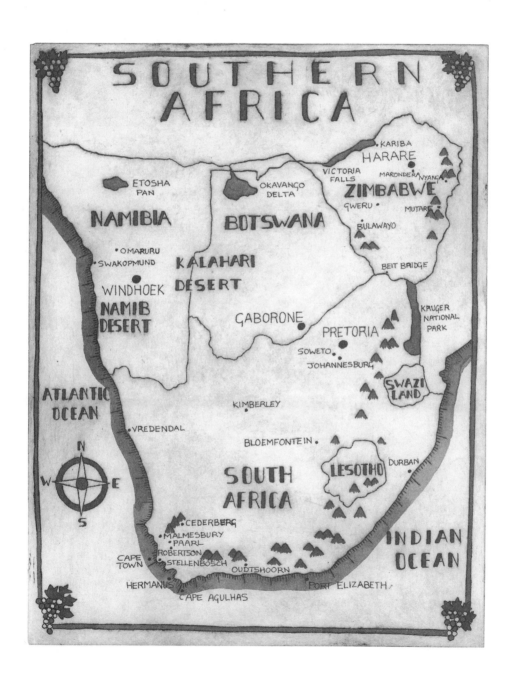

ZIMBABWE

There were hippos sploshing in the Limpopo below as we crossed the bridge from South Africa into Zimbabwe and turned left, heading for the vineyards of Bulawayo. They were making their usual deeply grumpy (hippos are always having a bad day) acoustic tuba sounds. Ominous allusions flitted into our minds: old war movies, troop ships being sent off by brass bands.... We weren't heading into normal wine-tasting territory. This was Zimbabwe, 2001, and times were bad.

It was the day after His Excellency The Hon. Comrade President Robert Gabriel Mugabe's 77th birthday. *The People's Voice* – 'Bold, Factual and Fearless' claimed its masthead – had put out a special edition. The headlines fawned: 'President Mugabe a great, inspirational leader… role model for the youth….' And in the sports section: 'President has great passion for cricket.' (At the height of cricket's match-fixing revelations, he had sympathised with the late South African captain Hansie Cronje.) On the front page, above a giant picture of the Comrade President in striped shirt and sharp suit: 'This eye-catching space is for sale.'

Meantime, judges had been forcibly retired; opposition newspaper presses had been bombed; journalists were being assaulted by police and farms invaded by 'war veterans'. Tourism had plummeted 90 per cent we were told – and you might as well have blown your nose on a Zim-dollar. The lights were on only because South Africa was manning the switches. There were petrol queues all over the country. Foreign exchange was a commodity so severely threatened it was heading for extinction.

The country was being bled to death to keep troops fighting in the Congo. Rumours flew thick and dark as a plague of locusts. We heard that 4x4s such as ours risked being hijacked and flown (literally) to the Democratic Republic of Congo from the airforce base at Gweru, next door to a vineyard we were to visit. Security forces on home ground were armed and twitchy. There were roadblocks everywhere. A friend taking her dog to the vet was turned back by police who claimed it was illegal to travel with a 'dangerous animal' in a car. The South African weekly, the *Mail and Guardian*, editorialised:

This cradle of a great, ancient civilisation, this most promising and beautiful of countries, is in the thrall of a lunatic who, in the service of his hubris, is willing to destroy himself and all about him....

Back in 1978 during the death-rattles of Zimbabwe's bush liberation war, John, then news agency UPI's Southern Africa bureau chief, had interviewed winemakers toting Uzis, in vineyards surrounded by electric fences, barricaded with sandbags. (After reporting that this was a war the white Rhodesian régime would never win, he was expelled from the country.) Now, wouldn't it have been more sensible to visit this region by e-mail? Did the wines of Zimbabwe warrant a hard, 2000-kilometre road-trip? Yes and no, perhaps, but beside the point. Because beckoning more seductively than any grapey bouquet was something we'd been lamenting as lost ever since we'd exchanged news-reporting for the (usually) softer options of wine-writing: a breaking story.

We picked up fuel wherever and however we could on our Zim wine journey.

So we packed 100 litres of petrol into jerry cans and headed along the Great North Road to the vineyards of Matabeleland. It was raining but we travelled with all the windows open; even a shifting-spanner didn't close out the presence of our fuel reserve. It invaded the car, taking wine-tasterly definitions of 'billowing aromas' to giddy new dimensions.

After Beitbridge we drove through ranching country. Mopanis – the favourite leafy green of elephants – msasas, multiple brands of thorn tree (knob, buffalo, giraffe and mimosa) dappled the long 'sweetveld' grass. En route, we bumped into the international buyer for a British meat company. He raved about the local beef. 'Best in the world after Argentina and New Zealand. But Zimbabwe these days has a stigma about it. We've had to develop a *nom de plume.*' Serious carnivores should have been looking for the South Crown label.

About 300 kilometres from the border, the landscape began to shrink to a more domestic scale – patches of maize, citrus, tobacco, ostriches, and fields of scarlet paprika (exported to Spain). We were in the fertile valley of Esigodini – the hole, it means – close to Zimbabwe's second city, Bulawayo. And there, suddenly, loomed some vineyards.

Errol Normanton, formerly the boy who made wine in his bedroom.

Bedroom wines

We turned off opposite the Chipangali Animal Orphanage (late patron of its Big Five and other wild waifs, Princess Diana), and took the 'Much Binding' road towards Worringham Estate. Here Errol Normanton had made some of Zimbabwe's earliest wines, in the mid-1960s. White-bearded now, he had no grand illusions about the winemaker as artist. 'Rhodesian wine was always known

for its sulphur,' he said. 'Sun-drenched? Ha! Our back labels should say: Made from rain-ripened grapes!'

Errol's wine career began in his bedroom, as a teenager, when he mashed some table grapes – Catawba, Isabella and Seneca – into 20-litre plastic containers and inoculated the juice with yeast. 'There were a few loud pops in the night, but I got some wine.' Its fame spread: he was made an offer he didn't refuse by a Corsican family firm in Bulawayo. Trading under Monis, a respected import label, they had the licences for various spirits and South African wines. They approached his mother.

'We have heard that your son makes wine. Tell him to make a lot of it.'

Errol gave up his book-keeping job on the railways. (Bulawayo is an important rail junction; its steam train museum is world famous.) The operation moved from the bedroom to a shed, with a small basket press, a hand-operated mangle, and some old barrels lined with paraffin wax.

'They didn't seem too fussy about quality, which suited me. I wasn't a great one for chemistry. They were a nice family, but Corsican. They kept buying and buying and we kept planting and planting. I suppose they were distilling it for port and things,' Errol mused. Not quite. The theory now is that wine from a network of unsuspecting growers and makers was disappearing into imported bottles. Bulawayo cheap was stretching pricey Cape.

'We really got going when the world slapped on sanctions,' Errol recalled. (From 1965, when Prime Minister Ian Smith declared UDI – Unilateral Independence – from Britain.) 'Anything we could make locally, we did. Because wine was so novel we weren't bothered by legislation.' Worringham's Lorraine range, and bottling line, were launched by the PM. The visitors' book, still in use, begins: *Ian Douglas Smith*. Address: *Rhodesia*. 'He was a perfect gent,' said Errol.

The Lord and the war vets

Worringham's current incumbent, Colin de Villiers, wore ankle-high farming boots, long khaki shorts, and a bush hat, indoors and out. He doffed it – revealing a pale dome above his tanned face – only to say Grace at the dining table. He and Jack Russells Cabernet and Merlot welcomed us to the electric-fenced farmhouse. Zimbabweans are famously hospitable, but they were more effusive now; they were feeling abandoned. Taped to the dining-room wall was a message in blue and red crayon:

Though our farms are taken away, though our country is ravaged by Aids… we must not lose faith and hope.

'We'll be guided by the Lord. We're safe in His hands,' Colin's wife Avis told us. Bluff, philosophical, Colin's credo was: Work as if you might die tomorrow, Plan as if you'll live forever.

With the country in economic freefall and mountainous foreign debt, he was increasing his vineyards. 'We're short of red wine.' A year before, he and Avis had driven to South Africa in a 7-tonne truck to pick up 30,000 grafted vine cuttings. The 5000-kilometre round-trip took eight days, with frequent stops to hose down the grafts. They were soon to repeat the exercise. Even though, since tourists stopped visiting, they're sitting on stocks like they've never had before, Colin seemed unquenchably optimistic. 'Now we'll see if our wines can actually age! It'll all come right in the end. Won't it?'

Worringham's winery is surrounded by 45 hectares of vineyards. They could have been anywhere; widely spaced, vertically trellised, carpeted with trimmed grass. But the frame – thorny acacia mimosa trees – was unmistakeably African. So were the biggest pests – warthogs and kudu. Plum-coloured starlings, red bishops, purple rollers flitted about glamorously as we inspected the Cabernet from Colin's Land Rover. Then his radio crackled. It was a neighbour.

    – We're being occupied, they've just come on to the farm.

    – Any contact?

    – Negative. But they've staked out claims and begun cutting trees to make their camps.

    – How many involved?

    – About 20, mostly male. I didn't engage.

    – Roger, then. Keep monitoring.

    – Over and out.

We'd heard a live report of war vets invading a farm. 'Touch wood, they've left us alone… maybe they don't understand vineyards and the winery,' said Colin.

A former cotton farmer, he'd been at Worringham Estate 20 years. Neither he nor any of the other farmer/winemaker/managers we met in the Zim group African Distillers had formal qualifications. (They were all white too, rather noticeably in a black majority country.) Consultants, principally New Zealander Clive Hartnell, dashed in for brief visits, and doled out step-by-step recipes: *Keep the fermentation cool for the first three days, thereafter turn off cooling and allow it to warm up…. Add sugar to give about 12.5% alc. if necessary…. The final blending and tweaking was done in Harare – 440 kilometres away.*

The flying winemaker

We caught up with Clive Hartnell later, and posed the irresistible question: Why? Why persist with wines in a climate so unsuited to the vine, for consumers so firmly wedded to spirits and beer? 'Because they can,' he said.

A former chemistry and sensory evaluation lecturer at the renowned Roseworthy College in Adelaide, Clive had been Zimbabwe's mobile wine guru since 1990, between annual flying winemaker stints in Hungary and South Africa. He was trying to coax cleaner, riper grapes from under-trained and often part-time wine farmers with a lot on their minds.

The soils aren't the problem. But it's not, as the modern wine cliché has it, 'all in the dirt'. Not in a country where 90 per cent of the high annual rainfall falls smack in the middle of the harvest. Such a French vintage would be declared a national emergency. The government would rush in aid and vignerons would block motorways and burn for-

The seconds and thirds winery at Worringham.

eign wine tankers. Zimbabwe's latitude, about 18–22 degrees south, doesn't help. Vines are hardy, but they prefer a Mediterranean climate's extended daylight hours during the growing season..

'Actually, the standard of viticulture in Zimbabwe is probably better than it is in the Cape. It has to be, if they're going to make any wine at all,' asserted Clive. 'When I first went in 1990, the stuff was undrinkable. But I can manage now.'

His upbeat view wasn't universally shared. Many of the otherwise fiercely patriotic locals were frank: We don't drink Zimbabwean wines. Tourists are more adventurous, and often pleasantly surprised. (A bottle of local red costs pence rather than pounds!) Except, there were no tourists now.

'Oh, they'll be back. It's got to come right. The troubles are a dream marketing opportunity with all the headlines about farm invasions. I compare it to Serge Hochar's story in the Lebanon,' Clive said bullishly. But Lebanese weather is kinder, whatever the political climate.

Clive tipped Merlot and Shiraz as Zimbabwe's grapes of the future. Yes, a little more sweetness in the wines was probably in order – sometimes we thought we were biting into a lemon not drinking wine. But forget these technicalities; didn't he have a stock of outrageous anecdotes? 'Plenty! But for stories like that I need some notice – and a lot of good wine first.'

Seconds and thirds

Winegrowing in summer rainfall regions is a blend of eccentricity and defiant masochism. In Zimbabwe, as harvesting winemakers prayed for the heavens to close, we saw traditional rainmakers, in masks topped with ostrich feathers, roaming the countryside in ululating bands. They were seeking heavenly aid for the tender young seedlings of the national staple, maize. They seemed to have better connections than the winemakers.

Back in Worringham's vineyards, in the rain, workers were trying to pick the Cabernet before it rotted. It had been pouring for weeks – 300 millimetres in February, a third of the national average in one month. We took shelter, and tasted some works-in-progress, in Colin's winery, a monument to unpretentiousness: no stainless steel, no barrels. Just a large shed with a corrugated iron roof. Brandy and other spirits (hard tack) pay the rent. 'Wine is really a by-product. The bread and butter is distilling. Accountants are our masters.'

The pomace, a murky mess of oxidised grape debris – squashed skins, stems, pips and pulp – is 're-used' in almost all Zimbabwean wineries, to produce something quite rightly not called wine, but 'seconds' and 'thirds'. Colin said: 'We can make as much as you like. Place your order.'

After the grapes yield their 'free-run' and first-pressing juice for wine, the leftovers are blended with a ready-mix of liquified sugar and water to induce fermentation. This grey gruel is later distilled into brandy. However distant the relationship to a grape this trumped-up substance is legal. And it explained the hectic pong, and the sugar bags piled high on the winery floor.

Chaptalisation is common (though regulated) in Europe in wetter, slighter vintages but banned in South Africa (the theory being that in the sunny Cape, grapes should ripen without the addition of any sugar to increase a wine's alcohol content). This tickled Colin: 'No rules and regulations here!' he boomed, wagging a finger.

A welcome drink? Justice Chazi on Camp Amalinda's airstrip bus.

We tasted the infant 2001s from the cement tanks. The Sauvignon Blanc had a terrific attacking aroma, but also the juddering tartness we generally found on palate and finish. The Sémillon wafted grass and peppery spice. (Other whites grown here are Chardonnay, Chenin and Crouchen Blanc, Muscat d'Alexandrie.) The bright maroon Merlot had been beefed up with tannin extract bought by the bag. All these would be tankered to Harare for tweaking and mixing with wine from other regions.

These were the first vines we'd seen, Colin the first winemaker we'd met. But we might have transplanted them and the challenges he faced to anywhere in the country. His parting remarks referred to winemaking, but encapsulated Zimbabwean life at the time.

'You duck and you dive and you make a plan. It's crisis management.'

Justice, Bagman and the art gallery

Camp Amalinda, our base for the night, was invisible until we got to the foot of a massive hillside and started climbing. Bit by bit, from colossal rocks and dense tree canopies, this extraordinary lodge emerged: growing organically out of – and inside –

the deep caverns and granite galleries of an ancient bushman shelter in the Matobos hills. We slept in an opulently furnished cavern; the bathroom was tucked between two rock-faces, so it felt as if we were showering in a waterfall. A suspension bridge swayed over the trees to our own gazebo. Two elephants – the airstrip buses, if you arrived by light plane – munched through the mopani branches below.

But tourists were an endangered species here; hotels were hanging on but only just. Assistant manager Justice Chasi was running this cross between a palace and a cave with aplomb, but the dream he'd once had – a lodge of his own – was fading. Amalinda had even de-commissioned its *cave* (a real one).

Bagman Chauke was Amalinda's expert on all and sundry – officially he covered flora and fauna, rock art and local history, unofficially, he ranged much wider. Bagman had been a teenage military scout – a *mujiba* – in the guerrilla war of liberation, tracking the Rhodesian army, informing on village collaborators, passing messages in coded whistles, moving barefoot through the undergrowth.

Traitors had their ears cut off in front of their families and the whole village, and they then had to dig their own graves, he'd told us nonchalantly at dinner, over the warthog *brochettes*. But he provided a brisk antidote to the general white farmers' take on Zimbabwe's land issue. 'How can they sit forever on most of our arable land? Our people are living like termites. We all need land… but we must not do it with violence.'

Bagman led us into the eccentric, mesmerising landscape of the Matobos: massive boulders defying gravity and geology in multiple balancing acts; lime-green lichen clinging like lycra to acid orange cliffs; granite domes like monumental hardboiled eggs – one of the meanings of *matobo* is bald head. Mist rose from the forests like gigantic hot springs. A tiny klipspringer bounced away as we climbed to the deep Bambata cave.

Bagman explained the ancient frescoes on the walls – the greatest density of rock art in the world is in these hills – lithe hunters and animals delicately drawn in animal blood and droppings, bark, ash and urine. 'Art,' he said, 'is the best means of communication. These paintings were notes from people who'd moved on: they showed the animals of the area, so newcomers knew which poisons to collect from the plants and trees to use on their arrows'.

The current Zimbabwean land invasions were old news, he insisted. 'Where are the people who painted all these things? They have been forced into the bloody Kalahari! No one can farm there! And not by white people. We, the black Nguni people, chased these little people, the bushmen, from these places.' His voice rose, he was playing to the gallery, and an arm swept westward, toward Botswana and its desert thirstland. 'So who owns what, really? It's not simple.'

The killing fields

It got even more complicated later, when poet-novelist John Eppel, and his psychologist wife Shari came to lunch. They live in Bulawayo, where the streets are still wide enough for a span of oxen to park under mauve jacarandas, vermilion flame trees or yellow-gold cassias. These flowering trees shade more pavement displays of masks and spears than can be humanly possible to fabricate without aid from Taiwan. The Natural History Museum boasts 'the second largest mounted elephant in the world'.

It feels terribly dozy. In other Southern African cities, minibuses take you on a swerving, spurting, dice-with-life road rampage. Here Commuter Omnibus taxis ambled along, sedate as old ducks in walking-frames. But Bulawayo means 'place of slaughter'; this region had always been soaked in blood.

As Bagman had related, the indigenous San or Bushmen people were driven out by the Shonas (antecedents of Robert Mugabe and most of his Cabinet). Zulu-speaking Matabeles later turfed out the Shonas. Then Cecil Rhodes, British colonialist supreme, swept in to claim not only the sacred Matobos hills – he's buried here – but the whole country under his own name. In the early 1980s Mugabe dispatched his North Korean-trained Fifth Brigade into Matabeleland, to root out pockets of resistance to his wing of the liberation forces. They slaughtered many thousands. Their red berets still coloured people's nightmares here. You didn't have to get out of your car to find the bodies, you could smell them, we'd been told over dinner the night before.

Shari Eppel told us more. Head of the Bulawayo-based Amani Trust, an NGO funded by Danish and German donors, she documents human rights abuses and violence. And counsels victims like the election agent for a young Opposition candidate who stood against – and defeated – a Mugabe henchman. The agent's house was subsequently torched. His family was trapped inside. The TV and furniture he hadn't yet paid off were also incinerated.

When her husband suggested emigrating to less grisly pastures, Shari was horrified. 'I told him I couldn't go to New Zealand. There are no torture victims there.'

We sat beside Camp Amalinda's swimming pool, carved out of natural granite, the water a sheet of silvery turquoise. John Eppel had brought a jug of Zimbabwean Green Valley plonk. 'The best accompaniment,' he advised, 'is five aspirins.' In the circumstances, the subject of wine seemed an irrelevance.

Where are the grape trees?

We had nearly 500 kilometres to travel from the Matobos to Harare, and a vineyard to visit en route, so we left not long after sunrise. Surviving yet another *Deadly Hazard!* – the ubiquitous Zimbabwean road sign warning of a narrow bridge ahead – we passed dozens of festive watering holes. The Hey Hey Bar, the Why Not Hide Out Inn, One For

1999

THE
MEADOWS ESTA
—Chenin Blanc—
DRY

Crisp and refreshing with a medley of tropical flavc

IMBABWE • Produced in Our Cellars at Mukuyu Winery, M

Top: *The Matobos Hills; Alan Carlson of Bertrams Estate; tobacco harvest on Tavydale Farm; Alsace-in-the-bush dreamer Dave Simleit.*
Middle: *Shari Eppel, human rights activist; Charles de Burbure's chef, 'Cookie', with baby duiker; Bagman Chauke; Gweru's Bata factory, once among the world's largest.*
Bottom: *Colin de Villiers of Worringham; Charles de Burbure in his Tinta Barocca vineyard in the Mazowe Valley; Camp Amalinda's pool; hand-printed Kudhinda fabric from Ros Byrne in Harare.*

The Road Cocktails and similar intimations of icy martinis and urban sleekness popped out of the bush.

On we pressed to Gweru, where there were 42 hectares of vines and a winery which 'looks like that Falcon Crest place on TV, can't miss it'. But no one we consulted on the streets of The Capital of the Midlands, Proud Hometown of Bata Shoes had the faintest idea about Bertrams Estate. Vineyards? An old man in a broad black hat, with a gaggle of wizened women in the back of his van, didn't know. Winery? He shook his head. Cellar? We finally realised that 'grape' was the crucial word.

'Oh oh YES!' he exclaimed. 'The grape trees! On the chicken farm next to the aerodrome, that's where they used to grow. Perhaps they are still there.'

Zimbabwe's vineyards are so whimsically situated that you might stumble upon them just about anywhere. Why not Viognier at Victoria Falls or Zinfandel on the Zambezi? And here at Gweru was a prime example of the bung-in-grapes-anywhere phenomenon. Overgrown by blackjacks, the Bertrams board was almost invisibly discreet, unlike the winery. It was as long as a rugby field, with a doorway wide enough for one tractor to overtake another when delivering grapes. Tuscan? Spanish? Whatever, it was an astonishing sight, looming out of the bush and floating above rows of soggy vines and fever trees.

We hadn't made an appointment because we had no idea when, or even whether, we'd get to Gweru. (Would we have enough fuel? Would the roads be navigable? Many bridges had been washed away.) Arriving at lunchtime, we wondered how welcome we'd be. In France, we'd not have dared disturb the sacred hours of *déjeuner*. But after Alan Carlson had fed his baby son and burped him, he took us to the winery.

The splendid edifice he ran for African Distillers was built in 1990, to handle major vineyard expansion. It echoed emptily now, its gleaming floorspace only half-tanked, a head office white-elephantasy, completed before permission to tap into a main water pipeline from Gweru had been secured. This was vital to irrigate new vineyards affordably. But permission hadn't been given; planting had stopped.

Alan, a photographer in the then Rhodesian Airforce, later in the South African defence industry, had swung the Bertrams job on the strength of some (dairy) farming experience and his hobby: 'Home-winemaking, from peaches and things. Now it's grapes. I love it.'

It had to be love. How else to explain why he and his colleagues continued to commit so devotedly to the fine wine crusade – defying logic, geography, chemistry, meteorology? But they had few illusions. There was no attempt to make a 'cool breeze' out of a few flaccid stirs of torrid air, or a mountain slope out of a molehill. They saw and admitted their problems.

'Basically, this is cattle country,' Alan said. The 40 per cent clay soil was wrong; grapes ripened only in a drought; local birds were addicted to them; vineyard diseases were rampant. Sémillon, Riesling, Cabernet, Chenin Blanc, Merlot, Clairette Blanche, Sauvignon Blanc, Colombard and Muscat d'Alexandrie: a whole fruit salad was struggling on in what sounded like a total disaster area. And yet. He shouted above rumbles of thunder, electric flashes of lightning, and drumming rain: 'I'm quite pleased with my Pinotage.' Racing along a catwalk, he drew a sample: it was a pleasant surprise.

We drove on to Harare, passing graveyards full of wreaths and processions of hearses and mourners. That night a Canadian researcher gave us the latest AIDS prognosis: calamitous. She had been training township residents as counsellors. They'd insisted on starting their programme at 7am. 'If we do not leave our houses early the people come and knock on our door to tell us about the funerals. There are too many. And then we have to go to them.' Her organisation was now moving to a 'more operational' country: Tanzania.

Alsace in the bush

Amid these constant reminders of the perilous health (and wealth) of the nation, David Simleit and the story he told us the next morning seemed all the more fantastic. And the dénouement all the more inevitable. He'd had a dream: an Alsace in the African bush. From the deep red soils along the Mutoko road in Mashonaland, northeast of Harare, aromatic Gewürztraminers and Muscats would flow in abundance and spicy intensity.

'We were going to be talking poetry here, old boy.'

In 1966, he spent a year in France, taking time out from a job as a game ranger. He worked as a cellar rat at Chx Haut Brion and d'Yquem. 'But when I arrived at Trimbach in Alsace, I knew I'd found my life's mission. There is nothing more beautiful than a cold, fresh fine Muscat, or Riesling, or Gewürztraminer from Alsace. Alsace is the pinnacle of everything.'

He has a bit of a Hemingway look, white hair, white beard, Havana cigar-smoked. In his youth he was an intelligence officer in the Selous Scouts – the small, shadowy, crack force which specialised in infiltration and counter-espionage behind black guerrilla lines in the bush war of the late 1960s and 70s. His family's firm, Philips Central Cellars, founded in 1944 – the country's leading wine merchants – weighed into the 'war effort' in other ways, too. He and his brother went into the sanctions-busting business, aiming to produce enough wine and coffee to make the country self-sufficient.

Rhodesian White Wine was his first effort, in 1967. 'Let's say it was simple.' But definitely an improvement on St Christopher, a blend of table grape varieties such as Black Prince and Muscat Hamburg, made by electrical engineer René Paynter, described by many as 'the father of Zimbabwe wine'. A passionate oenophile, Paynter imported vines from South Africa in 1953 and established 'Arlington Vineyards' in his back garden in the

Harare suburb of Umwinsidale. Only 300 survived. The next year, only 12 made it. And so it continued, before Paynter produced enough grapes to press through the mangle of an old washing machine. Many growers had caught the wine bug from him.

'We used to run for cover when his grey VW van approached, because we knew he had St Christopher in the back,' said Simleit. 'It passed no test of potability known to man.'

The Simleits' wine was made from table grape Seneca, with Colombard and Clairette Blanche. 'We invited all the political and society bigwigs to our underground cellar. Even the Governor-General came, with his ADC, and they were in their official finery, you know, and black ties. This was an important breakthrough, symbolic… telling the world they could boycott us, but we were all right jack. Thank God, my brother took the precaution of smelling the wine, in a corner of the room. He signalled to my father. *They've cocked it up.*'

In the bottling process, the wine had been racked into a tank previously containing woodnaptha – a paint stripper. The dignitaries were told there had been 'a bit of hitch' and plied with substitute Ch. Margaux. The 67 Rhodesian White was never released.

In 1986 Simleit turned his Africa-Alsace fantasy into Meadows Estate: modern vineyards irrigated by Israeli drip technology, classic wine varieties including his beloved Gewürztraminer and Riesling, plus Chardonnay, Pinot Noir and Merlot. He cited Bolivia, southern Brazil and the Atacama desert in Chile as evidence that vines thrived at the same latitude as Meadows Estate – 17° 42' South.

When the rains were late, he draped tractors with vine leaves, loaded up the drums and the rainmakers in feathered regalia and drove round the estate. Wines were launched with fashion parades in marquees, beauty contests, endless parties for Zimbabwe's multiracial high society. 'Frankly, our wine is for enjoyment,' he wrote in a local magazine. 'We frown on spitting in Harare.'

By 1992 the wines were winning silver medals at London's International Wine and Spirit Competition (IWSC). But Simleit ran out of funds and customers, who were running out of money, before he ran out of stamina. He had to sell in 1995. 'I cried the whole day.' Meadows Estate became an export rose farm.

Father Dave

Africa's most frequent judge at competitions such as the IWSC is Zimbabwean-born Dave Hughes. He lectures all over the world, writes books, wears T-shirts printed with slogans: *Remember, the body does not store alcohol. You need a top-up.* His letterhead exhorts: DRINK!

It was he who made the Simleits' ill-fated 67 Rhodesian White – not long before moving to South Africa, to become production manager of Stellenbosch Farmers' Winery. Not that the wine's dunking in the paint-stripper tank had anything to do with Hughes, the most experienced distiller-winemaker in Zimbabwe at the time (trained in Scotland, at Harvey's of Bristol, at Pernod in Marseille and at Mumm in Champagne). He was in the Nyanga mountains when the instructions he'd left for bottling weren't followed….

As he tells it, the big boom from backyard production to large vineyards was a panic measure, when sanctions were introduced against Rhodesia in 1965. 'They thought the bottom would fall out of tobacco. Grapes became an alternative.' He was commissioned to do a climate study, but 'in the end, we planted where the willing and best farmers were'. Grafted vines were trucked in from South Africa. Not all of them arrived. 'All these thousands of damp plants, they heated up terrifically and… yes, there was spontaneous combustion and they blew up. Pretty standard for Zimbabwe – a bit of farce along the way….'

Eventually, the country was exporting: 'Serious volumes of cheap stuff, quite acceptable sweet whites, to the Congo, in green beer bottles.' One, with a label depicting Victoria Falls, was called White Thunder. Meantime, despite sanctions, the tobacco industry continued to thrive. 'And frankly, I think they should stick to that,' said Hughes.

Classics and bullet holes

Peter Raynor, an ex-RAF pilot with an Oxford classics degree, followed a glamorous uncle 'who'd lost an arm in Mesopotamia' out to Zimbabwe in search of 'freedom, adventure, undeveloped country'. Until deep in his 60s he still piloted commercially for a dam-construction firm, and flew hunting parties into the Zambezi valley. Now in his late 70s, he'd just written his first novel – a tale of drug smuggling in a French village. And also his autobiography, entitled *Spilt Milk*.

This was a reference to his first dairy-farming venture ('disastrous'), which was rapidly followed by other calamities: the seed débâcle, for instance – someone foolishly left a Rhodesian label on a consignment of his morning-glory seeds exported illegally to the USA during the sanctions-era. ('Catastrophe.') Then there were the peaches. ('Hopeless. Had to ring-bark them.')

He resorted to teaching Latin, Greek and English at local private school, Peterhouse, and water-divining, before 'I stumbled on grapes. Well, I wasn't completely clueless. I knew what a grape was. We visited France when I was a kid, 1933; fished for *écrevisses* near Figeac. Wine – well, it was sanctions time here. People would have drunk anything.' So he planted the vines and began to make the wine.

'Mad, perhaps, but isn't sanity a comparative term? Our first crushers were six babies' baths, on the front terrace, with a worker in each.' For fermentation, winery

Humfrey and Peter Raynor make Fig Hill Chardonnay and much besides near Wedza.

operations moved to the bathroom. Where the juice proved it was strong stuff indeed. 'Buggered the bath. Took the enamel right off it.'

Thus began the rise of Zimbabwe's largest private grower. The Raynors' 80 well-groomed hectares in the Wedza area, each row finished with a rose bush, churn out both highs and lows. There's the individually vinified Fig Hill Chardonnay. There's 600,000 litres of what son Humfrey distinguished as 'proper wine'. And then there's the big end product – 3.5 million litres of 'sugar water', the seconds and thirds we'd met in Bulawayo. Three tankers a day shuttle in and out during the winemaking season.

Humfrey, big, beefy, and bonhomous, was wearing shorts and two bullet holes in his leg. These were souvenirs of a recent snatch-and-grab attack in Harare. Relatively, the 'little visit' war veterans had paid the farm had been no trouble at all. 'Your place is too small,' they'd concluded, and left. But Peter Raynor wasn't so easily persuaded that this was the end of the matter. 'Mugabe let slip the dogs of war,' he insisted. (Such talk went well with his prophet-of-doom long white beard.) 'He started a fire, now it's out of control.'

But who would really have known, sitting at the Raynors' table drinking an inky Cahors? (Peter was very severe on the quality of local wine – particularly the whites. Rubbish, he said, even of his own Fig Hill.) We had roast pork with crackling and many vegetables, excellent local cheese, and luscious butter and cream for the apple crumble from the farm's four Guernseys.

Soon, Peter would be off to England to visit his cousin, Colin Gillespie, founder of a leading English vineyard at North Wootton in Somerset. He planned to ring the bells at Wells Cathedral. Find a literary agent. And come home to the thatched house on the hill overlooking savannah, thorn trees and vineyards, to 'hang on until' things settle down. However, as he'd predicted, the heat of the land-claim process had intensified. By the end of the year the Raynors had been 'listed', and they picked their 2002 Chardonnay, Cabernet Franc and Chenin under threat of take-over. In the neighbourhood, 31 farms had been 'occupied'.

An aristocrat in Africa

Our next lunch was about the same distance from Harare – 75 kilometres – but in a different direction, down the Mazowe river valley, with winegrower Helin de Burbure de Wesenbeek. He's a lanky, languid Belgian of an uncertain age – well camouflaged by longish floppy hair in an autumnal tint, a youthful giggle, and a penchant for nightclubs and raves.

He arrived in Bulawayo after the Second World War, aged 16: 'Rhodesia was a paradise.' Changing his first name to Charles so his new schoolfriends could manage it, he then sportingly accepted their mangling of his surname. No one uses the Wesenbeek bit – the name of his family château on the outskirts of Brussels – or his title of 'Chevalier'.

For 50 years he's been Charles de Burberry. 'Alias Mackintosh,' he giggled.

A renowned young ladies' man, Charles might look as well-preserved as he does because he neither drinks nor smokes, despite Tavydale Farm's 20 hectares of vineyards and 400 hectares of tobacco lands. Why the grapes? 'Wine is the most romantic crop, and there was this land next to the river which wasn't good for tobacco.' He was also proving a point. When some South African experts dismissed Zimbabwean wine-growing Charles was on his mettle.

'They were mad! I had seen vines growing very well in people's gardens. The wine, of course, that was something else. I said to myself that if René Paynter could do it so badly and get so excited about it, well, I could do better!'

He study-toured France, Italy and South Africa, bringing back Chenin cuttings from 100-year-old Cape vines. The first crop in 1968 was trucked 500 kilometres to Monis in Bulawayo – 'I think then the longest distance in the world!' – in 44 gallon drums. The grapes – Tinta Barroca the latest – still do a long-distance haul, in an open truck, but now to Mukuyu Winery near Marondera.

The core business, in 84 red-brick barns, faintly dark satanic mill-looking, was tobacco: air-cured Burley – for the sort of kick and drag demanded by those who wear berets or Stetsons or a bush hat like Charles – flue-cured Virginia for the rest. The air was pungent with the smell of smokes-in-progress.

Outside tractors moved matronly through a shoulder-high sea of viridian green. Pickers bunched the ripe leaves onto stick-and-wire crosses, then dashed to the tractors, like standard bearers late for a religious procession. The hard-hatted supervisor brandished a walkie-talkie. She might have cracked a whip in the old days; now she was fuming because her status symbol, her authority totem, was no longer exclusive. In a bid to ratchet up productivity, Charles had allocated a radio to another supervisor.

The farm's 100 hectares of maize were being shared with a group of war veterans. The rows they'd permitted Charles to plant were as neat as braids. The vets' rows, planted with government aid money and French aid tractors, were quite the opposite. But Charles was remarkably sanguine.

'Our situation in Zimbabwe is not as precarious as in Africa in general. We are very resilient. Look, my grandparents owned 10,000 hectares of land in Romania, and lost it all, billions. No one must think it only happens here. My property in Brussels has been declared an historical building; now I can't do what I would like with it. Effectively, that has been taken away from me….'

Religious experiences

It was time to leave Harare, but fuel remained a problem. The week we arrived there'd been a trickle of petrol but the diesel had run dry; now it was vice-versa. There wasn't a drop of the unleaded stuff; pump attendants cunningly bent pieces of wire to gain entry to Green tanks such as ours. Now the petrol queues featured empty cars, and the attendants were earning alternative tips: for fuel-alerts by phone.

Spot-the-tanker had become a new national activity; seeing one of these precious vehicles a near-religious experience, leading to a general alert by cellphone: 'Follow the blessed vision'. Soon a conga-line of up to 600 cars would be snaking through town, tailing the tanker to its destination. But no tankers had been sighted in the past few days. (This was before Muammar Gadaffi came to Mugabe's rescue and poured in Libyan fuel.) Pumps weren't pumping. They were wrapped in mournful black plastic, sporting signs that read: SORRY. Our jerry cans didn't hold enough for the circuitous route we planned. Should we head straight home? Our reserves should (with luck) get us to the border....

Such feebleness was roundly scorned by the wine people we'd arranged to see. On no account were we to take the easy way out. They would find fuel for us. And they did, passing us from one friend with a few litres to spare to another, starting with a miraculous full tank from a benefactor in the natural Prozac business – Zimbabwe's biggest grower of hypericum or St John's wort.

Rural Ruwa, close to Harare, was our first destination. Here, on an earlier trip, we'd visited tiny Bushman Rock winery, owned by Rick Passaportis and his wife Sally. Rick had been a military adviser to the Sultan of Oman; his father Chief of Staff of the Rhodesian Army. And *his* father came to Zimbabwe from Cyprus as a 13-year-old, via neighbouring Mozambique. He had no passport, spoke nothing but Greek and could only repeat what immigration officials were shouting to him – Passport please! – which they mistook as his name. Passaportis it became and remains.

Sally's chief worry seemed to be keeping Witness Sakulu happy. He'd been making wines for the previous owners, the Bianchini family, for 15 years – about 65,000 litres a year, filled into large recycled bottles – for the Harare restaurant trade. His ingenious winery featured a converted tobacco press, drying racks made out of chicken-wire netting, and a drain fashioned from olive oil tins. Sally had enrolled for courses – and had asked consultant Clive Hartnell for help.

Just as well, perhaps, because Witness was a winemaker who had never tasted wine. He was a teetotal preacher – complete with prophetic beard – in an African Zionist church.

The garagiste of Ruwa

David Kirkpatrick would melt into the deep countryside and bar-tabacs of *la France profonde* without causing the slightest inquisitive twitch of a village curtain. He looks the part, in the sort of black cap passed on from Lenin to the French student firebrands of the 60s. He sounds the part – wry, dry, worldly. Here in Ruwa he was waging an elemental battle with a patch of vines.

It was the Zimbabwean wine struggle in microcosm: the enthusiasm, and in some cases – David's certainly – the passion, versus the depressing realities. A love-hate relationship. 'This physiological ripeness thing,' he sighed. 'What is it? All I know is I don't get it!'

He followed world wine affairs minutely, and dreamed of a land of plenty *vin ordinaire*. Regrettably, even on that modest scale, Zimbabwe didn't really rate. 'I used to hear Monty doing a vertical tasting of Mukuyu wines – on the radio, can you imagine – and I'd say: "Come on! You can't be serious!" But you had to admire his enthusiasm.'

David Kirkpatrick consults John on the patch of vines which is his no longer – it has been 'redistributed'.

A small digression here: Monty was ex-Senior Police Superintendent Montgomery Friendship, Commander of Zimbabwe's Presidential Mounted Guard, once to be found clopping alongside former President Canaan Banana's motorcade dressed in jodhpurs and spiked pith helmet. Latterly, he'd handed in his spurs to become a man of affairs and local wine guru. TV, print, radio – Monty was seen and heard everywhere. He concocted many sonorous phrases on his houseboat, the *Water Scorpion*, on Lake Kariba.

Resplendent in what he described as 'the toil position' – behind a PC on the sundeck – in nothing but moustache and swimming trunks, topping up his creative juices with a bottomless flute of Gosset champagne… Monty's interpretation of the job of wine-reporting was altogether fresh. We saw him in this office ourselves. While he tapped the keyboard elephants wandered past, considerately avoiding the houseboat's gangplank. A pride of lions patrolled the fringes of a herd of buffalo. After a quick, quiet, gold-black-vermilion African brochure sunset, Monty closed down his PC and had a little more champagne.

Just another view from Monty's houseboat on Lake Kariba.

Later he confided what we'd already noticed: 'I don't drink Zim wines myself. Generally.' (He has a cellar of European classics.) But he's a loyalist and had recently, with great stealth, organised a Zimbabwean wine tasting in South Africa. The tasters, including a Cape Wine Master and a Burgundy vineyard owner, didn't recognise any of the wines. Four scored an average of 15 or more points (Very Good); none rated below 13 (Good). 'There was much surprise when I revealed the wines' origin,' Monty reported. Some said that had they known it was a Zimbabwean tasting they wouldn't have come.

The luxury of refusing to drink local was one David Kirkpatrick couldn't afford. So he'd planted his own vineyard – in the wistful hope that it might become the next prodigy of the wine world, or at the very least, cut down his drinks bill. It represented a quintessentially Zimbabwean blend of determination, defiance and optimism. But he wasn't happy. He wanted a second opinion. We strode out through the long grass.

A minimalist weeding programme – the biodynamic approach? – appeared to operate. The Merlot and Cabernet were spaced to accommodate a landing strip. Poor soil, leafroll virus, voracious bul-bul birds and distinctly alternative pruning and trellising methods had slashed yields. We mentioned some new thinking in this field; David had read about it in *Decanter*. But he wasn't sure it met his needs.

'I'm just trying to get a few more f***ing grapes off the blighters.'

His winery was an extension of the tin-roofed, lean-to garage, sheltering an eclectic collection of near-vintage vehicles awaiting attention or further maturation. Parked next to a derelict fridge painted with marijuana-like leaves was a saucy pink Renault, both relics (surely) of the Kirkpatricks' bell-bottom, flower-child days when they were known as the grooviest couple in Harare. There was a mid-60s Volvo saloon, an aged Land Rover, two old tractors, a lorry, a rusting trailer. We wondered, briefly, about the similarities between this setting and those of California's hot new 'garage' wines.

Squeezing through the used-car lot we came to the press, operated via an old Nissan truck tyre jack. The pantry-sized winery was thoroughly padlocked. David jingled a large set of keys to open up the valuables: a motley array of plastic containers housing recently fermented, inky young wine. Air conditioning was via an open window. There were kitchen sieves and a colander ('to separate the skins') – and buckets of water. There was none on tap; he carted it in. A handbook, *Progressive Winemaking*, perched next to a tin marked Rat Poison. On the wall was an inspirational – or not – map of *La Route des Vins de Bergerac en Périgord*.

'This is when I lose control of the stuff,' he admitted, instantly destroying any resemblance to an authentic *garagiste*. No self-respecting Frenchman (or Californian) would ever exhibit such uncertainty. We recommended a quick racking, airing, and splashing the wine across some copper, an old trick to remove off-odours. Taking no chances, David later siphoned the wine *through* a 4-metre copper pipe; his wife Norma at the other end filled up 2-litre carafes.

'What a bloody business, wine all over the place, hands stained purple. But the smell's gone,' he reported. Such is the devotion of a true amateur of wine. There would indeed be a vintage of Ruwa Estate Red 2001. Limited release, of course. Like the fuel.

But what of 2002? Just before the harvest, David e-mailed: *We're f****d.* Their property, despite being zoned 'residential' and therefore officially not a candidate for take-over and redistribution, had become a casualty of the notorious Zimbabwean land-claim process. It was pegged out into 12 small plots, and never mind its core activity, a workshop where black artists and craftsmen were making their living from carving and painting.

The Champagne of Africa?

Zimbabwe's star winemaker, jaunty jolly, switched-on Sam Pfidzayi and his second in command Nelia Kanyasa are the creative powers behind Mukuyu winery - named after the Shona word for a fig tree - up the road from Ruwa, near Marondera. This property's 90 hectare vineyards, too, were 'listed' for take-over in 2001. Sam managed to get the listing revoked, but it was touch and go whether the country's leading wine producer – Sam also advises a string of supplier-farmers – would survive the land-grab frenzy.

The operation is sizeable: 185,000 cases (or nearly 3,000 tonnes of grapes) a year; 20,000 cases of 'quality', 165,000 cases of 'average, commercial' wine, and Sam's employers, Cairns Holdings, didn't expect him to squeeze grapes to extinction into 'seconds' and 'thirds', unlike his opposite numbers in African Distillers. Mukuyu was a rarity in Zimbabwe – a dedicated winery, no distilling. For the time being.

He gave us the lowdown in his authentically gloomy tasting room. 'You know the game, the winemaker can do only so much if the fruit's not up to it; our goal simply has to be good, clean, drinkable.' He laughed ruefully. 'My Australian classmates came to visit me here and said: 'What are you *doing*? If we had to work here we'd go home after a day!' I know… but who would want to make wine in Australia? It's so easy, you can't fail. Here it's a challenge, every vintage, it's all against you.'

Sam is a graduate of the New World's most famous wine-finishing school, Roseworthy. He was there in 1992, and had recently returned to give incredulous students a lecture on the struggle that is winemaking in Zimbabwe at the best of times. 'They couldn't believe we could make wine at all, in such conditions!'

Zimbabwean vintages seem to vary from the catastrophic (drought, 1991) to the less bad, with inevitable heavy downpours before and during the harvest. Sometimes (1998) there'd be a monstrous hailstorm. 'The vineyards were looking so beautiful; I was so proud of my canopies. Then the hail. In the middle of our summer, can you believe it? There was so much ice around, we could have been skiing down the rows.'

2001 had been a rare year: the Chardonnay, Sauvignon Blanc and all the reds came in ripe enough not to require chaptalisation. But later in the season, with an array of other varieties still to pick, the deluge had come; rot had set in.

'I don't know what to do. A rain dance? A sun dance? What I need is a waterproof spray!'

The cheery masochism got more complicated. Sam did his thesis on viticultural and climatic conditions in Zimbabwe. Conclusion: Bulawayo and Rusape, almost at opposite ends of the country, southwest and northeast, were most suitable for vines. But he'd ended up working in Marondera. Humid, hot, sandy soils, average rainfall 700–800 millimetres. a year. It's better country for cattle, and orange and yellow chanterelles.

One of Sam's local names is Mr Clean: the one who doesn't like shit in the vineyards. He spends so much time in them that his wife says: 'Take your bed, go and sleep there.'

N. DOBROPOULOS
WINERY
NO ENTRY
USAPINDE PANO

Top: *Pani Dobropoulos's
tobacco shed-turned
winery; Pani's imposing
trellising system; Gavin
and Sharon Patterson;
Monty brings up anoth-
er bottle of Gewürz
from his floating cellar.*
Middle: *Zim's leading
winemaker, Mukuyu's
Sam Pfidzayi; with his
assistant Nelia
Kanyasa; Ruwa Estate
garagistes: David and
Norma Kirkpatrick and
grandson; Gladys
Jongeling, maker and
keeper of Zim's highest
vineyard; Mount
Chinaka Vineyard.*
Bottom: *The Oldest
Winery in Zim; Mauro
and Marie Sacconi; The
Patterson farmyard:
lug-boxes for the
harvest and views
across the Odzi Valley;
Dr Arthur Dunkley,
owner of Mount
Chinaka Vineyard.*

He's been battling against a legacy of grape varieties planted for little other reason than that 'there were cuttings available' since taking over from two German oenologists, Gerd Stepp and Lothar Grimm, as chief winemaker in 1997. Passionate about Shiraz and other classic varieties, he began importing these for his growers to convert their vineyards from 'terrible' table grapes like Seneca.

'But vineyard management here is not about what's in a textbook, it's about what actually happens. We have to do everything differently. Really manipulate.'

University of Zimbabwe graduate Edson Gambara, a grower for Mukuyu, had recently been drafted in to the viticultural portfolio, and he and Sam were experimenting, coaxing Cabernet to bear twice a year. The second crop, ripening in the dry, cool month of June, had delivered 'excellent quality'. But still not good enough to warrant oak barrels. 'Much too expensive,' Sam sighed. 'I'm always fighting with the accountants – it's part of my job, I even enjoy it sometimes, but there's no foreign exchange now, except for essential spares.' Oak chips provide his vanilla and spice notes.

Now this restless innovator had come up with a smart new idea: a fizzy red from Cabernet Franc, slightly sweet-dosed à la Australia's popular sparkling Shiraz, and Italy's Lambrusco. Grapes for sparkling wines need to be picked early anyway – so dodging the heaviest rains – and the combination of perky bubble and sweetness would cover a multitude of sins. A brainwave but plain good craftsmanship too. A Mukuyu Brut – Blanc de Blanc Chardonnay sparkling – was already selling well: champagne authority Tom Stevenson compared it with 'a fresh, clean, fruity Veuve du Vernay *méthode champenoise*'. We thought the red could turn out even better, and could already see the slogan: Zimbabwe, the Champagne of Africa?

Mindful of the struggle to make wine here, the French connection mightn't be altogether inappropriate. Champagne was always a battleground. So too the former Yugoslavia, where Sam's assistant trained. Tall and imposing in gumboots and jeans, Nelia Kanyasa is fluent in Serbo-Croat. Of course, she told us, she'd had to learn. How else would she have got through her 5-year scholarship, in a town 75 kilometres outside Belgrade, and score her BSc in vini/viticulture?

Maize, mangoes, guavas and groundnuts grew on her family's farm; she'd never tasted wine before she went to Eastern Europe, and had the coin she spun landed heads, she might have specialised in flowers rather than vines. She arrived in the middle of a blizzard. 'I had never seen snow except on a Christmas card.' She was terribly homesick. 'People would come up to me and touch my skin and my hair. They had never seen a black woman before. One asked me if I really had feelings. But then I discovered polenta – it was like our *sadza* at home.' She soon fell in love with wine and travelled and tasted in Europe. At Mukuyu, she cuts herself no slack in the cellar: 'We have no women here, we're all men.'

Arthur, Gladys and the secret mountain vineyard

Another formidable woman was our next call, but before meeting Gladys Jongeling we had a session with her boss, Arthur Dunkley. Under his khaki bush hat he looked nothing like an eminent surgeon. Not that he needed the hat: the veranda where we drank coffee was wide and shady. It was what it suggested: authentic vinegrower not some dabbling dilettante of a doc. And it was also to guard against any jumps to the latter conclusion that Arthur had for five years stayed as secretive as a mole about his wine-farming venture at Juliasdale, in the northeast Nyanga highlands, 180 kilometres from Harare, near the Mozambique border.

This is cool, misty mountain country, a natural for forestry, apples and pears, trout-farming and sheep, hectares of export and wild flowers. St Joseph's lilies, barely affordable by the single stem, bloom here in great white sheets; indigenous yellow arum lilies mass in every gorge. In spring, it's more spectacular than Vermont in the fall, locals insist: mountains ablaze with the new orange leaves of the msasa trees. It's also prime hunting ground for porcini (*Boletus edulis*); four tonnes of *Boletus* a week are trucked out of the pine forests by Italian entrepreneurs during the season, and flown lucratively to Europe (local hunter-gatherers are paid the equivalent of about US$2.20/£1.50 a kilo).

In this remote, rugged area Arthur Dunkley had established his vineyard. And to his evident dismay, David Kirkpatrick tracked him down for us. 'How did you find out about my vineyard? No one here knew!' he fired off, as if to uncover some sort of Deep Throat. (We'd heard from some hikers who'd stumbled across it by chance.) He'd not wanted a word whispered until he was sure he wasn't making a fool of himself, trying to accommodate two different ambitions in one patch of land. But a brilliant harvest unseals any owner's lips, and he was soon in full flight.

'I'd always wanted to own a mountain, and I'd always wanted to own a vineyard.'

He bought Mount Chinaka in 1995, to run his dogs and fly his falcons; the vines were planted in 1997. He reasoned that what convention saw as a negative – the cold climate – could be a positive. The cooler and longer the growing period, the better the chance of ripe, healthy grapes. And so we found: all the vineyards we'd visited at the beginning of March had finished their harvesting in the rain, picking grapes, whatever their ripeness, before they rotted. Here in Nyanga, the Cabernet fruit was still hanging on the vines, sweet and luscious.

Arthur was delighted. 'It was a dream,' he said, 'but also an idea. I said to myself that we had to look at wine differently here, recognise our shortcomings from the start.'

The economic dire straits had forced him to postpone plans for his own boutique winery. Sam Pfidzayi was handling the first crop, at Mukuyu, and the lights switched on when he described the Sauvignon Blanc grapes: 'You'll be knocked out!' So we were. Impressed by the Chardonnay (eventually for a Chablis style), that Sauvignon

Blanc, the Cabernet Sauvignon (looking good), the Merlot and – Arthur's latest joy – Australian Shiraz.

There's enough mountainside here for 12 hectares 'with quite remarkable position and views,' Arthur said, inarguably. Range after range of mountains in fading shades of denim roll into a haze of distant horizon; up close, there are great balancing boulders of granite; msasas, umbrella thorns and giant cabbage trees… the essence of the African highlands. In fact, this vineyard, at 1800 metres, beats Europe's loftiest, in the Spanish Canaries, very handily.

Arthur, in the bleakest of times, was still optimistic: 'If things stabilise… we'll put in cold fermentation… only big barrels because I prefer my wines unattended by additional flavours… it'll be very exciting… Zimbabwe is full of people, black and white, with the pioneering sort of energy to get this sort of thing going.' Like Gladys Jongeling, maker and keeper of this extraordinary vineyard, hewer of wood, breaker of rocks.

At Nyanga's World's View site, where the angle was wide and deep enough to show a whole array of weather systems – an electric storm above, sunlight here, cloudbursts there, rain on the horizon – we'd established where we were in relation to a couple of other vineyards in Africa: 1550 kilometres from Madagascar; 3100 kilometres from Kenya. Oregon, where Gladys hails from, was definitely off the map. Her broad American accent and big laugh boomed around the boulders surrounding the vines. But under yet another bush hat, in worker's blue trousers, white T-shirt and bush-whacking boots, she looked entirely in place.

She and Africa first connected in Mozambique, where she arrived as a young medical missionary. Forty years on, most spent in Zimbabwe, she'd seen it all – tottering colonialism, shaky freedom, and, in her former fields of microbiology and haematology, terrible evidence of the double plagues of poverty and AIDS. But if anyone has developed traction in Zimbabwean soil, it's Gladys. She is the sort of truly imposing figure that used to grace the prows of Viking ships. Waiting for us to ford a stream and bump and grind up the rocky road to the vineyard, she looked as capable as the 4x4 she was leaning on.

Her retirement from a fulltime hospital job, where she'd worked with Arthur Dunkley, and his wine intentions, had been a fortunate coincidence. Gladys and her team heaved aside tonnes of boulders; uprooted forests of wattles; and clawed the first 4 hectares of vines out of raw granite and bush. Teaching herself viticulture from scratch – I knew nothing! Just how to drink wine! – she passed the principles on to her right-hand young man, Kudsie. He now prunes, suckers and trellises as competently as he lets fly with catapults to stone the Chardonnay-loving crows.

What about other 'visitors', as farmers delicately dubbed land-invaders? Gladys had just been elected head of 'security' for the Juliasdale area, and said: 'We're expecting trouble.' Surely, we thought, nothing that a woman who can move a bit of a mountain can't handle.

You are the ones

The temperature rose and the humidity intensified as we drove down from the cool mountains of Nyanga to Green Valley Vineyards, in Odzi valley. Towering folds of clouds outlined in streaks of gold and grey floated above these 55 hectares of vines towards a horizon fringed by thorn trees and the blue Jenya hills. It was a scene set in a garden of

temptation: African Distillers was making inviting offers to all its embattled, endangered winefarm managers, urging them to remain on the Zimbabwean front line. To continue pumping Afdis (an associate of South African liquor giant Distell) with its alcoholic life-blood.

Will the dream to make Green Valley Vineyards the centre of an Odzi wine route become a reality?

And this was a front line. Manager-winemaker Gavin Patterson, tall, strapping, bespectacled, and his wife Sharon, as slim and striking as a model, both in their twenties, with two young children, had been under siege – physical, emotional – for months.

It was quiet when we went to bed, except for the mosquitoes, a concerto of tree frogs and the obstinate trilling of fiery-necked nightjars. There were five Patterson dogs and a whole pack next door where Will Powell, a young Englishman, was training sniffer-dogs to detect land mines. His finished products were deployed all over the troubled world, including Kosovo. There were fences, locked gates, emergency radios. There were undoubtedly guns. But was it safe?

Just a stone's throw from where we slept, Gavin Patterson had been seriously beaten up by a gang of attackers. They broke two of his ribs, but he'd been lucky. 'There was a plot to kill me. They wanted me off the farm, so they could take over.'

'They' were the war vets who'd invaded the farm. Sharon described one of their leaders – 'staggering-drunk and blowing cigarette smoke into everyone's face' – warning Gavin he would be 'six foot under if you don't watch out'. And another, stating that Zimbabwe had been settled by British criminals and that whites should all be killed or driven out of the country now. It wasn't possible to pass the buck to African Distillers. 'When we said we weren't the owners, the vets said: "You are the ones!"'

These verbal barrages had taken place on the Pattersons' veranda, a bamboo-shaded terrace with a fountain and barbecue; two ponies grazed beside a dam; palms, roses and a tree heavy with avocadoes fringed the lawn.

Sharon Patterson reacted to such remarks by issuing challenges of her own. She counted herself a war casualty: in 1978 when she was 5, her father was shot and killed in an ambush set by guerrillas in the Nyanga mountains. Now she'd written a blazingly accusatory letter to the provincial governor, enumerating her bona fides: the workers' babies she'd delivered, the mouth-to-mouth resuscitations, the midnight dashes to hospital with desperately ill children in her car, and more.

'In my opinion, formed from living with the masses not above them, life under our government has deteriorated to the point of existence and not living… and we all deserve better.'

The war veterans had built grass huts, and planted a few patches of maize around the vines. But crowds were no longer dancing outside the gates, baying *'Bloo-dy-Patt-er-son, bloo-dy-Patt-er-son.'* A fragile modus vivendi held. Green Valley had just got through its latest harvest. How long would the lull last?

Queen of the vineyard

At a nearby vineyard, the sign outside read: Beware of the Dogs and the Lion.

Strictly speaking it should have been Lioness. She, Queenie, was prowling about a vast open-air paddock bordering the vines. The ultimate African night-watchwoman. 'She thinks she's a dog,' said her owner, Pani Dobropoulos. 'She only roars at night, because that's when the dogs bark. They have their supper together – she likes dog chunks, but her favourites are beef and fresh impala. She refuses to touch sheep, goat, zebra or waterbuck.'

No one except Pani had dared put Queenie's foodie fads to a personal test. 'I came back from town once and all my staff were up in the rafters. Queenie had dug herself out under the fence. Another time she got hold of my brand new motorbike. I came back from a party and it was lying in pieces in the yard.'

There were no war veterans on Pani's farm.

He stopped us outside the winery, a converted, red-brick tobacco shed. 'Listen, I wasn't trained in anything… no degrees *whatsoever.'* But he turns out 325,000 litres of wine a year, from 26 hectares of vines, which include the ubiquitous white 'Issor' (Raisin Blanc), and Muscat Hambourg, and now also Chardonnay and Shiraz. Most of the wine goes in bulk to African Distillers, but he sells a lot from the cellar door.

The press was a massive, mean piece of equipment, home-made from cannibalised D8 bulldozer parts and a Nissan truck chassis. The no-frills (whatsoever!) winery was cool and cleaner than most; the tasting room dark and obviously rarely opened.

Ceremoniously, Pani pulled out a wine made by his late father in 1983. 'He added something to it, I don't know what.' It was light amber, mildly sweet, the spicier edges of Muscat Hambourg well nipped and tucked, mellifluous, balanced in a way very unusual in Zimbabwe. 'Maybe I need to treat it with more respect. Perhaps we should even drink it,' Pani joked. 'Actually, I think it was a bit of honey my father put in.' So it wasn't altogether wine. But it was certainly a delicious Zimbabwean drink. His vineyards were different, too, featuring huge tree trunks for trellising anchor posts, and Queenie gazing watchfully through the fence. Pani's Shiraz and Merlot vine cuttings came from Israel, and in a few years, he would have commercial quantities.

Bacci: Italian kisses

The Odzi valley was once known as Rhotalia, and Mauro Sacconi, the ranking member of its previously numerous Italian community, was waiting for us. His wife Marie, who comes from one of Zimbabwe's Afrikaner settler families but looks vividly Italian, with long espresso-dark hair, had prepared her famous lasagne and focaccia. Our motorcade hurtled off over dusty farm roads, past an old red-brick Methodist church, recently commandeered by war veterans who'd smashed its Italian stained glass windows. The roof caved in but they'd thatched one corner for shelter.

Mauro was hosing down his winery – 'the oldest in Zimbabwe' – under a giant eucalyptus, on the last day of the harvest. His 500,000 litres of wine would soon be collected by tankers from Harare. 'We're still in the Stone Age here,' he joked, pointing out wax-lined cement fermenting tubs and the sunken pit around the grape de-stalker in a tin-roofed winery converted from stables by his father.

Giovanni Sacconi arrived from Italy in 1957. Now 88, he'd never visited home again, never left his adopted African country. A virtual recluse, he didn't learn to speak English either, managing on a mixture of Italian, Swahili and Fanagalo (a fusion of Southern African languages commonly used in the mines). He'd picked up Swahili in Tanganyika, before the Second World War, and left his post as an oenology lecturer at Padua University the day he was made an offer by Dr Rossi Compostella, a farmer in this valley.

Giovanni had invented a name for a variety he didn't recognise – inverting the name of his employer to Issor. It turned out to be ordinary old Raisin Blanc, still the country's main white wine grape, but not before causing all sorts of confusion. We'd hoped to meet him, the communication gap to be bridged by Swahili (John's second language), but it was his siesta-time, so 14-year-old granddaughter Deanna filled in some historical details. She told us her grandfather (Nono in Italian) was the first person to grow grapes and make wine commercially in Zimbabwe. When the wine was ready, people travelled from all over Zimbabwe with their own containers to buy Italian-style wine directly from the farm.

Mauro was surprisingly relaxed about the tobacco he'd lost the week before – six barns of it, after a storm took out the power lines – and the drought of 1991, which took out 40 hectares of vines. (He'd replanted 22 hectares, mainly reds, including Shiraz and Tinta Barroca.) Besides such calamities, the war veterans encamped outside the old winery were no trouble at all.

'They give me the Zanu-PF [pro-Mugabe] clenched-fist salute in the mornings and I blow them back kisses. It works fine, except when they occasionally shove boulders onto the track to make roadblocks.'

The Odzi wine route

At the Pattersons' that night the indulgences continued: farm-reared lamb with a very smart 98 Shiraz-Durif blend from Campbells in Rutherglen, Australia. And before dinner, a few sniffs and gargles of Green Valley's just-finished vintage.

Odzi had a relatively good year in 2001; the heaviest downpours came after most varieties were harvested. But the young whites – Sauvignon Blanc, Colombard, Clairette Blanche and Issor – were almost eerily staid. The reds had more bounce: a mildly fruity Ruby Cabernet and a Cabernet Sauvignon, both chaptalised to about 13%, were to disappear into Stapleford's 'Private Cellar' Cordon Rouge with reds from every other region. But there was one potential cracker, from a mystery variety locally known as Ferrazza, after one of the early Italian farmers here. It was very deep and inky, with a solid texture and berry-and-chocolate flavours. And it had ripened enough to reach an unusually powerful 13.8%. A tall red poppy in rather a weedy allotment. 'Next vintage I'm going to vinify this separately, traditionally, probably in barrels,' said Gavin.

At dawn the next morning we inspected his prize Smart-Dyson and Scott-Henry trellises, developed in Australia to optimise yields and flavour simultaneously. 'It's not a viticultural Eden here, but the challenges are part of the attraction.' He was thinking beyond the huge yields of 15–20 tonnes per hectare to quality estate-bottled wines. Which, the future permitting, would be for sale from the Madhara Winery, a rustic, small thatched barn on the farm with oxwagon wheel-rim windows, rough-plastered walls, and lots of spaces for tasting, eating, partying.

Sharon runs the ballet school in Mutare, and was planning tango lessons on the deck, looking over to vineyards and mountains. The old homestead adjoining was being renovated into a country lodge... nothing unimaginative about the Pattersons' ideas for the headquarters of the forthcoming Odzi Wine Route.

The war vets' huts were very close. One emerged with a catapult, raised the flag, and gazed up into the trees, looking for breakfast. 'Pigeons, lilac-breasted rollers, sparrows too. Because of the fuel shortages, supplies from Zanu-PF aren't as regular as they used to be,' Gavin explained.

Topping up our jerrycans at both the Patterson and Sacconi farms, we headed home.

Back home

On paper, it was six hours to the South African border. But the BBC had reported seven bridges washed away along this road. We might have to go cross-country and into South

Africa via Botswana. Hoping we'd find more petrol en route.

We bumped over the potholes in Mutare – filled with bricks because the country had run out of tar. Like most African border towns, it looked sleepy, but was full of smugglers, and the markets were throbbing, particularly the one dedicated to clothes donated to Mozambique's flood victims. Sharon Patterson and some of her friends told us they were kitted out from head to toe – down to their Playtex bras – in designer-label gear from this market. They explained: Mozambican flood victims themselves were exchanging donated clothes for money. This is how the international aid system worked.

Near the border, we bought palm-frond baskets woven with messages: *Noone is Perfect.* and another: *God Nose.*

The young salesman was pathetically grateful. 'There are no tourists,' he said mournfully. 'My president is not leading carefully.'

Three bridges remained down, but wooden planks had been thrown over the gaps, and we were on the border of the Kruger Park by sunset.

Just in time. A vintage later and a journey along the Zimbabwean wine route would have been mission impossible. Violence and land seizures had escalated, mass starvation loomed, foreign journalists had become objects of intense suspicion. We could imagine how happily the State Intelligence Service would have bought our unlikely story – but Officer, we're just here for the wine! No rain since the downpours during the 2001 harvest had terminally affected the national maize crop, but meant disease-free grapes for winegrowers. Amid all the turmoil, 2002 turned out to be one of the best in years, especially for red wines, reported both Gladys Jongeling and Sam Pfidzayi.

'I just hope the tourists come to drink them,' Sam added.

NAMIBIA

Welcome to the bush-desert winery in Omaruru.

Had we got to Omaruru a day earlier, or a day later, we'd have missed the Namibian wine harvest. In the vintage of 2002, 12 February was D-Day for mechanic, mineral and water drilling expert and, lately, wine farmer Helmuth Kluge at Kristall Kellerei, the one and only winery in this country nearly four times the size of Great Britain.

He and his team had started picking in the 4.5-hectare vineyards early that morning. They were loading the antique tractor – a 1946 Deutz which Helmuth found abandoned on a Namibian beach, just the steering wheel sticking out of the sand, and had meticulously restored. It was now trailing wicker baskets piled with sweet, mini-berried bunches of grapes back and forth from the riverside vineyard to the tiny, immaculately clean winery a few hundred metres away, past a prickly pear plantation (for Helmuth's Cactus Schnapps) and the asparagus patch. In season he slaps a special label featuring these edible spears onto his Colombard, and serves both to visitors as astonished as we were to find either here on the edge of the Namib desert, in Africa's most arid country south of the Sahara.

Machine man

This was Helmuth's ninth harvest at Omaruru, and he'd long graduated from his first amateurish attempts. Then, he admitted, he made 'telephone wine' – on the line to friends in South Africa every step of the way. ('Horrible' is Helmuth's own description of his first vintage. 'I made a lot of mistakes. Spent a lot of learning money.') Now the process flowed as smoothly as cream, and Helmuth was on his cellphone only to summon his wife, Uschi, for a photograph. By nightfall, the whole harvest had been delivered to his little home-made press outside the winery, and thence to the small stainless-steel tanks – also handmade, 'I'm a machine man' – within.

Easy pickings in more ways than one – the little oasis of Omaruru may appear to be in the middle of nowhere, but in this vast, empty country (only 1.7 million people), it's also in the middle of everywhere. Strategic, as Helmuth said. It's where all the tourist buses pull in for lunch en route from Swakopmund on the Atlantic coast, and the capital, Windhoek, to the shimmering salt pan of Etosha ('the big white place') National Park, one of the great game reserves of the world. It's a mainline station for Namibia's Desert Express cross-country train; Helmuth uses the local school bus to pick up passengers and transport them to the winery.

A tasting of wine, brandy, schnapps and Rappa (in deference to new EU regulations, he has dropped the G) costs 15 Namibian dollars (about US$3/£2). It's the most unexpected and extraordinary pitstop in Namibia, and such a raging success that he's now sold his borehole-sinking and mineral exploration business to concentrate on wine. Helmuth laughed merrily, as well he might: 'It's a bit of a goldmine, really, and I never, ever expected it!'

But. There has to be a significant 'but' in a climate that veers from a severely frosty minus 12°C in winter to a searing 40°C in summer (it was a mere 30 when we visited). And in a place so chronically short of water – 45 millimetres of rain only in an exceptionally wet year. The grey clouds which gathered mid-afternoon looked promising to us; Helmuth took one look skywards and dismissed them. It hadn't rained here for two years and it wasn't about to. 'There's no weight in those clouds', he said, 'we're in trouble.'

The Omaruru river was bone-dry. Its underground reserves were almost exhausted. The powerful pumps operating a massive well Helmuth had sunk near the river were idle. They must have been, at the best of times, a bone of contention with the neighbours and the townsfolk downstream – that classic French tale of water-rights and village-feuds, *Jean de Florette*, transplanted to Africa. Especially since Helmuth wasn't only drip-irrigating his vineyards; he was also bottling his own brand of water, which he maintained was the best in the world, hence the label Brilliant.

Now he planned to rip out the enormous blue-gum (eucalyptus) trees which fringe his vineyards – they swallow 3000 litres of water every four hours in drought conditions. But unless it rained, even this emergency measure wouldn't help. Were we observing our first and last Namibian vintage? In which case, the neighbours might be spared some of the other idiosyncrasies of viticulture in Omaruru.

As we strolled into the vineyards, there was an ear-shattering explosion and we prepared to throw ourselves to the ground (clay, granite and quartz) to avoid a barrage of what sounded like machine-gun fire. Helmuth reached into a cabin and flicked off a switch. It was his gas-cannon, primed to fire every five minutes to scare off marauding, grape-addicted birds – wattled starlings, green wood-hoopoes. (His next-door neighbour had, he said, recently bought another 'quieter' farm.) Equally problematical were the birds who prefer to forage at ground-level – francolins, guinea fowls and (a bit of tit-for-tat?) his neighbour's turkeys. And the porcupines. Helmuth had therefore constructed his trellising unusually high – 'so they can't jump up'.

Then there were the 44-gallon half-drums at the ends of the rows. These are Helmuth's ingenious defrosters: the *boere-raat* – old-fashioned farmer's remedy – method of warming up his icy vineyards in winter. He fills them with sheep manure, sets them on fire, and the ensuing 'hell of a cloud' wafts warmingly over the vines. We could only imagine what urban pollution-police might make of this when, as happens at critical times, about 60 of these contraptions are in simultaneous operation.

This vintage, these emergency forces had fought a losing battle. The crop had been drastically frost-bitten – all the Merlot wiped out, and from the rest, Helmuth estimated he might coax only 750 litres instead of the usual 5000. His 20,000 litre-capacity winery would be yawning even more emptily than usual. He'd tried to infect nearby farmers with his wine-bug, but so far hadn't been successful. The nearest vineyard – 1000 recently planted Shiraz vines – is 250 kilometres away at Otavi, near the Etosha National Park.

Far from the Rhine

A chunky, jolly, third-generation German-speaking Namibian (like about 30,000 other citizens of the country), Helmuth grew up on a cattle farm at Gobabis, on the edge of another desert, the Kalahari, which perhaps explains his stoicism in the face of Omararu's climate. It was in fact the dryness which led him to transfer his business here, from the foggy coast at Swakopmund: 'All my machines were rusting.'

He planted a few hundred vines 'just as a hobby – I've always drunk wine not beer', and far from giving up when they all died of sunstroke, became more determined to beat the odds. Having consulted 'all the books' and winemakers on the Orange River, he realised that the first variety he'd tried, Chenel – a cross developed for conditions in South Africa – had been the worst imaginable choice: practically its only claim to fame is that it withstands torrential rain better than most, hardly applicable in Omaruru. Ruby Cabernet, Colombard, and Cabernet Sauvignon are his success stories, and it was his young son, Michael, trained in South Africa and with a Masters degree in oenology and viticulture from Germany, who was to write the next chapters at Kristall Kellerei. Tragically, Michael succumbed to cancer a week before he was due to take over.

Meantime, Helmuth had built a *weinstube* to give all his visitors lunch. You approach via a little bridge over a dry river bed. 'It's my Rhine,' he says, 'and there's the Lorelei.' Which is a seal conjured from a large, weathered tree-root by Omaruru's other main attraction, the carver-craftsmen of Tikoloshe Afrika, who work under the camel-thorn trees at the entrance to the town. Sitting amid a fallen forest of dry tree trunks and roots, they sculpt whatever is suggested by the natural forms and sizes of their 'found materi-al' – a skyscraper giraffe from a lofty curved trunk, a coiled python from a whorl of roots, a graceful gemsbok, a sleeping leopard. Much of the work, specially if you can stop them varnishing the sun-bleached wood, is happily unkitschy. Helmuth's collection stands out-side the winery, where every second year he hosts the Omaruru Wine Festival, complete with choirs, bands, wine princesses, *braaivleis* (barbecuing meat) and barrels of Colombard.

Inside, there's lots of dark, polished local wood, beams from an old bridge at Walvis Bay, railway-sleeper furniture, a fireplace for winter. Which is the ideal season for perhaps Kristall Kellerei's strongest suit, Helmuth's schnapps. Made in an antique copper still from the Black Forest – acquired via a visitor who came to Omaruru on a hunting trip. (Namibia is infested with game farms and hunting lodges.) 'I asked him to see what he could find for me in Germany when he went home, and a few months later, the still arrived at Walvis Bay!'

The prickly pear schnapps is the tourists' favourite – and we thought it very fine and smooth too, with a definite taste of this delicious desert cactus fruit. Helmuth's fanati-cism about quality rather than quantity in the distilling process is evident – 'you cannot be greedy, you must throw out everything but the purest spirit'. He makes up for quan-tity in variety: distilling just about anything that grows here, from lemons to dates to the fruit of indigenous trees, as well as his Rappa and an oak-matured brandy. Some Ruby Cabernet which wouldn't ferment dry he's labelled Gluhwein.

With festive travellers in mind, he's also turned out an attractive, classically bottle-fermented bubbly from Ruby Cabernet (which we tasted very dry, before dosage – adjusted sweetness). It's the exact, champagne colour of the tourmalines which are the semi-precious speciality of this area. Prospecting and polishing gemstones is another of his activities. Visitors here and at a handful of lodges lap up everything he produces, and he's cannily raised the odds by packaging in half-bottles. 'Tourists used to refuse the standard bottles, said they were too bulky; now they look at the smaller ones and say: "I'll take two!"'

We could taste why. These are honest wines, with their own personality, reflecting the unusual *terroir*. More than curiosities, and at around US$3/£2 a snip for foreigners (though their built-in rarity value makes them quite cheekily-priced in local currency). The oak-chipped Ruby and the Cabernet were respectably drinkable, the Colombard crisp and refreshing. It cried out for Namibian oysters, which we knew weren't on the menu at Omaruru's Hotel Staebe, the admirable small, family-run – for the past 41 years – country hotel where we were staying that night. No problem, we decided, we'd just drive down to Swakopmund on the coast for lunch next day. What's two and a half hours between oyster lovers, over possibly the best roads in Africa? Even the dirt roads in Namibia are as smooth and broad as landing strips.

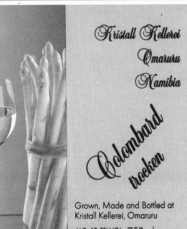

Kristall Kellerei
Omaruru
Namibia

Colombard
trocken

Grown, Made and Bottled at
Kristall Kellerei, Omaruru

ALC. 12.5% VOL · 750 ml
PRODUCT OF NAMIBIA

BRILLIANT

MINERAL WATER
ONE OF THE PUREST IN THE WORLD

Other desert flavours

The Staebe's menu, which we'd first encountered a decade earlier, on a birding trip from one end of Namibia to the other, had remained comfortably familiar. There were *kornflocken* for breakfast, *hausmacher geflugelsalat* for lunch, and *bratwurst mit bratkartof-feln* for dinner. That sort of hearty German fare, still being cooked up by chef-patron Siegie Wagner, with the best beer in a country famous for it, the Hansa draught personally drawn by Frau Ute Wagner in the Staebe's atmospheric bar.

On our first visit, we'd spent hours rock-clambering in the nearby Eronga mountains in a finally successful search for the raucous but infuriatingly stealthy and rare Hartlaub's Francolin. We'd brought our own wine of necessity, the nearest vineyard to Omaruru then being at Upington on the Orange river in South Africa, 1000 kilometres south. Our bird-party leader, Ian Sinclair, scored the first bottle from our stocks at the back of the bus '3 for temperature'. We all fell instantly and uncharacteristically silent. Any forthcoming comments, even from the winemakers in our group, were bound to sound absurdly pretentious. We have refrained from wine-speak on our birding safaris ever since.

After a fairly sleepless night – hordes of francolin clattering around on the dry river bed sounding like a football crowd waving rattles en masse; plus a throng of giant rats having a thundering party on the roof – we took a drive through the town, past the Franke Tower, which commemorates a battle in 1904 in which German troops 'quelled the Herero Rebellion', meaning they slaughtered rather a lot of local inhabitants in the interests of colonial rule. We also noticed – not that there was any connection, was there? – that Omaruru's Beware of the Dog signs were a breed of their own. *Enter and be Eaten* read one; *Pit Bull – Is there Life after Death? Come In and Find Out* read another.

The warning signs en route to Swakopmund, through the Namib, were far less fierce. *Keep Our Desert Clean* we were exhorted, *Beware of Kudu* (a leaping antelope) and *Switch on Lights*. This, in broad daylight, presumably to ensure road safety in the face of frequent, distance-distorting mirages, dust storms, and the thick fog that rolls in from the Atlantic. We heard just about nothing but German in Swakop, and apart from a sprinkling of tourists in Peter's Antiques, known for its unusual collections of African art and German (including Nazi) war memorabilia, these were locals speaking. The architecture, the confectionery, the charcuterie, everything except the palm trees and the surrounding desert dunes transports you straight to a small town in Bavaria. However, the oysters at the Lighthouse Bar on the beach were all-African, and as fine a fusion of ocean and cream as ever, a soulmate for Helmuth's wine. We had the most restful of nights because the Prinzessin Rupprecht Heim, the B&B we'd chosen for its pretty garden courtyard, turned out to be an old-age home which rented out rooms on the side!

We drove back to the airport via the 'Moonscape' road – a bowl of rocky craters

Top: Beware of bouncing buck, a local road hazard; desert dunes outside Swakopmund; Helmuth and his vines. Middle: Swakop has a German look; Helmuth's riverside pump; Namibia is hunting, shooting, trophy country; wine-partner for desert asaparagus; Namibia's vintage chugs in. Bottom: Siegie and Ute Wagner in the Staebe bar; Tikoloshe wood carvers at Omaruru; vineyard workers Gabriel Dausab and Martin Petrus; 'the best water in the world'.

and canyons in the middle of the desert – and stopped at Okapuka Game Ranch for another taste of Namibia – springbok and green 'desert' asparagus salad for lunch. Passing on the *lowenfutterung* and *pirschfahrten* (lion-feeding and game drives), we pressed on to Windhoek where we drove down Nelson Mandela and John Meinert Street – the latter named after a famous forebear of Stellenbosch winemaker Martin Meinert. It was as orderly and uncongested as it had been when we arrived. As if Namibia is one long Sunday or public holiday.

The surrounding mountains, wrinkled and folded into the shapes of reclining dinosaurs, looked as though they were now at rest after millennia of upheaval. There were more of the Germanic forts and faux-schlosses you find all over the country. A roadside advertising billboard for First National Bank featured a massive leopard in a tree and urged: *Feel at Home in our Branches*! The Bismarck river just before the airport was as dry as the Omaruru, the veld bleached to blond. We hoped the rains would again begin to smile on Helmuth's pioneering efforts.

SOUTH AFRICA

Now we were back on home ground, in the wine region where we'd lived and worked for more than 20 years. We've sometimes wondered how it is, in the face of hundreds of vine-covered Capes and Caps all over the world, some with much longer wine histories than a mere three-plus centuries, that this southern tip of Africa seems to have copyrighted this generic name, but there it is. And the remarkably beautiful, politically stormy Cape wasn't going to be the easiest trip. Because it was almost too familiar; because we already knew and loved – and often irked – many of its key players. We'd owned vineyards, we'd grown and made wine ourselves, for two decades we'd written an annual guide to Cape wines – in which we'd tried to include everyone (and how do you not irk people sometimes doing that?).

But this time, this book? How were we going to approach it? We couldn't possibly touch all bases. There were, by 2002, some 6000 labels, more than 350 wineries (barely 100 when we began in 1980). The volume and quality completely dwarfed the rest of Africa. With 105,000 hectares of well-managed vineyards and an annual harvest of more than a million tonnes of grapes, South Africa is the world's eighth largest wine producer. And among the New World's oldest. Did it even fit into 'Extreme Wine Territory'?

Comparatively speaking, perhaps not. For a start, the going is good: the broadest and best roads (though on dirt tracks, Namibia is supreme), and the only designated wine routes, with all the sophisticated accessories of board and lodging, in all Africa. There are no war-zones to avoid, no active volcanoes to traverse, no hippos at the end of vine-yard rows. But what's not extreme about the vines in the diamond fields of South Africa, 1000 kilometres from the traditional wine heartland? Or the most southerly vineyards in Africa? And the human extremes: pioneers pushing at all the perimeters? No, there's no shortage of character here. It's the vast choice which is daunting.

But, we reminded ourselves, we weren't writing a normal wine guide. Yes, it would be a fine thing to report that, since the last time we'd looked and tasted in depth, South

African wine had a new batting order. That the Cape's quest for globally acclaimed wine icons – like Grange of Australia or Opus of California – had been successful. But that would – or wouldn't – come along the way. It was the something-else factor we'd go after.

Involuntarily almost, and this is part of its disordered charm, South Africa nurtures a unique diversity of wine, a kind of eclectic abandon. While Aussie Shiraz or New Zealand Sauvignon is always good, it can be predictable. Whereas South African wines – against the tide of globalisation – stubbornly resist stereotyping. In the Cape you still can strike rich seams of the unexpected, come across incredible, barely known bargains – and not only because of alarming exchange rates. Probably nowhere in the wine world is there such a rich array of options, and people making and taking them.

This was what we would try to reflect, we decided. Zig-zagging around for six weeks, with no rigid programme, we sought out the unusual, but also called in on the 'usual suspects'. And? We were dumbstruck.

A new generation is asserting itself, and it showed in altogether finer wines – much less clumsy and tough, riper, more subtly oaked. The global wine quality renaissance had hit home. The men and women in charge now have thrown off, with the bravura that youth reserves for its elders, the confines and conformism – and complacency – of the past. They're shaking up an over-regimented, over-protected wine industry. Management and ownership is still virtually all-white, but it's a lot more cosmopolitan now; the traditionally Afrikaans-accented winelands buzz with many tongues, have been injected with many currencies.

King protea, the national flower (and emblem of South Africa's cricket team), blooming at Boekenhoutskloof in Franschhoek.

Less weighed by the baggage of the past, the new generation is freer to focus on wine's intrinsics, more confidently assertive, better travelled, much less reluctant to analyse and confront shortcomings. One example: in the past everyone strained to claim 'cool climate' conditions (sea breezes, mountain slopes, shaded valleys); the new bunch isn't wasting time on often suspect subterfuges; they accept the Cape is a warm wine region and are finding ways to make terrific *vins de soleil*.

There's still not a whole lot of 'transformation' evident. There are still accusations of poor labour conditions. But they've become the exception, and, not that it's an adequate excuse, Cape wine does make much of the rest of Africa look pretty shabby on this score. As one wine farmer told us: 'The apartheid past will be with us for a long time. Until we get our whole house in order, we'll always be eyed more closely – and judged by weakest link. Actually, perhaps that's not such a bad thing.'

Coast-to-coast, and then various ventures into the interior was how, very simply, we plotted our course. We began on the left-hand – Atlantic – side of the map.

The bold and the beautiful

Spring – August, September – is when there may not be a more ravishing wine route in the world than up the Cape's West Coast, to the semi-desert region of Namaqualand. Then it's a psychedelic rainbow-trip: billions of daisies, gazanias and vygies surging across the veld in rioting mobs of orange and yellow, purple and pink, blue and white. We were at the other end of the continent, in the Sahara, at prime-time, but this is always a magnetic landscape.

The 300-kilometre road northwest from Cape Town to the drowsy little wine town of Vredendal flashes through bleached blond wheatfields, green pastures and glossy orange groves. The sea crashed in on our left, strings of ochre, amber and denim blue mountains unrolled on our right; then long stretches of dry red earth, plains spiked with grey thorn bushes, and suddenly, luminous green splashes of vineyards, fringed with red roses and date palms.

If size matters, Vredendal winery measures up. This is the South African giant, gathering in the equivalent of the entire New Zealand crop: 100,000 tonnes of grapes, supplying 10 per cent of all Cape wine exports to the UK. The country's largest single wine tank stood here, out in the open, barely dwarfing its gleaming neighbours. From afar, Vredendal resembled an oil refinery. And even close-up, red wine chief Len Knoetze, a substantial figure, looked like a tiny fly as he climbed the stairs spiralling round the 1.3-million litre colossus. It was built in just five days during the 2001 harvest – when the crop threatened to swamp the cellar – and filled to the brim with Shiraz.

'That's how we get consistency,' Len explained. 'We need all the components of a wine blended in the SAME tank before we begin bottling. But,' he pulled a face, 'a bugger-up on this scale is a multi-million bugger-up.'

Vredendal's very remoteness was its major galvanising force. Beyond every fringe, the winery might still be stagnating in the backwaters of the Olifants River had it not been for the marketing chutzpah and political nose of former manager Giel Swiegers. He foresaw, before many local peers, that South Africa was about to re-invent itself, and that his extension cord should be plugged into European supermarkets.

He dreamed up wildly Afrocentric labels – spotty leopards, high-kicking giraffes, variations on a rock-art theme. He gave the wines pointedly indigenous names. Goiya Kgeisje and Goiya G!aan, replete with clicks pronounceable only by speakers of Kung – the language of the San people who once herded their cattle and goats here – were soon unstiffening British lips. Baby ostriches, bare-breasted maidens, sponsorship of the 1993 Miss South Africa contest, the first in history to be open to – and won by – a Soweto beauty: Swiegers' publicity stunts were legendary. Curiously, he'd gone rather quiet after the giant national co-op – since privatised – the KWV, poached him away to Paarl. But the legacy survived.

'The first thing you do when you come here,' said Len, 'is trade in your 4x4 for a really fast BMW. We can't afford to sit around. We've got to *move*.' Len and his three winemaking colleagues drive and fly furiously around to keep up to speed; he'd been to five different wine countries in 2001, most recently Australia, and had a steely resolve in his eye.

'Irrigation,' he said, 'it's all about rationing and controlling irrigation, managing moisture. That brilliant softness in their wines, that width – we can do that. What's there is here! We can improve by 100 per cent! We can make better Shiraz than the Aussies! I'm so, what's the word, excited!' The Tintin quiff on his closely shaven head stood up and quivered.

Local farmers were bracing themselves for yet more shocks to the old system. Having British chains like Tesco, Sainsburys and Oddbins as their big customers meant change all round. In 1997 the BBC happened to catch an incident of labour abuse on a Vredendal farm. They might shoot such film again – workers' exploitation has outlasted apartheid – but not here. From a perceived bad boy of the old South Africa this winery had become a shining light.

'We are the leaders by far,' claimed Len, of the Ethical Trading Initiative (ETI) launched in Britain in 1999. This is a carrot-stick scheme which keeps supermarkets out of damaging headlines ('Child Labour Shock Horror!') by financially motivating better working conditions on their suppliers' factory floors and farms. 'Our farmers must meet certain wage and housing standards, and improve their workers' lot by 4 per cent each year – as monitored by independent inspectors. If they don't, they know we can't take their grapes. Simple as that.'

In the vineyards, 'you have to speak through their wallets too. We've forced them to pull out varieties like Raisin Blanc yielding 60–70 tonnes of grapes per hectare – can you believe it? – by paying them virtually nothing. That's when the deafness suddenly leaves them. We've got our 'policemen' – our two viticulturists – watching them.'

'But,' Len added darkly, 'there are still people whose minds are too small. We tell them they can't think volume, that's crap. They must think quality. Hey, I'm 33, I can't wait forever for things to change. We're not competing with Stellenbosch here, we're competing with the world!'

The latest decision was to zoom in on individual vineyard blocks. So that top-of-the-range wines were grown rather than made. The farmer would be paid accordingly, but under minute scrutiny. 'If he does *anything*, we must be there, from irrigating to pruning to the lot. I want to, like, *sleep* with those vines.' Meantime it was big, bulk business-as-usual, including quantities that go into one of New Zealand's most popular boxed quaffers.

'Attitude – it's all attitude,' said one of the 'policemen', viticultural consultant Jeff Joubert. 'That's my big problem, the farmers' attitude. And there are 170 of them here!

Getting them to think small is my job. Small berries, smaller yields equal higher quality, bigger profits. 'Fertigation' – that's what I call the old way of wine-farming – is out.'

In such a semi-desert, almost disease-free climate, the crop is virtually organically grown, 80 per cent of it machine-harvested. But the meagre 120-millimetre annual rain-fall got farmers into the habit of irrigation-flooding to pump light yields up to heavyweights. 'Now,' announced Jeff, 'it's all CDI.' We pictured the old-timers, besieged on all fronts, with this final pill to swallow: farming by acronym. It means controlled deficit irrigation; allowing vines scientifically prescribed doses of water to influence the size of each berry, each bunch, and ultimately, fruit concentration.

'In one word, quality!' Elementary to Jeff, mumbo-jumbo to some of his flock. He wasn't counting his chickens yet. But – a cautious smile – they'd cut average yields from 28 to 17 tonnes/hectare overall, and to 12 tonnes for premium varieties like Cabernet, Chardonnay and Shiraz.

The challenging, dirt-road Niewoudt Pass climbs up from Clanwilliam into the Cederberg mountains.

'Look' said Len, holding up a glass of Goiya Kgeisje and making the ritual gargling noises over this Sauvignon Blanc-Chardonnay blend. 'This isn't fantastic-fantastic, but it's clean, crisp, fresh. What more do you want? For the price of a cappuccino?' It was effortless summer glugging. But it was Shiraz that was firing his cylinders – 2 million litres a year. The Aussies, he said, had liked 'that bit of sweet mint' in his 99 Mount Maskam. We did too. We bought. Back in Cape Town, expert noses couldn't guess its origins, and were amazed by the rock bottom price.

On the horizon were some new-age wines, from coastal Koekenaap and, 300 metres from the Atlantic breakers, Strandfontein beach. South Africa's national al fresco activity, *braaivleis* (barbecuing meat) routinely becomes the much classier crayfish or *kreefbraai* here. Jeff was mulching the upcoming bio-vineyards with the leftover shells – and seaweed. If the wines didn't make a perfect partner for crustaceans and sushi, nothing would.

Len sounded a caution: mind the labels! He'd just been to Japan and had been asked why Cape Rock, a wine Vredendal bottles for one of its producers, had a cockroach embossed on the bottle. 'Man, but it was a really nice *kreef*!'

Clean your mind

Our next stop was deep in the Cederberg mountains. Knowing the last 50 kilometres would be on a precipitous dirt track, slow and slippery, we ignored the rural charms of the little town of Clanwilliam: like the handmade *veldskoene*, bush-shoes; and the Red T Company sign pointing to a farm growing a wild bush (*Aspalathus linearis*) with rosy-tipped leaves, cultivated nowhere else in the world, but in global demand for rustically aromatic *rooibos* tea. We turned off the tar and began to climb.

At 1100 metres the Cederberg Cellars vineyards are the loftiest in the country. We crawled up there on the red mud Niewoudt Pass, with the Olifants river a slender snail's trail perilously far below. Eventually, through a gap in the mountains, we reached a sliver of plateau, a patch of wheat, a bit of vineyard: tiny man-made marks in the natural scheme of things in this fantastic wilderness.

More sandstone crags reared into the clouds; they turned from saffron to coral as the light changed; they'd crumbled and weathered into astonishing shapes – a cow, a regiment of Red Guards, a cathedral with gargoyles. One named the Maltese Cross, depicted on Cederberg Cellars' label, is a feature of the family farm we'd now reached. As are buck, leopards and black eagles. And pristine *fynbos* – the indigenous plants which make the Cape mountains the richest botanical area on earth. Universal garden plants like sparaxis, agapanthus and watsonias grow wild here; so do many rarities, like the snow protea. The sky is so clear that photographs taken from an observatory on the farm illustrate many leading reference works. There are scores of caves interior-decorated with ancient rock-art, including one so huge it's called *Stadsaal* (Town Hall).

'You can clean your mind here,' said David Niewoudt.

The sheer isolation of the place is its beauty, but for an ambitious winemaker like David, it's a challenge. His brochure artfully glosses over the long-distance rally-driving necessary to get in and out of this mountain eyrie ('250 increasingly scenic kilometres from Cape Town'). Staying in touch, for this 29-year-old graduate of Elsenburg in Stellenbosch – the agricultural college alternative to university for aspiring oenologists – means perpetual motion. 'I attend every important tasting; I must.'

In the winery was a photograph of a beaming David, aged 5, in enormous bow tie, alongside his grandfather, David Josephus 'Pollie' Niewoudt, and a large trophy. Some 25 years ago, South Africa's Champion Cabernet Sauvignon was made in this extreme spot. But it was always regarded as a bit of *bizarrerie*, turning out quaint quaffers for hardy hikers, until young David began to refashion it into a more modern, sophisticated label and scoop double golds at the national show.

He took us to his newest vineyard, and laughed as our mouths dropped open. It looked as if he'd dumped a huge load of slate crazy-paving on the hillside. This was *soil*? We couldn't believe it. You could have laid a million garden paths with this lot. Some infant Sauvignon Blanc vines were bravely peeping through the slaty shale.

This is the sort of natural obstacle he faces in turning the farm from fruit, vegetables and table grapes into – eventually – 35 hectares of Cabernet, Shiraz, Merlot, Sauvignon Blanc and Chenin. And then there's the fundamental payback for living in the middle of a national treasure. The family put down roots here in 1835, when nature

A formidable soil-challenge: Cederberg Cellars winemaker David Niewoudt in one of his new slate-and-shale vineyards.

conservation was a rather futuristic concept. Now, the authorities demand total environmental impact studies before David can establish a vineyard or replace an orchard. He was resigned: 'Rome was not built in a year.' And anyway, he's the last to threaten his own home ground.

'Look, look!' he blurted as we skirted his soon-to-be organic vineyard, where workers were mulching the vines with heaps of straw and *rooibos* leaves. 'At those very very lovely rocks.' The understatement of someone who'd grown up in wall-to-wall scenic splendour, but who still marvelled at it all. So his plans are small-scale, eco-sensitive. They include some port varieties, maybe some Petit Verdot, Malbec and Viognier.

We drove back down the Niewoudt Pass with purchases of Sauvignon Blanc (Erica), Barrel-Matured Chenin (John), Cabernet (both) and a glamorous bottle of V Generations, David's forthcoming special release Cabernet. We spoke sternly to each other. This was the first day of our Cape wine journey and already our car was clinking. We couldn't continue like this. We must resist.

This had been, mostly, easy to do elsewhere on the continent. But here, even right off the beaten track, even under obscure labels, dud wines are becoming an endangered species. Rising out of the 'sea of vapid mouthwashes', as Jancis Robinson once described the deluge of dull Cape Chardonnay, is a new wave of wines, a new breed of winemaker.

Country house japes

We stayed the night with Julian Melck, whose business card introduces him as 'farmer, pig-killer, aviator' and (in smaller print) 'Advocate of the High Court of South Africa'. His speciality is plane-crash cases, and the pigs are fearsomely tusked wild boars – released only to proceed in crackling roasted mode to his 22-seater dining table. Except on Hannes Myburgh's 40th birthday, when Julian arrived with two squealing piglets under his arms to throw the party into incredulous disarray. Hannes owns Meerlust Estate, the Cape equivalent of a classic Bordeaux château. What do you give someone who has everything like that? asked Julian. Possibly not a fresh deposit of baby boar manure on the Persian carpets in his hall…

Another branch of the Melck family owns Muratie, a recently regenerated Stellenbosch estate; its signature Ansela van der Caab Cabernet-Merlot blend is named after the slave freed in 1695 who married the farm's first owner and helped establish its vineyards. (Its 2000 Shiraz is the current star.) Martin Melck House – now the national gold museum – was the home of the first family member to emigrate from Holland to Cape Town. (Julian's farm, Kersefontein, was originally a cattle-post supplying meat to sailors on the Spice route. Located on the Berg river 150 kilometres away, it's handily between the Olifants River, Swartland and Darling wine areas.)

On this 6000-hectare spread, this eighth-generation Melck still raises Herefords, wheat and sheep; the swirly gabled Cape Dutch homestead (a national monument) and farm buildings are now a distinctive guest house, with the aura of a place caught in colonial time. Local flavour was the dinner theme – butternut soup with orange zest, infant artichokes, water-lily and lamb casserole, all farm-grown. Plus copious regional wine: Cederberg Barrel-fermented Chenin Blanc, Kloovenburg Shiraz from a winery (and olive-oil press) near the hamlet of Riebeek Kasteel.

The place teems with old-fashioned roses, books, family memorabilia and venerable copies of *Country Life*. Julian's forebears were hoarders; he simply raided the attics for his décor. Herds of wildlife trophies stare beadily from the walls; a set of rhino horns tops the living-room door. Racks of antique guns included one used in 1869 in what a newspaper of the day headlined 'A Sad Accident on the Berg River' – when 'the last hippo in the river took a bather' and had to be shot. The hippo's skull sat forlornly on the floor in the passageway.

A US magazine photographer had recently come to Kersefontein with the brief: *No dead animals* and spent hours scouring the place for the few nooks unadorned with such Africana. Julian hooted with laughter: 'This was huntin'-shootin'-fishin' country in the old days.' The garden rolls down to the river, and a bright purple gallinule against a back-drop of wild white chinchirinchee flowers might be your best shot today.

Spice and soul

In the fifteenth century, when Portuguese galleons first sailed round Africa in search of a route to the spices of the east, the Cape was still prowled by African game. It was the rhino's favourite snack of dark-leaved *renosterbos* which gave the west coast hinterland its local name of Swartland – the black country. The odd small antelope or porcupine is now as wild as it gets. As we approached Cape Town, the same silhouette of Table Mountain that confronted those early seafarers hove into view. We were less adventurously on the N7 highway, looking for a contemporary Spice Route – the winery of this name near the town of Malmesbury, a green punctuation point amid golden wheatfields.

Erica dreamed up the name Spice Route for a quixotic partnership founded in 1998, on not much more than hunches and laughter. Jabulani Ntshangase, who'd been in exile for 12 years in New York, most of it in the wine trade, had been pestering us to find him a farm. He wanted to be the first black South African to own a vineyard. We'd looked at scores; consulted inveterate risk-taker Charles Back, of Fairview in Paarl, and persuaded Gyles Webb of Thelema Mountain Vineyards in Stellenbosch to join the party.

Charles had some vineyards and an old tobacco shed at Malmesbury. The shed was converted – in a record three months – into a 30,000-case winery, the harvest (mainly Pinotage) supplemented with handpicked Cabernet, Merlot and Shiraz formerly sent to

Robben Island

```
             VAT R
TOUR NOV 2
* * * D E P A R T * * *
   FERRY: MAKANA
DEPART FROM: JETY 1
   DATE: 25/11/2000
   TIME: 09:00

* * * R E T U R N * * *
   FERRY: MAKANA
   TIME: 12:00
   RATE: Adult
   PRICE: R60.00
PLATTER
```

Top: *Rugged rocks
round Cederberg
vines; clock tower,
Cape Town Waterfront;
Klein Constantia's
Ross Gower; Cape
Town harbour.
Middle: Eben Sadie,
ex-Spice Route; old
tractor, new role;
Vredendal vineyards;
don't miss Robben
Island; architect Johan
Wessels (left), founding
Spice Route partners
Charles Back, Gyles
Webb, Jabulani
Ntshangase (and
behind the camera,
John Platter).
Bottom: Kersefontein
homestead; Vredendal's
big red chief Len
Knoetze; Swartland
wheatfields; dinner
with Julian Melck.*

a co-op by a neighbour. The hunches were vindicated: treasure lay buried in these deep red soils. Jabulani was in charge of marketing, Charles general factotum and production chief, Gyles responsible for wine quality and John, with no specific duties, was relegated to chairman.

The first vintage was a cracker, the lot bagged (and paid for!) before it was even bottled by London wine company Enotria. We were still glowing, and thinking about an encore, when Charles sprang a surprise: 'Guys, I'm restructuring Fairview, can I have Spice Route?' A long party – and Fairview absorbed the company.

To make the Spice Route wine, Gyles had recruited a young man of exceptional ability and cool. It was Eben Sadie we were now visiting and he too had a surprise. In South Africa, with no movie industry to speak of, winemakers rank with soccer players and game rangers as lifestyle icons. And for four heady years, Eben had been the artist behind the Spice Route wines; they and he had shot from nowhere to overnight stardom. The Flagship Merlot, Syrah and Pinotage had received rave international reviews. But out of the blue, he'd just resigned.

'Look, fame means nothing to me; rising stars become falling stars,' said Eben. He'd already moved on – emotionally – to a new love, Carignan: the supposedly second-division red wine grape rescued from ho-humdom most spectacularly in the Spanish wine region of Priorato, near Barcelona. Eben had been there, and lost his heart. He'd made five barrels of wine there in 2001; they were maturing in the village of Porrera. Was this soulful, romantic young Afrikaner, a surfer in his (limited) free time, considering a South African transplant of these feats?

What a question! What is wine if not an unvarnished, untarnished reflection of its own unique soils and climate? Eben is a purist. And the Cape no longer defined the limits of his universe. 'South Africa,' he drawled, 'deserves a great wine. It still doesn't have one. But Spain! Now there they grow real vines, old, hard vines, on rocky hillsides. To make great wines. And I mean great. Here,' he said, nodding at the lushness outside, 'we grow vegetables.'

We'd long learned to wait for Eben to adjust the free-style thoughts that habitually tumble out of his head. Clearly he'd not been growing any old vegetables in this patch. But he stayed in dreamer-hyperbole mode. 'Now let me tell you about the spiritual path to my wine.'

We adjourned to a next-door shed to taste his Sadie Family creation. He wouldn't give us its proper name 'because it's so fantastic someone might steal it'. He'd sold his pick-up truck to buy 17 super-expensive, thinly staved French oak barrels for this wine, and – with Charles Back's okay – done his personal thing here. His wife joined us and their ambitions and philosophies poured out in jumbled torrents.

'Wine is all about passion,' she said. 'Ag no, Maria,' he said, 'every beggar on the street's passionate. You must just do the business! You have to get inside the mind of the vine, know how it thinks.'

We tasted from the barrels, in huge Riedel glasses. The wine was a 2001 Syrah (usually called Shiraz in the Cape) from three vineyards with different soils: 'Slate for power, granite for finesse, gravel for minerality. The only thing they have in common is they're all from under the same sky.' A soupçon of Mourvèdre topped it up. He'd pruned and canopy-managed personally. At harvest, workers checked 'not just every bunch, every berry; you'd be surprised how much we threw out. I hate raisins, I don't want even one in my wine. If I want jam, I can buy it in jars, not in a wine bottle.' The wine was fermented in oak, matured in oak, bottled from oak.

'It's extreme,' Eben allowed. 'But to make a wine like this means going all the way. No wine has ever shown me the power of blending as this one has: great individual wines from different vineyards into one, achieving the power of many more.'

It was seduction at first sight, sniff, swallow. We instantly ordered a case. Then asked the price. About R300 a bottle. Brazenly high in local terms, not immodest when speaking an international language. We gulped and confirmed the order. And wondered what it would take to acquire a drop of his Priorato, to keep abreast of his Spanish labours. That was clearly his idea, post-Spice Route: annual vintages in each hemisphere.

Ah yes, Spice Route! Eben's heart no longer seemed to be in it, but he drew us some barrel samples. Would these Flagship wines be upstaged by his private endeavour? Perhaps, perhaps not. The Spice Route Merlot was a beaut; among the Cape's best without doubt. : The Syrah was still top-league, and from the cellar at Fairview at less than half the price of Eben's wine, better value.

Later that week, we heard that proprietor Charles Back had already filled the gap his freedom-seeking, admin-loathing, wild-child of a winemaker had opened up. Charl du Plessis, another young meteor, had been lured from Rijk's Private Cellar in the mountain valley of Tulbagh to take over at Spice Route.

Wine on the waterfront

For inveterate long-distance travellers like us, South African wine country is – mostly – a pleasure. We enjoy the possibility of encountering a vineyard anywhere from the Orange river in the north to Cape Agulhas in the deep south. But it's ideal for those allergic to perpetual motion too. You can sit in Cape Town with Table Mountain peering into the window and know there are strings of glamorous cellars right on the doorstep.

The mother of all South African wine areas, Constantia, is only 15 minutes from the centre of the city; from the Houses of Parliament, the street markets and clubs, and the unmissable – if you want to get under Cape Town's skin – District Six Museum. But you can be even more indolent, and simply amble down to the Waterfront.

There, the world seemed to have docked just outside Vaughan Johnson's front door. His eponymous wine and cigar emporium reverberated with foreign accents, all ashore from the Cunard liner moored down the quay in Table Bay. Last week it had been the *QE2*. During the summer, 38 more cruise ships were due, sleek white decks and giant funnels amid the ferries and tugs, fishing boats and dive-schools of seals in Cape Town's throbbing harbour. Today there were no trapeze artists soaring above the crowds, or dancers leaping around the outdoor stage (we'd once had the St Petersburg Ballet with our lunch), but the jazz quartet was playing. These resident buskers have such swing that a smitten visitor recently flew them to Germany for a weekend party. They launched into 'I'm in Heaven' and Vaughan was.

He'd been thrown into jail a couple of times in the bad old days, for having the audacity to flout the apartheid regime's Never on a Sunday liquor-selling laws. Now things were different. He'd delivered five truck-loads of wines and spirits to passengers on the *QE2*, who'd clearly done their sums. The difference between the liner's corkage fee of $13 a bottle and the cheapest *vin very ordinaire* on its list made it economically ludicrous not to invest in some liquid Cape take-aways for drinking later on the voyage.

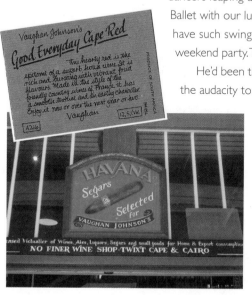

Top marques and no-frills quaffers at Vaughan Johnson's Waterfront wine and cigar emporium.

This is the store where visiting presidents shop (the Clintons fell for the local equivalent of Sauternes, South Africa's Noble Late Harvests); where former liberation strug-gleniks now enjoying the better life they deserve pick up their cigars; where locals find Vaughan's own troops in his battle against price-inflation: house wines which flaunt their cheap chic with brown-paper labels and take-the-mickey names. Seriously Good Plonk was one we dreamed up for him, but the user-instructions were his own: 'Decant this wine and fool your friends.'

Cape Town's suavest shop-keeper, in Hong Kong-tailored shirts, emerald green-rimmed Italian specs, and vast white Merc with the WINE-1 numberplate, Vaughan also has tentacles in Dublin's Temple Bar area, where there's another VJ's stuffed with his best-of-the-Cape selections.

On a knoll directly behind, overlooking the harbour, is a mellow old stone house, once the Port Captain's residence, now the HQ of Flagstone Winery and Vineyards. Underneath, cut into the hill, is a 100m long barrel-vaulted brick tunnel burrowed while Cape Town's breakwater was being constructed, and later designated as a bomb shelter. This is Flagstone's maturation cellar. Outside in the bright summer sunlight traffic roared, inside it was as gloomy and atmospheric as an old *cave*, though this was misleading. When nearly all your 250 barrels are high-toasted American oak your wines aren't speaking French.

'We're definitely a New World winery,' said towering winemaker Matt Orton, right-hand man of Roseworthy oenology graduate Bruce Jack, whose father was the driving force behind the transformation of shabby, sleazy Cape Town harbour into today's swanky Victoria and Alfred Waterfront. Bruce is 32, Matt 25 – but the team's not all young, said Matt. 'Our viticulturist Dudley Wilson is about 40.'

Big doors hid all this from the Waterfront throngs, but on the drawing board were plans to convert this space into a scale-model of a winery, with a see-through roof and observation platform. Meantime, the main, no-frills winemaking area was in a less gentrified part of the harbour, though still with full-frontal Table Mountain views. A large yard was jumbled with containers, presses and open fermenters. Steel tanks stood under an open roof; bottling and labelling was happening al fresco. Nearby was a commercial plant formerly used to freeze tuna for export to Japan and now to chill down Flagstone's grapes.

This most urban of wine operations was buying grapes from 39 vineyards, spread from the West Coast to the Karoo. Its Free Run Sauvignon Blanc, which had just won a top, 'Blue-Gold' medal at the Sydney wine show, came from Africa's most southerly wine district – the Land's End vineyards near Cape Agulhas. Bruce and Dudley hurtle between all these parcels, grooming them like Parisian poodles for a range of 14 wines, many destined for the shelves of UK chain Oddbins. In under five years, Flagstone had become a new South African success-story, with novel labels to match.

BK5, the brash, friendly signature wine in its Poetry Collection range, was sten-cilled with a paean to Pinot Noir by local laureate Stephen Watson:

This pinot on your tongue, you'll find
your planet becomes a planetarium
roofed once more, now richly hung
with the star-clusters of the taste buds

Writer's Block is the name of the Flagstone Pinotage, not that this affliction was evidenced on the back labels. They rippled with phrases like 'summer-squeezed smells of *fynbos*' and, recalling the pressing of the Strata Wild, Barrel-fermented Chenin: 'It was the sort of day that could make you softly scratch beneath the surface of this land, like a child healing damaged, adult angst with a suddenly power-ful belief in the possibility of tomorrow'.

National treasures

Leaving Flagstone, we waited for a fishing boat to motor below a raised draw-bridge, and crossed to the Nelson Mandela Gateway – part museum, part mall, part ferry station. This is where to catch the boat to The Island – Robben Island, but no need to specify (the name means 'seals'). Here, this is the only island which counts. And while

Never a dull label at the winery on the Waterfront, Flagstone.

you might not, in other wine countries, include a visit to a (former) maximum security prison on your itinerary, this is South Africa. Wine history here began with Dutch governors and French Huguenots, but it would never have risen from the dead without The Island's most famous inmate.

When Nelson Mandela beamingly, photogenically, raised a glass of South African wine soon after his 1990 release from 27 years' imprisonment, he liberated Cape wine to pour into an international marketplace which had been virtually closed during the days of apartheid. With his 'sporting endorsement – he's practically a teetotaller, drinking no more than a sweet sip or two – brand South Africa almost instantly lost much of its stigma.

On The Island you see Mandela's anchovy-tin cell, the hard labour quarry, and that taunting view of the freedom of the city just across Table Bay, and it's almost impossible to understand how he and his comrades emerged so unembittered. Now the whole place is a World Heritage site; poignantly, former inmates guide the tours. And Ahmed Kathrada, Mandela's close soulmate and fellow-prisoner, has redefined it: 'A monument reflecting the triumph of the human spirit against the forces of evil.' It is moving, shaming, outraging, uplifting and not to be missed.

Cape Town's Kirstenbosch, the botanical garden on the slopes of Table Mountain, is a national treasure of a different sort, the one-stop answer to the question of why the Cape is classified as one of the six Floral Kingdoms of the world. In its glasshouse grow plants from every corner of South Africa, desert to sub-tropics. The al fresco sunset concerts here – Ladysmith Black Mambazo, perhaps, or local diva Sibongile Khumalo – are a summer glory. We dropped in en route to the wineries of Constantia and Cape Point.

The Emperor and the handsprings

Our first Constantia call was on Ross Gower, the barrel-chested teddy-bear who runs the cellar at Klein Constantia Estate. Years before globe-trotting became both fashionable and crucial for local winemakers, Ross had just about done it all. Qualifying at Stellenbosch University, he collected more credentials at Weinsburg in Germany; worked in New Zealand, Australia and France; and study-toured other European wine countries. In Italy he discovered a particularly flavourful Cabernet clone, and imported it to the Cape, where it strengthened a depleted 'gene pool' at the time.

Klein Constantia is a modern relic of the winefarming past. Now surrounded by *haut gratin* suburbia, with its highest vineyards creeping up the backside of Table Mountain, overlooking False Bay, it was part of the property holdings of Simon van der Stel, the Dutch Governor who was the Cape's first bigtime vineyard owner. A subsequent proprietor was a Pittsburgh steel heiress who married a milliner from Paarl, and served her guests champagne in watermelons. The estate was bought by an old Cape wine family, the Joostes, in 1980. It needed a complete overhaul – new vineyards, new winery. Both became industry models, and the burly Ross a fixture on the local awards rostrum.

His powerful, figgy-gooseberry Sauvignon Blanc is a stand-out, but no KC has, for us, ever quite matched a one-off 87 Blanc de Blanc, a blend of Chenin and Sauvignon Blanc with a faint touch of botrytis. This is called *pourriture noble* in France, noble rot, signifying grapes which have been attacked by the *Botrytis cinerea* fungus, which shrivels them almost into raisins, concentrating their sweetness. This 'fault' – in a dry white – was meant to be obscured by the blending – and apologetic pricing. It had quite the opposite effect – and the ripe-apricot botrytis scents simply grew and grew in the bottle.

We bought 20 cases and drank the last bottle eight years later with Johnny Apple Jnr of the *New York Times*. 'Whoa, a discovery wine,' he beamed. 'The whole orchestra.' The *Times* has an admirable policy on wine writing: you seem to graduate to those frivolous heights only if you have been a hard-news reporter first. Apple and Platter had covered Uganda and many other African coups and hotspots together. (Frank Prial, the *Times*' long-time official wine columnist, arrived via the United Nations beat – sometimes a war zone, too.)

Klein Constantia sadly never repeated that fabulous, fabulous Blanc de Blanc aberration. But they made amends by becoming the first – still only – Cape estate to resuscitate the fabled Constantias of two centuries ago. These were then – and in Klein Constantia's case from 1987 onwards, are – luscious, beguiling, golden dessert wines, finished in barrel (as they were before, pitching on the ocean across the equator on their journey to European ports).

Vin de Constance is made from Muscat de Frontignac, which has a much finer Muscat flavour than the commoner Muscat d'Alexandrie. These vines were propagated from descendants of those originally imported from western France in 1656 by the first Dutch Commander of the Cape, Jan van Riebeeck. Vin de Constance's deliberately misshapen, squat, opaque bottles – replicas of the originals – add to the lustre of this trip back in time. Even the French import it now, calling it the Emperor's wine, tickled by the fact that Napoléon, exiled on St Helena, chose to drink Constantias above (and only marginally less pricy than) Hungarian Tokaji.

Ross long ago vowed to stop any further study 'because it only confuses me', and the Joostes are happy. 'Sure-footed' they call him, and we've seen him playing interesting variations on this theme – doing his party trick, a series of flick-flack handsprings, once, famously, across the town square in the French wine village of Sancerre. Late-night strollers watched in amazement, then broke into applause.

The neighbours

Klein (small) Constantia's neighbours include Groot (big) Constantia, a major Cape Dutch architectural gem, surrounded by a much larger vineyard and winery. For decades it has been under State management – and its overall wine record has been patchy. To the south is Buitenverwachting – 'beyond expectation' – another successful rescue mission from run-down to immaculate. (The concept of a modern South African wine renaissance is very visible in Constantia.) The graceful historic buildings and haute-cuisine restaurant here are matched by an increasingly organic wine list, crafted by a perfectionist, Hermann Kirschbaum. Its Sauvignon Blanc, a model of late-developing decorum, is seemingly unrelated to Klein Constantia's billowing, come-hither number.

A third neighbour, the handsome wine and golfing estate of Steenberg, produces another distinctive Sauvignon, more flinty-gravelly. And round the corner, from Constantia Uitsig, comes yet another. Sémillon and Chardonnay had led the pack here, but the Sauvignon is in hot pursuit. All of which makes for difficult wine choices at two of our favourite Cape Town restaurants, both on the Constantia Uitsig property. It's the Franck and Frank show here – Franck Dangereux from Provence via the Caribbean at La Colombe, Frank Swainston inspired by the new Italian *cucina* in the Uitsig manorhouse.

A portion of the estate had just been put up for sale when we visited. If we'd had many millions to spare we might have succumbed, especially as the private cricket oval was thrown in. Instead we ate the best steak tartare this side of Paris, and eventually drank elegant Steenberg Merlot, then headed over the Silvermine mountain – wild flowers spectacularly in bloom – towards the end of the Cape Peninsula.

Not quite the end of the continent

Cape Point is disputed territory. It's uncertain whether it was these craggy cliffs or, round the corner, the Cape of Good Hope, which had Sir Francis Drake spouting in 1580: 'A most stately thing and the fairest Cape that I have seen in the whole circumference of the earth.' (Imagine his endorsement fee today.) The argument shouldn't but does continue to rage over whether the warm Indian and icy Atlantic Oceans meet here at the tip of the Cape Peninsula, which crooks a rugged finger behind Cape Town into the sea. Actually, they converge at Cape Agulhas, a few hours' drive away, slightly southeast.

The latest controversy lay in vineyards recently planted here above the beach villages of Noordhoek, Scarborough and Fish Hoek. Their claim to singularity was officially recognised in 1998, when the new appellation of Cape Point was declared, but big, bluff Emmanuel Bolliger was candid. 'They're still giving us uphill.' 'Manny', the founding winemaker on this property, was shortly to move to Rongopai Wines in New Zealand (one of the countries in which he'd trained). but right now he was concentrating on jolting us up to a very steep vineyard indeed (4-wheel drive obligatory), clinging to one of the rocky vertebrae in the spine of mountains running along the Peninsula.

'They' were nature conservation officials and local Greens, who charged that the kaolin mining activities of Emmanuel's boss, Sybrand van der Spuy, were defacing the area; 'they' were not completely mollified when he announced a trio of vineyards formed part of his 'reclamation' plans. 'They' contended that mine-ravaged land should be returned to nature – to the indigenous flora and fauna that make the larger part of this Cape Point peninsula one of South Africa's most beautiful national parks.

Tucked into mountains rearing back from the sea, the Cape Point Vineyards form an official wine-ward all of their own.

We love its op-art bontebok, its mountain zebras, its Jackass penguins wobbling about like tipsy comedians in an old black and white movie, its ostriches, running on the beach. There are as many wild-flower species here as in the whole of the British Isles. The mountains crash dramatically into the sea. All this and now vineyards too: Cape Point must become one of the great wine-drives of the world. And 'they' should be happy, because Emmanuel was colouring the picture even brighter.

'Look,' he said, crouching down between rows of Pinot Noir. He was up to his knees in a cover-crop – not the normal rye and grasses planted elsewhere to hold and shade soil and give rampant vines some competition. This was a riot of shocking pink, yellow and lime – pelargoniums, arums, ericas, miniature proteas. A simple, sympathetic, natural strategy. 'The vines will be taking up only a tiny bit of space!' he said happily. 'The mountain will still be full of flowers! It's going to be interesting… I firmly believe that what grows around a vineyard has a bearing on its flavour.'

The wide-angle view was as remarkable as this floral close-up: over Noordhoek's 8-kilometre curve of silver strand, fringed by mountains, wild milkwood trees and the Slangkop lighthouse, to the ultramarine ocean. Far less picturesque is the winery. Plush estates and grand cellars might be executive toys in his boss's circles, but, said Emmanuel, 'I don't believe in over-capitalising. One of the kaolin bunker-stores became redundant; we converted that.'

The 35 hectares of vineyards, producing 400 tonnes of grapes, would soon become 45, none further than 5 kilometres from a beach. The wines have already started to build a distinct personality profile, different from the neighbours. The plan is to target (by manipulation if necessary) admirers of big, brash New World styles with the second brand, Scarborough, but for the Cape Point label to remain true to whatever the *terroir* throws up.

We took the seaside road back to Cape Town. Whales cavorted near the naval base of Simonstown. The fishing boats in Kalk Bay harbour had sold out their catches of Cape salmon and yellowtail, and our favourite coastal café, the Olympia, was overflowing for supper.

Bubbles

The 160-kilometre road from Cape Town to Robertson winds up from the lush green floor of Paarl and cuts through the Huguenot Tunnel in the Du Toitskloof mountains: we emerged from the dark into another country. There's a rampantly untamed look to these mountains – great shards and boulders heaved into colossal piles, range after range, stretched along every horizon. Robertson snoozes on the banks of the Breede (Broad) river between the Riviersonderend (River without End) and Langeberg (Long Mountain) ranges. Locals call this hot hinterland the valley of wine and roses. Its vineyards were once rather disparagingly consigned to the B-stream. But it now slots convincingly into the modern definition of 'hot' – rather cool – and we were visiting a venture which dramatically illustrated its re-invention.

Growing out of orange earth, pink wild flowers, grey veld scrub and braided green vineyards, is an apparition painted in the same colours. Environmentally faithful, but startling nonetheless. This is the Graham Beck Winery, and 12 years after it flew out of architect Johan Wessels' imagination its acute angles and sinuous curves in stone and steel, glass, wood and corrugated iron, remain the South African winelands' sharpest construction statement. A love-hate object: some visitors turn away before even tasting the wines. Others find its cutting-edge suggestiveness irresistible.

Pieter Ferreira, chunky, blond and twinkly behind his round John Lennon specs, looks far too cherubic to suit his lofty title of Cellarmaster. It was this then raw young man whom mining and horse-breeding magnate Graham Beck (with a stud in Kentucky too) had plucked out of obscurity and charged with the unthinkable. Pieter was to transform a portion of Beck's huge mixed farm, Madeba, into a corner of Champagne.

A rich man's folly of an idea, sceptics scoffed. Beck was simply trying to pump up his portfolio to become the biggest private player in Cape wine. Torrid Robertson was bulk and fortified dessert wine territory, no place for delicate sparklers. Yes, giant Danie de Wet of nearby De Wetshof Estate had steamed ahead with Chardonnay (is still steaming). But Danie had bottled his first wines way back in 1973! What made novices Beck and Ferreira (he has a microbiology and economics degree) think they could succeed where others had wisely never even tried?

The question should have been who, not what. The matchmaker here was former Springbok rugby player Jan Boland Coetzee, of Vriesenhof Estate in Stellenbosch (currently a new, dark and promising horse in the Cape Pinot Noir stakes). 'He dragged me away from work (at Achim von Arnim's sparkling wine cellar in Franschhoek) saying that this crazy coal miner wanted to make something different in Robertson. We met, and Graham Beck said: "OK, you're part of the family now. Go off and make me a cellar." Then he got up, poured himself a large whisky, and we got on with it.'

Here we were in that much-expanded winery, its brutal lines now softened by the foliage of fever-trees, wild restio grasses and bananas. In the elevated glass tasting gallery, we looked over a reflecting pond to vineyards lined with Iceberg roses and the inevitable mountains beyond. Matching the décor, red-winged, steel-blue-plumaged starlings swooped around the deck.

Pieter poured the fruits of Graham Beck's folly. The only fools now had to be the wet, grey and cold-climate diehards. Instead of going into denial about the givens here, Pieter had embraced them. 'We *are* a warm region. That's not a minus, it's a plus. The challenge is to manage the warmth. And make sunshine wines.'

He'd done this so notably that he'd become known as Bubbles Ferreira. The South African equivalent of champagne, a name which the French insist on keeping to themselves, is Cap Classique. Graham Beck joined the Big Five in this park.

First into the local bottle-fermented bubbly market had been Simonsig, with its Kaapse Vonkel (Cape Sparkle) 30 years ago. Then came Villiera's Tradition, a great-value sparkler. Its maker, Jeff Grier, remains (with Simonsig's Johan Malan) probably the Cape's best all-rounder, incapable of turning out a disappointing bottle of anything, and there were now another three bubblies in the Villiera stable, including new star Brut Natural. Nicky Krone of Twee Jongegezellen in the mountain hamlet of Tulbagh, had won even French acclaim for his Krone Borealis Brut. Pieter's former boss, now Baron von Arnim, was doing the business with six Pierre Jourdan bubblies. In Devon valley, Stellenbosch, young Melanie van der Merwe was sparkling for the big merchant-producer firm of Distell, at the chic cellar and oyster bar of The House of J C le Roux.

And now the festivities had spread to Robertson. (Nearby, on Bon Courage Estate, young Jacques Bruwer had dived deep into bubbly, too.) Pieter's latest experiment was due to become the fourth sparkler in the Graham Beck range. Two-thirds Pinot Noir, one-third Chardonnay, to be named Synergy: the grapes were harvested and crushed together. Another innovation, an all-Pinotage bubbly, was his answer to the question of how South Africa should approach its home-bred grape. (Short of UK wine writer Robert Joseph's advice: 'Pull it all out and plant buchu!' Buchu is a nasty-tasting wild herb much in demand for medicines and hangover cures.)

'I was very naughty,' Pieter owned up. He entered his bubbly in the very serious Top Ten Pinotage contest, and befuddled the judges. They threw it out on a technicality – though it complied with the rules which called for a dry ('and it was, in Champagne terms!'), 100 per cent Pinotage of the vintage. 'I'm told one judge even thought it was still fermenting! But at the awards ceremony, they served it as an apéritif. So I was happy.'

Bubbles still drive him, but 'Shiraz is creeping up in my blood'. The keynote version here, The Ridge, is a single-vineyard wine from a block rooted in red limestone, and had recently been picked by *Decanter* magazine as one of the top Shirazes in its price bracket (under £10). A Shiraz, Pieter predicted, would eventually become Graham Beck's 'super-premium' label. His colleague Charles Hopkins, winemaker at Graham Beck's Coastal Cellar at Franschhoek – supplied by the company's farms at Firgrove near False Bay – is an ace with Cabernets Franc and Sauvignon, and might not agree. But he turns out a pretty good Shiraz himself.

We went through the smart conference room (table featuring spittoons hidden in drawers) and into the cellar to barrel-sample two different renditions of 2001

'Bubbles' Ferreira, Graham Beck's Robertson cellarmaster, taste-testing his sunshine wines.

Shiraz. Pieter is an indefatigable experimenter, and was testing the theory that small, concentrated berries produce greater wine. On the palate, in this infant stage, it was the 'standard-berry' wine, which had not been manipulated by CDI (controlled deficit irrigation) in the vineyard, that took our vote.

'So we can't jump to conclusions,' Pieter said. 'We're still finding out. Before we spent on cellars; now we're pouring millions into the vineyards.'

They'd also gone the distance up the model employment track. Graham Beck was the first South African cellar to appoint a black winemaker: Manie Arendse, in charge of their white wines. He had since moved on, but a future star, young Jakob Booysen ('remember that name,' said Pieter) had risen through the ranks.

We sampled Graham Beck's Railroad Red and Waterside White: 'bistro wines' said Pieter, budget models of food-friendly drinkability, a crucial consideration for him and PR wife Ann, both outstanding cooks with global repertoires. We were due to have dinner with them later – at the next best table in the valley after their own. But first, a call on a Robertson original.

About turn

'So what's new?' we asked Abrie Bruwer, whose towering, bulky build we'd never dream of comparing to that of a rugby player. He's the only South African winemaker we know who loathes the game. Fishing and flying his own light plane are his sports, and he doesn't do that other macho winelands thing – hunting – either. The herd of 50 springbok, led by a rare black ram, grazing in the scrub along the driveway to Springfield Estate is a purely decorative touch; the ducks, marched into the vineyards during the snail season, are not.

'Everything's new,' Abrie replied. He pointed at a family tasting under an umbrella on the edge of the dam next to the winery. 'Even one or two years ago, it was rare to find black people doing the wine route. Now you can't believe how interested they are.'

In the winery it was all-change too, and typically rather alternative. Since 1998 grapes had been gently conveyor-belted into the action, after mechanical harvesting and de-stemming. No pumping, and absolutely no crushing before natural, wild-yeast fermentation. Keeping the berries intact was the crux of the matter. Abrie's highly complicated explanation seemed to boil down to this: if you crush berries, you release a flood of tannin into the juice. If the tannins' only escape-route is the tiny hole left after de-stemming, your juice will be less bitter. 'You'll coax out 10 different flavours, not just a single chord,' said Abrie. 'Like Bob Dylan – he's better with a band than solo.' So his berries are permitted to keep their skins for anything from six weeks to two months – most winemakers don't extend the process beyond a couple of days. Only then are they (gently) pressed.

It's a radical, risky approach, and we sniffed one tank which had turned into 'world-class vinegar'. But if you can pull it off, you can then name your wine Whole Berry Cabernet Sauvignon. Or Merlot. And taste the difference.

Did we swallow his story? Well, yes. After he'd clambered from barrel to barrel – and come crashing down – to draw samples, we had

Flying, fishing winemaking original Abrie Bruwer at his cellar, Springfield, on the Breede River, Robertson.

to. Robertson farmers had recently been working diligently to challenge the traditional wisdom that this was white and sticky wine country. And Abrie was making some cracking reds.

His whites are equally extreme – the Méthode Ancienne Chardonnay 99, left to its own devices, took an agonising 55 days to ferment in barrel. (A week or two is more usual.) Springfield's Life from Stone – the vines growing in a glinting carpet of quartz – is uncompromisingly flinty; no louche, easy-lay this Sauvignon Blanc.

No quarter given in the vineyards stretching along the Breede river either. They looked different because they were. Abrie was ripping them out and realigning the rows with the trajectory of the sun – despite the success of the status quo, which had produced wines good enough to fly onto international airline lists. Abrie was adamant: no longer would a single sunbeam 'hit the grapes side-on, so they get those golf ball indentations'. He was also narrowing rows. 'I believe in that old French rule-of-thumb: the more vines per hectare, the higher the wine quality.' (There are few more passionate francophiles in the Cape winelands.)

This tighter spacing (and stricter pruning) had already slashed yields. 'In the old days, we'd harvest 2000 tonnes from 120 hectares – today we get 540 tonnes from 160 hectares.' Though if his marketing weapon, sister Jeanette, had her way (and we thought she would, she is a former dentist and knows how to pin people down), they'd not be uprooting their unfashionable old Colombard. She had Dutch customers begging for it.

As a child Abrie – 'never passed any exams; used to leave my satchel and homework on the road when the school bus dropped us' – spent much of his time taunting his sister. When she took refuge in her bedroom, he'd stick needles through the keyhole, jiggle the key out (jabbing her fingers if she tried to resist), and use his duplicate to storm in. Now they've made peace and a formidable team. (Abrie's English wife is the local GP, busy with daily doctoring, and leaves the business to them.) Every morning they hop onto a motorbike to check the vineyards and the fancy radio-signal irrigation system.

But, said Jeanette, when it came to tough decisions, 'he just throws me the cellar keys, says "get rid of the problem" and goes fishing!'

Once a year, Californian viticultural guru Phil Freese (he and wife Zelma Long, ex-Simi Winery, own a small vineyard near Paarl) came to consult. 'It's like a shrink session,' said Abrie. 'He lets you work out your own problems, find your own solutions. Then we have his favourite – curry – for lunch.'

Country feeling

Fraai Uitzicht is a two-centuries old farm in the verdant Klaas Voogds valley running into the foothills of the Langeberg. It was a picture of its Cape-Dutch thatched homestead – under the obligatory venerable oaks – that Axel Spanholtz and Mario Motti, Stockholm-based German vacationers in the Cape in 1998, spotted on a Farms for Sale ad. Visiting it the next day, they were irrevocably smitten.

'It gave us this warm feeling round the soul.' The small patches of vines on the 173-hectare property had been the final temptation. Returning to Sweden, Axel sold his apartment before he'd even got back into it – to someone he met in the lift going up. Enquiring at the South African Embassy about permanent residence formalities, he encountered a young woman who seemed to understand why he was throwing up his high-powered pharmaceutical company career to head into the backwaters of the Cape. 'Oh yes,' she said. 'You will be neighbours of the friendliest man in South Africa, Abrie Bruwer of Springfield Estate.'

A few months later they arrived to begin Fraai Uitzicht's sweaty makeover into a rustic charmer of a guest farm, with a table to match. Mario grew an abundance of lavender, red, white and Blue Moon roses, and herbs and vegetables to infuse a menu starring an almost all-local star cast, from the lamb, beef and quails reared nearby to farm chickens of indecent plumpness. He's untrained – 'a chef by fun' – but we'd never have known.

Now the pair had made their own Merlot 2000 from their own vines, in the ancient stables leading off the restaurant and bar. Very artisanal, with a small basket press, the old feeding-troughs re-deployed into tanks and a few oak barrels. Pieter Ferreira had helped. But Axel wasn't too happy with its rating in the latest South African wine guide.

'Traditionally-made… deliciously rich… presently hidden depths': it read well, but his face didn't. It had been rated 3 stars out of a possible 5; he'd been hoping for more. We consoled him: début vintage, maybe their upcoming Shiraz and Cabernet were destined to lead the pack. He soon cheered up: 'It's all sold anyway,' he said. 'Our guests love it.'

Ostriches on route 62

Even if travellers between Los Angeles and Chicago no longer get their kicks on Route 66, that now rather elderly hit song was still playing in the Cape hinterland. It had inspired the tourism bureaus of 21 rural towns and hamlets to embark on diversionary tactics. For years they'd languished in obscurity while tourists shuttled along the highway between Cape Town and Port Elizabeth, peering hopefully through bus windows in an attempt to establish why this had been sold as the Garden Route. Now the communities off this beaten track were fighting back, flaunting the 'adventure' and the 'unexpected pleasures' of the 'better alternative to the N2', their back-road Route 62.

Though we're normally unconvinced by brochure-hype, this 'stunningly beautiful, longest wine route in the world!' revived our faith in exclamation marks. This is the way to go if you're to get the point of the Cape winelands – their diversity.

We had a 300-kilometre or so drive into the Klein Karoo, so we zipped through the village of Ashton, where Shiraz specialist Paul de Wet, of Zandvliet Estate, had once neglected to check for oncoming trains at a level crossing. He and his car had been ploughed 340 metres down the line; he'd miraculously survived with broken ribs and a few missing teeth. Passing some intriguing signs: 'Wine sold at Cellar Price at Total Garage', and 'Final Choice Hair Salon', we sped on to the hamlet of Montagu. Big notices warned: 'Do Not Feed the Baboons'.

Montagu is famous for its hot-water springs and annual Muscadel Festival but we remember it best for the nurseryman we'd once visited. The old-fashioned radiogram in his office was a scale-model of Afrikanerdom's most emotionally charged architectural symbol, the Voortrekker Monument. More recently, an outrageously politically incorrect (and it turned out, illegal) brandy had made a brief appearance here. Labelled Fo'K'ol, the back label noted, in Afrikaans: *Specially manufactured by people who own Fo'K'ol for people who could not care about Fo'K'ol in a country where money is worth Fo'K'ol.*

We were heading for ostrich country, and on cue the first big birds with their feather-duster tails strutted onto the scene. Tractors and trailers transported workers towards Saturday-morning shopping; we stopped only for a herd of Jersey cows. Very stylish, commented John (whose first love is cattle). Such beautifully formed udders.

The special at the steakhouse in the next town of Barrydale was frog's legs, with which the local co-op's wines might have gone down well, followed by a snifter of its Joseph Barry Potstill Brandy. But we pressed on, resisting too the R62 Chardonnay and Cabernet-Merlot from the only private cellar in the area, Joubert-Tradauw Winery.

Top: Axe Hill vineyards;
no sex, just Ronnie's
cunning ruse to stop
traffic at his roadside
pub; another local
grape product; Domein
Doornkraal's Pieter
and Alice le Roux
and babies.
Middle: Graham Beck's
Robertson Winery;
from portocrats Tony
and Lyn Mossop's front
garden to (Below, right)
the back; the beach at
the end of Africa;
ostriches and vineyards
at Domein Doornkraal.
Bottom: Gourmet food
and wine on Route 62;
the Le Roux family
homestead was sent
out from the UK in
kit-form around a
century ago; Fraai
Uitzicht means, more
or less, 'charming view'.

We were in starker country now, vegetation more stubble than crew-cut. Donkey carts clopped onto the road from the old mission stations of Zoar and Amalienstein, recently restored to suitable quaintness. Down another vertiginous pass, the mountain-sides were thick with aloes, pink flowering *spekboom* (bacon tree) and the yellow lanterns of the *berg-granaat* (mountain pomegranate). At the Domein Doornkraal Beste Wyne roadside stall outside De Rust we were directed to the ostrich-wine-vegetable seed-tobacco-allsorts farm which makes these 'best wines'.

Owner Swepie le Roux is a former director of the KWV, but seemingly unrelated to the narrow-gauge establishment of the organisation that previously ran South African wine. Though he and his wife Ann both descended from Afrikaner aristocracy – National Party Cabinet Ministers on both sides – Swepie's politics appeared to be of a freer, easier sort.

He'd taught himself to silkscreen to make his own port labels. He attached a cerise home-grown ostrich feather to his sparkling wine and called it Tickled Pink. His naïve-art labels – ostriches partying madly under a full moon – stood out from the wine-is-deeply-serious crowd. His travel itineraries – Bulgaria, Romania – were alternative. We looked forward to seeing him at home in his ostrich palace.

We arrived with a drove of other cars, waved in by two women dressed in full clown suits – red noses, the lot. Swepie hurried up to explain: they were hosting the AGM of the local Parkinson's society. Many of the passengers took an agonisingly long time to get out of the cars. Swepie delegated the new generation, his son Pieter and daughter-in-law, Alice, to Meet the Press.

The burnt-umber and white family house, on a gentle slope of green velvet lawn, is pure Edwardiana. It was chosen from an English catalogue at the turn of the twentieth century by Swepie's grandfather, and sent out in kit-form. It has all the wide verandas, frilly woodwork, decorative domes and mock-Gothic towers of that *troukoekerige* (wedding-cakey) genre, as Alice, an accountant with her own practice in Oudtshoorn, put it. A Scottish engineer had been imported to build and run the irrigation pump-house. 'My great-grandfather didn't have a clue,' said Pieter. 'When the engineer moved on, and the pump broke down, he'd ring my grandfather in Parliament who'd have to drive through the night to restart the engine. All the children had governesses too.'

Those were the days, and every wall was crammed with portraits and sepia photographs capturing them and the family in old-fashioned finery. It's all different, yet in some ways much the same now. Pieter reads *The Spectator* on the Web in his office amid Boer War memorabilia, and Doornkraal is still an oasis of gracious living in the semi-desert of the Klein Karoo.

The finest tables in the neighbourhood are at Jemima's in the nearby ostrich capital of Oudtshoorn, run by two of Pieter's five sisters, Annette and Celia – and here at

Doornkraal. His mother Ann is a legendary cook, and her chicken liver paté is oral heaven. The farm produce – chillis for their own harissa; pomegranates for Swepie's grenadine; olives for his oil; Swiss Brown cows, ostriches, chickens, turkeys, pigs (Celia has a degree in animal husbandry) – nearly all ends up on the menu here or at Jemima's. The ostriches are especially versatile, game for anything from eggs for multiple meringues to fillets for carpaccio.

'To have your own wine on the table, too – that's for me the embodiment of the good life,' said Pieter. Selling the wine, and winning double gold medals at the local show (most recent star their Pinta, a chocolate-fudge siren of a dessert from Pinotage and Tinta Barocca made by another sister, Maria) seemed almost an accessory after that fact. Pieter followed his agricultural degree at Stellenbosch University with a 5-month cellar-rat stint at Robert Mondavi in California ('the first vintage of Opus!'). He was enthusiastic about the new South African Muscadel Society – formed to raise the profile of the fortified dessert wines that are this region's forté. But there was too much happening on these 150 hectares to concentrate his mind narrowly on wine. Especially when vines were such a struggle against the odds – the chronic lack of rain, the strictly policed irrigation rights.

'Here people don't marry for money, they marry for water,' he said.

Portocracy

Water is the crux of the matter too, in the hot, dry Klein Karoo town of Calitzdorp, 385 kilometres from Cape Town. This is the Douro of the Cape, home to South Africa's smallest and only specialist port-winemaker. Tony and Lyn Mossop, our hosts that night, have only a single hectare of vineyard on their Axe Hill property – named because it's not soil the vines struggle through here, it's a prehistoric factory floor – layers and layers of Stone Age tools! But they've been forced to buy another patch of land nearby purely for its water rights. Now their Touriga Nacional, Tinta Barocca and Souzão vines – traditional port varieties – aren't dying of thirst. On the other hand, we thought, why pamper them when they clearly thrive on deprivation?

Small was sensational here from the start. Every vintage from the début 97 had been 5-star-rated by the South African wine guide judges; the 400-case production is booked practically before birth. Awards had been showered on the elegant packaging. (Though Tony was a bit worried: his German supplier was discontinuing the ruby-coloured glass which had given the slender, sleek bottles their lustrous depths; 'when it's half-empty, in all these fancy back-lit bars in San Francisco and Miami, it won't look as good.... But we'll make a plan.')

The Nel families had originally encouraged him to take the port plunge. They're the eminences of Calitzdorp – even the river that runs through it is named after them. Carel

Nel of Boplaas had made the first connections with the Portuguese winemaking luminaries who'd become frequent visitors and advisers here, nudging locals towards a more classic, drier, more powerful style of Cape port. Carel liked to survey his vineyards from his microlight, in streaming scarf and Biggles goggles. (John once went up with him and survived.) Carel and his cousin, Boets, of Die Krans, are Cape Wine Masters, like Tony Mossop.

The Mossops became the newest members of this portocracy, and were married in the local church. It was decorated with sheaves of grasses and arum lilies; the bride clopped up in a donkey cart driven by a wonderfully toothless local.

Axe Hill's grapes are hand-sorted, foot-stomped. The Mossops used to invite mates to share these duties, but the crowds quickly became riotous. Now this part of the process is kept in-house, and done in stages. Lyn likes to read while doing her tramping bit.

The miniature cellar is over the dust road in front of their white-walled, khaki-shuttered old cottage, its front *stoep* (veranda) framed by tumbles of ruby bougainvillea and beds of blue plumbago and indigenous irises. Behind the cottage is a little rockery of semi-desert succulents; stands of grey cacti with white flowers big as pudding basins, cerise flowers small as coffee-cups; and then the vineyard.

Dinner, under a rustic reed roof, was whipped up in minutes by the formidably organised Lyn, who spent years sailing and cooking on the Med and the Caribbean and now runs one of South Africa's top catering companies. Tony's cigars came out with the port and we puffed away contentedly. The daytime temperature of around 40 degrees had dropped to a manageable 20, and the Axe Hill Cape Vintage 97 was so good we opened another (half) bottle.

To the end of Africa

Leaving Calitzdorp, and mindful of the sign which urges motorists to watch out for tortoises, we turned coastwards over the Tradouw Pass. It was hot semi-desert going up, cool green valleys going down. As Pernod-Ricard international development director Robin Day – the Aussie behind the blast-off of the Jacobs Creek range – had discovered.

The most southerly wine region in Africa lies around the mission village of Elim.

Scouring the Cape for sources of prime fruit he found the remote vineyards tucked into these mountains, and instantly snaffled a share for P-R's South African label, Long Mountain. A couple of years after he'd persuaded the locals to go for quality rather than quantity, up lumbered the KWV behemoth and bore away the fruits of his labours. Understandable from the farmers' point of view – 'we couldn't take all their grapes,' explained Long Mountain winemaker Jacques Kruger. So he'd now winkled out other cool spots, and Long Mountain was up to 250,000 cases a year, mostly for UK supermarkets.

Ostriches were still a high-stepping feature, and now there were blue cranes too, posing in elegant pairs in pastures and wheatfields. The wheat snaked over the hills towards the sea in sinuous patterns. We were heading for the new winegrowing ward of Elim, the most southerly vineyards in Africa, not far from the official endpoint of the continent at Cape Agulhas.

Elim is a rustic little mission village of thatched cottages and churches, and some rather big Cape players were busy pushing vineyards to new extremes here. Distell, the giant merger of Distillers and Stellenbosch Farmers' Winery; Hein Koegelenberg of La Motte; and a new force, transplanted Scottish businessman Dave King. His consultant, Kiwi Rod Easthope, is overseeing developments here beyond the traditional winegrowing fringe: 40 hectares of Cabernets Sauvignon and Franc, Pinot Noir, Pinotage, Merlot, Petit Verdot, Chardonnay, Sauvignon Blanc and Sémillon had been planted on Boschkloof, King's mountainous 3000-hectare farm.

A sign on the dirt road showed a bunch of grapes and a protea. It's not all that close to the oceans – 22 kilometres in fact. But it is in another climate zone – cool and misty, more prone to summer rainfall, which was why the tractors were out on a Sunday, spraying against downy mildew. Gas cannons were popping off to chase baboons away from the fledgling vineyards, along with grysbok, duikers and flocks of grape-eating birds.

The first harvest was in 2001: 30 tonnes of grapes were picked early in the morning, sent to Stellenbosch in refrigerated trucks, and baptised Dave King's spanking new winery there. We were to visit it later in the week, and also taste a Sauvignon Blanc from his neighbours' 35-hectare Land's End vineyards down the road. These are closer to the sea, not far from the Cape Agulhas lighthouse. The beach was so white it seared our eyes, and in the little fishing village of Gansbaai we ate Cape salmon just out of the bright turquoise sea, with chips.

Keep our grapes clean: instruction along the dirt road leading to new vineyards at Boschkloof, inland from Cape Agulhas.

God's own mountain

Driving back back to Cape Town, our imperative (minor) detour was into the valley ringed by the Helderberg and Hottentots Holland mountains which is André van Rensburg's considerable sphere of influence. And this big, beefy winemaker was grumbling. He's sick of being called an *enfant terrible*. First, he's not a spring chicken. And second, if there was a vote among peers and consumers for the Cape's best winemaker, he'd stand a good chance of winning. Conversations about him usually start something like: Whatever else you may say about André, you have to admit....

Yes, perhaps the finest wines of the Cape are being made by this complex, obsessive perfectionist whose bachelor life is dominated by three dogs. A lot of the time he seems angrier than he probably is because he tends, in a big, booming voice – and with an intense, bespectacled stare – not to bottle things up. The bark is worse than the bite – he's usually all heart and charm.

But why he elected to work in the most corporate of environments – form-filling, memo-flying Anglo-American, the giant mining house that owns Vergelegen – was a mystery to those who watched his earlier progress through various establishments where free-spirited leeway was what he craved. Typically, he probably thought he could buck even Anglo's tight systems – and he may have.

Vergelegen (meaning far-flung) had always been a bit of a folly. The Dutch planted their own flag of corruption and graft in Africa here – back at the start of the eighteenth century – when the colony's gifted but wayward second governor, Willem Adriaan van der Stel assigned himself, illegally, the sprawling property. He planted the first vines and, equally illegally, siphoned off 600 slaves to build what is still one of the glories of Cape colonial architecture, the centrepiece of this estate. His tenure was brief. Amsterdam recalled and sacked him, and the Cape lost an outstanding horticulturalist and winegrower.

The estate has been a plaything of the wealthy down the centuries and even Anglo wasn't immune. In the 1980s they let French architects loose, pointed them to the top of a hill and had them sink a huge hole into which was lowered a four-storey winery – so that only the offices peeped above the windy skyline. All at probably three times the cost of a 'normal' winery. The idea was this would be one of the first virtually pump-free cellars. The views are magnificent. But: 'Shocking place, a nightmare to work in' said Van Rensburg. 'I'd rather make the wine outside.' (On the flat, instead of having to hare up and down stairs all the time.)

He arrived in 1998, after it was built. His wines have been triumphs ever since, and he'd set the bar high. At his previous post at Stellenzicht, on the other side of what he calls God's own mountain, the Helderberg (he's vowed never to leave its slopes), he isolated a small block of Shiraz vines. From 1994, he tapped into this to turn out the Syrah which became a Cape superstar wine. At a famous taste-off against the Australians in 1997, it scored more highly than the Aussie icon, Grange – the international tasters included Australians! But there were 100 wines from each country in that contest and the Cape lost abysmally: 78–22. In the ensuing uproar, Cape winemakers cried foul almost en masse.

Van Rensburg's was a lone voice against this chorus. If they couldn't take defeat and raise their game, 'they should go and grow vegetables instead,' he charged in an angry letter to a local wine magazine. There'd never been a re-match.

The Vergelegen line-up is now led by a Cabernet Sauvignon-dominated Estate wine that, especially in 1998, effortlessly lived up to that over-ambitious claim: world class. The supposedly second-string 98 Cabernet is one of our personal favourites. The Sauvignon Blanc Reserve is world class too. The small range also includes a Chardonnay and an ultra-fine botrytis dessert from Sémillon. A wine that isn't top of its class doesn't graduate here. Van Rensburg knows he's dished out enough criticism of others not to risk exposing himself.

Over the Helderberg, the rollcall resonates with some of Cape wine's most notable modern names. Wineries like Cordoba, Grangehurst, Eikendal, Longridge, JP Bredell, and closer to Stellenbosch, boutique cellar De Trafford, and Waterford. This is a very exclusive neighbourhood, and now we were off to taste with an immigrant from up north who'd stormed the place.

Bottled Jung and the epicure on a bike

Big Ken Forrester's wine journey started in the middle of Africa, in old British-run Zambia, on the copper belt bordering the Congo. 'I used to ride to school on a bicycle every day through the bush.' His father was a mining engineer in this epicurean desert. Hard tack ruled, interesting cuisine was off the radar (unlike in French colonies). Such early deprivation motivated later compensation – wine and food are Ken's passions now. 'And I wanted my own business – from day one.'

By the age of 19 he was a restaurateur in Johannesburg's most cosmopolitan quarter, Hillbrow – now a much wilder, sleazier place. Just over 20 years later he 'retired' – as the South African hotel and restaurant organisation's chief spokesman – to the Cape.

He wanted to make a mark and has – by stamping his name, and staking much of his savings, on two underdog grapes, Chenin Blanc and Grenache. He hunted down old vineyards of both – while upgrading his own vines at the rundown estate of Scholtzenhof, beneath the Helderberg range, whose fine old home he restored. In the mid-1990s when others were still emphasising deep, inky, opaque density in their reds, he bottled an almost translucent Grenache, cut with a bit of spicy Shiraz. It wasn't an easy sell at first. And his evangelism for Chenin seemed a missionary donation to a feeble cause when whacking Sauvignons and Chardonnays were all the rage.

But a decade on, Ken Forrester wines are an established part of the scenery – due in no small measure to his friendship with Martin Meinert, the most travelled, over-qualified, cerebral of winemakers (a newspaper sub-editor in another life). Martin's is a love–hate relationship with wine. He abhors the hard-sell and self-promotion it entails, and seems to bottle only when the mood takes him. But invariably with talking-point results.

He is Forrester's partner in the buzzy 96 Winery Road restaurant, a kind of high-class canteen by appointment to the Stellenbosch (and visiting international) wine fraternity. It had been our table from home for years, just down the mountain from the vineyard we used to own. Meinert makes his and the Forrester wines at his compact, model winery in Devon valley – the restaurant, their virtual joint office, and wine point of sale, situated conveniently in between their vineyards.

Seated at the grand table in the Forrester homestead, Ken nudged the reluctant Martin and said: 'Take it away, the show's yours.' The California-based wine correspondent of the *Dallas Morning News*, Rebecca Murphy, had arrived and was all ears. Martin poured his latest Meinert 2000, which he'd just named 'Synchronicity' (he hand-writes his labels). This signified more than its blend of Cabernet Sauvignon, Merlot, Pinotage and Cabernet Franc. It had been inspired by 'the meaningful Jungian coincidence of the mental and physical states of….'

Martin Meinert and Ken Forrester deep in wine speak.

The voice tailed off. He grinned.

'Actually my ex-wife used to say it was a meaningful coincidence whenever I got a wine into a bottle.' He laughed again. And then explained how he added tannin to soften a wine! It's about polymerisation: added tannin reduces the tannin effect by accelerating the process of smaller molecules combining to form bigger ones (which eventually drop out as sediment in old mellow wine). What's more, he explained, tannin addition 'helps colour wine because it binds the anthocyanins'.

We wondered how this would play in the *Dallas Morning News*. But soon we were drinking. A gorgeous wine – spicy with the Pinotage (which might have swamped its more refined partners) well-buried. Then the individual Meinert Merlot and Cabernet Sauvignon, also 2000s: both strong, purposeful wines – good for the next 10 years at least.

Ken soon took over: never mind that he had an audience of one, Rebecca; he was in big-crowd presentation mode. A short history of the Cape. Then the Chenin Blanc story. 'We plan to change the world's view of Chenin Blanc… er, make that South African Chenin,' he said. He poured some delightful, waxy, honeyed older vintages which made his point. Even Meinert, who'd made them and hadn't tasted them for a while, became uncharacteristically chuffed.

By the time he moved onto a recent signature red, the 2000 Grenache-Syrah, Ken was in full flow. 'Evocative of gypsies dancing around flickering fires,' he rhapsodised. This was a long way from polymerisation. But like his Chenins, this wine plays well in Britain, especially in Scotland – to which he returned frequently to claim his roots; it was served at the banquet which marked the inauguration of the Scottish Parliament. It also harmonised with 96 Winery Road's creatively modern Cape menu (the restaurant has the best wine list in Stellenbosch). We repaired there to thrash out the world's problems.

Parties and porcini

Stellenbosch was to be our stamping ground the next day, an easy 25-minute trip from Cape Town if you stop nowhere en route. Inevitably, we took a great deal longer. Some of the most beautiful old wine farms fringe the R310 which leads off the highway.

First up is white-gabled Vergenoegd (far enough) Estate, so close to False Bay that tasters often swear they pick up a sea-salty tang in its wines. We find more eucalyptus, herbs and plums, with the Shiraz perhaps the most exceptional in the red line-up.

We called next door, up a fat palm-fringed driveway, at another Cape-Dutch architectural treasure, Meerlust. There are even more romantically roccoco swirls to the gables here, and the front door has been framing Table Mountain – exactly – for more than 300 years.

Inside, handsome, urbane eighth-generation owner Hannes Myburgh has shocked the purists, banished any resemblance to a museum piece, and filled the house with wit, glamour and Art Deco. We'd been to countless parties in the hub of this home, the vast kitchen with its fireplace and 30-seater table: tripe-cooking competitions for example, and extenuated festivities after the annual Nativity Play, performed by the farm children. (Memorably, the little inn-keeper had once not turned Mary and Joseph away. He'd piped: 'Come in for a drink.')

Top: Sally Simson, author of the classic Cape of Good Cooks, *Meerlust owner Hannes Myburgh, and Vineyard Ventures super-guide Gillie Stoltzman. Below: Meerlust's Giorgio Dalla Cia, recipient of the next best thing to a knight-hood from the Italian government for 'services to wine'.*

There'd been countless feasts of fungi foraged by the Cape's finest Italian import, rubicund Giorgio Dalla Cia, Meerlust's winemaker since 1978. Giorgio had recently suffered withdrawal symptoms so acute he threatened to return to his roots in Friuli. His annual fix of porcini, growing wild in the Stellenbosch forests, had dried up. But 2001 was a splendid vintage for wine and the 'queen of mushrooms'; he unpacked his bags.

Naturally – nowhere in the Cape is there a more natural, everyday celebration of the culture of wine than at Meerlust – every gathering here is lubricated by the expressive, individual house-wines. If there's one local label diners at stylish restaurants as far apart as London and San Francisco recognise and call for, it's Meerlust.

Their Eurocentric styles – Giorgio is a classical fundamentalist, Hannes Myburgh has a degree in French – are clearly part of the appeal. From the restrained Rubicon Bordeaux blend to the forest-floor Pinot Noir, the minerally Merlot and the weighty Chardonnay (Meursault the benchmark here), none of these wines are too foreign for foreigners.

A new generation is making its mark here, too. In his mid-twenties, George Dalla Cia is continuing his family's tradition of making grappa. So well that crucial South African trade talks with the European Union were log-jammed by protests from Italian competitors, unnerved by this African challenge to their turf. In 2002 the Cape lost the skirmish to use the names port, sherry and grappa on labels, but won crucial EU trade concessions. And, by any other name, Meerlust's grappa remains a very smooth *digestif*.

Today, though, only the supporting cast was home. The Dalla Cias were in Italy, Hannes was flitting between Europe and the US. And anyway, it was far too early, though an espresso and a shot of George's finest would have fortified us for the dangers that might lie ahead. Just up the road, at Spier, we were going to taste with a cheetah.

Dreaming with cheetahs

Nyana, holder of the world record for the 100-metre sprint – 6.34 seconds, and who knows how much faster he'd have run in chase of something more succulent than a fluffy toy? – was waiting for us, draped glossily over a tree trunk at the Cheetah Outreach Centre at Spier. Vineyards climbed up the hill behind, traffic hummed up and down the Stellenbosch road past the Spier station.

We were just too early for the annual Arts Festival, between mid-November and March, when we might have steamed out here from the Cape Town Waterfront on a 1950s vintage train and heard, in the open air amphitheatre, anyone from the Soweto String Quartet to Senegalese heart-and-soul singer Baaba Maal and *Dido and Aeneas* African-style. We were just too late to watch Anna Kournikova battling local heroine Amanda Coetzer on the Spier tennis courts.

But our timing was spot-on to marvel at the cultural revolution that's transformed this 310-year-old wine estate in under a decade. Conservatives who'd reviled owner Dick Enthoven when he was an MP, lambasting the old South African régime from the Opposition benches, had changed their tune. So had those who lamented Spier's passing from an old family farm into this business tycoon's portfolio.

The trouble was that Enthoven's vision for Spier was so wildly grand, went so far beyond restoring its wine fortunes, that it defied understanding. His crusade for the performing arts, the multiple restaurants, the hotels, conference centres and golf course, the picnic-friendly lakes, riverbanks and gardens – the tourist theme-park corner of the picture, all that was digestible. The idea of cheetahs in the winelands – not so incongruous, are we not in Africa? – was rather delightful and educational. It raises money and environmental consciousness for the Cheetah Conservation Fund.

But when Enthoven spoke about eliminating poverty, building eco-villages and schools, organic farming, rural regeneration and land reform, an institute for 'the theory and practice of sustainable living', and, for heaven's sake, a unique sewerage system based on hessian bags and earth-worms – not just re-inventing the estate but the whole neighbourhood – well, the consensus was that he'd gone mad. And that he'd never see a return on his multi-million – in any currency – investment.

Maybe not for some time. But the bravery and generosity of his dream are stuttering towards a working reality. The prophets of gloom are now silent, some even (grudgingly) admiring. The wines had improved too: the Spier Private Collection range shining brightest. Meantime, Enthoven had also come to the rescue of a couple of other wineries. These bunched under the Winecorp umbrella labels like Naledi and Sejana (consultant Alain Mouiex of Pomerol) and Longridge, whose brilliant young winemaker Ben Radford had just resigned. He was off home to Australia's Barossa Valley, but wouldn't be altogether lost to Cape wine. The Radford-Dale range – a partnership with half-Brit half-Burgundian mate Alex Dale which had already produced some crackers – would continue.

Chris Keet of Cordoba – its vertiginous vineyards climbing the Helderberg range in front of our eyes – had dropped in to bring us a bottle of his Crescendo red blend. We toasted Nyana's world record, and he purred throughout. You won't get this sort of start to a day in the winelands anywhere but in Africa.

Stellenbosch continued…

Stellenbosch is the pretty wine and university town which had turned out most of South Africa's apartheid-era prime ministers and was soon to cap the country's first black oenology graduates. It's not the sort of place to zip through, as we did this time, in a hurry.

Stellenbosch is for strolling under ancient oaks and lilac jacarandas (the affectionate Afrikaans name for it is Eikestad – Oak City). It's for soaking up gracious colonial architecture. For dipping into museums and galleries. For classical concerts at the conservatory or cabaret at the Dorp Street Theatre: forthcoming attraction, we saw from the posters, our former neighbour, winegrower and national singing icon Lesley Rae Dowling. Pavement café cappuccinos, pasta at De Cameron or grilled calamari at Wijnhuis are Stellenbosch too. And Oom Samie se Winkel, with its authentic whiffs of an old-time general store, purveying anything from fly-swatters to home-made puff pastry.

But Stellenbosch stretches beyond town and gown. This neighbourhood is the Napa of the Cape and we had a choice of 86 cellars to visit. This was far too many – oh for the simplicity of Egypt with its single winery! We had to be as subjective as tasting itself about our pit-stops… some oldies, some new blood, we decided, and we'd get our youthful transfusion first.

Young bloods

It was in our face everywhere. A young and unstoppable force was re-occupying the winelands. It was smart-bombs vs the cavalry. And it was only a matter of time before

– see Afghanistan, see South Africa itself – the old guard adapted or died. Our next book might very well have to carry an age-restriction.

We short-circuited the protracted expedition that would have been involved in documenting this youth revolution in its entirety by plugging into Rootstock. This is a group established by Michael Ratcliffe and like-minded mates after he returned from post-graduate studies at Roseworthy in Australia to take over the family farm, Warwick, from parents Stan and Norma.

'Our voices weren't being heard in the established wine industry bodies,' Michael said. Probably because the *ancien régime* doesn't take kindly to being challenged by youngsters barely out of school. Ergo Rootstock, age limit 35, which now had 140 members. They meet monthly to debate and strategise. They are a powerful new lobby in Cape wine, and we could see why when we met a small sample on the oak-shaded veranda of Warwick's tasting room.

The young ones. Standing to attention: Bruwer Raats (Delaire), Michael Ratcliffe (Warwick), Lizelle Gerber (Avontuur), Jean Engelbrecht (Rust en Vrede). At ease: Adi Badenhorst (Rustenberg), Victor Sperling (Delheim), Rianie Strydom (Morgenhof).

They were formidable. Eloquent, forceful, determined and committed. Highly critical of how the previous generation had managed South Africa's re-entry to the international stage: they'd not been market-driven, they'd fragmented their forces instead of devising a national battle plan like the Australians, they'd pumped out a flood of ill-conceived bulk wine. It was the sort of hard-talk which not long ago might have had them accused (as we'd been) of 'sabotage' and 'treason'.

Jean Engelbrecht, former airline pilot, new-generation owner of Rust en Vrede Estate (at 37 over the limit but on this occasion permitted to deputise for his younger winemaker, Louis Strydom): 'I'm not interested in how things were done in the past. We were so on our little island then. It's the present and the future that count.'

What are the problems you face, we asked? Michael Ratcliffe, 29, quietly detonated a grenade: 'Pinotage?'

The rest of the gang exploded; this was something they'd thrashed over before. In the hubbub, we didn't catch exactly who said the following, and probably just as well: 'It's crap! When some a***hole gets up and says there HAS to be Pinotage in a blend to make it South African… No no no!'

Rianie Strydom, winemaker of French-owned Morgenhof, 31: 'There may be 10 exceptional Pinotages; the rest are mediocre. People get the wrong impression of our wine from them.'

Everyone with Pinotage vineyards indicated they were cutting down on them. Bruwer Raats, winemaker of Delaire, 31: 'It's a little niche market. Now Chenin, there's something we can make our own….

Bruwer, perhaps the philosopher of the group, elaborated on what UK wine writers Robert Joseph and Tim Atkin had concluded after recent visits: that post-apartheid South African wine had entered its third modern stage. 'First there was defensiveness; then there was a lack of confidence. Now we're doing it. Our foundations are sound. There's energy and excitement. Things have changed.'

We could personally second that, with special reference to Delaire. The farm used to be ours: we'd named it; John converted the cellar from a shed; he planted some of the vineyards, including the one from which Bruwer drew his (stunning) Merlot, marketing it as coming from (ouch) 'very old' vines. It had moved right up the evolutionary scale from our original poacher-turned-gamekeeper efforts.

Michael Ratcliffe: 'In the past, we were trying to cook on a two-legged pot. Just viticulture and viniculture. Marketing has to come in to achieve the right balance.'

Jean Engelbrecht: 'We can't be the Mom and Pop show any longer – you know, doing everything themselves from pruning to delivering the cases to a restaurant on the tractor. Wineries which want to be relevant internationally must have specialists handling each part of the operation.' He was adamant that 'we have something that everybody has underestimated: tourism. We're Africa *and* Europe here.

So – Old World, New World, where was the Cape positioned, we asked? Firmly in its own space, they all replied, in a new, not old South Africa.

Rianie: 'I've just been on a tasting trip to France, second growths, and was really disappointed. We've advanced while they've stood still! We were forced to travel to learn, and that's paid off. The French in general have never thought it necessary to investigate what's happening in other wine countries.'

What is the South African brand, then, we asked?

'Exceptional value,' they sang out. 'And diversity, one of our strengths,' said Michael. 'The Australian show system has improved the breed, but it's also homogenised it. Because we have such individuality all in one country here, we have more strong selling points.'

Staff-training was making a difference. Ten workers had just returned from a visit to the vineyards of Burgundy, courtesy of the French government. 'A changed man,' said Michael of his French-seasoned employee, now greeting everyone with a cheery *Ca va*? Winemaker Louise Hofmeyr of red-wine Welgemeend Estate near Paarl was battling, however: her staffer now refused to drive the tractor; he considered it beneath the dignity of someone who'd been on foreign TV! But this was an advanced programme: for many, there's still the hurdle of literacy to climb. Rianie's right-hand man in the cellar could neither read nor write.

Individual farmers had to make an effort, Michael said. Last vintage he'd laid a trestle table in Warwick's Cabernet block with white cloth and wines, and invited his staff to taste 'what you're working for. The wine you helped to make is now on the table of the British Prime Minister.'

Bruwer was about to employ the first black student to graduate from Stellenbosch University (via a bursary from the Natural Corporation wine company). He'd been head-hunted by one of the giants, but refused the job. 'No, they just want to use me for window dressing. And I just want to make wine,' he said. 'I'm coming to you.'

They moved on to two viticultural problem areas: virus in the vineyards, and the knock-out alcohol levels in many of the modern wines. 'Really good dating wines' was how Adi Badenhorst, 29, winemaker at Rustenberg, described these.

Lizelle Gerber of Avontuur, 27: 'Phenolic ripeness; we didn't know what it WAS six years ago. But all wine countries have viruses. We must just learn to manage what we've got. We're still winning international competitions.'

Of more concern seemed to be the inexperienced winemakers and viticulturists (yes, even younger than this lot!) swarming all over the winelands. 'New cellars are pop-ping up all the time,' said Rianie. (One every 9 days was the count during 2001.) 'And they're hiring guys straight out of university! It's totally wrong. A viticulturalist is only going to know the vineyards after at least 5 or 6 years....'

At Warwick, this is why Norma Ratcliffe – whose first vintage was in 1984 – continues to work the harvests. 'I'm the only one who knows the vineyards from experience. The hotspots, the cold spots, the G-spots.' At least some of the older generation still had something to teach the new. But the blood at our next port of call was decidedly young.

Transfusion

First impressions of De Toren, the newest sensation on an upwardly mobile block in the Polkadraai hills outside Stellenbosch, were unpromising. The vineyards looked fine, the views to the Helderberg range and over False Bay were gorgeous. (The Cape really is outrageously scenic.) But if the lofty aim is to produce a Mona Lisa here (young wine-maker Albie Koch's romantic contribution to De Toren's rather lush publicity literature) what was a derelict abattoir doing slap in front of the winery?

That's what it looked like, that's what it had been when Emil and Sonette den Dulk decided to scale down their direct-mail empire, move from Johannesburg to the Cape, and buy a thatched farmhouse. The neighbours are certainly the right sort. To name but two: there's Jordan, recently rated the Cape's top cellar for 'overall quality' by WINE magazine (its Chardonnay one of our enduring favourites). And there's Kanu, whose winemaker Teddy Hall had turned dowdy Chenin Blanc into a sex bomb; he'd just walked off with South African winedom's equivalent of the Best Actor Oscar – the Diners' Club Winemaker of the Year award (for his second-string Chenin!).

But right in front of their 'little piece of heaven', the Den Dulks found to their dismay, was a shed in which 10,000 chickens were slaughtered daily and sold from the door. Convoys of buyers bumped up and down the dirt track in a continuous stream. 'One Saturday morning there was a gun battle, AK-47s, the lot,' recounted Emil.

This was taking neighbourly tolerance to the extreme. Complaints were filed, the slaughterhouse was closed, and its site and some vineyards came onto the market. The Den Dulks hadn't intended braving the crowded wine scene. Emil's idea was 'just to be a sort of country squire'. But the experts kept telling him: 'You have a unique *terroir*. Why send all your grapes to the co-op [nearby Vlottenburg] when you've got your own little Château Ausone here?' His business antennae began quivering.

Niche-marketing is his forte. Like the service one of his companies provides – the secure delivery of credit cards from banks to customers. He searched for a similarly simple gap in the wine business, one which matched the varieties which grew best in his 20-hectare soils. When one of his mates (a top Cape winemaker who must remain nameless) began musing about a one-wine-only estate, Emil knew he'd found his slot.

'I also knew how risky it would be. With only one wine, you have only one bite at the market.' He made Albie Koch, just 24 at the time, but with local, Californian and French experience, 'an offer he couldn't understand. And from day one it all clicked.' Albie knew the area, having worked with another local hero, Nico van Rensburg, who makes explosive reds at nearby Saxenburg and at Château Capion near Montpellier in France.

Denying any allusion to Latour, Emil insisted that De Toren had been named after the ingenious tower-cum-liftshaft which dominates the winery. No pumps (instruments of torture he calls them) here; instead, juice gravity-feeds into a tank which moves between floors. No crushers either. The rites of passage for young wines could hardly be smoother. But when the 99 registered a startling 90 out of 100 on the Richter scale of international wine – Robert Parker's rating, practically unheard of for a début vintage – the French connection was made for him.

Blazing out of nowhere, De Toren Fusion had local critics raving: an instant Cape First Growth. Made from the classic Bordeaux red varieties, with Cabernet Sauvignon leading the rest of the orchestra (Merlot, Malbec, Cabernet Franc, Petit Verdot). Emil's gamble had paid off.

Take it softly, make it personal seemed to be the slogan here. Albie told us his favourite French word was *tranquille*, and that his unfrantic approach had been encouraged by 'the way my French friends in the cellars paused for proper meals; they were always telling me to stop rushing around and take it easier.'

Emil, who admitted he was so clueless previously that he was under the impression that 'a blend was down-market', had now become such a technical authority that when

A FUSION OF FIVE NOBLE VARIETIES

DE TOREN
W.O. COASTAL REGION
FUSION V
1999
De Toren Private Cellar
Polkadraai Road
Stellenbosch
75de   SOUTH AFRICA   13.5%vol

De Toren's Emil den Dulk and Albie Koch, powers behind a sensational upstart, the Fusion blend.

Albie slipped off to attend to some UK customers, it was the boss who gave us the guided tour.

We began outside, where Emil stations himself during the harvest. Few if any winery proprietors are this hands-on: he personally eye-balls and helps sort every crate of grapes. They are spread out on a conveyor belt and rolled slowly along: 'Anything suspect, anything blemished, I reject.'

In the chic tasting-eyrie looking into the barrel cellar, over the winery, and to the view beyond the abattoir (happily soon to be demolished) we sat on zebra-skin ottomans and sampled the Fusion. It was terrific. No wonder Mr Parker had been impressed. The 99 was long sold out; the 2000 overbooked before birth. We put our names down just in case a vacancy came up, and headed off to investigate the other side of Stellenbosch and a couple of winemakers who hadn't arrived yesterday.

Traveller's rest

'Thank God we've moved on from the era of 'white-coat' wines, designed and fixed up in the cellar, technically correct but boring,' said Neil Ellis. This was even before we'd sat down in the vast loft office above his barrel-vaulted cellar. 'But you know, these youngsters… jeez, can they waffle! They sound as if they've got degrees in talking bulls**t. Waffle, waffle. On the other hand, there's no denying there's some frightening research now, really complex, useful stuff.'

Ellis was more prosperous about the girth than when he and we lived on Delaire – we'd all moved on several times since then – but he'd lost none of his earthy philosophy and intensity. His wines are intense too, among the smartest, tidiest, most focused of all ranges in the Cape.

He came from nowhere – barely a bean to his name after he graduated from Stellenbosch University in the mid-1970s – but snaffled the pick of the jobs at the time: winemaker at the government showcase, national monument, tourist magnet of Groot Constantia Estate. He had a fairly hectic career from there: Zevenwacht, Louisvale, Neethlingshof, all respected wine names, all pit-stops. Then he ran a travelling show – with barrel halls, crush facilities and cartons scattered all over the place – until finally bringing them to rest at the secluded vineyards owned by friend and wine enthusiast Hans Schroeder. Here in the Jonkershoek valley, a narrow channel between towering mountains just outside Stellenbosch, he'd established Neil Ellis Wines. Geese splashed about in the dam, waterways coursed through the buildings.

In 1985, Ellis had stunned the wine establishment by importing a simple, obvious idea from abroad: he tracked down parcels of exceptional vineyards in obscure areas and brought the grapes to Stellenbosch, making regional, vineyard wines under his banner. He was the first to put Elgin – an area known mainly for apples – on the wine map. Previously its grapes had disappeared anonymously down merchants' gullets. He quickly expanded to 16 different suppliers. It was the Burgundy négociant idea, and also the California practice of sourcing grapes from scattered, specialist growers. He never looked back.

'To make great wine, the winery matters about 10 per cent – the rest is all in the vineyards; if you get a few winery basics right, you're simply optimising what your vines give you… but it takes 10 years to get to know your vineyards, and 10 years to know how to fine-tune the fruit. I can't understand the youngsters these days on the merry-go-round, leaving and joining new wineries all the time.' He'd obviously forgotten his own peripatetic youth!

'Wine is about feel, gut feel, knowing your fruit and your area so you can produce wine that's true and not forced.'

His underlings and understudies soon get to know about his obsession with detail. 'There's only so much democracy you can tolerate in this business and there's that point in every season where everything has to become a military operation, otherwise you'd find yourself playing 2nd team in the national quality stakes. And I like playing in the 1st team,' said Ellis.

Few are more respected by their peers in Cape wine. Neil Ellis Sauvignons are a byword for bold freshness; lately his Shirazes had become triumphs too and the Cabernets remained rock-steady, solid, powerful, gutsy. Like himself. Those who might suggest they could be a touch gentler would be asking for something less 'true' to their maker.

The one to beat

Gyles Webb, at Thelema Mountain Vineyards in nextdoor Banhoek valley, and as quality director of the launch vintage of Spice Route, had been about the smartest name in Cape wine for nearly a decade. Now he'd embarked on perhaps the trickiest phase of a glittering career. He was lending his lustre to a swanky new venture, Tokara, without the prerogative of unfettered decision-making he enjoyed at Thelema, the family farm across the road. He was also contending with a rampant crop of college-fresh viticulturalists and winemakers eager to dislodge the 'old guard'. Gyles, though in his youthful early 50s, knew he was a prime target. Thelema was the standard to beat.

His lovely manners and persistent humour disguise a highly competitive streak – to the point where many miss it altogether: this wiry, compact man was a scratch golfer and a chartered accountant before becoming a fully degreed oenologist, with a post-grad stint at one of the best finishing schools in Napa, California, in the 1970s, Heitz Cellars. His lightning quickness and fabulous memory make him a lethal wine taster, birder, storyteller. He plays a mean game of *boules*, has a penchant for puns, enjoys his Monte Cristos. An inveterate browser of CD shops, he had the aged maestros of the Buena Vista Social Club booming out of giant speakers from his veranda long before they became music-world darlings.

This evening, Piero Conté's gravel-throated cynicism wafted over the peacocks stalking the front lawn, above mauve jacarandas and into the blue of the Groot Drakenstein mountains. As usual, Gyles' generosity extended beyond Thelema's own lovely wines, this time to Lynch-Bages. As usual too, the choice provided a talking point – though wine discussions are never obligatory at the Webb table. The wine bore gets short shrift here.

Gyles knows that the sleek easiness that's the hallmark of his wines, specially the reds, ('accessibility') probably explains Thelema's phenomenal appeal. But it might also be its Achilles heel. The Lynch-Bages' characteristic dense firmness, its trademark among Médocs, was a counterpoint to Thelema's luscious, sweet-ripe mintiness.

Squaring the elusive circle of grace and power – of succulent fruitiness and firm tannin in wine – remains his constant goal. The Thelema Cabernet (which usually has a little Merlot) vied with the Lynch-Bages. (The Thelema Merlot usually carries a little Cabernet. 'Actually,' he confided, 'on this farm Cabernet and Merlot seem to be pretty much the same!'). 'I think I could do with a shade more austerity and dryness in my wines,' he said, perhaps revealing a desire to be classified (a shade?) more classic Old World than easy-to-understand, juicy New.

Driving through the modest gates at Thelema, with the Simonsberg slopes looming behind the Victorian-styled homestead, along the corrugated, red earth road lined with eucalyptus and pine trees, between rows of vines ending alternately with red and white roses, is like entering a room of freshly arranged flowers. The sense of very personal attention is strong. The winery is a model of functionalism and simplicity; it's the vineyards that really matter here.

All through the 1990s, the country's top accolades regularly ended up in Gyles' lap, which shook the neighbours, because until the early 1980s, when the Webbs moved in, Thelema had been a fruit farm. Gyles still wears a mask of mild bemusement – or measured modesty – at his success.

And he still, out of habit more than necessity, balances the books himself, in longhand, late at night (when not the life and soul of parties and tastings). But however hard the night before, he doesn't miss his dawn therapy session: a time for reflection and solitary creativity in his 50-hectare vineyards. Pruning it used to be called. It's 'managing the canopy' now. The idea is to draw dappled sunlight into the bunches: the leaves and canopy are arranged, the rows aligned, to let in more morning sunlight (infra-red, less sunburn) than afternoon (ultra-violet, more sunburn).

The deep red, decomposed granite mountain soil is known for water-retention, but Gyles nevertheless built a large dam (cum-trout pool) to drip-irrigate his vines. The taps are turned on and off scientifically: to 'tease' the vines into developing optimum berry size and foliage-to-bunch ratios (16 fair-sized leaves ripen one bunch of grapes properly). It's a carrot-and-stick approach to bring canopy and crop into balance. And balance is the mantra of techno-wise growers. Even infant vines, they say, can be engineered into producing outstanding wine quality. The old vines–great wines correlation could soon become passé.

Gyles' life had been full enough scampering around at the head of a competitive pack but then a few years ago, Johannesburg banker G T Ferreira bought the farm next door. He liked what he drank from over the fence (and didn't object to the music). So he planted vineyards and olives. Gyles agreed to oversee the new project's wines, while meantime, Ferreira became chairman of South Africa's biggest bank, First National (to which he'd sold his own bank, Rand Merchant).

The new winery perches at the top of the Helshoogte Pass with Cape Peninsula and ocean vistas glittering below. A ritzy restaurant launched by the chef who unleashed nouvelle cuisine on the Cape some decades ago, Etienne Bonthuys, is incorporated. Instant, Napa-esque chic all round. Tokara (a name from two names – those of G T Ferreira's children) epitomises the sort of business in which fortunes are made by starting with much larger ones.

What *had* it all cost? Guesstimates varied, but the bottom line was constant: more than any other Cape winery so far – and judging by that always reliable gauge, the ablution fittings (not to mention the boss's private bouledrome on the top floor) they might not have been too far off the mark. All for a relatively modest target of 50,000 cases a year. Ferreira acknowledges that this is a venture where ROE doesn't stand for return on equity, but return on ego.

And still, by 2002, not a single bottle of wine under the Tokara label.

Gyles maintained his insouciant banter in the face of great expectations. The grapevine had it that Ferreira insisted his first release should emerge in a blaze of glory – a guaranteed 5-star wine. As his cellarmaster's Thelema Cabernet, Merlot and Chardonnay had been, but individually, recognisably Tokara. He was prepared – had the resources – to wait it out. But young Miles Mossop, second in command to Gyles in Tokara's cellar, was quoted as wondering whether he'd still be around to see D-Day. And meantime the competition had proliferated wildly. Gyles represented an ever larger target for the snipers.

Though not for pop star Sir Cliff Richard. He'd tasted Thelema's Ed's Reserve in the UK and fell for this high-voltage Chardonnay. From a clone which reverberates with

THELEMA

Ed's Reserve

A DRY WHITE

1998

WINE OF ORIGIN STELLENBOSCH

PRODUCED AND BOTTLED BY THELEMA MOUNTAIN VINEYARDS,
HELSHOOGTE, STELLENBOSCH.

% Alc.Vol. PRODUCE OF SOUTH AFRICA   750 ml

exotic Muscat scents, and spiced honey flavours, it was named after Gyles' mother-in-law Edna, whose sepia baby-picture adorns the label. Sir Cliff had recently visited Thelema unannounced, and asked to meet Ed, who runs the tasting room. She was off for lunch. So he came back the next day.

We were reminded of Gyles' near-miss with the Queen of England (we specify because in Africa we have our own royalty). A persistent caller insisted on speaking to him rather than Ed or his wife Barbara, the marketing dynamo when she's not giving physio and aromatherapy to athletes like herself (twice World Triathlon Champion). The caller was after Thelema Sauvignon Blanc. This usually sells out the moment it's released.

'No,' said Gyles patiently, 'Even if it was for the Queen, I couldn't help.' The volley was returned. 'But it IS for the Queen!' Gyles hadn't known that Elizabeth II was due in town, and Thelema was required for a reception on the royal yacht *Britannia*. He winkled some wine out of his personal reserves…

Watch those waves

Some months before, we, the Webbs, and wine producers James and Tanya Browne had survived another near-disaster involving a boat. Scouring the rainforests and beaches of Gabon, under the sweaty armpit of West Africa, for birds, we had set out to sea in a small (much too small) pirogue. Narrowly avoiding the monstrous tree trunks which float about these shores (escapees from nearby logging operations), treacherous sandbanks, ravaging mosquitoes and the rest of the givens on such expeditions, we were about to beach and rush to the bar of Gabon's most delightful hostelry, Ekwata Lodge.

A huge freak wave crashed in; we were thrown backwards into the bottom of the boat, and pinned there, helplessly, as set after set of breakers pounded over us. The water level in the boat surged, it was up to our noses before we managed to crawl out. We tottered to the bar. Wine failed us at such a time. We ordered stiff Stolys all round. Though had the Brownes packed a bottle of their rustic, strapping Pontac – unique in South Africa – that might have hit the spot.

The langorous, lanky James, inevitably accessorised with rakish neckerchiefs, looked seriously bedraggled. They'd never have recognised him at the smart wine stores in Britain and Australia where he honed his marketing edge, but failed miserably to acquire any Aussie brashness – or chirping skills. Even Tanya's famous wit deserted her.

She and her sister Fiona Mackenzie own 105-hectare, 40,000-cases a year Hartenberg, an estate in the Bottelary hills behind Stellenbosch. Their winemaker (and white-water kayak expert) Carl Schultz has driven a change in the estate's traditional – think front-row rugby forward – style of Shiraz. Its savoury trademark is still there, but in more classic form, on a riper, softer fruit platform. We are also fans of the sturdy, delicious Merlot, the mature Zinfandel and one of the Cape's most attractive off-dry (Weisser) Rieslings. And of the oak-dappled charms of the vintner's lunch on the terrace below the cellar.

The interloper

Now we were off to catch up with a young man who, perhaps more than any other, personified the new wave engulfing the Cape.

Foreign coaches are entrusted with the fate of national sports teams with hardly a murmur but it was more radical than chic back in 1996 for venerable Rustenberg to call in a brash (his word) 24-year-old New Zealander, Rod Easthope. Fresh out of Roseworthy College in Adelaide, he'd taken charge at the only Cape estate where wine has been made uninterruptedly for more than a century.

Rustenberg's national monument homesteads and rolling fields are emblematic of a settled order and unhurried grace that often seems very unattached to much of tumultuous, chaotic Africa. The reaction was predictable. A foreigner! In these hallowed vineyards! Xenophobia rippled through the winelands.

The wealthy Barlow family who own this estate in Idas valley, on the fringe of Stellenbosch town, have sometimes appeared more interested in their internationally acclaimed Jersey stud herd. (Their second label, Brampton, refers to a prolific Canadian bull.) But heir Simon Barlow, with the resources to be adventurous, insisted on a complete makeover. With Easthope, he built a swish new winery in the old cattle byre. The Jerseys were moved across the road, not entirely out of sight or mooing range, but cowpats no longer decorate the cellar doorway. Simon built his office in a tower atop the old silage pit. He can now see everything in the winery and paddocks.

'We're preparing this show for the new century and we intend to play up there with the world's best,' he said. His targets are ambitious: the Rothschilds and Mondavis. The wines and vineyards have been transformed, and the most prestigious label now is reserved for a single-vineyard Cabernet Sauvignon named after his father, Peter, who restored the estate a half century earlier.

The strapping, forthright Easthope soon flayed his critics with excellence in bottle and take-no-prisoners verbal combat. His first signature wine, the 96 Peter Barlow, earned 92 out of 100 from the fearsome Robert Parker. 'May be the finest red wine I have ever tasted from South Africa,' this guru pronounced.

While Rustenberg's vineyards might have been revamped, Easthope's merciless eye didn't find a great deal to recommend in the Cape in general. 'I was appalled,' he said now, 'at the standard of viticulture. There are still too few skilled people and those skills are deployed too thinly. The wineries were very well equipped, even over-equipped. But the hygiene! The level of attention to detail....' He shook his head.

'If you have great grapes, you need no one in the cellar. It's when you have bad grapes

Previous pages
Top: Welcome,
Welkom, Bienvenue:
the young generation
of Franschhoek greets
visitors; in the garden
with Nellie, Gyles and
Barbara Webb; Kiwi
consultant Rod
Easthope – in the
Glenhurst winery he's
designed for Scottish
businessman Dave
King; Boekenhoutskloof
in the Franschhoek
mountains.
Middle: Dave and
Felicity Johnson preside
over their kreef feast;
exhausted by the wine
business: James and
Tanya Browne of
Hartenberg; Wine and
roses below
Simonsberg,
Stellenbosch; Sir Cliff
Richard's pick of
Thelema's Chardonays,
features baby Edna
McLean; mother and
son – Sebastian and
Jayne Beaumont.
Bottom: Train-spotting
in Africa: John and
Gyles Webb, begin a 4-
hour wait for the
trans-Gabon express;
Johann Krige and
Beyers Truter of
Kanonkop; Corner shop
on the Paarl wine
route; wine writer Oz
Clarke at an early vin-
tage of the Johnsons'
annual kreef feast.

that you need effort. It takes more effort to make bad wine.' He insisted he'd 'calmed down now' and that 'I've tempered my degree of arrogance… maybe I've already been here too long'. He paused, smiled, then couldn't help himself. 'But the poor quality of labour and management is only South Africa's No 2 problem. No 1 is virus in the vineyards, and it's in the plants when they come from the nursery.'

He extended the charge-sheet: 'At Roseworthy we tasted, tasted – water, acid, tannin, everything – for eight hours every week for four years. This is a hobby horse of mine about the Cape, no palate-training. And then these "qualified graduates" identify grim wine-making in the bottle as "individuality". Even worse, they go into the business and hire their old tutors as consultants!'

His next step seemed inevitable: backed by the evidence of his talents at Rustenberg, he'd built up a following, and with Barlow's blessing, he then set *himself* up as a consultant. His chief preoccupation now was launching a new venture – Glenhurst, just over the ridge. The investor was businessman Dave King (whose vineyards near Cape Agulhas we'd visited earlier). 'He understands great wine and wants to produce it.' No virus or any sort of sloppiness would be tolerated here.

'It's the small wineries that will produce the outstanding quality,' Rod predicted. Clearly not yet – he admitted he didn't 'risk a punt too often' on local wines. Though he admired some of the West Coast's 'thick, chocolatey shirazes', they weren't to his personal taste.

On the far horizon is his end-goal: 'I've spent my life dreaming about my own winery… in New Zealand of course. And I came up with this idea.' He was standing next to a tank on a lift platform in the winery he'd designed for King. He pushed some buttons and it levitated. Five floors! He could manoeuvre wine with velvet gloves, without a pump, from the very depths of his cellar. 'Even if it makes a 2 per cent difference, you've got to try it,' he said.

Though he dislikes the term, his consultancy business is all about 'reverse wine-making'. First, the producer targets the price and style of a wine; then Easthope works out how to achieve this end-result, beginning in the vineyard, knowing the budget. It's usually the other way round in the wine world – producers wait and see how the vintage turns out, and only then make their marketing moves.

The homegrown iconoclast

At Rustenberg, another youngster, Adi Badenhorst (one of the Rootstock members we'd met earlier), had slipped into Easthope's shoes. They worked in tandem for a while and still interact. Opting for homegrown this time, Simon Barlow nonetheless deliberately hired another confident, passionate, impatient iconoclast. Even Adi's hair – a wild tangle of Gustavo Kuerten curls – is free-style. He is 'a survivor', he said, of 'Boerassic Park over there', pointing in the direction of his Stellenbosch alma mater, Elsenburg College, which hadn't prepared him for work 'on the outside'. He'd had to dig and learn for himself.

His wine vocabulary bristles with techno-cool phrases, interspersed with frequent guffaws: green picks, bunch-tagging, deficit-irrigation, vibrator-berry selection. And now – he thought this might be a first – oak-anonymity. Removing all identification from the thousands of French barrels in the cool Rustenberg vault beneath the old milking parlour.

'The trouble is you come down here, and you can read: Alliers, medium-toasted from Séguin-Moreau; Nevers heavy-toast from Nadalie – the oak forest, the degree of toasting, the cooper. Immediately you're conditioned by that info, when you shouldn't be; it's got to be blind tasting.' Barlow smiled, Adi moved on to the obvious jokes about the 'vibrator' they'd introduce next vintage. After de-stemming, berries would be sized and graded on a perforated, vibrating conveyor belt – normally a manual process.

Winemaker Adi Badenhorst and owner Simon Barlow, of Rustenberg; Simonsberg mountain behind.

In the best, very long 18 rows of the Peter Barlow Cabernet vineyard, they tag individual bunches early in the season – marking those positioned to benefit most from sap flows and photosynthesis (no weakling, 'hind-tit' bunches). This tagging comes after the first of several 'green picks', geared at eliminating unwanted bunches. Less-than-perfect berries now stray into their flagship wine with utmost difficulty.

The best since the famous 96 (which we thought already needed drinking) is the 99, perhaps the finest Cape wine of that year – at the top of the tree, anyway. 'True physiological ripeness' of the grapes was possible 'due to a few years of sustained viticultural improvements,' explained Easthope.

'Yes and only R130 a bottle – a steal in sterling,' chirped Badenhorst.

Fine or funky?

On nearby Kanonkop, there was a robust rejoinder from the 'Prince of Pinotage' the mercurial, shrewd – and very political – Beyers Truter when we told him we'd detected some dissent in the ranks; some questioning of Pinotage's title as the 'national' grape. He was not mollified when we added that even these non-believers agreed that but for Kanonkop's dogged determination, this difficult cross between Cinsaut and Pinot Noir – a plodding workhorse-nervous thoroughbred mix if there ever was one – might have languished among thousands of other discarded genetic fiddlings. And that they recognised that Pinotage's 'conception' here in Stellenbosch – by accident almost, in 1926 – did make it a 'marketing tool': South Africa's contribution to the alternative red-wine grapes of the world.

'I don't know who they think they're bloody kidding,' said Truter, 'if you took a proper poll, you'd find 70 per cent believe it's the national grape. These people don't understand that Cabernet and Merlot and the rest are like men: you don't have problems with them. Pinotage is like your wife, there are always problems!'

The variety can show a particularly acerbic – the euphemism is distinctive – acidity (it has a much higher proportion of sharp malic acid than other reds). But it can also ripple with juicy flavours. With a wrapping of expensive barrel maturation, it's been known to present a tamer, calmer version of itself. He took it like the seasoned politico he is – he leads a multi-racial, anti-ANC local party – when we suggested Pinotage is never better than when it doesn't taste like Pinotage.

The obsession with Pinotage would be easier to understand if Kanonkop grew nothing else. But the estate is one of the grandees of Cape wine mainly because of its Paul Sauer blend of the two Cabernets and Merlot. It's the wine that won Truter strings of international trophies, including an unmatched feat, twice judged the world's best red blend at London's International Wine and Spirit Competition.

A stroll through the stick-to-basics winery, essentially unchanged in the 25 years we've known it, was an affirmation of faith in unfussy tradition. Dazed by the glittering new temples elsewhere, the visitor might wonder how wines of such class can be made here. Truter's answer: You don't need much more than ripe fruit – and maybe a fine oak barrel.

An existential crisis

The annual crayfish season had just opened, and next day we were off to celebrate this auspicious day in the foodie calendar with Dave and Felicity Johnson, of Newton-Johnson and Cape Bay wines, at their winery on a hill overlooking the two essential producers of lunch – the sea, and the vineyards of the Hemel en Aarde valley behind the beach resort of Hermanus.

The drive out is stunning whichever way you go – hugging the coast on the edge of vertical cliffs, or via Sir Lowry's Pass in the Hottentots-Holland mountains, through Elgin's pine forests, rose gardens, apple orchards and, since 1984, when Neil Ellis was the first independent Cape winemaker to outsource his grapes, elegant cool-climate vineyards. Brain surgeon Paul Cluver is the big player in Elgin, but every fruit farmer seems to be diversifying; Ross Gower, winemaker of Klein Constantia, had just bought land here.

Our first tasting of the day was a little further on, in Bot River, at the foot of the Houwhoek mountain pass: a small corner of the Overberg wine district, which encompasses Elgin and Walker Bay. Here we were to sample the discreet charms and quirky character of Compagnes Drift, a 500-hectare wine and fruit farm now owned by the Beaumont family, and formerly (in the eighteenth century) an outpost of the Dutch East India company. In 1993 they'd stared the future in the face: replant their tiring vineyards to boost their contributions to the local co-op, or give the old cellar on the property – last used in the 1950s to make a wine called Rooi Perd (Red Horse) – mouth-to-mouth resuscitation.

'We lived in a permanent existential crisis in those days: didn't know which route to go,' said Jayne Beaumont.

Neither she nor husband Raoul were winemakers. She's a fine artist by training, he's a fruit farmer by vocation, yachtsman and Harley-rider by inclination. (His biking club admits only members over 40; its motto is 'Growing Old Disgracefully'.) Their cellar was deeply upholstered with cobwebs and mould, its cement tanks so dark and satanic-looking it might have served as the set for a horror movie. Their vineyards were bulk- not fine-wine producers. The Beaumonts were insane even to think about it....

But this is no conventional family. Even the farm dog looks like danger – he's half-wolf. They dived in. Jayne's Pinotage was an immediate rave. By the time son Sebastian (epitome of young cool) graduated from Elsenburg College with all the viti-vini qualifications, his parents and Niels Verburg, the winemaker they inspanned once success became too much to handle on their own, had stamped Beaumont on the modern Cape winelands map.

Now the cellar sports new equipment, stainless steel, oak, but – we'd known and rather loved it in its chamber of horrors days – remains agreeably agricultural. They've kept the old sign officially permitting the farm to 'sell and dispose of alcohol'. The barn, once stuffed with mouldering tractors, rusting spare parts and general junk is now a rustic-chic office. Sebastian had got onto intimate terms with the 50 hectares of vines, and his next step was into the cellar, to become assistant winemaker.

'The hardest bit', he said, 'was getting my Dad to relax and leave the vineyards to me! He comes from the generation when you picked at exactly the same point each year because you were penalised if your sugar was too high or too low. You didn't taste the grapes and the pips!'

Sebastian, unlike many of his young peers, has a soft spot for the 'home-grown' Pinotage, because 'here in Walker Bay it's distinctive. It doesn't scream out of the bottle.' This applies to their rather serious Chenin Blanc, too, but not to their showy Mourvèdre – first single-variety bottling in South Africa, more proof of Beaumont's membership of the Cape new wave. Speaking of which, how had the Winemakers' Classic gone the day before?

This is a surfing contest open only to winemakers. An astonishing number had turned out, Sebastian reported. Ross Gower (on but mostly off his old-fashioned longboard) had won the prize for the most spectacular wipe-out; Gunter Schultz of Waterford Wines in Stellenbosch retained his title. The Johnson Brothers – our end-destination that day – had 'styled'.

We previewed the atmospheric landscape paintings Jayne had made for a joint exhibition with jewellery-designer daughter Ariane – now admin-manager at Beaumont – before moving on. But not too fast. Cape school-leavers had just finished their exams, whereafter they traditionally converge on the beaches of Hermanus to party. There would be roadblocks. There were, manned by gun-toting police. We were waved through, while unfortunate students were pulled over for licence-inspections, contraband-searches. The rare advantage of age….

Heaven and earth

South Africa's Oregon, some have called it, or Burgundy by the Sea. Back in the late 1970s, J Walter Thompson ad. agency chief Tim Hamilton Russell had defied the system to establish vineyards here in the Hemel en Aarde (heaven and earth) valley, outside the official Grape Cordon. He was harassed by the wine police of the time, the

KWV (sometimes referred to as the KGB by its victims), taken to court – and convicted! – for mentioning Burgundy in his publicity material. Officially he'd flouted an arcane trade agreement with France; unofficially his liberal politics and aggressive marketing had got up the establishment's nose. But he kept on waging a fierce battle to change the mind-set of those who decreed grapes should be grown only where the powers-that-were allowed them to be grown, and not where they might – who knew? – grow best.

Now, with new vineyard areas opening up everywhere, and social-responsibility an un-negotiable bottom-line for any producer, the establishment's stubborn hold-out in the face of the inevitability (let alone desirability) of change seemed all the more absurd. The past was another wine country.

Today this once-renegade valley bulges with respected wine names: Hamilton Russell Vineyards (HRV) and Southern Right, Bouchard Finlayson, WhaleHaven, Newton-Johnson and Cape Bay, Sumaridge, Bartho Eksteen. Nine more vineyards were in the pipeline, including one to be developed by

Artist Arabella Caccia's studio high on a hill; the Hamilton Russell Vineyards above Hermanus.

Gyles Webb for Tokara's GT Ferreira, and a joint venture between Dave Johnson and the wine-lover to whom we'd sold our South African wine guide, Andrew McDowall.

Tim Hamilton Russell's son, Anthony, now owns HRV; he was at a trade fair in Munich; winemaker Kevin Grant was at a seminar; but the power behind the property's most striking labels, for special auction wines, was in: the artist Arabella Caccia. Her fingers were suitably paint-stained: she was working towards an exhibition. After a tasting update in the cellar (Chardonnay and Pinot Noir in fine fettle) we followed her Land Rover between manicured cypresses, standard roses, precision-trim vines, neat olive groves and beehives, past a community centre, crèche, and horse-paddock (she rides daily) to a rough stone building, rather like a chapel, high and lonely on a hill.

Amid a sea of *fynbos* – blush pink and cream proteas, drifts of snowy white and deep pink everlastings – a sign read Studio: Private. How can she not spend all day gaping out of the windows? On one side are the Babylonstoren mountains, on the other the ocean. Where – we could see even without binoculars from the clifftop – Southern Right whales were breaching.

Arabella's latest works were sizeable creations too: glass panels and sculptures based on 'the spaces between nude figures'. They were to be installed around a pool, and viewed, among other angles, from a swing overhead. Buddha Bar 3 and Nirvana Lounge music would play – 'because it's what I listen to while I paint'. It was no wonder to us that Anthony, formerly buttoned-up in tweeds and brogues, had recently modernised. 'He's now wearing what an Englishman wouldn't be seen dead in,' Arabella reported. 'Not quite lycra, but nylon at least. Funky. I think it's a huge relief.'

Whale-spotting in Walker Bay – from the Hamilton Russell farm.

Down the hill, overlooking a dam patrolled by blue cranes, is Braemar House, mellow stone and colonial pillars, shades of a venerable Randlord's mansion. There were hammocks on the veranda where we sipped cool Chardonnay. In an enormous gallery – and party space – upstairs, Arabella's work could be viewed by appointment. Anthony's collection of Stone Age tools found on the estate features in an adjoining study.

Over the hill, another cellar is on the drawing board, for Southern Right wines (dignified Pinotage and sparky Sauvignon Blanc). This is a joint venture of Anthony H R and Kevin Grant; part of the proceeds funds research into the whales who mate and calve in Walker Bay.

Past next-door Bouchard-Finlayson's thatched winery – more evidence that classic Burgundian varieties are probably this valley's strong suit – we drove deep into the valley to dinner. Distinctly farmyardy smells wafted outside Moggs Country Cookhouse. Inside, under a ceiling made of chicken wire piled with pine cones, we ate great modern-rustic food. We drank local wine, of course, but beer-aficianados are well served too, by the Birkenhead Brewery in the nearby village of Stanford. This is not noted for taking the matter of gender seriously. Its slogans (apparently devised by a New York ad-executive) have included 'Helping ugly women have sex since 1869', and 'Get some head!'

The kreef feast

'Because local bottling facilities were so appalling' Dave and Felicity Johnson put up their own small winery and bottling line here. Dave's long marketing career with Stellenbosch Farmers' Winery had been followed by a foray into the packaging field. A maestro with wood, he's done every bit of carpentry in their home, from the pearwood dining table with a hologram grain ('a low-life son of a bitch to work with'), to the cupboards in the guest-wing, conjured from wine cases: Chx d'Angludet, Ducru-Beaucaillou, Lynch-Bages, De Pex. But now the whole family is in the wine business.

They bought in and bottled the first vintage of their Cape Bay label in 1992; it took off and flew, from just over 50,000 cases to today's 150,000. 'We owe everything to Nelson Mandela,' Dave said. 'He made us respectable. Then the boys said let's plant some vines.' Their family-only Newton-Johnson range was born. (Felicity's maiden name was Newton; it's also the middle name of sons Bevan and Gordon, both in their twenties.)

They had some midwifely assistance at first: the boys' degrees from Stellenbosch University were in economics, not oenology; Dave, though a Cape Wine Master (his thesis on Pinot Noir), was no winemaker either. Neighbour Bartho Eksteen lent a hand and still makes his own Sauvignon Blanc here, but the youngsters are now on their own. Final arbiter of taste remains Felicity, her palate decisive when the rest of the family dithers.

It was house Pinot Noir, Chardonnay, Sauvignon Blanc we drank at lunch, among sundry burgundies and champagne. But the wine was a side-show to the main event, the Kreef Feast.

Felicity drives the boat, Dave fishes, nets, dives for booty. Dave steamed the crayfish to coral-coloured succulence; Felicity whipped up aïoli. There were tiny *perlemoen* (abalone) with an extreme green dipping sauce of wasabi and soy. Dave had picked mussels off the rocks. There was a Cape salmon caught that morning, and simply *braaied*. Along with thick slices of equally fresh tuna, marinated à la Union Square Café in New York, grilled very pink. (John had become hooked on this recipe when in the US to give the first big tasting of South African wines after Mandela was released.) The rest of this catch was in the air; tomorrow it would be sushi and sashimi in Tokyo restaurants.

With the Johnsons' newest neighbours, Andrew and Moysie McDowall, we ate and drank for hours, and Dave apologised constantly for the absence of oysters. Next year, he promised. He was having a shellfish tank built. 'For when we can't eat everything we catch in one sitting.'

We kept an ear on the TV in the background. Italy were playing the Springboks in a rugby Test match. John, whose family's vineyard roots are in the Alto Adige, became over-excited when Italy surged into a (short-lived) 9–0 lead. Georgina, the Johnson's pointer, began to sing. Her usual inspirations were Bob Dylan playing the harmonica or Yehudi Menuhin the violin; today it was the operatic Italian crowd.

Much later, after visiting the fledgling McDowall-Johnson properties up the valley, and when the *fynbos* garden and the sweeping views of the sea had disappeared into the night, Dave persuaded us to have 'another little something'. Foie gras and Sauternes. Next morning, feeling surprisingly strong, we headed inland, to the vineyards of Paarl and Wellington.

Wild things in Wellington

'If you can weld an inch, you can weld a mile,' said Edmund Oettle as we threaded between four dogs, a gaggle of geese, assorted chickens, and followed him into the oak-shaded dimness of a cross between a shed, a scrapyard, an agricultural jumble sale and a mad inventor's workshop. It was his ingenious and extremely functional Upland winery. Apart from a small filter and some barrels, Edmund had home-made every bit of equipment himself.

He'd cut down the frame of a cast-off Vaslin press and concocted his own mean crushing machine. He cast concrete to make some tanks, scoured industrial yards for stainless-steel offcuts and scrap to knock up others. Not dinky little things either: 50,000-litre jobs. 'With an angle grinder, a welding machine, and a jigsaw you can make anything.'

Bach bounced off the rafters as his staff finished bottling the 2000 Upland Cabernet. Depending on their mood, it might have been rap or rock. The decidedly manual process involved plastic jugs, funnels, bowls, and a bedside lamp ('quality control,' said Edmund) shone onto each bottle to check the level. He was about to re-invent another discard, a mangled corking machine, but for the moment closure came via a smart tap with a padded hammer.

The cost of the whole set-up? We were speechless when he told us. If he'd added three noughts we'd still have thought it absurdly cheap. Now and then Edmund had an eccentric genius look – the wild eyes, their disconcertingly piercing, fixed gleam. But now they were crinkled up in laughter. This was a man who (some might think) had thrown his career away to vegetate in the backwoods of the Hawequa mountains near Wellington, and he couldn't have been happier.

A research scientist in the in-vitro fertilisation field, his invention of a stain to isolate viable embryos had been patented – and was in use – worldwide. He was trained as a vet; and avoided active military service during South Africa's war in Angola ('didn't fit in, had to get out') by using those qualifications. If the army released him to develop his research, he'd find a way of preserving the bloodline of their best canine trackers. 'The top dogs would invariably be on the frontline and get clobbered. The poorer ones lurked at the back and survived.'

Artificial insemination was Edmund's answer, his field, and later his university lecturing discipline. It applied to humans too: most of the babies born over the past decade in South Africa using the in-vitro technique are – he hesitated – 'speaking scientifically of course, mine!' His second PhD, was in electron microscopy, the thesis written during the harvest of 2000. By then 'I'd followed my dreams.'

To this green, Darling Buds of May refuge, less shambolic but just as pretty when the almond orchards are in bloom, and as celebratory of country life. Here he pottered and tinkered and dreamed on. He and wife Elsie were giving their son and daughter an idyll of a childhood, which included not having to leave the farm to go to school. Home-educating was the Oettlean way – 'because we remembered how miserably bored we were at school'.

So, this was not your average farmer. Nor did the diminutive Elsie fit the usual iden-tikit. She is an electrical engineer. Not much scope for that in the neighbourhood, so she'd started her own business, Hand Africa, making greeting cards which tourist shops gobble up en masse. Her office was piled with feathers and seedpods, animal-print cloth and beads. Two of the Oettles' five employees were industriously gluing and cutting. Elsie finishes off with her own drawings.

Elsie and Edmund Oettle of Upland in Wellington - charming, inventive - and that goes for their cellar too.

Next door was another of Edmund's babies. His brandy and grappa distillery under a rustic reed roof; his tiers of 86 barrels filled with Chenin Blanc, Colombard and Cape Riesling – 'my kids' inheritance'. And yes – the still was also home-made. His doctor brother did the complicated maths, Edmund built it. 'Now that was HUGE work! All from flat sheets of copper.' The brandy is a partnership with his mate and mentor Danie Steytler of Kaapzicht Estate near Stellenbosch.

Edmund hadn't been a total winemaking rookie. He'd started as a schoolboy, 30 years ago, despite a teetotal mother. But those were garden products: his biggest success ('what a perfume!') a jasmine wine. His children had just made their first vintage from the elderflowers that rampage around the cellar. But for his reds, Edmund turns for advice to a man who makes poetry of Pinotage where many churn out doggerel.

Quite by chance, Danie himself arrived, bearing a young Barn Owl with an injured wing. Edmund whisked it into his surgery off the farmhouse kitchen. He still sees animal patients (by special referral or in an emergency), and barters his expertise with his dairy farmer neighbour. He delivers her calves, she supplies manure for his 13 hectares of vines. Everybody was going organic, but Upland turned green in 1994; the farm was one of the first in the Cape to be awarded international certification.

'Don't miss them,' had insisted Zimbabwean Arthur Dunkley of the Oettles – it was Edmund who'd inspired him to plant his vineyard in the Nyanga mountains, which we'd visited earlier in the year. They shared another passion.

'Come and meet Guinevere,' Edmund invited. 'She supplies us with 80 per cent of our meat.'

Entering a cell (roomier than those on Robben Island) through several security doors, we found a large and dishevelled bird, a cross between a Peregrine and a Gyr falcon. (Arthur Dunkley, up on his mountain, also bred and flew falcons.) Guinevere was moulting; even Edmund couldn't handle her for six months. 'Her hormones are all out of balance.' But in full-feather and flight she's a superb hunter. The Oettles' deep-freeze was crammed with her hauls of guineafowl and yellow-billed duck, which Edmund removes from her grasp by offering a ready-to-go substitute – this the fate of the farmyard chickens.

On the 100-point charm scale, the winery hovered around the top. But what about the wines? We approached the Cabernet with trepidation. By the time we'd sniffed and gargled our way through the 98, 99 and 2000, a dash of smooth, slightly wooded grappa, and a soupçon of 3-year-old brandy, we were cheering. This was – no reservations – good stuff. And it wasn't only us: at a top South African competition, the 2000 Michelangelo awards, the 99 had won the only gold medal for Cabernet. Plus, reported Edmund, 'a French buyer asked me, after blind-tasting the brandy, which XO Cognac it was!'

'Now this was really difficult to make!' says Edmund of his still, hand-hammered out of copper sheets, and now producing one of the Cape's finest brandies.

Ever the rigorous scientist, to pinpoint his house-style he'd made each vintage of the Cabernet differently – reductively, oxidatively and in-between – a comparative exercise. The reductive 98 was our unanimous favourite.

We wanted to carry off Edmund's Director's Reserve, slightly sweeter and gentler than the standard brandy, in a special decanter. But it cost R600 – 'I was advised to give one product in the range an outrageous price ticket; just for marketing!' The Cabernet, though, at a sixth of the price, was irresistible.

Running late – we'd rather prolonged this rare encounter – we dashed off to Paarl. To sample some reds in quite another price bracket.

Praise singer

'A wine is an aria captured in the bottle.'

Such wine-speak normally makes us roll our eyes. But this was Deon van der Walt, using his own business language. He owns miniature wine estate Veenwouden, but his work description is international tenor: have voice, must travel. To fulfil a 10-performances-a-year contract with the Opera House in Zurich, his European base, and freelance gigs all over the world. He dashes back to his vineyard, a 15-hectare tranche of Pomerol on the outskirts of Paarl, between engagements and recording sessions.

'Munich, Barcelona, Vienna, Munich again, Barcelona again, Valencia, and back to

Zurich....' He sounded like an airport departures board as he reeled off his diary for the next three months. We were talking and tasting in Veenwouden's winery-cum-auditorium (raked seating, a chorus line of stainless-steel tanks), with the choc-box backdrop of the Du Toitskloof mountains. Up in the gods were offices for father Charles (farm manager), mother Sheila (all-round fixer) and winemaker brother Marcel, a former golf-club pro.

Coached initially by Meerlust's Giorgio Dalla Cia and then by French guru Michel Rolland, Marcel teed off in 1994 after a season at Château Le Bon Pasteur and other luminous Rolland consultancies. 'Because I knew nothing, my mind was open. I was like a dry sponge, just soaking everything up. And, you know, winemaking is rather like golf. If you stick to the basics and then keep practising, you have to get better and better.'

The basics were fanatical cellar hygiene and Rolland's mantra: 'only the finest, cleanest, ripe fruit'. From the Bordeaux Right Bank varieties that had captivated Deon when he first ventured abroad to sing for his supper. 'I fell in love with the classics.' When he bought the small vineyard he'd dreamed about since student days at Stellenbosch University, he knew he wanted to specialise in Merlot, Cabernets Franc and Sauvignon, and Malbec. All to be given the tough-love treatment – severely disciplined to yield like misers but produce a wealth of flavour.

The wines were uncommonly adult from the start, startling older pros in the game. 'They kept on saying we'd made flukes.' Marcel now allowed himself a brief flare of annoyance at such mean-mindedness. The vines matured, the wines grew in sophistication and reputation. Gold medals and silverware piled up. People began speaking of the Veenwouden Classic blend as a cult-wine, and the Merlot was right up there on the green too.

Part of the formula was the flying bottle factor: Deon picked up numerous 'aspirational wines' on his travels and sent them back to be tasted against their home-produce. The comparisons grew less shabby by the vintage. Recently, Veenwouden had been the only South African winery invited to the swanky Swiss show put on by *Vinum* magazine. He and Marcel did their double-act next to the Château Angélus stand. 'People were quite flabbergasted that such wines were coming out of South Africa. Some said they even preferred ours to the Bordeaux!'

Luciano Pavarotti owns a small vineyard near Modena, and when they were singing together at the New York Met, Deon invited some visiting Cape winemakers to meet the maestro. Beyers Truter of Kanonkop and Gyles Webb of Thelema arrived, uncharacteristically trussed up in dark suits and ties. 'Are they your bodyguards?' Pavarotti asked Deon.

So where would this teenage-faced 43 year-old fit in when he eventually retired his voice? Would he add to the patch of Shiraz and Cabernet they'd acquired nearby for their new Thornhill label? Expand from minor to major? 'Definitely not. It's a way of life for us, and this is as big as we want to get. Each wine is a work of art, and art is not a mass product. There is only one Mona Lisa.'

But he'd be devoting time – in his role of Honorary Professor of Music at the University of Port Elizabeth – to nurturing local protégés: 'wonderful young Xhosa singers'. And to kickstarting wine and music festivals in wine-country towns.

We drove around the back of Paarl (Pearl) Mountain, which is lavishly embroidered with vineyards and olive groves, to another family cellar, where it's the pops rather than the classics that play full-blast.

Dancing with goats

Charles Back, South African wine's most effective advertisement for the entrepreneurial free spirit, is also into goats and cheese, cows and sheep, and previously, pigs, chickens and eggs, even imported French guineafowl. But despite the revolving door of original farming experiments – his father flew in sheep from Germany; they became the first in vitro fertilised flock in the Cape – wine has always occupied top place at Fairview, ever since his grandfather, a penniless immigrant from Riga in Lithuania in 1906, bought the farm in the 1930s.

'I spend 90 per cent of my time on wine… though it represents about 10 per cent of the income,' Charles said, with an I-must-be-crazy laugh. Athletic (he and wife Di drive into nearby Paarl at dawn daily for gym sessions), with a wide moustache and a mop of gingery hair that at 45 was beginning to silver in rather a distinguished way, Charles is strenuously unorthodox, a congenital tinkerer.

He lost a thumb years ago 'adjusting' his bottling line. When pricy stainless-steel and glass designer gadgets became de rigueur to observe the change from clarity to murkiness while pumping wine from barrels or tanks, Charles simply spliced see-through garden hose into his system. 'There's my quality control,' he said triumphantly. 'Why waste money and burden the consumer?' The knowing, darting look was meant to reinforce Fairview's value-for-money policies. Would this man miss a marketing opportunity?

Charles knows a lot of animal-farm stuff. He can do half an hour – easy – on the best sitting position for a laying hen. But it's the goats that twin with the wine. Fairview's tower emblem transpired after a holiday in Portugal, where he'd spotted goats walking up and down a spiral staircase girding a tower. He promptly built a replica in front of his tasting quarters. The finest specimens of long-bearded white Saanen goats were herded into the enclosure. But they refused to scale the stairs, refused to entertain the visitors. 'I soon taught them; I put the water and food at the top and they were getting plenty of exercise in no time.'

Château Latour, or some such, of course, might just have been at the back of his

inventive mind, but no, actually (he smiled) it was about 'towering quality… tower of quality… take your pick.'

In the early 1990s after Mandela's release and the lifting of international boycotts, when Australia, California, New Zealand and Chile had already cornered the market in modern, early-drinking wines, South Africa had to re-launch itself as an international brand. There ensued much self-flagellation about 'the authentic Cape wine style', which Charles characteristically ignored. Eternally impatient and independent (he's never joined any voluntary farming organisation) he dismissed the idiotic appeals to 'patriotism' invoked in favour of an austere, less fruity 'Old World' style to differentiate Cape wines, with their three centuries-long history, from the competition. This was transparent hogwash, rationalising a general shortcoming in many Cape reds at the time – tannic hardness, which rarely mellowed into complexity. The main problem was extensive viral infection in vineyards, inhibiting grape ripening.

Brightest sparks in the winelands? Di and Charles Back (with their totem-icon, the Fairview goat-tower) probably own that title.

Charles looked out, not in for direction. 'We had untrained local palates, starved of international experience, awarding 'character' to faulty wines,' he said. 'I decided that those much maligned British supermarket buyers were the meanest, smartest educators, with the sharpest palates in the business; and their advice was free for heaven's sake! I'd have been an idiot not to listen to them. I was staring at a bargain! Changes to meet their specs might be costly, but the upgrading lesson was free.'

This meant a major make-over. Out went swathes of Cabernet. Climatically and temperamentally, Charles was more suited to Rhône grapes and styles. In went more Shiraz and he led the now stampeding herd with varieties rare to the Cape: Mourvèdre, Viognier included. He tracked down long-neglected pockets of Grenache, Carignan and more: sometimes buying the grapes, other times the vineyard.

From this frenetic 'work-in-progress' grew a long, scatter-gun list of labels. He added off-beat blends to a range already featuring many tributary rather than mainstream grapes: Shiraz-Merlot, Zinfandel-Cinsaut, Crouchen-Chardonnay, Shiraz-Gamay. There were pinks and blushes, sparklers and fortifieds, including a very sweet Shiraz at 18% alcohol – labelled Sweet Dessert Red – which was such a hit he had to limit buyers to three bottles apiece. Every vintage saw radical revisions. Like the best of chefs, Charles ensured that regulars wouldn't be bored by a rigid menu.

Some critics pronounced querulously on the frivolity of his approach, and there were some brutes in the bunch – like a 97 unfortified Zinfandel at 16%. It took an unusually strong constitution to survive that one, but the judges at London's International Wine and Spirits competition didn't flinch – they awarded it top honours!

Now, under a general 'Wines of Charles Back' umbrella, you can find numbing blockbusters and refined elegance. His inaugural (98) Viognier was a triumph – Jancis Robinson hailed it as one of the few authentic New World examples. His penchant for Shiraz, both in the Fairview and Spice Route ranges, has produced bullseyes.

He was forever re-inventing his winemaking methods too. He was the first in the Cape (at many things, including the now fashionable barrel-fermented Chenin Blanc) to experiment with gentler 'whole bunch' pressing – he adapted an existing machine to achieve more delicate fruitiness. 'Look, when you move from rough pressing to a gentle fondle, you get results,' he said. He has an uncanny touch.

In 1998, before launching a new red, Goats do Roam – a saucy play on Côtes du Rhône – he sent us the proposed back label. It featured a tall tale about his son Jason naughtily releasing the animals into the vineyards; with unerring good taste, they allegedly nibbled only the ripest bunches of Carignan, Grenache, Cinsaut, Mourvèdre, Pinotage, Shiraz and Gamay Noir. Hence this 'Rhôney concoction'.

We were unconvinced. It had Charles' audacious DNA. But, we pronounced loftily, it was 'too corny'. Oops. Fundamentally a lone ranger, Charles took absolutely no notice. Within months Goats do Roam was an international smash-hit. Within two years it was a 40,000-case brand including a white and a rosé.

How could we have doubted Charles' market-savvy for a second? Here, after all, was the man who'd multiplied his inheritance from 2000 cases a year, when he took over from his father, to 200,000! Who'd foreseen the potential of his vineyards near Malmesbury, and created the Spice Route range. Whom Algerian wine chief Said Mebarki, after just one meeting – we brought him to dinner at Fairview – was intent on luring to Mascara to wave his wand over North African grapes.

Real tower, real goat, and really good wine and cheese in the Fairview tasting quarters.

'Yes,' said Charles with satisfaction, 'I've got a bone to pick with you…. You know that story about Jason and the goats? Well, it was true!'

He's built a new red wine cellar to cope with the roaming goats phenomenon – complete with a tower, and a spiral staircase which rises dizzily up to a glamorous tasting gallery: stupendous views over Di's gardens – lavender, roses, long reflecting pools – to the vineyards and Table Mountain on the horizon. The massively heavy central chandelier came crashing down during building operations, missing Charles by centimetres.

Menus here would obviously mix and match the Fairview cheeses and wines. Would goat or cow go better with the tributes to his late parents – Cyril Back Shiraz and La Beryl Blanc? The latter, a straw wine, we found very good with the gorgeous, decadently stinky, heart-shaped La Beryl cheese (the first washed-rind specimen in South Africa). Fairview is – we think – South Africa's best cheese range. Like the wines, commercial, but without sacrificing their rustic soul. Di gave us a pre-release taste of their latest creation, Roydon Handcrafted Camembert. Sensational. The secret is a tiny proportion of goat in the mostly cow's-milk recipe.

Now Charles is hunting down another quarry: the ultimate South African icon-wine. So are others. But gamblers wouldn't be taking too great a risk if they backed Back.

The French quarter

Driving through Franschhoek, we thought back to when we threw up our journalists' jobs in Johannesburg, poured our savings into a tiny patch of vines, packed up our new-born baby – now a strapping 23 – and began our journey into the wine world. Not that this sleepy little valley, then, was the least bit worldly. Our language and career combination was viewed with deep suspicion: 'die Engelse Pers' – the English Press – was the bogey of apartheid-supporting Franschhoek folk, inciting the disenfranchised, fomenting rebellion. Even John's efforts to write about the wines made by the local co-op – the only show in town – were rebuffed. His column was, after all, in the crusading, anti-government Rand Daily Mail. We felt like fish out of water.

But illuminating the scene were some memorable characters. The Standard Bank manager who, unlike the doomsayers at the KWV, saw the point of our idea of writing the first South African wine guide, and backed us. The local Sendingkerk dominee – the Dutch Reformed Church was racially divided then, and this wine-loving, gourmet-cooking, bridge-playing intellectual (he read Larousse in the French) administered to an all-Coloured flock – kept our brains in trim. When we moved to Stellenbosch, in search of a vineyard with better soils to make our own wine, this narrow valley was beginning to open up. Now it's unrecognisable.

The only restaurant in town when we lived there, Chez Michel, has been joined by umpteen others, and the best all have French names too – Le Quartier Français, Bijoux, Monneaux, La Petite Ferme and a trio making their own excellent wines – Cabrière, La Petite Ferme, Matin Soleil and Cabrière, where formidable party animal Baron Achim von Arnim's Cuvée Belle Rose (from his Pierre Jourdan range) is our favourite sparkler; his Pinot Noir is a fine specimen too. We were sad to see that our favourite roadside cafe was gone – run by two doughty old sisters, it had been named, in deference to Franschhoek's Huguenot roots, La Teas. This part of the country had been a sort of refugee camp for persecuted Protestants fleeing from France in 1689 who'd brought in the area's signature white grape, Sémillon. The old familes here – De Villiers, Le Roux, Marais, Malherbe, Bruwer – are their descendants. Everything else has been Frenchified too.

Franschhoek now proudly banners itself as Food and Wine Capital of the Cape. Floods of tourists sail obliviously past the shacks and shanties at the entrance of the town. The finest chocolates in the land are made here by young locals who might have become casualties of the farm-labour system in the old days, but whom journalist-restaurateur Penny Gordon – an old colleague – organised into a new venture sponsored by the Belgian government. Penny, her writer-photographer husband Dennis, and their sons, ace-chef Matthew and IT-wizard Greg, are among the wave of new residents who've transformed the town. The Cape's liveliest wine guide, Gillie Stoltzman, of Vineyard Ventures, commutes to Cape Town from here. There've been hundreds of foreign imports, including a couple of alleged Mafioso and a shady African President; at one time, semi-retirement in Franschhoek became almost obligatory for the CEOs of South Africa's top companies.

Today we could have visited 22 cellars, most with Gallic names. But first stop was the new winemaking sensation of the valley.

Rhône ranger

Marc Kent was on a bit of a high. In a just-published pocket wine book, *The Wine List 2002*, UK writer Matthew Jukes had called him 'a genius, an alchemist' and had gone into such raptures about the Boekenhoutskloof Sémillon 2000 that he gave his readers a health-warning: watch out for RSI – repetitive superlative injury. The Sémillon was one of Jukes' top 250 wines of the WORLD.

Actually, we'd come because of his reds. Along a winding dirt road through forest and deep into mountains, to see how Marc had rescued some rather singular vines from the brink of extinction. It began in 1997 when he made a stupendous Syrah – a genuine ringer for a high-toned northern Rhône – with a fragrant, spicy delicacy rarely encountered in the New World. There was almost mass hysteria among local *snifferati* when he announced it could never be repeated. He'd bought the grapes from a vineyard near False Bay in Somerset West which had since disappeared beneath a business mall.

But Marc rescued a few cuttings. He propagated 1000 baby vines, grafted them onto American rootstock, and planted them on a rocky mountainside behind the winery. A bit of Côte Rôtie. In the meantime, the wine had to come from a vineyard he'd located in hotter Wellington. How would he manage anything like his triumphant 97? Incredibly, the 98 wasn't too much of a departure.

His Cabernet, one of the Cape's very best, had won heaps of laurels, a 90-point rating from Robert Parker, and listings in London restaurants. The Sémillon, infused with a bracing squeeze of Sauvignon Blanc, was a hit. As too the second-label range named Porcupine Ridge. These creatures, like the Cape beech trees (Boekenhoutskloof means Beechwood Gorge), thrive on the property. Who wouldn't? It's completely beautiful.

Whether you're looking from Marc's chef's kitchen over a rose-fringed lawn where his dogs Pétrus and Gaia (after the French and Italian wine icons) are gambolling, or you're playing *pétanque* outside the winery, dusky blue mountains gaze down on you.

Marc has a reputation for scattering targets with very short words. But he was unusually benign today. He'd just remodelled and expanded the winery. It now featured a designer bar in the kitchen-cum-tasting room. There were two coffee machines (at board meetings, seven partners need their espresso fix; the wine label features seven different antique chairs). He had a new office. 'Since 1994 my office has been the front seat of my farm truck.'

His upcoming 'concept' wine was to be a Syrah with a dash of Viognier. ('my heart is in the Rhône.') But this reminded him of the endless trouble he'd had getting hold of this white variety; others who'd ordered long after him had jumped the queue, it was all totally unacceptable.... We left reassured. He was still an angry young man.

Marc Kent, rebel for the new Cape wine cause.

Battles and bottles

Our Cape round-trip completed, we hit the long road home to the coast of KwaZulu-Natal. But our wine explorations weren't over. En route, 1000 kilometres north of the vineyards of Stellenbosch, we were in wine territory again. And meeting up with a wine-maker last encountered in 1978, in the vineyards of then-Rhodesia. The scene was still vivid.

Crouched behind sandbags, Uzi at the ready, young Ian Sieg had been guarding his vineyard. The bush war – white army vs black freedom fighters – was in its death-throes, but there was no cease-fire yet. At Avis and Hertz you could, and sensibly did, hire an armoured car to drive into the countryside. Ian had been running the Mateppe (now Mukuyu) Winery under siege. Pruning and harvesting had become para-military manoeuvres. John wrote this story of wine in a war zone for UPI, and it was carried round the world.

Now here was Ian in another vineyard, in the middle of a far older battlefield. The tiny town of Jacobsdal, on the flat red plains between the Modder and the Riet rivers in the Orange Free State is so quiet it might be on tranquillisers. But it had been at the bloody centre of the Anglo-Boer War. A short march from the siege of Kimberley, and between the battles of Magersfontein (1899, a crushing British defeat) and Paardeberg (1900, the first major British victory of the campaign). Its graceful white church was the Boer commandoes' field hospital. In its graveyard lay the fallen brave of both sides: Scottish Highlanders – who'd worn aprons for camouflage over their green tartan kilts – and Afrikaner guerrillas.

Ian's guided tour of the town took five minutes: cemetery, abbatoir, bottle store, church, schools, bank or as he put it '24-hour overdraft centre', supermarket, supermarket owner's Greek-colonnaded swimming pool. Then the vineyards. It had been the extraordinary sight of rampant rows of green which had beckoned us off the N7 Cape Town–Johannesburg highway, just before Kimberley.

We'd driven all day through the bleak, arid Karoo. Strictly speaking, we'd have been likelier to find diamonds than vines (in nearby Hopetown the first big rock was discovered, leading to the Kimberley diamond rush in 1870). But there they were, with signs blaring Gewürztraminer, Cabernet and Pinotage. Here Ian was, beefier but still winemaking on the edge, at Landzicht Winery. And here was the key: a network of canals, fed by a 120-kilometre lifeline from a dam on the Orange river down south.

'Our climate isn't all that different from the Breede River Valley. It was just water we lacked,' Ian said. Now they were swimming in it, and celebrated an annual Wine and Water Festival in and out of it – tractor inner-tube races down the canals, hole-in-one golf contests targeting an island on their balancing dam ('for the guys whose eyes are still OK despite everything'), grape-treading competitions. 'A bit of fun. I organised it because this area doesn't have a wine tradition – the farmers here were into brandy and beer.'

No wine tradition had long been the South African wine establishment's excuse for the absence of black growers in its ranks. A decade post-liberation, 99 per cent of vineyards were still white-owned; the handful of 'empowerment' ventures routinely trotted out as evidence of 'transformation' was pitiful. This issue was not very visibly on the front-burner in the traditional Cape winelands. But to our astonishment, here in the Afrikaner heartland of the Free State, they were taking it very seriously indeed.

Surprise: vines 1000km from Stellenbosch, just short of the diamond fields of Kimberley.

Perhaps the province's grim tally of dead farmers had concentrated minds. 'Getting along in a small town is all about job creation.' said Ian Sieg. Security here came in the form of the abattoir, the ground-nut plantations for the local Yamado peanut butter and – the big surprise – black vineyard-owners.

Landzicht had established 'practice blocks' on the edge of town, where a group of black locals had learned how to manage a vineyard. On a 60-hectare spread donated by the winery, they were now planting their own vines, and passing on their knowledge to others. Soon, Ian beamed, Landzicht would have more grapes from black suppliers than any winery in South Africa. 'And everyone will be having a better life. It's time whites shared. We kept everything to ourselves for too long. We were like donkeys with flaps over our eyes.'

Walking down rows of Cabernet and port varieties, we could see why he enthused about the soil. The prevailing bright orange sand is only a top layer – 'blown all the way from the Kalahari millions of years ago'. But visibly unearthed during the making of this vineyard is a bottomless reserve of limestone. No artificial soil adjustments needed.

The owner of this vineyard was one of Landzicht's first black growers: Mosiuoa Lekota. Previously known as Patrick, and, as a young hero of the anti-apartheid struggle, 'Terror'. He was the first post-liberation Premier of the Free State, and he took a personal interest in the curious oasis of vines in his territory. He and Ian became friends; he brought Nelson Mandela along to talk to farmers (current Deputy President Jacob Zuma had popped in just the day before we visited); he organised international trade trips.

Lekota was now South Africa's Minister of Defence, but his groundwork was bearing fruit. Ian had just returned from China, having tied up a trade-exchange agreement. Soon Chinese winemakers would be coming to learn from this 3000-ton winery, and Landzicht would be launched on the market the whole wine world was desperate to crack.

'We sat for three days, talking, drinking tea, eating strange things – lots of hairy crabs – until they were ready to sign. There was exactly the same food at breakfast and dinner. But I got used to it. Then they gave me a hell of a fright. They had this pot filled with coals and they threw a bottle of wine into it and then some live prawns. It was so hot they jumped straight out. Prawns were flying round my head!' Ian related.

We drove back to town past wheatfields, a Boer War blockhouse, and the Gravel Road Theatre. 'Where we have shows, cabarets. It may look quiet out here, but we are like moles, we move in the evening.' There were more luxuriant vines, a forest of Colombard, a jungle of Shiraz – Ian's big battle here is to check rampant growth. Well, one of them. Since he'd arrived in 1984, just about every plague seemed to have been visited on these 325-hectare vineyards. Locusts, drought, hail, floods. Only the nondescript variety Chenel survived the deluge of 1988: 'It ripened with its feet in the water!'

At the winery, under willow trees, a *braai* designed to take 60 steaks was smoking, and South African Brandy Foundation chief Pietman Retief was hosting a tasting. He'd last been here for the centenary of the Battle of Magersfontein: he and the Black Watch, he said, had marched across the battlefield under a full moon, with bagpipes. 'Lots of people came,' Ian said. 'Battles and Bottles, we called those tours.'

We adjourned to Ian's house, where Cliff Richard sang 'Please Don't Tease' while Ian poured samples: the labels were covered with ingenious little waistcoats, sporting bow ties and buttons. These didn't disguise the identity of the Cabernet, Shiraz, Merlot and Pinotage, all most respectable, if a bit light-coloured (the result of summer rains). The Shiraz was specially attractive – 'it was this wine that convinced the Chinese we knew what we were doing!'

But one bottle stumped us. It was such a genteel specimen we couldn't believe Ian had made it. He hadn't. It was Great Wall of China Cabernet.

Amandla!

Jabulani Ntshangase had been an embalmer and a shoe salesman in Scotland, a business student and store shelf-packer in New York. That was where he'd picked up his most impressive – but most problematic – credentials. The store sold wine. The bottles Jabu packed bewitched him. He began to devour wine literature. The manager invited him to join the in-store tastings; soon this young Zulu exile was advising customers.

Struggling at first with traditional comparisons ('I'd never tasted wine back home, and fruits like redcurrants were foreign to me') he quickly invented his own. Blackcurrants were similar to the wild *ijigijolo* berry or the fruit of the indigenous *umdoni* tree. He became an acute taster, specialising in Burgundy and the Loire. But the apartheid-era South African wines of the time were a closed book: banned from the US.

Our mutual contact had been Joe Lelyveld, an old friend and former foreign correspondent who became Editor of the *New York Times*. Joe went into the store – Neal Rosenthal's, on Lexington Avenue; Jabu served him; Joe recognised his accent; Jabu was thrilled to meet the writer of Move Your Shadow, classic reportage of life under apartheid; Joe gave Jabu our name. When Mandela was freed, John went to New York to give the first major tasting of Cape wines after sanctions were lifted. It had been organised by André Shearer, a former international model, who recruited Jabu to his Cape Classics company. (In 2001 André was voted wine importer of the year by the American magazine *Food and Wine*). This good-looking young duo gave South African wine a new face in the US.

Even before he came home permanently, we knew Jabu's desire to change the complexion of local wine would be no easy ride. His capabilities were often questioned. In Sweden once, on a sales-trip, he was asked by an agent to blind-taste a Bordeaux. 'I was being tested,' he said. 'I might have come quite close anyway, but someone was holding my hand that day. I'd tasted the same wine in New York the week before! I drew it out a bit – which commune, which bank, which château and vintage – but I knew. The guy was amazed.'

In the Cape, he was scrutinised even more narrowly. We'll never forget the faces of the matrons at an adjacent restaurant table in Stellenbosch when Jabu swirled, sniffed, gargled and then spat a perfect stream of wine, before pronouncing: 'A little tannic?' A black man with a palate? When he visited us at our Stellenbosch vineyard, Clos du Ciel, and went out for an early-morning run in his New York Marathon T-shirt and Nikes, he was accosted by the farm manager next door: who was he, where had he come from? His explanation was rejected. No, the Platters had only one house, so how could Jabu possibly be staying with us?

Top: VIPs at Landzicht:
vineyard-owning
Cabinet Minister
Mosiuoa Lekota and
former President
Nelson Mandela with
Landzicht's chaiman
Dr Christo van Graan
and Ian Sieg; Marcel
and Deon van der
Walt of Veenwouden
Middle: Ian Sieg and
assistant Emden
Viljoen, midwife of
Landzicht's first shiraz;
Boekenhoutskloof's
ringer for a vineyard in
the Côte Rotie; Thabani
Wines mover and
shaker Jabulani
Nsthangase.
Bottom: We queued in
the vineyards to vote in
South Africa's first
democratic elections;
general shop in the
Karoo owned by for-
mer Springbok rugby
player Mannetjies
Roux.

Wine people with nothing like his broad palate were amazed when he joined the team for our wine guide. But can he really taste? they asked. Yes he can. He can also sell. But he'd set himself a larger task. Transformation, training, ownership: these processes were going on in other fields all over post-liberation South Africa. Jabu felt it was his responsibility, his calling, to drive them in an overwhelmingly white-dominated industry.

Aggressive, abrasive, he whirled about the winelands, cutting many corners, veering dangerously near various verges, offending all and sundry – particularly pillars of the establishment like the KWV and Stellenbosch University – and pushing for 'his' students, the budding black oenologists on a bursary scheme whom he made it his business to shepherd through the system. The first crop graduated in 2001–2. Jabu had brought some of them to our farm before they enrolled. They were thirsty for education, but wine was as foreign to them as it had been to him.

'Please,' one asked, 'why do you call wine dry when it is very wet?'

Lately, excited by our tales of North Africa, Jabu had flown off to take the wine pulse there. Instantly observing that Algeria was recommissioning scores of cellars, he called in the stainless-steel tank manufacturer who'd equipped Vergelegen and constructed Vredendal Winery's super-tank. A massive contract was clinched; banks and development companies came on board.

He'd also sewn up a winemaking agreement with the Algerians. Joint cellars there (in Mascara) and here. No, not in the Cape. Between Johannesburg and Durban, in the foothills of the Drakensberg! His home ground, and certainly not traditional wine territory. This was beside the point, though. Wines would be trucked up from the Cape, sailed down from Algiers, and a unique African blend would be bottled. Some Cape grapes would also make the long-distance journey (as often done in Australia). And in time they'd join the harvests of vines recently planted here as part of an initiative by the KwaZulu-Natal agricultural ministry. (Probably no less feasible than vines in other summer-rainfall territory round the world, and the soil analysis was excellent.)

So Landzicht Winery wasn't the end of our odyssey. Here we were 500 kilometres on, driving past the grasslands, thorn trees and aloes where the new Thabani wine cellar was to be built. The last word of our South African wine story was written in Zulu.

Wines **Landzicht** Wyne

Van links na regs: MINISTER MCP LEKOTA, DR CH VAN GRAAN,
OUDPRESIDENT NELSON MANDELA & IAN SIEG

THE END?

More than most books this is an incomplete one. We didn't set out to be comprehensive but there are many intriguing vineyards we haven't visited. Nigeria, we hear, feels the need (half-Muslim and winter-less notwithstanding) to augment its oil wealth with wine; and Chad (desert and more desert); and Mozambique (steamy and tropical). A South African winemaker recently nipped over to Angola to show a couple of generals what to make of their vines. Uganda has its own vinous plans.

High on our 'still to-do' list is Libya. There's been a 30-year ban on alcohol by the Gadaffi regime. But there are vineyards, well-established ones. The vines – some planted by the colonial Italians – flourish on the Mediterranean coast as you'd expect. 'They are of course all grapes for eating, not drinking,' the country's ambassador to South Africa told us. 'But,' he added after a long pause and a meaningful look, 'what some people might make of them in the privacy of their baths… we do not know.' How you both criminalise wine and turn a blind eye to its making bears investigation – and sampling.

Cesaria Evora's rich profundo-afro-fado cadences alone would be enough to lure us to the Cape Verde islands too – in the Atlantic Ocean but off and of Africa. There, we're told, are just the sort of precipitous volcanic vineyards we like; the wines, unlike the people, are bound to be edgy, or at least dodgy.

And there's other unfinished business too. When irrepressibly doughty wine warrior Sam Pfidzayi of Marondera in Zimbabwe finally gets his Cabernet Franc red fizz to hit the spot – he's almost there – we'd like to be there too, to toast it and, perhaps, a brand of new-vintage Zimbabwean politics.

Nor will we stop following the fortunes of Faith Rutto's Yatta Plateau Cabernet Sauvignon in Kenya – her vineyards are getting excitingly close to producing the right stuff. Richard Leakey's Ngong Hills Pinot Noir – astounding in the circumstances – should only improve in succeeding vintages. We'll need to monitor that too – though, actually, his existential ruminations, on that wide veranda, gazing down at one of the great vistas of Africa, the Rift Valley – Maasai herdsmen and their spears glinting in sunset – require little lubrication.

Then there's Ramilla Ramguendez, whose blinder of a wine from the hills behind Oran in western Algeria was the most masculine of the 'new wave' reds we tasted (in its early, in-barrel, state). Will she or won't she bottle it? Will it be blended away, written off as another small-scale experiment in Algeria's gathering vinous recuperation? We must revisit mischievous surfer Jacques Poulain in Morocco to retaste the fruits from the immaculate fledgling Atlas vineyards of his stately farmer-friend, Abdelsalam Moulbled. On our visit, only the Chardonnay, tantalisingly, was ready. The reds should be thrilling.

And will engagingly cocksure Frédéric Chaix in Madagascar shame the present keepers of that country's wine fortunes, the extraordinary, cut-off but intact community of Chinese Malagasy *vignerons*, with entirely new and more drinkable wines? He's made the threats. The answer will not be long in coming now.

These may sound like intrepid investigations but of course they are self-indulgences too, and besides, such far-flung 'playing away' is made all the easier by the close comfort and superb choices from home team South Africa. But even here the ground is shifting and the shock waves of innovation from a generation impatient after decades of barely incremental progress, offer a growing and spectacular challenge. No one, least of all the Cape, wants to be left out of the world's great wine revolution.

Did we, can we, come to anything as simple as a conclusion, or, more vulgarly, do we have a 'message' after all these peregrinations? Were it not for the publisher's deadline (deadlines, the infernal nuisances!) we might still be airily slurping, sipping, spitting and laughing our way around the continent, taking notes, making friends, on the trail of more wonderful oddballs, the kinds of men and women who seem to think life without adversity loses its deeper purpose.

They seem (to us, not to themselves of course, they're oblivious) too inured to living on the edge. To us, it's these brave spirits and their ideas that matter as much as the wine. And, as they eke at the margins – a metaphor for the African condition? – their defiance becomes heroic. Auberon Waugh divided the world into the reckless, the brave, the amiable – and the rest. The wine community of Africa is on the A-list.

So… if not a message, perhaps an observation or two? First, a journey through the African winelands is a salutary antidote to the pretentious angst and reverential (and self-reverential) absurdity that often surrounds the subject of wine. Wine's simple and honest glory is enduring and reassuringly universal. Even in this exasperating, least tamed (but most beautiful) of continents, it renders almost everything easier, funnier, profounder.

Its everyday power to cast the day's highs and woes – to bathe Africa itself - in a new and tempering light is anything but commonplace, but as strong in Antananarivo as it is in New York. We love our friends as much for their failings as anything else after a glass or two, and with more passion, whether in Paris or Alexandria. Wine – *kileo kifanyizwa cho kutoka maji ya zabibu* – the intoxicant from the water of the grape – is no less magical, ultimately, in Swahili than it is in English, French or Chinese. And, as elsewhere, wine seems so much 'wiser' somehow than Africa's great thirst-quencher, beer; or scotch or vodka, which get you there too quickly (though it might be wise to pack some stronger stuff on a safari such as ours – a sort of emergency drip for when the going occasionally gets too desperately non-vinous).

Like Africa generally – perhaps it will become our continent's great gift to a mad world rushed off its feet in technological stampedes – we prefer not to arrive too soon, in a hurry. There's much more to savour, other flavours to explore. This book can't mark the end of our travels.

ALGERIA

The **Medea** region stretches into the hills behind Algiers; whenever we did a cross- Algerian tasting, its wines did something extra for us. Like **Ch. Tellagh**, a mellow red of fading – though agreeably so – fruit, rounded off with some barrel-ageing. The **Rosé** under this label a notch above average too: invariably fresher than the ubiquitous, middle-aged (sometimes oxidised) **Gris d'Algerie** which occupies a staple, fallback position in Algerian wine.

Dom. Ouzera 96 was one of our favourites, earthy, but with more grippy tannin, more grapey substance and spine, and a longer (slightly rough but not unattractive) finish than most. Amid the usual throng of grapes, the Cabernet Sauvignon managed to assert a presence (the 'spine' part). Mostly, varieties are harvested and pressed together in Algeria; in this wine, the Cabernet evidently is gathered, pressed and vinified separately before a final whirl in the blender. **Dom. de Djendel 95** (a decent Algerian year) was another **Medea** stalwart: chewy texture, unusual length, varied fruit (ripe, ripe plums and a bit of paw paw) with nuts, with a peasanty perimeter.

Mascara, in the high rocky moonscape of the hinterland east of Oran, provides the wines our Algerian friends fancied most. **Doms de Mamounia** and **El Bordj**, with senior partners Carignan and Grenache grapes presiding over just about the entire Algerian fruit bowl (even some 'indigenous' white-grape varieties in the latter) were usually good bets in a ripe, unaggressive way. Assisted by a little unobtrusive oaking. (Unobtrusive because the Algerians were still hesitant about importing new barrels – hesitant about the price as well as the effect on the wines.)

But we preferred **Ch. Beni Chougrane**, a Carigan-Grenache-only show, with a brief stint of old-oaking. It was variable, but when on song an engaging performer: a bit deeper-coloured and fuller than the norm, some ripe cherry flavours off-setting characteristic Algerian rusticity.

From the coastal **Dahra** region, our star red was **Ch. Tajna**, a full mouthful, nicely fleshed out.

Ch. Mansourah gets the local nod as the pack-leader from the **Tlemcen** region, near the Moroccan border, but again, we found our palates tuned to a slightly different wavelength: we were equally taken by the supposedly humbler but most amiable **Coteaux de Tlemcen** generic red, made up of the usual ensemble of four or five varieties.

EGYPT

Ch. Grand Marquis Pinot Blanc is not personality-packed, but fresh and clean (and a 1000 per cent or so improvement on the vintages of the immediate past decades), plumped by unobtrusive – still tastes dry – soupçon of sugar (6gm/l). We preferred this to the leaner-finishing (muscat-scented) **Cru des Ptolomées Pinot Blanc**. Best in this **Gianaclis** range was the **Ch. Grand Marquis Cabernet Sauvignon 2001**: if standard wine labelling legislation were in place the wine couldn't substantiate the Cabernet claim, but this was a very pleasant red, much more sophisticated than many we tasted elsewhere in North Africa. Plums the operative fruit association here – deep ruby-plum colour, sweet plum flavours and nose, a good (maybe even over-generous, if you want to be picky) dollop of vanilla and spice from oak chips. A new sparkling wine in this range – still in infancy when we visited – could be the ticket for sunset toasts on the Nile.

ETHIOPIA

Awash Winery's Cristal Chenin Blanc was low-alcohol but still a bit of a toughie, with fairly whopping sulphur when we tasted, though the country's fiery cuisine does a good decoy job. We preferred the gentler local **Soave**. The **Dukum Red** was more of a guava juice colour, with a supremely rustic nose – we could hear the cocks crowing in the farmyard – mixing comforting rural smells and fusty old barrels (18 months ageing). The low acidity offered pros and cons: less bounce and freshness, but no fear of sandpapered throats. **Gouder Red** appeared darker and deeper, and was also interestingly scented.

KENYA

Yatta Vineyards is the most visible label; the **Chenin Blanc 2001** was perfectly drinkable if a bit dusty-tasting. Probably the better bet, with spicy food, was the light, crisp, off-dry (but still fairly tart), equally spicy **Muscat Alexandria 99** made from the dual table-wine Hanepoot variety, imported from South Africa. **Ruby Cabernet 2000** was very nearly a good *vin ordinaire* with its attractive ruby hue and earthy nose. But palate and finish a bit hollow and cardboardy – not enough fruit to carry the alcohol or the high acidity. However, the future looks much rosier. An 'experimental' Ruby Cabernet matured in American oak was very different, richer and with a delightful bouquet. A barrel-aged Cabernet Sauvignon was even more promising.

Richard and Louise Leakey's wines, from the Ngong hills outside Nairobi, stole the Kenyan show. **Ol Choro Onyore Pinot Noir 2001** was our pick of the reds from the African tropics; unwooded, with inviting, juicy, authentic Pinot character, nicely filled out and fleshy on the palate. Nit-pickers might focus on the slightly attenuated finish, and the rather quiet nose, but a triumph in the circumstances. **Ol Choro Onyore Sauvignon Blanc 2001** had some of the power and fresh flinty thrust, but wasn't (when we tasted) yet offering classical Sauvignon gooseberry-grassiness. Most respectable nonetheless.

MADAGASCAR

Grand Cru d'Antsirabe How we wished we'd bought a case of this bottle-fermented sparkler the instant we tasted it, to see us through the rest of our journey. Nothing we drank subsequently was nearly as nice. Dressing grapes up in the camouflage kit of bubbles and sweet dosage (20g/l) is clearly one solution to the problems of winemaking in the rain (or rather, the cyclone). The bead was fine and busy, the sheen gold-green, the flavours quite complex, yeasty and gently fruity enough to hint at some desirable toastiness. And all winkled out of the very lowly Couderc Blanc grape! The second-string **Rosé** sparkler from hybrid Seyve-Villard was sweeter and thinner, but still a whole lot more drinkable than most of its compatriots.

Clos Malaza Gris Not grey, of course – colour closer to California's blush wines – a mere tinge of apricot-pink. Dry, clean, the best of the rash of this style of wine made on Mad, but still more damp squib than fireworks (though this should change with recent innovations in the cellar). From Alicante Bouschet.

Côte de Fianar Vin Blanc Still whites are not Mad's strongest suit, but this lean but clean thirst-quencher, at a low 11.5%, gave us no headaches.

MAURITIUS

Wines made in Mauritius – from imported grape concentrate – are hardly classics. Nonetheless, at bargain prices, labels like **Eureka, Chaptalin** and so on put some of the wines-from-grapes we tasted elsewhere to shame. **Capinella** is a respectable, finished-in-Mauritus (bought from Bellingham in South Africa), everyday plonk. Born in Mauritius is our tag for wines from **L'Avenir Estate**, in Stellenbosch, South Africa, whose proprietor Marc Wiehe is island-bred. Waves of tropical fruit roll right the way through the loud and luscious **Chenin Blanc 2001**, broadened by a stir of sweetness from a tiny percentage of 'noble rot' grapes and generous alcohol (14% plus), off-set by fresh acidity. A food and party wine. The **Pinotage** doesn't mince about either: a ballsy, deep purple, plum-banana-cinnamon-flavoured extrovert – and frequent award winner, as is the cool **New World Chardonnay** and fine **Cabernet**. (The Maingards, who own Dieu Donne vineyards in Franschhoek, also hail from Mauritius.)

MOROCCO

Atlas Vineyards 2000 range from French company Castel's Meknes property: the **Merlot** in approachably juicy New World style but with more clench and length than many front-of-mouth South American seducers; two impressive **Cabernets** (one made for Sainsburys, UK) with proper cassis and coffee nuances. A Sainsbury's **Syrah**: delicious – even if it doesn't shout Syrah spice and heft. All these oak-chipped, so essentially commercial. Plus a minerally, barrel-matured Cabernet-Merlot blend, **Private Reserve El Baraka 99** oozing jammy black cherries. Good stuff.

Beni Snassen Doms de Chaudsoleil Gris Palest flamingo pink, light, dry, fresh, from vineyards near the Med: a natural with fish on warm, salad days.

Les Celliers de Meknes Cabernet Sauvignon Rosé A cut above the mostly boring multitude of rosés spilling out of North Africa. Deep pink, soft-fruit texture and flavour, fresh and clean enough to stand up for itself before and through a meal. In the same range: a **Merlot** opening with spicy-minerally attack, leading into soft, sweet prune fruit and some complexity on the palate. The **Cabernet** similar weight, mettle, just a little firmer. Barrel-matured experimental versions of **Cabernet** and **Syrah** were deeper-coloured, more richly fruited

– the oak playing (as it should) second fiddle. Recent blends from the same stable – **Cabernet-Syrah** (gutsy, a bit tarry) and **Cabernet-Merlot** (shyer, more straightforward) were trying to raise the quality bar and widen the taste selections on offer.

Thalvin is the producer to look for if you (like us), begin to sink in Morocco's sea of reds. The finest white wine we tasted in North Africa was **CB Chardonnay** (standing for Chardonnay Barrique). A limpid but also sassy representative of the world's most ubiquitous dry white: some spice, some fudge, some lemon-marmalade tartness to hold your attention. Until we discovered **CB**, we were disappointed in every white we tried except another Thalvin label, the **Semillant**, which was nothing grand, but simply, unlike its peers, full, balanced, fresh, clean and mildly fruity. Exactly what the fabulous seafood at places like the throbbing Restaurant au Port in Casablanca's fishing harbour screamed for. Another belated discovery in this range was a frisky and surprisingly rich-flavoured **Sauvignon-Ugni Blanc** blend. None of the reds was the least bit shabby either: a cracker of a **Dry Rosé**; an incredibly grown-up **Cabernet-Merlot** blend from infant vines – crammed with prunes and spice and that minerally inky quality that spells quality. And all those stampeding towards Spain for newly trendy and formidably pricey Carignan might well look over the water to Morocco's more affordable version, labelled **Siroua Rouge** – deep violet-ruby, concentrated, rich.

NAMIBIA

If the wines from **Kristall Kellerei** weren't individuals, something would be drastically wrong. You can't originate from the edge of the Namib desert and taste like other wines. For want of new descriptions, 'earthy' and 'rustic' will have to do for the oak-chipped **Ruby Cabernet**, but it is its own man. Lovely colour, nice grapey bouquet, punchy acidity, snatches of chocolate on the finish. No blockbuster, but a convivial *braai* partner. And seems to grow with a bit of maturity: we preferred **98** to **2000**. No guava (or any other) scents emanated from the very crisp, clean **Colombard 2001** but there was a touch of honey on the palate. An agreeable food companion, well-chilled to counteract spikiness. The traditionally bottle-fermented **Sparkling Ruby Cabernet** was fresh and festively zippy. Star turn: the outstanding **Desert Cactus Schapps**.

REUNION

A most professional **2001** trio from the **Chai de Cilaos** featured a **Rosé** from Malbec and Pinot Noir. An unlikely but successful combination – some limpid earthiness from the former, and an engagingly fruity, raspberry bouquet from the latter. The **Chenin Blanc** showed a lively, fruity complexity that begged more than a glass. (Both these wines off-dry – on the drier side of sweet – the sugar expertly balanced to plump out each mouthful without compromising the fresh acidity.) Then the **Moëlleux**, the Indian Ocean answer to Sauternes with foie gras. This a fresh, light, sweet, tingly Chenin (a charmer in any country), born to be married to Madagascan duck livers. At about 12% (like the other wines) made for drinking rather than cautious sipping.

SOUTH AFRICA

Vredendal Mount Maskam Shiraz blows muted notes of ripe-sweet mint rather than a blast of spice: Shiraz with the volume turned down. Price low-key too. Altogether easy to get on with, specially **99** (sampled end-2001, ready).

Cederberg Chenin Blanc (barrel fermented) and **Sauvignon Blanc** are naturally crisp, bracing, tinglingly fruity-fresh – what else from South Africa's highest-altitude winery? You can almost taste the astonishing slaty 'soil' (see our picture!) too. Very individual. As is stunning **V Generations Cabernet 2000** – mashed ripe plums, all-spice, a side-order of cranberry sauce.

Two ranges at **Spice Route**, take your pick. We'd head for the upper-deck **Flagship Syrah** and **Merlot**. Towering – fill in all the big adjectives – sunshiny, definitely don't-drink-and-drive wines. The Syrah oozes spice, the Merlot spoons up inky minerals; both wrapped in plush fruit. Some over-hyped New World – or even Old – competitors have been put on notice here. We're special fans of the **98s**.

Flagstone Longitude (and other wackily named Flagstone labels), loads of passion in these 'new-comers' and a brave, groundbreaking project; the opposite of 'little grey' wines. We rather like the **BK5 Pinot Noir**.

Klein Constantia Vin de Constance – irresistible history, luscious music in a bottle – smooth, soft, silky and very sweet, with a twist of lime marmalade in the tail. Comforted Napoleon in exile; just about the only alcohol Nelson Mandela allows past his eloquent lips but – unlike Napoleon – only in hesitant sips: see what it's done for him – and us! **Sauvignon Blanc**, and **Sauvignon Blanc Noble Late Harvest** always terrific too.

At **Buitenverwachting**, determinedly iconoclastic winemaker Hermann Kirschbaum insists his wines offer 'deeper communication'. So, the slow-release **Sauvignon Blanc**, a considered, flintily elegant, complex (after a couple of years in the bottle), unflashy intellectual studiously avoids the company of all the jocks in this class. The **Merlot** can turn on the charm in good year (like **99**); Bordeaux-blend **Christine's** spice and mineral upper-cuts 'communicate deeply' enough for most.

Steenberg Sauvignon Blanc Reserve is a Cape Unmissable. All serious class, steely glint, stony flint. Dazzles – especially **2001** – without cheap shock-effects. Cracking **Merlot** too, **98** our favourite. Loads of fruit and charm, ripples sinuously over tongue and down throat. (Yes, we could say it has a 'pliant mouthfeel', but no. We are trying to avoid such – awful! – winespeak.)

Cape Point Sauvignon Blanc-Sémillon, a cool new kid on the block, isn't shouting the odds – this is a low-key blend – but not deferring to older residents either. Many have tried to use Sémillon to fill out the crisp bite of Sauvignon but haven't pulled it off nearly as well.

Graham Beck 2000 Blanc de Blanc (all-Chardonnay), bubbles from a semi-desert source. Fresh, even a bit creamy – none of that sharpness which often adds sandpapery throat-torture to the ordeal of a long, rainy – or even sunny – wedding in a marquee. The **Brut** is classic Pinot-Chardonnay, fuller, hints of the elusive, decadently biscuity pong

of mature champagne. The **Ridge Shiraz** is squaring up to take on the Aussie benchmarks.

Funky wines from risk-addict Abrie Bruwer at **Springfield**. His **99 Whole Berry Cabernet** is rather like a sumptuous cushion stuffed with blackcurrants.

Axe Hill has scaled in three vintages heights the Portuguese took three centuries to reach – well, we exaggerate, but not completely wildly. Owner Tony Mossop, a prolific wine writer and permanent member of umpteen tasting panels, can pronounce (unlike many peers) not from a lofty perch but from the ground. We asked him for his picks of the Cape port bunch:

Ruby: **Die Krans**; Vintage: **Bredell**, **Boplaas**, **Landskroon**, **Die Krans**, **Allesverloren**, **Axe Hill**; Tawny: **Boplaas**, **Monis 89 Special**. Our own tasting of Axe Hill revealed oozy layers of expensive sweets – soft toffee and chocolate; the finish hangs about an age. Plus – big bonus – doesn't seem to leave a sore head next day, on our test drives anyway.

Vergelegen is desert-island stuff. Even if you were in a plaster-cast you'd want to dance to the trio of reds: **Cabernet Sauvignon** (Cab S.-Merlot), **Vergelegen Estate** (Cab S.-Merlot) and **Cabernet Franc-Merlot** (reserved for auctions mainly). All super-smart, super-fine, super-succulent, especially from **98**. The 'Estate' label is the flagbearer but forget the pecking order: drink, buy, hoard any/all. Same for whites-only drinkers: terrific **Sauvignon Blanc** and **Chardonnay Reserves**, and **Noble Late Harvest Sémillon**.

Ken Forrester produces a rare Super-**Chenin** in an ocean of mediocrity: worth waiting 3–4 years

to get the full grown-up, ample, dry-honeyed effect. **Grenache-Syrah** is for seekers of originality: deceptively light, supple, savoury.

Meinert Wines, released sporadically, erratically, by philosopher-winemaker Martin Meinert. Grab anything from **98** onwards with both hands. Serious stuff here: full, expressive, rich; as if he's stirred crushed blackcurrants and blackberries with cedary lead-pencils. Particularly in the **Cabernet-Merlot**.

Grangehurst begs the question: is a 'Cape blend' obliged to contain Pinotage? (Are you authentically Californian only if you have Zinfandel blood?) And then dismisses it. Never mind the birth certificates of the varieties in Jeremy Walker's **Nikela** (Pinotage, Cabernet, Merlot): if they didn't, together, make a class act it wouldn't matter. They do.

Cordoba Crescendo, once ambitiously, now propitiously named. If this is how well Cabernet Franc (with a splash of Merlot) can play in the Cape, why's there so little of it about? A fine, taut, minerally spicy specimen, with two vital statistics for icon-status: rarity (only 500 cases a year) and mystery. No one knows what it'll taste like after a decade, even winemaker Chris Keet, who constantly exhorts us to abstain until then. First vintage was 95!

The stately **Meerlust** galleon sails on... resolutely (anachronistically some charge) outside the modern fleet of full-frontal fruity wines, and why not, if demand for your patented brand of unshowy restraint, of savoury-nutty-brambly (adults only) flavours remains so strong? We have a soft spot for claret-style blend **Rubicon**; and **Merlot**; forest-floor-with-fungi **Pinot Noir**. And the '**grappa**' for a *digestif*. Watch for upcoming Viognier.

Warwick, where top-listed **Trilogy** is all bespoke vinosity, a two-Cabernets and Merlot blend made to the brief: 'Some claret classicism please.' So, quite herby and tailored, with some fine details – violets, blackcurrants, good oak, a grind of pepper. **Three Cape Ladies** (Pinotage plus claret varieties) more playful: chocolate, sweet plums.

French ownership, crossover Franco-Cape architecture at **Morgenhof.** Outstanding **Merlot**, **Cabernet Sauvignon Reserves** and Bordeaux blend **Premier Selection**: bold, dark, well-groomed, like the leading ladies of this production: proprietor Anne Cointreau-Huchon – yes *the* Cointreaus – and winemaker Rianie Strydom.

Rust en Vrede, long a heavyweight red estate, now with a new resolve: to fly only one (fabulous, distinctive, all that) R&V blend in future. Cabernet with Merlot and Shiraz. It's well en route. Super stuff. (More proof of our contention that with most serious Cape reds, the recent years – **99** onwards – are the ones to seek.)

The Platters might well have crooned over the flamboyant **Delaire Merlot**, a stream of rich coffee and sweet prune. The reds from this up-and-down (topographically-speaking) farm on the crest of a mountain pass are all juicy ripe limpidity. No meek **Chardonnay** either. Brawny, brainy young Bruwer Raats is the new Cape winemaker personified.

De Toren Fusion V has the briefest of track records (only two vintages!), but here's a red wine advisory: this is buy-and-accumulate stock. No inflated p/e ratios yet, no gimmicks, few frills, a package of carefully culled, five-sorts-of-Bordeaux berries in a bottle (after some character-building in barrel).

Give the nod only to the mighty, gong-laden **Neil Ellis Shiraz** and **Cabernet Reserves**, and you'll miss out. Neil doesn't tolerate stragglers in his list. **Groenekloof Sauvignon Blanc** can take on the very best; ditto **Chardonnay**, ditto **Pinotage**. There's real value in his Stellenbosch range. But the Reserves *are* irresistible, if grand and taut and powerful are you.

The Cape would be an infinitely poorer (wine) place without **Thelema:** simultaneously sleekly professional and unostentatiously home-spun, in and out of the bottle. **Ed's Reserv**e (super-spicy Chardonnay) is something else. **Cabernet** and **Merlot** have been national clarion-calls for a decade – supple, deep, juicy, napped with chocolate, sprinkled with sweet spices, topped with sprigs of mint. Those who think it's not pukkah for top reds to be so shamelessly drinkable are welcome to go elsewhere for a pucker-fix. There's no shortage of tough, tannic, that'll-show-the-grandkids sort of stuff in the Cape.

Hartenberg is now reaping the rewards of sustained viticultural improvements. A label that's always had rather decorous devotees should now prepare for ravers if our preview of the new millennium **Cabernet**, **Shiraz** and **Merlot** is on the spot.

The flavours in **Kanonkop's** famously show-winning Bordeaux blend **Paul Sauer** vary by the vintage (sometimes more oaky, sometimes smoky-cinammon, sometimes more rustic) but the style – weighty, full, rich – is constant. And while this once uncontested **Pinotage** champ no longer struts the ring solo, it retains its title to rugged honesty and power.

The **Newton-Johnson** family's early models of a new **Pinot Noir** point steeply upwards as Walker

Bay continues to stake its claim to Pinot territory every bit as appropriate as patches of Burgundy, Oregon and New Zealand. Début N-J vintages smouldering with funky, organic forest undergrowth; oak-spice and cherries on top.

Beaumont's barrel-reared grande dame of a **Chenin Blanc**, original **Pinotage** (less brazenly acidic and gawky), and inky, opaque, chewy **Mourvèdre** are the ones to watch.

Much renewal and reconstruction at **Hamilton Russell Vineyards**, as virus-infected vines are systematically replaced in Anthony Hamilton Russell's tireless quest for 'a sense of place in the bottle'. The essential character of this **Chardonnay** – a classic, edgy lime tartness, the antithesis of frothy, fruity simplicity – will doubtless continue. It's certainly there in the **2001** we previewed. Winemaker Kevin Grant thinks **2000** is his 'best vintage yet' of **Pinot**. We found more forest floor, more everything – damp leaves, mushrooms and cherries – swirling in our sample of **2001**.

Watch out for: **Waterford** winemaker Kevin Arnold's 'concept' wine from southern European (warm country) varieties – Tempranillo (Spain), Mourvèdre (France), Barbera (Italy) and others, seven at least, all red. Those grapes weren't just plonked there, he argues; they fought hard for their places over centuries, so doesn't it make sense to transplant them in the similar climate of the Cape? (The architecture of the Waterford winery has this Tuscan-Provencal-Spanish-Cape ambience.) He aims to mix and match grapes, oaking, winery and vineyard techniques – for a blend of European tradition and New World science. While we wait there's a fine, cassis-suffused **Cabernet**, a heady, mocha-and-spice **Shiraz**. The property is a tangible product of South Africa's IT boom – co-owned by one of the gang which took the Didata group international, Jeremy Ord.

Doing his gifted thing at **Mulderbosch** is the Cape's only Serb winemaker, chemistry boffin Mike Dobrovic, one of the 'older' generation winemakers revered and consulted by the young posses now riding into town. Few have his measure of **Sauvignon Blanc**, though he torments his fans: his landmark racy, crisp, explosive, gooseberry-and-

grassy style isn't an annual given. We don't care, we buy and are never disappointed, even in the so-called down years. Mike struggles with a wayward vineyard, on an exposed, windy unirrigated ridge. If you want an expression of vintage and place, this is it.

When an investment analyst decides to switch careers (and rushes straight through a BSc Oenology to a MSc) anything's possible. At **Kanu,** cigar-chomping Teddy Hall wants to teach the Loire a lesson. Oaked, unoaked, dry, sweet, **Chenin** is his mania; he's won all the local silverware; we predict he'll burst onto the international scene soon. Kanu **Cabernet** and **Merlot** show he's an all-rounder; he's even poured Hungarian grape **Harslevelu** into a temptation of a Noble Late Harvest dessert.

Veenwouden's duo of **Classic** (Cabernet-Merlot blend) and **Merlot**, combine power and grace. Every vintage since breakthrough **96** up a notch.

Stamina needed to navigate the ever-changing **Fairview** list of about 30 labels, from an incorrigible experimenter. Exhausting but essential if you want Cape wine's Breaking News. Prices ungreedy enough to allow for investment in a bottle or two of each; then pick and choose at home. **Shiraz** – at least two now, often more (two of everything it seems!) – are good bets, sturdy but supple, packed with ripeness. The monster **Zinfandel** is way over the top (just the ticket for rowdy events though). Our household regulars are **Viognier**, **Chenin Blanc**, **Chardonnay**, **Sémillon** and **Goats do Roam** (seven red varieties).

Boekenhoutskloof Syrah doesn't mess about blowing your socks off. It's the full Monty. Unmatched for individuality; probably best dry **Sémillon** in the Cape (serious relief from the boredom of tame Chardonnays, belligerent Sauvignons). We also like the fine texture, and ripe berries and plums of the **Cabernet Sauvignon**.

Husband-and-wife team Gary and Kathy **Jordan** simply do not – cannot – make second-rate stuff. Latecomers to wine (trained in the US) they're both brilliant and reliable. Others discarded the oaked **Sauvignon Blanc** style, they persisted – it's called **Fumé**, we like it. Their single vineyard

Bordeaux blend **Cobblers Hill** jousts with Cape's finest. Their **Chardonnay** should convert even fundamentalist members of NABCO (the international Not Another Boring Chardonnay Organisation).

Delheim Vera Cruz Shiraz is a smoky, smouldering blockbuster; its **Grand Reserve** (Cabernet from the same vineyards) oozes power.

De Trafford epitomises the boutique winery idea; tiny, tucked away on a Stellenbosch mountain crag, determinedly alternative styles (without funky fireworks): architect David De Trafford's eight labels all display hand-crafted individuality: **Chenin**, **Shiraz**, **Cabernet** and **Vin de Paille** dessert are our picks.

If balance, depth, smooth power are your tall order – the kind of wine that'll etch deep in your memory – then you'd not suffer too much angst if you picked **Rustenberg Peter Barlow 99 Cabernet**. The rest of the range not shabby either: **John X Merriman** (Bordeaux blend) magisterial; **Stellenbosch Chardonnay** rises above the herd.

The vitality and originality of everything Edmund and Elsie Oettle do is completely beguiling, and it spills over into their juicy, rounded **Upland Cabernet 99**.

At **Avontuur** the names may be trying – Luna la Miel, for **Chardonnay**, Above Royalty for **Riesling Noble Late Harvest**, Baccarat for **Merlot** (they're called after racehorses) – but the contents are finely sculpted works by an outstanding young winemaker, Lizelle Gerber (with a nod to grapes from the upper-crust Helderberg area).

At **Villiera** the Grier family spreads itself – but never too thinly – across the whole range of cellar and vineyard disciplines, labels and styles: sparkling to port and everything in between. Deliciously modest prices for some of the Cape's best wines: we specially like the **Merlot Reserve**, **Cru Monro** (Bordeaux blend), **Bush Vine Sauvignon**, **Brut Natural Chardonnay**, **Reserve Chenin**.

Walter Finlayson's pose of humorous grumpiness – the Cape's Walter Matthau? – is no longer a highlight of local wine conclaves now he's spending more time with his cows (excellent Cap Salut

cheese). Son David has talent in his genes, and now does the driving at **Glen Carlou**. His wide-bodied, front-row rugby forward **Shiraz** is ready to roll straight over any mincing French delicacy. The **Pinot Noir** shouldn't be but is always a surprise – this is supposed to be hot country; the **Chardonnay Reserve** is indubitably world class (and the original reason why Napa's Donald Hess (Hess Collection) is a partner here).

L'Avenir Estate (see under Mauritius).

Backsberg One of the few – and first – estates to have come up with an in-house 'transformation' program, offering black workers share-options in a vineyard scheme, from which equity can be transferred into house ownership, a huge leap after the tied staff housing on most farms. Michael and Gill Back shun the limelight, their trips are more likely to be into Africa than off to flashy wine markets – they've actually driven from the Cape to Ethiopia and back! But for dependable value – and some crackers like **99 Shiraz** or, most years, their Bordeaux blend **Babylonstoren** – they have few peers, and across a range of styles. Fine **Chardonnay Reserve** too.

TANZANIA

Tanganyika Vineyards Makutupora Red 2000 might be made from a mystery and not specially flavourful grape but no debate about its respectable natural alcohol of 13% and no-headaches sulphur levels. However, lots of promise in new plantings of recognised cultivars. **Chenin Blanc 2001** under the same label has a rich sheen (more gold than green, and ageing), subdued bouquet, crisp taut taste. Yes, the finish hangs about a bit awkwardly after a couple of glasses, but give it a spritz and away you go.

TUNISIA

Almory Rouge from Carignan-Syrah – light, super-juicy, uncomplicated – and **Rosé** from Grenache – ditto.

From the SICOB company, **La Vieille Cave Grand Vin Rouge**, a pleasant, supple Carignan-Syrah-Merlot blend with a notably good finish; also **El Kahena**, the nicest gris we tasted, from Cinsault,

Carignan and Mourvèdre; and an amiable everyday white, **Cristal Blanc** (including Chardonnay and a local grape, Beldi).

Watch out for the wines from **Tardi,** another private producer, with its own 'domaines' (we visited one near the coastal resort of Bizerte): they're on the up.

The national co-op, the UCCV, produces masses of labels, but perhaps none as charming – in an utterly unfancy, non-serious way, than the **Muscat Sec de Kelibia.** The contrast of its wafting Muscat d'Alexandrie scents and light dry palate made it a winner as an apéritif and with Tunisia's fabulous seafood. Much more ambitious, but still with a way to go to crack international standards, were the country's first single variety wines: **Chardonnay, Syrah, Cabernet Sauvignon, Merlot.** The hot climate, despite maritime moderation, seems to denude these of deep flavours or varietal definition: they're good, straightforward and one-dimensional. But bound to improve. Especially as newer oak barriques are used more widely – starting from **2000.** Even so, the **Dom. Magon 98 Merlot** and **Syrah** more than adequate quaffing, the latter smoother, but simpler.

Traditionalists, hankerers after the grape unvarnished (by oak) should try **Ch. Mornag.**

ZIMBABWE

African Distillers is the local wine (and spirits) giant. **Cordon Rouge Private Collection 98**, a no-airs companion at a bush *braai*, is our pick of the bunch. This an oak-chipped fruit salad from Ruby Cabernet, Pinotage, Merlot, sometimes Tinta Barroca, even a mystery variety locally known

as Ferrazza. **Fig Hill Chardonnay**, Zim's first single-vineyard wine, has more substance than other local whites (American and French oak chips), but it's not (yet) text-book stuff. Wacky very ripe melon aroma. **Private Collection Muscat d'Alexandrie**, off-dry, spicy, goes well with chilli, ginger, anything curried (which cancel out its sharp nettly aftertaste); its dash of Gewürztraminer wafts about attractively.

Cairns (Mukuyu Winery) is the other wine player. Its **Meadows Chenin Blanc**, in the good-average, no-histrionics, off-dry zone is probably your most dependable Zim white. **Mukuyu Select Merlot 98** is the pick of recently released reds: oak chips stick out less obviously than in the Select Cabernet and Cabernet-Merlot. Presentable, and though quite tannic, fine with food. But the best Zim wines of the lot come with a sparkle. **Mukuyu Brut – Blanc de Blanc** is genuine bottle-fermented dry bubbly from Chardonnay at significantly less than US$1 a bottle in 2001 (so why quibble that it's not overly fruity?) Brightens a party, complements freshly caught Kariba bream. A gutsy, jolly-natured **Cabernet Franc Sparkling** still on the drawing board in 2001 could be the answer to Zim wines' big problem: unripe grapes (leading to thinness, sharpness). Fizz, even in Champagne, doesn't require full ripeness. With the bubble for freshness, the red grapes for an ampler feel on the palate, the sugar dosage to disguise aftertaste-aggression, a good excuse for a celebration.

Ampelography
The scientific study of the vine, in all its parts.

Botrytis.
This is called *pourriture noble* in France, noble rot, signifying grapes which have been attacked by the *Botrytis cinerea* fungus, which shrivels them almost into raisins, concentrating their sweetness. A botrytis wine is an intensely sweet wine made from nobly rotted grapes.

Cépage
The French word for grape variety.

Cru
The French word for 'growth'. The terms Grand Cru and Premier Cru are denote top wines in France.

Chaptalisation
The dosing of fermenting grape juice, or must, with sugar (or grape syrup or other sweet concentrate) to increase the alcohol content of a wine.

Dosage
The addition of a mix of wine and sugar to champagne to reduce or smooth its acidity. Sweetening is essential for most styles of champagne and other sparkling wines.

Lees
Sediment which settles at the bottom of a fermentation tank or vat. Usually denotes dead yeast cells but also includes other debris of the winemaking process, such as remnants of skin, pulp, pips etc. The term on the lees refers to leaving wine in contact with some of this sediment so that it can pick up more complex, richer flavours.

Must
What grapes become after they have been crushed – more of a grape pulp (including skins, pips etc) than grape juice – in preparation for fermentation into wine.

Négociant
Merchant who buys grapes, must or wine from growers to sell on or to make/blend into his/her own-label wine.

Terroir
The natural vital statistics of a vine site – soil, sunlight, topography, hydrology, climate – which combine to influence and individualise the flavours of a wine.

Vin de cépage
Wine made from a single grape variety.

For any other unfamiliar wine terms, consult, as we did and do, the authorities:
The Oxford Companion to Wine, edited by Jancis Robinson (Oxford University Press, Oxford 1999)
Vines, Grapes and Wines, by Jancis Robinson (Mitchell Beazley, London, 1992)
The World Atlas of Wine, fifth edition, by Hugh Johnson and Jancis Robinson (Mitchell Beazley, London, 2001)

Note: an indispensable travelmate all over Africa (and other offbeat parts of the wine world) is a bottle of cassis liqueur: a few drops turn tart or otherwise irredeemable wine into a potable Kir apéritif, or, added to a sparkler, a Kir Royale.

Grape names: The names and spellings of grape varieties vary widely in winemaking countries.
To take but two: Cinsault is spelled Cinsaut, while Tinta Barroca becomes Barocca, in South Africa. Syrah and Shiraz are one and the same: Shiraz is often the New World name used for the wine made from the Syrah grape.

INDEX

ACKNOWLEDGEMENTS

Many extraordinary people illuminated our wine odyssey. Africa's warmth and hospitality are not clichés. Our very deep appreciation goes to these stars of the show – we provided the outline but the wine community dramatised it. We set out to discover African wines; you opened our eyes to much more. Your passion and initiative, often in the most challenging circumstances, underline how resourceful and creative our continent can be. If not all the wines – yet – then certainly the wine people of Africa are an inspiration.

We are also indebted to those in the deeper background who believed this was a marathon worth running and gave unstinting support: Kader and Louise Asmal; Graham Boynton; Sally Carney; Mary Hope; Julian and Jenny Larby; Gayling and Margaret May; Judy Olivier; Jane and Hugh Patrickson; Vy Raharinosy; Les Saunders; Moe Shaik; Gillian Slovo; Johnny and Maureen Wroe; and our pan-African bird watching party.

Cameron Platter's indulgence of his peripatetic parents has been admirable.

Special thanks to Hugh Johnson for his longtime support of our beyond-the-fringe wine writings and his generous foreword; and to Jancis Robinson, Stephen Brooks and Frank Prial, who gave us their backing before we began. Jancis also directed us to our agent, Clare Alexander of Gillon Aitken, in whose stable of best-selling novelists we are the oddities. She found us the perfect publisher in Kyle Cathie, who as a student hitchhiked from Cape Town to Khartoum and was instantly on our wavelength. The pleasure of working with her enthusiastic team, designer Vanessa Courtier, copy-polisher Stephanie Horner and specially super-editor Sheila Davies, has been all ours. South African co-publisher Bridget Impey was most encouraging, as was her decision to lead the launch-list of the new Juta DoubleStorey imprint with Uncorked.

Rainbow Tours, UK specialist in trips to the Indian Ocean islands, arranged our travels there impeccably. Their Derek Schuurman is the co-author of the *Bradt* guide to that part of the world. Their African focus includes 11 other countries on the continent.

Most of the airlines we approached clearly thought we were the sort of lunatics they didn't want on their flights. The efficient exceptions were Air Madagascar, Air Australe, Air Algérie and Air Namibia.

Recommendations for R&R on the African wine routes: Le Vieux Cep in Réunion, from the Anthurium Group's portfolio of charming island hotels; Jean-Marc Harel's palmy Paradise Cove in Mauritius, the balmy Le Paradisier and Tsara Guest House in Madagascar, the gracious El-Djazair in Algiers, the rustically luxe Camp Amalinda and Wild Geese Lodge in Zimbabwe and the relaxingly informal Driftwood Club in Malindi, Kenya. South African winelands options are outstanding.